noted cookery

COMPILED BY THE
JUNIOR GROUP OF THE
DALLAS SYMPHONY ORCHESTRA LEAGUE

ILLUSTRATIONS BY
BILL GOLDSMITH

NOTED COOKERY was compiled by the Junior Group of the Dallas Symphony Orchestra League to benefit the Orchestra. The entire membership worked in some capacity to make this book possible. We have gathered, tested, typed, and proofed recipes from friends of the Symphony in Dallas as well as throughout the world. We sincerely regret that it was impossible to include all of the over 1400 recipes received and tested. For the editorial liberties, we ask your indulgence. Compiling **NOTED COOKERY** has been our pleasure; we hope using it will be yours.

The Cookbook Committee

First Printing—October, 1969

Second Printing—December, 1969

Third Printing—March, 1972

Dedicated to Helen Corbitt

With gratitude for years of continuous support of the
Dallas Symphony Orchestra and with special affection.

GUEST CONTRIBUTORS

FOREWORD

There was only one Mozart, there is only one Picasso, but the virtuosos in the kitchen have talents even they do not recognize and their creations are endless. They are masters of their own destiny, their imagination knows no bounds, their enthusiasm can be as great as the time they devote to it.

The genius behind many a home is a good cook who keeps everyone well-fed and healthy and who recognizes the great influence that good food exercises on all members of the family.

The enthusiasm of family and friends for a well-laden table is recognition enough for a talent that must not disappear from our daily living.

Travel today has influenced enthusiasm for different foods. We are no longer happy with plain mom's cooking. It has become a symphony of colors with the array of pots and pans of all the colors in the spectrum. It is a fun thing to do with the many gadgets that intrigue the inquisitive mind today. One talks of recipes and menus as one used to make small talk about things that really counted for nothing. Today the gossip over the back fence, the bridge table, has resolved to "Is She or Is She Not a Good Cook?"

These recipes are signatures of people concerned with people, their families, their friends, and a philosophy that may be simply translated into "loving arms around you" through good food.

HELEN CORBITT

ACKNOWLEDGEMENTS

Any qualities **NOTED COOKERY** may possess, like in any civic effort, were largely generated by enthusiastic contributors outside the sponsoring organization. For their extraordinary help the Cookbook Committee extends very special thanks to:

Helen Corbitt, author and Director of Food Services at Neiman-Marcus, who wrote the foreword as well as the menu chapter, and in addition, contributed several unpublished recipes. Among Miss Corbitt's many popular books is **Helen Corbitt's Cookbook.**

Bill Goldsmith, artist and illustrator, who created and generously contributed the original illustrations. Mr. Goldsmith, a friend of the Symphony who now makes his home in New York, illustrated **The New York Times Menu Cookbook.**

Chuck Gruen, commercial artist, for his contribution of the art direction. Mr. Gruen is former Art Director for Neiman-Marcus and now heads his New York studio specializing in fashion advertising and greeting card design.

Victor Wdowiak, Director of the Neiman-Marcus Wine Cellars, for his contribution of the wine chapter. Mr. Wdowiak has gained wide admiration for acquainting Texans with the nuances and pleasures of wine.

All of those who have graciously shared their favorite recipes.

The many other contributors, though unnamed, who have given of their time and talent to this book.

THE COOKBOOK COMMITTEE

Chairman: Mrs. Jimmy T. Lontos

Vice Chairman: Mrs. Joseph D. Zimmerman

Committee Chairmen: Mrs. Thomas S. Davidson

                             Mrs. Richard A. Erb

                             Mrs. Fred F. Johnston

                             Louise Kent Kane

                             Mrs. Jack W. Lively

                             Mrs. Robert H. Mitchell

                             Mrs. Manfred E. New

                             Mrs. William R. Newsom, III

                             Mrs. Robert D. Rogers

                             Mrs. James F. Rose

                             Mrs. Alex F. Weisberg, Jr.

                             Mrs. Joseph D. Zimmerman

Advisors: Bill Booziotis

                             James F. Gilbert

TABLE OF CONTENTS

TABLE OF CONTENTS

MENUS

There are many good cooks all around the world. They plan and enjoy cooking for their families, but hesitate to feel at home in the kitchen when guests are expected. The Symphony League hopes these menus will make the way easier.

BRUNCHES AND BRUNCHEONS

First courses are easier served in the living room or patio from a punch bowl or tureen, or poured from a pitcher.

Orange Juice and Champagne
Ham Loaf with Mustard Sauce
Hominy Casserole
Warm Pumpkin Bread with Apple Butter
Coffee*

Consommé on the Rocks
Crêpes Corelli
Baked Fruit with Chutney
Asparagus Mold
Butter Biscuits
Lemon Chess Pie

Cucumber Soup
Coquilles of Deviled Crab
Quick Tomato Aspic Rings
       filled with Cottage Cheese and Green Onions
Never-Fail Popovers
Apricot Tortoni

---

*Every hostess should decide her beverage, but shouldn't make her guests unhappy by being dictatorial. Coffee is accepted (use Stanley Marcus' guide), but if someone prefers tea, have it available.

MORNING COFFEE
(Strictly a Texas institution!)

Hot Peach Surprise
Corn Meal Biscuits
Orange Muffins
Frosted Cashew Cookies
Sugar Honey Pecans
Coffee   Grapefruit Drink Appetizer

Melon Balls with Fresh Fruit
Hot Cheese Biscuits with Ham
Blueberry Muffins
Coffee Cake
Date Balls
Coffee

AFTERNOON TEA

Banana Bread and Cream Cheese Sandwiches
Chicken Salad in Tiny Rolls
Viennese Pastries
Rum M M M Cake
Never-Fail Fudge
Tea Punch, Coffee
Sherry

LUNCHEONS

Luncheons today are more informal than not. These could be either buffet or seated.

Crabmeat and Artichoke Casserole
Greek Green Beans
Mango Salad decorated with Slices of Melon
Butter Cream Crescents
Assorted Cookies, for instance,
    Date Cookies, Mama's Orange Cookies,
    Pat's Snicker Doodles

Chicken Herbed Rice Casserole
Spinach Patties
Mushrooms with Bacon
One-Cup Salad in Boston Lettuce Nests
Hot Blueberry Muffins
Angel Food Delight

Quiche Lorraine
Eggplant and Rice Casserole
Jellied Cucumber Salad
Corn Meal Biscuits
Grapes with Sour Cream

BUFFETS

Come and go parties that designate a cocktail buffet on the invitation mean enough food to satisfy the inner man, not necessarily expensive, and cocktails mean good appetites; so the buffet table should have ample food for everyone.

Chicken Enchiladas
Polynesian Sweet Sour Shrimp
Chafing Dish Meat Balls
Cold Vegetable Salad with Dressing
Cheese Biscuits
Hot Citrus Fruit Salad

Luau Ribs
Cold Veal with Sauce Miramare
Cheese Salad Ring filled with Chicken Salad
Relishes with Curried Crab Dip
Small Whole Wheat Rolls
Rum M M M Cake

Spaghetti with Meat Sauce Tucci
Thin Sliced Thyme Tongue
Shrimp and Avocado Mousse
Twenty-Four Hour Slaw
Thin Sliced and Buttered Rye and White Bread
Black Forest Cake

Cocktail buffets can be a holdover for a dinner somewhere else, or just enough to keep your guests with you. Prepare enough!

Mushrooms Montemare
Grilled Garlic Shrimp
Stuffed Edam Cheese with Pumpernickel Slices
Curried Egg Dip with Raw Vegetables

Beef Tartare with Thin Sliced Onions on Rye Bread
Rumaki Pâté with Salted Crackers
Noche Specials
Cold French Artichokes with Sour Cream to dip

Crabmeat Supremes
Meat Balls Special
Miniature Pizzas
Curried Tuna Mold with Unsalted Crackers
Pickled Black-Eyed Peas
Spiced Miniature Beets

BUFFET SUPPERS

Buffet suppers are gaining in popularity, especially when entertaining for larger numbers — Fork food too — Or provide tables — Men do not like to balance a plate on their knees and try to manage a knife and fork.

Hungarian Goulash
Green Noodles
Glazed Sweet and Sour Green Beans
Maurice's Artichokes
Marinated Kraut Salad
Hard Rolls, Split and Buttered
Orange Wine Jelly with Sabayon Sauce
    and Chocolate Chip Brownies

Tureen of Minestrone Soup
    somewhere around
Worsten Broodjes (Meat in a Pastry)
Asparagus and Peas Casserole
Rye Bread
Salmon Mousse with Cucumber Dressing
Raw Relishes
Sherry Baked Bananas

Bengal Curry with Pineapple Rice and Chutney
Marinated Shrimp
Asparagus Saute'
Molded Grapefruit Salad
Assorted Breads
Lemon Chess Pie

DINNERS

Jellied Madrilene with Red Caviar and Sour Cream
Roast Leg of Lamb in Paste
Creamed Spinach
Minted Glazed Carrots
Green Salad with Avocado Dressing
Hot Rolls
Lemon Ice Cream
Swedish Gingersnaps

Pork Chop and Rice Casserole
Spiced Apple Rings
Buttered Peas and Little White Onions
Green Salad with Artichokes
    French Dressing
Homemade Bread
Warm Quick Fruit Pudding
    with or without Whipped Cream

Chalupas
Mexican Stuffed Roast
Spanish Rice
Refried Beans
Green Salad with Cherry Tomatoes
    French Dressing
Mexican Cornbread
Fresh Pineapple
Pralines

Individual Molded Cherry Salad filled with Fresh Fruit
Chicken Richelieu
Hattie Mae's Corn Saute'
Green Asparagus with Melted Butter and Lemon Juice
Butter Biscuits
Brandy Ice

Avocado with Shrimp Remoulade
Cheese Straws
Quail Madeira sur Canapés
Wild Rice Casserole
Slivered Green Beans and Fresh Carrots
Grapefruit and Boston Lettuce with French Dressing
Hot Rolls
Warm French Apple Pie

Quiche Lorraine, this could be served in the living room
Escalope de Veau à la Normande
Squash Casserole
Artichoke Hearts and Spinach
Old-Fashioned Wilted Lettuce
Orange Wine Jelly with Chocolate Chip Brownies

NEW YEAR'S EVE BUFFET

New Year's Eve should cater to many desires, those who imbibe of celebration drinks and those who don't.

Split Pea Soup
Swiss Fondue
Gourmet Corned Beef for Sandwiches
Beef Tartare
Pickled Black-Eyed Peas
Lipari Island Dessert

MENUS

BIRTHDAY PARTY FOR CHILDREN

Cream of Tomato Soup with Whipped Cream Floating
Peanut Butter and Jelly Sandwiches
Molded Ice Cream
Cutout Cookies holding Candles

SUPPER FOR WATCHING TELEVISION

Breast of Chicken Papillote à la Paillard
Creamy Corn
One-Cup Salad
Buttercream Crescents
Peppermint Brownies

OUTDOOR SUPPER

Shish Kebab
Eggplant Casserole
Mustard Beans
Dill Casserole Bread
Baklava

FOURTH OF JULY PICNIC

Barbecued Brisket with Buns
Confetti Salad
Cold Relishes in Ice
Peach Ice Cream Cones
     and
Sour Cream Chocolate Cake

THANKSGIVING DINNER

Pink Grapefruit and Shrimp Cocktail
Roasted Tom Turkey with Cornbread Dressing
Cranberry Sauce and Pickled Peaches
Glazed Sweet Potatoes
Hot Rolls
Fresh Green Beans and Little White Onions
Celery Hearts and Olives
Pumpkin Chiffon Pie

CHRISTMAS DINNER

Strained Oyster Soup — Toasted Crackers
Roast Duckling
Rice and Mushroom Casserole
Buttered Peas
Cranberry Salad
Plum Pudding with Hard Sauce

APPETIZERS

MUSHROOMS MONTEMARE

12 large mushrooms	2-4 tablespoons horseradish
½ cup butter, melted	4 tablespoons mayonnaise
12 clams or oysters	12 drops hot pepper sauce or Worcestershire sauce

Preheat the broiler. Remove mushroom stems and wipe with a dry cloth. Dip the caps in butter. On each cap place a clam or oyster. Cover each clam or oyster with ½-1 teaspoon horseradish, 1 teaspoon or more mayonnaise, and 1-2 drops hot pepper sauce or Worcestershire sauce. Place in pan. Broil 6 inches from heat until tops begin to color. Serve hot. Buon Appetito! Serves 6-12. *Mrs. Tozzi served this dish to me. Later the same evening I proposed to her. Perhaps this should be entered as a prescription rather than a recipe!*

Giorgio Tozzi

MUSHROOMS ARNY

2 boxes bite-sized fresh mushrooms	½ cup grated Parmesan cheese
4 slices bacon, finely chopped	¼ cup ripe olives, chopped
1 medium onion, finely chopped	1 tablespoon Worcestershire sauce

Fine dry bread crumbs or packaged corn flake crumbs

Wash and stem the mushrooms, drain. Fry bacon with onion until crisp. Do not drain off the grease, as it binds together the filling. Combine cheese, olives and Worcestershire sauce in a bowl, and blend. Add bacon and onion directly from skillet while still hot. Blend all ingredients thoroughly and stuff mushroom caps. Place caps in a shallow pan and sprinkle with bread crumbs. Broil about 3 minutes, watching carefully. Serve hot. Makes about 32.

Mrs. Edwin E. Harrison, Jr.

MARINATED MUSHROOMS HORS D'OEUVRES

½ cup salad oil	1 teaspoon salt
½ cup olive oil	¼ teaspoon ground pepper
½ cup lemon juice	½ teaspoon dry mustard
1 medium onion, chopped	3 bay leaves

2-3 cans (4 oz.) button mushrooms

Mix all ingredients except mushrooms in a jar with screw top. Add mushrooms. Let stand 12 hours or more. Serve on tooth picks.

Mrs. Hector P. Boncher

CHAMPIGNONS FARCI
Cheese-Stuffed Mushrooms

12 fresh mushroom caps, 2-3 inches in diameter

7 tablespoons butter, melted

Salt and pepper to taste

3 tablespoons onion, finely minced

1 tablespoon oil

3 tablespoons shallots, minced

¼ cup Rainwater Madeira

3 tablespoons fine dry bread crumbs

½ cup natural Swiss cheese, grated

¼ cup grated Parmesan cheese

4 tablespoons fresh parsley, minced

½ teaspoon dried tarragon

3 tablespoons heavy whipping cream

Remove stems from caps. Brush caps with 3 tablespoons butter. Place them, hollow side up, in a shallow, large oven-to-table dish. Sprinkle lightly with salt and pepper. Sauté onion in 2 tablespoons butter and oil for 3-4 minutes without browning over moderate heat in a large skillet. Mince mushroom stems finely and squeeze through a towel to extract juices. Add the shallots and the stems to the butter and onions. Sauté over low heat, stirring, for 6-8 minutes, or until the mushroom pieces begin to separate from each other and brown lightly. Add the Madeira and boil it down until it has almost entirely evaporated. Remove from heat; mix in the bread crumbs, ¼ cup Swiss cheese, ¼ cup Parmesan cheese, parsley, tarragon, and salt and pepper to taste. Blend in cream to moisten, but keep the mixture sufficiently stiff to hold its shape. Fill the caps with stuffing. Top each with a pinch of Swiss cheese and drops of butter, using 4 tablespoons grated Swiss cheese and 2 tablespoons butter in all. They may be done ahead to this point. Bake in upper third of 375° oven, 15-20 minutes, or until stuffing has browned lightly. These mushrooms make wonderful hot hors d'oeuvres or garnish for a meat platter. Serves 6-8.

The Cookbook Committee

QUICK HORS D'OEUVRES

¼ cup onion, minced

½ cup mayonnaise

¼ cup Parmesan cheese

White bread

Combine onion, mayonnaise and Parmesan cheese. Cut bread into small squares or rounds. Spread ½ teaspoon of mixture on each piece. Place on baking pan and brown in 450° oven 5-8 minutes. Sprinkle with additional Parmesan cheese before baking, if desired. Makes 8 dozen.

Dorothy Kirsten

21

TIROPITES

4 eggs

1 pound butter, melted

½ pound margarine, melted

14 ounces cream cheese

1 pound feta cheese

1 pound filo (pastry sheets)

In electric mixer beat egg whites thoroughly, then add yolks. Crumble cream cheese and feta cheese into the size of marbles and drop into well-beaten eggs. Mix well. Cut each sheet of filo across the width, not the length, into 6 strips each about 2 inches wide. Place the filo under a slightly damp towel to keep it from drying out until you are ready to use it. Place 1 strip of filo on the working board perpendicular to the table edge and brush it with the butter and margarine mixture. Place a second strip over the first and brush with butter mixture. Place 1 teaspoon of the filling on the end of the pastry strips nearest you and fold the corner over the filling to make a triangle. Continue folding from side to side in the form of a triangle (like folding a flag) until the end of the strip is reached. Brush folded tiropita with butter and margarine mixture to seal it. Place the uncooked tiropites in a foil-lined box with a sheet of foil between each layer of tiropites. These may be kept frozen until about 25 minutes before you are ready to use them. Place the number desired on a cookie sheet (straight from the freezer) and cook at 350° until they puff up, then reduce heat to 325° and cook until golden brown, 20-25 minutes. Makes 6 dozen. *Tiropites are served either as appetizers or on buffet tables.*

Mrs. Jimmy T. Lontos

ROLLED CHEESE SANDWICHES

18 slices white bread, thin sliced and decrusted

1 cup sweet milk

½ cup butter, melted

2 egg yolks

½ pound cheese, grated

1 tablespoon flour

Mix all ingredients except bread and cook over boiling water until thick. Spread mixture on bread slices. Roll each slice into a log. Brush with butter. Cut in half and toast in oven until brown. Makes 36 sandwiches.

Mrs. Hawkins Golden

CHEESE STRAWS

1 cup butter

½-1 cup Cheddar, American or Swiss cheese, grated

2 cups flour

Salt to taste

Cayenne to taste

Mix soft butter, cheese, flour and seasoning. Put through a cookie press with star blade onto cookie sheet. Dry out in 350° oven for 10-15 minutes. Do not brown. Makes 4-6 dozen.

Mrs. Bogan Gist

CHEESIES

20 slices sandwich bread
1 cup butter

1 egg
1 jar Old English cheese

Cut crusts off of bread. Butter all slices on one side and make sandwiches, then cut each sandwich into three strips. Combine ½ cup butter, egg and cheese. Beat until smooth. Ice all sides of strip sandwiches except bottom. Put in 350° oven for about 15 minutes, or until toasty and slightly brown. Can be frozen before baking. Makes 30 sandwiches.

Mrs. Richard C. Bower

HOT BACON CHEESE BITES

6 slices crisp bacon, crumbled
1 cup American cheese, shredded
¼ cup salad dressing

2 tablespoons green onion, finely chopped
¼ teaspoon Worcestershire sauce
Dash of hot pepper sauce

Sliced white or rye bread

Combine all ingredients except bread. Mix well. (Spread may be made ahead of time and refrigerated.) Cut bread into twenty 1½-inch squares. Spread with additional salad dressing. Top with cheese mixture. Broil until bubbly for 1-2 minutes. Makes 20 squares.

Mrs. Barry A. Thompson

The olive tree has been cultivated for hundreds of years and is recorded as grown in Egypt in the 17th century B.C. There are trees in the districts near Nice and Genoa believed to be more than 2000 years old. Green olives are essentially a relish, ripe olives constitute a wholesome and very nutritious food.

CHEESE BALLS

1 jar Kraft Old English cheese
½ cup margarine

1 cup flour
¼ teaspoon red pepper

Small stuffed green olives

Mix cheese and margarine in bowl. Gradually add flour and red pepper. Place in refrigerator until firm. Pinch off small amount and mold around olive. Place in covered box in freezer until you want to bake them. Bake 12 minutes or until brown in 400° oven. Makes 24.

Mrs. Leo F. Corrigan

STUFFED EDAM CHEESE

1 whole Edam cheese
1/2 cup dry sherry
1 1/2 teaspoons prepared mustard

1 teaspoon Worcestershire sauce
Dash of cayenne pepper
1/4 cup heavy cream

Remove red wax coating of cheese. Cut a 2-inch piece off the top. Carefully scoop out the cheese, leaving a 1-inch thick shell. Grate the cheese and blend with ingredients in order given. Stuff the shell. Serve with crisp crackers, thinly sliced pumpernickel or Scandanavian hardtack. Will keep 4-6 weeks in refrigerator.

Mrs. H. J. Rasmussen

PINEAPPLE CHEESE BALL

2 packages (8 oz.) cream cheese, softened
1 can (8 1/2 oz.) crushed pineapple
2 cups pecans, chopped
1/4 cup green pepper, minced

2 tablespoons onion, minced
1 teaspoon salt
Crackers
Pineapple slices
Maraschino cherries
Fresh parsley

Beat cream cheese with a fork until smooth. Gradually stir in pineapple, 1 cup pecans, green pepper, onion and salt. Shape into a ball and roll in remaining nuts. Wrap gently in foil. Chill overnight. Place cheese on board with crackers. Garnish, if desired, with pineapple slices, cherries and parsley. Serves 35.

Mrs. W. Lee Moore, Jr.

BEER CHEESE

1 pound aged natural Cheddar cheese
1 pound natural Swiss cheese
1 garlic clove, mashed

1 teaspoon dry mustard
1-2 teaspoons Worcestershire sauce
1 cup beer (approximately)

Finely grind or grate cheeses. Mix with garlic, dry mustard and Worcestershire sauce. Gradually beat in beer until mixture is well-blended and of a spreading consistency. Store in crock or covered container in the refrigerator. Serve at room temperature. It is especially good on rye bread with beer.

Mrs. Cullis R. Reese

CHEESE ROLL

1 package (8 oz.) Cheddar cheese

1 package (3 oz.) cream cheese

½ cup pecans, finely chopped

½ teaspoon garlic salt (optional)

3 teaspoons paprika

Dash of cayenne

Pinch of chili powder

Let cheese stand at room temperature until soft. Blend with fingers. Add garlic salt and pecans. Scoop up about half the mixture, holding it in your hands, form a roll about 1¼ inches in diameter. Place the roll on a piece of foil sprinkled with paprika, cayenne and chili powder. Spread the paprika mixture out on the foil about the length of the cheese roll, and roll. Wrap in the foil and chill. Makes 1 cheese roll.

Mrs. Donald D. Smith

BROCCOLI DIP

2 packages frozen broccoli, chopped

1 large onion, chopped

4 tablespoons butter

2 rolls garlic cheese

1 can mushrooms, chopped

1 can mushroom soup

Red pepper and salt to taste

Cook broccoli according to directions on package. Drain well. Sauté onions and mushrooms in butter. Place onion and broccoli in top of double boiler; add the garlic cheese, mushrooms and mushroom soup. Mix well. Add salt and pepper. Cook until melted. Serve hot with Fritos or Doritos or both. Serves 20-30.

Mrs. William B. Oliver

CHILI CON QUESO

4 large onions, chopped

3 large green peppers, chopped

4 tablespoons Crisco

1½ teaspoons salt

1½ teaspoons pepper

3 cans (1 lb.) tomatoes

3½ pounds Velveeta cheese

3 tablespoons flour

½ cup water

4 cans (4 oz.) green chili peppers, chopped

Sauté onions and green peppers in Crisco until tender, but not brown. Add seasonings and tomatoes. Cut cheese into pieces; add to tomato mixture, and stir well to melt. Make a paste of flour and water; add to sauce, and cook until desired thickness. Add chili peppers. Serve as a dip. Serves 20.

Mrs. Phil J. Schepps

CURRIED CHICKEN DIP

1 can (5 oz.) boned chicken

1 can (3 oz.) broiled mushrooms, chopped and drained

1 cup sour cream

2-3 teaspoons curry powder

½ cup cashews, finely chopped

Combine all ingredients except nuts in blender. Switch blender off and on until mixture is smooth. Chill. At serving time stir in nuts. Makes 2 cups.

The Cookbook Committee

CURRIED EGG DIP

4 eggs, hard-boiled

½ cup mayonnaise

½ cup celery, chopped

¼ teaspoon Tabasco

¼ teaspoon dry mustard

½ teaspoon salt

½ teaspoon curry powder

1 tablespoon onion, minced

Cut up eggs and mix in the rest of the ingredients. Serve with potato chips or pieces of raw cauliflower. Serves 4-6.

Mrs. James R. Friedberg

DEVILED DIP

1 jar (5 oz.) pimento cheese spread

1 can (2¼ oz.) deviled ham

½ cup mayonnaise or salad dressing

2 tablespoons parsley, minced

1 tablespoon onion, minced

Dash of Accent

4 drops of Tabasco

With electric mixer thoroughly combine cheese spread, deviled ham, mayonnaise, parsley, onion and seasonings. Chill. Serve with assortment of crackers, potato or corn chips. Makes 1⅓ cups.

Mrs. Joseph E. Smith

HERB-CURRY DIP

1 cup mayonnaise or salad dressing

½ cup sour cream

1 teaspoon mixed herbs, crushed

¼ teaspoon salt

1 tablespoon onion, grated

1½ teaspoons lemon juice

½ teaspoon Worcestershire sauce

1 tablespoon parsley, minced

2 teaspoons capers, drained

⅛ teaspoon curry powder

Blend all ingredients and chill well. Serve with carrot sticks, celery sticks and cauliflower buds. Serves 18.

Mrs. Jean T. DeSanders

FRIED SQUASH

3 pounds yellow, crooked
   neck squash

Corn meal

Salt and pepper

Garlic salt

Mazola oil

Slice squash lengthwise. Put in bowl, salt, cover and leave for at least an hour. Roll in corn meal seasoned with salt, pepper and garlic salt. Fry in oil in large skillet about 10 minutes. Serves 8-10. *May be served as an appetizer or vegetable.*

Mrs. Eugene Jericho

SHRIMP DIP

6 pounds shrimp, cooked

2 quarts Hellman's
   mayonnaise

2 cans (1/4 oz.) parsley flakes

2 cans (2 oz.) frozen chopped
   chives

1 small jar Kraft horseradish
   mustard

Juice of 2 lemons

2 tablespoons onion salt

Cut shrimp into small pieces. Mix the shrimp, mayonnaise, parsley flakes, chives, horseradish mustard, lemons and onion salt well. The last 3 ingredients can be added to taste. Serve with crackers, potato chips or Fritos. Serves 40.

Mrs. Henry L. Foster

TAPENADO
A Provençal Appetizer from France

1 bay leaf

Pinch of thyme

1 clove garlic

10 anchovies

2 cups black olives, chopped

2 cups capers, chopped

2 spoons olive oil

2 spoons rum

French bread

Put the first 6 ingredients in a mortar. Pound until very well crushed and mixed. Add, little by little, olive oil and rum. Serve with toasted French bread. Serves 10-12.

Zino Francescatti

TURKISH EGGPLANT

3 eggplants, round if possible, or sliced diagonally	3 tomatoes, peeled and chopped
Salt	1-2 cloves garlic
Olive oil	1 teaspoon ground allspice
3 large onions, thinly sliced	Pinch of sugar

Cut the unpeeled eggplant into slices ⅓ inch thick. Sprinkle with salt. Pile in colander, cover with a small plate and a weight to hold down, and leave for an hour. Press dry in a cloth. Fry in moderately hot oil, turning once, until both sides are golden brown. Remove from pan and in same oil cook onions until soft and pale yellow. Add the tomatoes and the garlic, mashed to a paste. Season with salt, allspice and sugar. Cook until this makes a thick sauce. Lay the fried eggplant slices on an oiled baking sheet or shallow oven dish. Put a generous tablespoon of the sauce on each slice and bake in a 350° oven for 20-30 minutes. Serve hot or cold. Serves 4. *Use as vegetable or hors d'oeuvre.*

Clifford Curzon

The Greeks had great respect for the aromatic plants we list under the heading of herbs. They believed the herbs had great power upon mental development. They also had some very practical benefits, too . . . Parsley would delay drunkenness (the Greeks always wore garlands of parsley on their heads before a drinking bout), chervil would cease one's hiccups, and dill seeds, when chewed, would certainly stimulate the brain and keep one awake.

RELISH DILL DIP

⅔ cup salad dressing	1 tablespoon parsley flakes
⅔ cup dairy sour cream	1 tablespoon dill seed
1 tablespoon onion, minced	1 teaspoon Beau Monde (optional)
	1 teaspoon salt

Mix in order listed. Serve with assorted chilled vegetables. Serves 20.

Mrs. Richard Wray, Jr.

FRIED ZUCCHINI FLOWERS*

2 dozen zucchini or squash
   flowers

1 cup olive oil or peanut oil

Flour

2 eggs

½ teaspoon salt

Use only the flowers of the zucchini, removing any stem parts. Cover with water and soak for 1 hour. Drain thoroughly and shake lightly in a wire basket to remove moisture. Heat oil to smoking point in a deep skillet. Place several blossoms at a time in a paper bag with a few tablespoons of flour and shake until lightly dusted with the flour. Dip each cluster into the eggs, beaten with salt, and fry quickly in the hot oil. They need to be cooked only about 2 minutes or until golden. Drain on absorbent toweling and serve hot. Serves 4. *My grandmother used to fry the flowers and serve them as an appetizer. Variation: Try dipping them into a beer batter and frying them in deep fat.*

Licia Albanese

ARTICHOKE BOATS

1 can (14 oz.) artichoke
   hearts

2 eggs, hard-boiled

3 tablespoons mayonnaise

1 teaspoon mustard

Salt and pepper to taste

1 teaspoon sugar

¼ teaspoon dill weed

Black olives

Drain artichoke hearts and cut in half lengthwise. Chop eggs fine; add mayonnaise, mustard, salt, pepper, sugar and dill weed. Top artichoke hearts with egg mixture. Decorate each with sliver of black olive. Serves 6-8.

Mrs. Richard A. Wells

*From *The Bel Canto Cookbook* by Peter Gravina
Published by Doubleday and Company

FRENCH ARTICHOKES

4 artichokes   1 clove garlic

1 tablespoon salad oil   1 pint sour cream

1-2 tablespoons caviar

Wash artichokes carefully and soak 30 minutes in salt water. Cut off stems and bottom tough leaves. Cut off ¼ of tops. Cook artichokes upright, covered, 45 minutes or until tender, in boiling water with salad oil and garlic. Drain and remove choke from center of artichoke with spoon, scraping gently when cool. Mix sour cream and caviar, and fill. Serves 4. *Variation: Poach 4 eggs with soft yolk and place in artichoke. Pour homemade mayonnaise with vinegar over artichokes. You can add pepper pickles, thinly chopped, along with chives and parsley.*

Mrs. Howard W. Dunham, Jr.

The Jerusalem artichoke is not to be confused with the French artichoke which is an edible thistle. The Jerusalem artichoke originated in North America and the roots were eaten by the Indians long before the arrival of Columbus. This root has the firm consistency of a potato and somewhat resembles the French artichoke in taste. The Jerusalem artichoke may be cooked in butter and covered with hot cream. San Francisco is famous for the dish, Chicken Jerusalem.

RED CAVIAR SPREAD

1 tablespoon water   1 small onion

1 large lemon, peeled and quartered   ½ cup olive oil

1 jar (4 oz.) red caviar   ½ loaf Pepperidge Farm bread

French bread

Place water, lemon, caviar, onion and ¼ cup olive oil in blender. Remove crusts from Pepperidge Farm bread, tear into small pieces. With motor running add bits of bread and remaining olive oil. Blend until mixture is pale and has consistency of heavy cream. Serve with crusty French bread.

The Cookbook Committee

QUICK BLINI

¾ cup flour
⅓ teaspoon baking powder

½ cup milk
1 egg, slightly beaten

2 tablespoons sour cream

Sift flour and baking powder together. Add milk, egg and sour cream. Stir well. Fry in butter in large skillet, making each cake very thin, and no wider than 1½ inches. Serve with caviar and sour cream. Makes 10-12 blini.

Alexander Kipnis

TARAMOSALATA
Poor Man's Caviar

¼ pound fish roe (Tarama)
8 slices day-old bread, moistened
¾ cup olive oil

¾ cup salad oil
Juice of 2 lemons
Garlic salt to taste

1 teaspoon onion, grated

Place fish roe in bowl. Add bread which has been squeezed well. Beat with electric beater until well-blended. Gradually add mixture of olive oil and salad oil alternately with lemon juice, beating constantly to make a paste of medium consistency. More lemon may be added if desired. Season with garlic salt. Add onion only to the amount used immediately. Serve on small slices French bread or crackers or use as a cocktail dip. Refrigerate remaining spread in a tightly closed jar. Makes 3 cups.

Jimmy T. Lontos

CRAB APPETIZER

1 pound lump crabmeat
1 small jar black caviar, whole grain
4 tablespoons mayonnaise

2 tablespoons chili sauce
Salt and white pepper to taste
Celery salt to taste

Melba rounds or Ritz crackers

Combine all ingredients except crabmeat and Melba rounds. Fold in crab and serve on white Melba rounds or Ritz crackers. Serves 8.

Mrs. Ted Strauss

CURRIED TUNA MOLD

1 can (7½ oz.) white chunk tuna

1 cup celery, finely chopped

½ cup onion, finely chopped

½ cup sweet pickles, finely chopped

Salt and pepper to taste

1-2 tablespoons curry powder to taste

Dash of Tabasco or jalapeno juice (optional)

2 envelopes gelatin

¼ cup cold water

1½ cups hot chicken stock

½ cup Miracle Whip

Drain tuna and add all chopped ingredients, salt, pepper, curry powder and Tabasco. Soften gelatin in cold water and add to hot chicken stock. Mix Miracle Whip with tuna mixture. When the gelatin has cooled and begun to thicken, pour a little gelatin in bottom of 1-quart mold and decorate as you desire. Allow the gelatin to set, and then pack the salad into the mold. (If your mold will not hold all the mixture make another smaller one, for second helpings.) Place in refrigerator until firm. When ready to use, place mold in hot water up to the rim for a few seconds until gelatin melts at the top edge. Turn out on serving platter and garnish. Serve with spreaders and shredded wheat crackers. Serves 25.

Mrs. John R. Hensley

ESCARGOTS BOURGUIGNONNE
Burgundian Snails

1½ cups butter

2 tablespoons shallots, finely chopped

1 clove garlic, mashed

2 tablespoons parsley, finely chopped

¼ teaspoon salt

Dash of pepper

Pinch of nutmeg

48 snails

48 snail shells

Bread crumbs (optional)

2 tablespoons dry white wine

French bread

Cream butter in a mixing bowl. Add shallots, garlic, parsley, salt, pepper and nutmeg. Mix until you have a smooth green paste. Preheat oven to 400°. Wash and drain snails according to directions on can. Wash snail shells thoroughly according to directions. Put a little snail butter in the bottom of each shell. Add a snail. Fill shell with butter mixture. Place shells in snail dishes or in flat baking dish, with open ends up. Sprinkle with bread crumbs. Pour wine in bottom of each dish. Bake in the hot oven for 8 minutes. Serve with thick slices of French bread to mop up extra sauce. Serves 4-8. *Variation: Combine snails with butter mixture and stuff into large mushroom caps and bake until hot.*

The Cookbook Committee

SARDINE CANAPÉS

1 can (3¾ oz.) Norway
   sardines

2 tablespoons butter

1 tablespoon flour

½ cup milk

⅓ cup mayonnaise

½ teaspoon vinegar

1 tablespoon stuffed olives,
   chopped

1 tablespoon sweet gherkins,
   chopped

1 teaspoon onion, minced

2 teaspoons capers

6 slices white bread

Paprika

Salt and pepper to taste

Lemon slices

Radish slices

Drain the sardines and set aside. Melt butter in top of double boiler over simmering water. Blend in flour. In a separate bowl, combine milk, mayonnaise and vinegar. Add gradually to the butter and flour, stirring constantly until mixture is smooth. Season to taste. Continue to cook until mixture thickens. Remove from heat and stir in olives, gherkins, onions and capers. Toast bread lightly on one side, trim and cut into thirds. Arrange a whole sardine on each toast strip and spoon hot sauce over the top. Sprinkle with paprika. Broil for 5 minutes, or until canapés are lightly browned. Garnish with thin lemon slices topped with thin slices of radish. Serve piping hot. Makes 18 large party canapés.

Mrs. William D. Humphrey

MARINATED CHICKEN WINGS

1 cup soy sauce

1 cup brown sugar

½ cup butter

1 teaspoon dry mustard

¾ cup Sauterne

3 pounds chicken wings

Combine and heat soy sauce, sugar, butter, mustard and Sauterne until butter melts. Spread wings in 13 x 9-inch baking pan and pour hot mixture over them. Marinate in refrigerator for 1 hour. Bake at 350° for 1 hour. Turn wings once after 30 minutes. Serves 10-12.

Mrs. Andrew F. Shannon, Jr.

RUMAKI PÂTÉ

½ pound fresh or frozen chicken livers

2 tablespoons butter

6 slices lean breakfast bacon (beef)

1 teaspoon onion, grated

1 teaspoon soy sauce

½ cup sour cream

Freshly ground black pepper

1 can water chestnuts, chopped

Sauté livers in butter until tinged with brown but still moist and slightly pink inside. Chop fine. Add crisp, crumbled bacon, water chestnuts and other ingredients. Blend well. Taste and add salt if needed. Mold in a small bowl and chill. Bring to room temperature. Unmold and serve with crackers or Melba toast. Serves 12.

Mrs. George E. Wilkin

BRAUNSCHWEIGER ROLL

2 large packages Braunschweiger

5 packages (3 oz.) cream cheese

2 bottles (5 oz.) horseradish, drained

Dash of cayenne

Dash of Worcestershire sauce

Dash of Beau Monde

1 teaspoon dry mustard

6-8 drops of Tabasco

Salt to taste

Remove covers from Braunschweiger. Mix cheese, horseradish and seasoning to a whipped texture. Ice Braunschweiger loaves. Sprinkle with paprika. Garnish with parsley. Serve with Triscuits. Serves 20.

Mrs. W. Lee Moore, Jr.

KOREAN-STYLE BEEF CUBES

⅓ cup soy sauce

3 tablespoons fresh ginger, sliced

4 cloves garlic, sliced (about 3 teaspoons)

1½ teaspoons sugar

Tops of 3 green onions, sliced

4 small hot red chilies, seeded and crushed

1½ pounds boneless beef sirloin or high quality top round, cut in ¾-inch cubes

2 tablespoons salad oil

1 tablespoon chopped black sesame seed, toasted, or standard sesame seed, toasted

To make the marinade for the beef, combine ¼ cup soy sauce, ginger, garlic, sugar, onions and chilies. About 30 minutes before serving, stir beef cubes into the marinade; let stand for 30 minutes, stirring once or twice. To serve, heat salad oil in an electric frying pan. Add the drained meat cubes and brown all sides for about 2 minutes or until done as desired. Turn out on a warm plate; sprinkle with remaining soy sauce and with sesame seed. Makes about 4 dozen appetizers.

Mrs. James J. Ling

BEEF TARTARE

2 pounds very lean ground beef, sirloin or round

12 capers (optional)

2 anchovy filets (optional)

3 tablespoons olive oil

1 teaspoon Worcestershire sauce

¼ teaspoon garlic salt

½ teaspoon ground pepper

1 teaspoon salt

1 medium onion

Small party rye bread, thinly sliced (2½-inch size)

Finely chop the capers and anchovies, then mix with the oil, Worcestershire sauce, garlic salt, pepper and salt. Mix to the consistency of a paste. Add paste to the meat and thoroughly mix together. Mold into a loaf and let set until it comes to room temperature. Serve with paper thin slices of onion on the rye with salt and pepper alongside. Let people serve themselves. Serves 8-12.

Richard A. Erb

MEAT BALLS SPECIAL

1 pound ground beef
1 can (8 oz.) minced clams,
   drained

Butter
1 package Lawry's, or other
   spaghetti sauce mix

Mix beef and clams. Roll into small balls, brown in butter, add spaghetti sauce and the juice from the clams, and bake at 350° for 30 minutes. Serves 8.

Mrs. William Andress

PIROSHKI

1½ cups flour
1 teaspoon salt

¼ cup butter
4-6 tablespoons sour cream

Sift flour and salt together. Cut in butter, leaving coarse lumps. Add sour cream a little at a time, just enough to hold dough together. Roll out dough. Fold in 3 thicknesses. Chill 1 or more hours. Roll out thinly. Cut in rounds 3-4 inches in diameter.

FILLING

1 tablespoon onion, minced
1 tablespoon butter
1 cup minced ground meat
   (beef, lamb or chicken)
Salt and pepper to taste

1 hard-boiled egg, minced
¼ cup mushrooms, minced
¼ tablespoon Worcestershire
   sauce
1 teaspoon dill, parsley or
   dill seed, chopped

Beaten egg or milk

Sauté onion in butter until soft. Add remaining ingredients. Cook 5-10 minutes over low heat. If dry add 1-2 tablespoons bouillon. Cool. Put 1 teaspoon filling on each round. Fold over and pinch edges together carefully. Paint with egg or milk. Place on greased baking sheet. Bake at 425° for 15-20 minutes or until golden. Makes 15-20 3-inch Piroshki.

Mrs. Morris A. Galter

MINIATURE PIZZAS

2 cans biscuits

1 pound sausage

1 jar Cheese Whiz, medium-sized

1 can (6 oz.) tomato paste

Split biscuits in half, flatten, press down in center. Mix sausage, cheese and tomato paste, and spread on pastry. Bake at 350° for 10-12 minutes until sausage is done.

Mrs. Peter S. Chantilis

DEVILED HAM PUFFS

½ package (8 oz.) cream cheese

1 teaspoon onion juice

½ teaspoon baking powder

1 egg yolk

Salt to taste

24 bread rounds

2 cans (2¼ oz.) deviled ham

Blend cream cheese, onion juice, baking powder, egg yolk and salt. Toast the bread rounds on one side. Spread the untoasted side with deviled ham and cover each with a mound of cheese mixture. Bake at 375° for 10-12 minutes or until puffed. Makes 24 rounds.

Mrs. Anderson S. Hurst

CORNED BEEF ROLL-UPS

1 can (12 oz.) corned beef

5 tablespoons mayonnaise

5 tablespoons prepared mustard

½ teaspoon salt

¼ teaspoon pepper

½ teaspoon garlic salt

3 dashes of Tabasco

1 loaf thin-sliced fresh bread, 24 slices, crusts removed

3 tablespoons butter, melted

Grated Parmesan cheese

Flake corned beef, add mayonnaise, mustard and seasonings. Mix well. Roll out bread slices thinly with rolling pin. Place bread slices on board. Divide mixture by spoonfuls to center of each slice. Using fork, evenly distribute mixture down middle third of each slice to both edges. Roll firmly twice, having fold on bottom. Line up on cutting board, brush with butter and sprinkle generously with cheese. Cut in thirds and place on ungreased baking sheet. Bake at 400° for 10-12 minutes until light brown. For luncheon, may be left whole and served with soup and salad. Makes 6 dozen hors d'oeuvres or 24 luncheon rolls. *This is my original recipe and was the result of needing hors d'oeuvres in a pinch. I created the recipe on the spot.*

Ruth Tears

PIPING PIGS

1 package weiners   1 cup prepared mustard

1 cup red currant jelly

Cut weiners into bite-sized pieces. Put in 1½-quart oven casserole. Mix mustard and jelly together, and pour over cut-up weiners. Put in 300° oven and cook until bubbling hot, about 20 minutes. Put in chafing dish and serve hot with toothpicks. Serves 12.

Mrs. Robert S. Addison

The hot dog probably had its quiet beginning in Frankfurt, Germany. Its red, white and blue explosion occurred in 1880 when Antoine Feuchtwanger introduced the hot dog to customers in St. Louis. Because it was eaten without a bun, Mr. Feuchtwanger provided his customers with white gloves to prevent burned fingers. The entire world then heard of the American "Red Hot" from the shouts of Mr. Harry M. Stevens, a concessionaire at the Polo Grounds in New York.

BOCCONCINO DI CAMOGLI*

8 paper-thin slices Italian prosciutto, or ordinary ham

⅔ cup Mozzarella cheese, diced

Flour

1 egg, beaten

3 tablespoons olive oil

Arrange 4 slices of prosciutto so they overlap slightly, and place half the cheese in the center. Lightly roll the prosciutto and tuck in the ends so that the cheese will not run out. Dredge lightly in flour and dip in the egg. Fry quickly in very hot olive oil, turning only once when golden brown. This should take no more than 2 minutes for each side. Repeat process with remaining ingredients. Serves 2. *Bocconcino literally means tidbit. Serve this for Sunday brunch instead of a cheese omelet or bacon and eggs. With it I usually serve broiled tomatoes topped with bread crumbs, grated cheese and a pinch of powdered ginger.*

Peter Gravina

*From *The Bel Canto Cookbook* by Peter Gravina
Published by Doubleday and Company

SOUPS

FRUIT SOUP

6 very ripe peaches or   1 tablespoon white wine
   8-10 very ripe apricots

1 pint sour cream

Mix in blender and serve cold. If sweeter mixture is desired, use Cointreau instead of white wine. Serves 4.

Mrs. Sawnie R. Aldredge, Sr.

RED CHERRY SOUP

1 can (1 lb.) red, sour, pitted
   cherries

¼ cup sugar

2 teaspoons cornstarch

¼ teaspoon salt

½ teaspoon cinnamon

½ cup orange juice

½ cup claret wine

Sour cream

Reserve a few whole cherries for garnish. Put remainder of cherries plus liquid from can in electric blender. Blend for 2 minutes. Combine sugar, cornstarch, salt and cinnamon in saucepan; stir in puréed cherries and orange juice. Cook over medium heat, stirring constantly, until mixture comes to a boil; boil 1 minute. Remove from heat and stir in claret. Serve hot or cold, garnished with a spoonful of sour cream and whole cherries. Serves 4.

Mrs. S. Morris Evans, Jr.

SWEDISH FRUIT SOUP

1 cup dried apricots

¾ cup dried apples

½ cup dried peaches

½ cup prunes, pitted

½ cup dark seedless raisins

2 quarts water

¼ cup sugar

3 tablespoons quick-cooking
   tapioca

1 3-inch piece stick cinnamon

1 teaspoon grated orange peel

1 cup red raspberry or strawberry fruit syrup

Whipped cream

Slivered blanched almonds

Rinse the fruit well in cold water. Put fruit into a large sauce pot with a tight-fitting cover and add water; cover and soak 2-3 hours. Add sugar, tapioca, cinnamon and orange peel. Bring to boiling; reduce heat, cover and simmer about 45 minutes, or until fruit is tender. Remove from heat and stir in syrup. Chill. Serve with cream and almonds. Makes about 3 quarts. *This soup is usually served cold and is equally delicious as first course or dessert.*

The Cookbook Committee

ICED LEMON SOUP

4 cups chicken stock
2 cups light cream
2 teaspoons cornstarch

6 egg yolks
8 lemons
1 teaspoon MSG

Dash of cayenne

In saucepan, combine chicken stock and light cream. Heat mixture gently, stirring constantly. Stir in cornstarch. Cook soup over low heat without letting it boil until it begins to thicken. Beat egg yolks lightly and gradually pour a little of the hot soup into them, stirring briskly. Pour egg yolk mixture into soup and add juice of lemons, MSG and cayenne. Let soup cool and chill for at least 8 hours. Serve the soup very cold, garnished with thin slices of lemon and chopped parsley. Serves 12 generously.

Mrs. Anthony Briggle

ASPARAGUS CREAM SOUP

⅔ cup celery, chopped
1 small onion, chopped
3 tablespoons margarine
2 tablespoons butter
2 tablespoons flour

1 can (10½ oz.) asparagus,
   cut in small pieces
1 cup light cream
1 drop green vegetable
   coloring
Salt and pepper to taste

Sauté celery and onions in margarine until tender and set aside. Melt butter in double boiler and add flour and asparagus juice drained from can. Cook until thickened. Combine the above mixtures and add cream, salt, pepper and coloring. Heat and add asparagus. Serve with croutons. Serves 4. *This soup is delicious served with ham loaf, grapefruit salad and baked potato with sour cream.*

Mrs. Mauva D. Reese

AVOCADO SOUP

1 large avocado
1 can jellied chicken
   consomme'
½ cup sour cream
1 teaspoon scraped onion

Salt
Dill
Ham
White Grapes

Purée avocado in blender and fold in consommé, sour cream, onion and salt. Serve topped with dill and julienne of ham or split grapes. Serves 4.

Helen Corbitt

AVOCADO AND CRAB SOUP

4 tablespoons butter	4 ripe avocados
1 onion, finely chopped	1 can (8 oz.) crabmeat
1 clove garlic, finely chopped	1 pint light cream
1 tablespoon flour	Salt and pepper
1 quart chicken stock	2 bay leaves

Sauté onion and garlic in butter, add flour and chicken stock. Whip until smooth. Mash avocados and crabmeat and add to the soup. Simmer for 20 minutes. Finish by adding the cream and seasonings to taste. Serve either hot or very cold.

The Cookbook Committee

Soup predates the Middle Ages. It comes from the words "supper", "sup", or possibly "sop" (sopping up of soup with bread). It is known that primitive men hollowed out a stone and placed it in the middle of the fire and proceeded to cook a liquid broth for his meal.

BEET SOUP

1 can (1 lb.) beets	½ cup sugar
1 beet can water	½ cup lemon juice
1 teaspoon salt	3 eggs, slightly beaten
	Sour cream

Place beets and juice in electric blender on low until well puréed. Put beets and water in saucepan with salt, sugar and lemon juice and heat to boiling point. Add small amount of beet mixture to eggs, mix well and return to saucepan. Heat over low heat 8-10 minutes until thickened. Do not let mixture boil. Remove from heat and strain into bowl. Chill thoroughly and serve with a teaspoon of sour cream on top. May be frozen. Makes 1 quart.

Mrs. Alex Camp

BROCCOLI SOUP

1 package (10 oz.) frozen chopped broccoli

1½ cups milk

3 tablespoons margarine or butter

1 tablespoon instant minced onion

Pinch of oregano or parsley flakes

¾ teaspoon curry powder

1 tablespoon lemon juice

Salt and pepper to taste

1½ teaspoons cornstarch (optional)

Cook broccoli as directed on package. Drain. Purée broccoli in electric blender. Add milk, butter, onion (soaked 10 minutes in 3 tablespoons water), oregano, curry powder, lemon, salt and pepper. Sample and adjust seasonings. Serve hot. May be thickened with cornstarch, if desired. Serves 4.

The Cookbook Committee

CREAM OF CAULIFLOWER SOUP

1 large cauliflower

4 tablespoons butter

2 tablespoons onion, chopped

3 celery ribs, minced

4 tablespoons flour

4 cups chicken or veal stock

2 cups milk or cream, scalded

Salt

Nutmeg

Paprika

Cut cauliflower into florets and cook until tender. Drain and reserve liquid and ⅓ of florets. Put the remaining florets through the blender. Melt the butter and sauté onion and celery until tender. Stir in flour. Slowly stir in stock and bring to a boil. Add strained cauliflower and milk. Add the reserved florets and seasonings. Serves 6. *Variation: Grated cheese, chopped chives or parsley make a delightful change.*

Mrs. William Plack Carr

CUCUMBER SOUP

5-6 cucumbers, peeled and sliced

4-5 scallions, trimmed and sliced

4 cups chicken stock

Salt and pepper to taste

1 tablespoon flour

1 cup hot cream

Unpeeled cucumber, finely chopped

Put vegetables in a saucepan with 1 cup chicken stock, salt and pepper. Simmer for 15 minutes or until cucumbers are soft. Stir in flour, mixed to a paste with a little cold water, and 3 cups chicken stock. Cook soup, stirring until it comes to a boil. Simmer the soup gently for 10 minutes and stir in cream. Turn soup into tureen and sprinkle the top with cucumber. Serves 6-8.

Mrs. Wendell H. Roquemore

GAZPACHO SOUP

1 medium onion, quartered

1 medium cucumber, peeled and cored

1 medium bell pepper, seeds removed

1 quart Italian-style tomatoes, drained

1 quart tomato juice

1 can beef consommé

4 tablespoons olive oil

¼ cup lemon juice

Dash of Tabasco

Salt and pepper to taste

Lemon slices

Chopped parsley

Blend onion, cucumber, pepper and tomatoes in blender. Place in large bowl and add tomato juice, consommé, oil, lemon juice, Tabasco, salt and pepper. Stir well. Let sit at room temperature about 3 hours to blend flavors well. Chill 6-24 hours to meld flavors. Garnish with lemon slices and chopped parsley at serving time. Serves 8.

Mrs. Richard D. Eiseman

GREEN PEA CREAM

1 package (10 oz.) frozen green peas

1 teaspoon salt

2 cups water

1 envelope instant chicken broth or 1 chicken bouillon cube

1 cup whipping cream

1 tablespoon fresh mint, chopped, or ½ teaspoon dried mint leaves, crushed

1 teaspoon onion, grated

⅛ teaspoon bottled red-pepper seasoning

Combine peas, salt and 1 cup of the water in a small saucepan; cook 5 minutes, or until peas are tender. Stir in broth or bouillon until dissolved. Pour into an electric blender; cover, blend until smooth. (If you do not have a blender, press mixture through a sieve into a medium-sized bowl.) Stir in remaining 1 cup water, cream, mint, onion and red-pepper seasoning. Serve hot or chilled. Serves 6.

Mrs. Dwight M. Simmons

LENTIL SOUP

1 pound dried lentils, washed
1 cup carrots, chopped
1 cup celery, chopped
1 teaspoon dried parsley
1 tablespoon salt
Pepper to taste

3-4 buds garlic, pressed, or
1 teaspoon dried minced garlic
3 ounces Contadina tomato paste
⅓ cup olive oil

Place all ingredients in heavy Dutch oven and fill with water up to 1 inch from top. Cook over medium heat until lentils are done. Soup should be of mushy consistency. *Serve with hot French bread, tossed green salad and fruit or berry cobbler for dessert. Very nutritious and high in protein.*

Mrs. Henry E. English

MINESTRONE SOUP

2 cans chick-peas
4 tablespoons olive oil
1 cup onions, chopped
2 cloves garlic, minced
¼ cup celery, chopped
½ cup carrots, diced
1 cup green beans, cut
1½ cups zucchini, diced
1 cup potatoes, peeled and diced

1½ cups cabbage, coarsely chopped
2 tablespoons tomato paste
8 cups boiling water
2 teaspoons salt
½ teaspoon pepper, freshly ground
½ teaspoon basil
2 tablespoons parsley, minced
1 cup cooked macaroni

Parmesan cheese

Drain the canned chick-peas. Heat oil in large saucepan. Sauté onions, garlic and celery for 5 minutes. Mix in the carrots, green beans, zucchini, potatoes and cabbage. Cook 5 minutes. Stir in the tomato paste; then add the chick-peas, water, salt, pepper and basil. Bring to a boil, cover and simmer 1 hour. Mix in the parsley and macaroni, cook 5 minutes, and taste for seasoning. Serve with grated Parmesan cheese. Serves 12.

Mrs. Peter S. Chantilis

MUSHROOM SOUP WITH CHICKEN STOCK

1 hen	Salt to taste
1 pint sweet milk	1 bay leaf
1 can mushrooms, chopped	Red pepper to taste
1 tablespoon flour	Whipped cream

Boil hen until very tender, making 1 quart of stock. To the stock, add milk, mushrooms and half of the chicken breast, finely chopped. Boil all together and add flour for thickening. Flavor with salt, bay leaf and red pepper to taste. Serve in cups garnished with a teaspoon of whipped cream.

Mrs. George N. Aldredge

ONION SOUP IN MUGS

4 cups onions, thinly sliced	6 cups water
5 tablespoons butter	2 teaspoons salt
6 beef bouillon cubes	½ teaspoon pepper
½ cup cognac	

Sauté onions in butter until a very light golden color. Bring bouillon cubes and water to a boil. Add sautéed onions, salt and pepper. Simmer, covered, for 1 hour. Just before serving, add cognac. Serve very hot with warmed crackers in any type of mugs. Serves 6. *Hostesses, like chefs, are often famous for their unique specialties — "the sauce and the soup make the cook" was never more true than in this day of frozen fare, punctuated by electronic easiness. The individual flair is achieved by serving this delicious hot soup from charming old porcelain mugs from a teacart as the preprandial surprise to a seated dinner. You may serve from the cart in your living room, or line the mugs up buffet style for summoning your after-the-game-crowd to the dining room. The aroma is divine and adds immediate interest to your dinner, no matter how simple. It is sure to please the simple soul or the authentic sophisticate who comes to your home.*

Mrs. Morris J. Fogelman

RED ONION SOUP

1 pound red Italian onions, thinly sliced	1½ quarts rich chicken stock
2 tablespoons butter	Salt and pepper to taste
1 tablespoon flour	French bread
	Parmesan cheese

Sauté onions slowly in butter in large pan until onions are slightly brown and clear, about 1 hour. Sprinkle with flour and stir until onions are coated. Cook for a few minutes. Add onions to chicken stock. Season with salt and pepper. Serve with French bread rounds which have been sprinkled with Parmesan cheese and toasted. Serves 4.

Mrs. Arthur A. Collins

SPINACH SOUP

3 cups chicken broth	½ teaspoon salt
1 cup cooked spinach	¼ teaspoon nutmeg
1 tablespoon soft butter	¼ teaspoon pepper
1 tablespoon flour	Sour cream

Put half the broth and all the spinach in blender. Cover and process at high speed until smooth. Empty into saucepan. Put all remaining ingredients except sour cream into blender container. Cover and process at high speed until well-blended. Add to ingredients in saucepan. Bring to a boil, stirring constantly. Lower heat and simmer 10 minutes. Serve hot, topped with sour cream garnish. Serves 4. *This makes a nice Christmas soup. If one wishes to carry the red and green theme — just sprinkle a tiny bit of paprika over the sour cream.*

Mrs. Pepecha Booziotis

SPLIT PEA SOUP

1 large onion, chopped	1 clove garlic, chopped
4 stalks celery, chopped	1 carrot, chopped (optional)
Ham hock bone, with some fat	2 quarts water
Parsley	1 package split peas
Salt and freshly ground black pepper	

Sauté onion and celery in ham fat. Add parsley, garlic and carrot. Add salt and pepper to taste. Add ham hock, split peas and water to vegetables and simmer on top of the stove until thoroughly done, or process in the pressure cooker about 20 minutes. This may be frozen and is really more flavorful after freezing or if it has been in the refrigerator overnight. Serves 6.

Mrs. Hubert B. Braden

CLEAR TOMATO SOUP

¼ cup celery, diced
¼ cup carrot, diced
¼ cup onion, diced
2 tablespoons butter
2 sprigs parsley

4 cups tomato juice
6 whole cloves
1 bay leaf
1 teaspoon salt
⅛ teaspoon thyme

2 cups hot consommé

Sauté celery, carrots and onions in butter for 5 minutes. Add the remaining ingredients except consommé. Bring to a boil. Cover and simmer over low heat for 1 hour. Strain. Add consommé. Serves 4.

Mrs. Mark Schooler

COLD TOMATO AND CHIVE SOUP

2 cups canned tomatoes
1 tablespoon onion, diced
1 stalk celery, chopped
Sour cream

Chopped chives (optional)
Avocado slices (optional)
Melon balls (optional)
Julienne ham (optional)

Put tomatoes, onion and celery in blender. Add equal parts of sour cream and mix. Serve with chives, avocado slices, melon balls or julienne ham, or any combination you wish. Serves 4.

Helen Corbitt

TOMATO-CHEDDAR SOUP

1 can (10½ oz.) tomato soup
1 can (10½ oz.) Cheddar
  cheese soup
1 small can ripe olives,
  finely chopped

1 tablespoon curry powder
Pinch of marjoram
Pinch of basil
1 tablespoon parsley flakes

Mix soups according to directions on cans and bring to a boil. Add rest of ingredients. Serves 4.

Mrs. Sawnie R. Aldredge, Sr.

VICHYSSOISE

4 leeks, finely chopped
1 medium onion, chopped
3 tablespoons butter
3 cups chicken bouillon or consommé
¼ cup dehydrated mashed potato powder

Salt
Pepper, freshly ground
1 cup light cream
Chopped chives
Paprika

Sauté leeks and onion in 2 tablespoons butter until tender, but not brown. Put in soup pot with chicken bouillon. Cook about 15 minutes; strain through sieve. Add dehydrated potatoes, stirring until smooth. Season with salt, pepper, 1 tablespoon butter and light cream. Heat over low heat (do not boil). Cool soup before chilling in refrigerator and serve ice cold. Garnish with chives or paprika. Serves 4. *Variation: If served hot, garnish with grated cheese or diced crisp bacon.*

Mrs. James F. Rose

One would think this French titled soup had its beginning in France . . . But not so! In 1910, when the roof garden was opened at the Ritz-Carlton on 46th Street and Madison Avenue, chef Louis Diat presented Manhattan society with a brand new soup. It was an old French leek and potato soup, cooled with rich milk. The chef made several refinements and named the soup Vichyssoise after the famous French watering spot Vichy. He presented his new soup to Charles Schwab, the famous steel magnate. It became an instant favorite among his patrons.

JELLIED MADRILENE WITH RED CAVIAR

3 cans (10 oz.) Madrilene
½ small can (2 oz.) red caviar

Sour cream
Lemon wedges

Remove Madrilene from can and stir in red caviar. Chill until jelled. Top with sour cream and lemon wedges. Serves 6. *An excellent appetizer for dinner parties*

Mrs. Fred M. Zeder

CRAB BISQUE

1 bunch green onions or shallots

1 pound lump crabmeat

½ cup butter or margarine

2 cans mushroom soup

1 can tomato soup

½ cup sherry

3 cups milk

Parsley, chopped

Sauté onions and crabmeat in butter. Add soups and blend. Add sherry, milk and a lot of parsley. Serve hot. Serves 6-8.

Mrs. Henry L. Foster

CRAB BISQUE

2 cups milk

1 tablespoon flour

2 tablespoons butter

1 teaspoon salt

1/16 teaspoon pepper

⅔ cup cooked or canned crabmeat

Few sprigs fresh celery leaves

Sherry

Place all ingredients in blender in order listed, except sherry. Blend about 15 seconds. Heat in double boiler or over direct flame, stirring occasionally. Add sherry to taste. Makes 2½ cups.

Mrs. Phil J. Schepps

BAKED OYSTER SOUP

6 cups half and half or 3 cups milk and 3 cups light cream, combined

2 tablespoons butter

1 large rib celery, diced

12 salted soda crackers, lightly crushed

Salt, cayenne and black pepper to taste

Generous pinch curry powder (optional)

2½-3 dozen large oysters, shucked (reserve liquor)

Sweet paprika

Preheat oven to 350°. Put half and half in a large saucepan and heat to just under boiling point. Reduce heat to a simmer and add the butter, celery, crushed crackers and seasonings. Drop in the oysters and add their liquor, strained through a triple fold of cheesecloth. When liquid is just under the boiling point, pour soup into oven-proof tureen or large casserole. Put in oven and bake until top is brown. Then stir under. Repeat the process 3 times until the soup is golden brown. When stirring for the last time, add a light dusting of paprika. Serve directly from the tureen. Serves 6.

Mrs. Barron U. Kidd

CAPE CHARLES OYSTER CHOWDER

1 can (10 oz.) frozen condensed oyster stew

1 soup can milk

1 can (10½ oz.) cream of potato soup

½ soup can water

½ cup cooked green beans, cut

1 tablespoon parsley, chopped

Dash of thyme

Chopped pimento

Combine oyster stew and milk. Heat until soup is thawed. Blend in cream of potato soup and water. Add green beans, parsley and thyme. Heat, stirring occasionally. Garnish with pimento. Serves 4-5.

Mrs. Norfleet Figuers

OYSTER STEW

2 tablespoons butter

3 green onions, including tops, finely chopped

1 tablespoon flour

3 cups milk

1 pint large oysters, drained

¼ cup parsley, minced

1 tablespoon Worcestershire sauce

½ teaspoon salt

½ teaspoon ground black pepper

Dash of Tabasco

In top of double boiler, melt butter. Sauté onions slowly until soft, but not browned. Add flour and make a roux; do not brown. Add milk and heat slowly, stirring with rubber spatula until well-blended. Do not boil. Place pan over slowly boiling water. Add oysters and seasonings. As soon as edges of oysters curl, the stew is ready to serve, in about 10 minutes. If over-cooked, it will curdle. Serves 4.

Mrs. Maurice E. Moore

KOTA SOUPA AVGOLEMONO
Egg and Lemon Soup

3 pints chicken stock

1 cup cooked rice

3 eggs, separated

Juice of 2 lemons

1 tablespoon cold water

Salt and pepper to taste

Bring stock to a boil, add rice. Season stock and rice with salt and pepper. Beat egg whites, then fold in yolks until frothy, add lemon juice and water. Take a ladleful of the hot stock and add it slowly to the egg mixture. Add another ladleful, then pour this back into the pan and stir well, keeping the soup away from the fire. Serve at once. Care must be taken not to let the soup boil once the eggs and lemon juice have been added or it will curdle. Serves 6-8.

Mrs. Frank Nick

TURKEY SOUP

Turkey carcass
Celery
1 onion

¼ cup rice
Turkey meat
Salt and pepper

Crack bones. Simmer bones in enough water to cover. Add celery and onion. Simmer 1 hour or more. Add rice, meat from turkey, salt and pepper, and let cook until rice is done. Serves 4-6.

Mrs. William W. Lynch

BEAN AND SAUSAGE SOUP

¼ pound lean salt pork, finely diced
1½ cups tomato juice
1 can condensed black bean soup
1 can (15 oz.) red beans
1 cup raw carrots, diced
1 cup raw celery, diced
1 cup cabbage, shredded
1 cup green onions, chopped (tops included)

6 beef bouillon cubes
1 teaspoon sweet basil
1 teaspoon Accent
Salt
Freshly ground pepper
2 quarts water
¾ cup spaghetti, broken in 1-inch pieces
1 loop (12 oz.) Polish sausage
2 packages (5 oz.) smoked cocktail sausages

Combine salt pork which has been sautéed until brown and crisp, tomato juice, black bean soup, red beans, sauce included, carrots, celery, cabbage, onions, bouillon cubes, all seasonings and hot water in a large soup kettle. Bring to a boil and simmer for 1 hour. Add spaghetti and sausage. Simmer (do not boil) for an additional 30 minutes. Serve along with slices of German black bread spread with cream cheese that has been mixed with small amount of mayonnaise, lemon juice and salt. Serves 8.

Mrs. Thomas W. Massey

BOUILLON

4 pounds round steak

2 turnips

3 carrots

2 onions

1 head of celery

3 bay leaves

Salt

Cover steak with cold water. Cook slowly 1½ hours. Add turnips, carrots, onions and celery, all finely cut. Add bay leaves and very little salt. Cook 7-8 hours. Allow to stand overnight. Next morning skim fat and strain. Salt to taste, and it is ready to serve.

Mrs. George N. Aldredge

At breakfast, Joan of Arc dunked her bread in wine, while the French peasants dunked theirs in broth.

IRISHMAN'S BARLEY SOUP

2 pounds disjointed oxtails

1 cup pearl barley

2 quarts cold water

1 large onion, chopped

2 stalks celery, sliced

2 large carrots, sliced

½ cup fresh parsley, chopped

1 bay leaf

1½ teaspoons salt

½ teaspoon freshly ground pepper

Place oxtails and barley in a large kettle and cover with water. Add remaining ingredients. Heat to boiling, then reduce heat, cover, and simmer 3 hours or until meat is so tender it falls from the bones. Remove meat from bones; return meat to soup. Remove bay leaf; skim off fat. Taste and correct seasoning for salt and pepper. Serves 6-8.

Orline Woodward

BEEF AND VEGETABLE SOUP

3-4 pounds center shank shin bone with meat left on

2 quarts water

2 teaspoons salt

1 teaspoon cracked pepper

⅛ teaspoon dry mustard

⅛ teaspoon paprika

⅛ teaspoon oregano

2 large stalks celery, cut thin, crosswise

1 medium onion, cut radially in thin pieces

1 medium white turnip, pared and diced, or ½ cup cauliflower florets

1 large or 2 small yellow summer squash, peeled and thinly sliced

1 large potato, peeled and diced

2 carrots, pared and sliced ¼ inch thick

2 cans (14 oz.) Italian-style peeled tomatoes

1 regular package frozen mixed vegetables

Place shank, water, salt, pepper, mustard, paprika, oregano, celery and onion in a 5-quart, enameled, iron pot. Bring to boil, cover, and simmer over low fire for 4 hours or until meat is done and loosened from the bone. Take meat from broth, removing all bone, fat and gristle. Set aside to cool while adding turnips, squash, potato, carrots and tomatoes to simmering broth. Add more spice if individual taste desires at this point. Return meat to broth in small hunks. Cook 1 hour or more. Serve with crackers, French bread and butter. Can be made days ahead and reheated as desired. *This is a hand-me-down from my French maternal great-grandmother. A great way to top it off is with quartered pears or apples and dessert cheese, the kind that spreads at room temperature on the fruit.*

Mrs. Edward L. Wilson, Jr.

SALADS
& THEIR DRESSINGS

MUSHROOM SALAD

1 pound mushrooms

Scallions

White truffles if available or
  black olives

¼ pound imported Parmesan
  cheese

Vinaigrette dressing

Slice mushroom caps, tops of scallions and truffles. Coarsely grate or dice Parmesan cheese. Toss with dressing. Serves 4-6. *I have had this salad with beautiful orange, egg mushrooms and fresh truffles several times in Rome. This was part of one of the best dinners of my life at Il Passetto.*

Bill Goldsmith

The truffle, a root-like fungus, is one of the most curious and least understood foods. It grows in clusters, a few inches under the ground . . . somewhat like a potato, but without roots or upper parts of any kind. The secret of its production has never been ascertained, though it has been eaten and enjoyed for centuries. Truffles so freely absorb the nutriment of the soil that nothing except the trees that give them shade is able to grow in the vicinity, so one recognizes a truffle-ground by its bare and somewhat cracked surface. As the truffles themselves show no sign above ground, they are generally located by trained dogs and hogs, held in leash, who find them by the peculiar aromatic odor which ascends through the soil above them.

SALADE NIÇOISE REGINA

Iceberg lettuce, torn in large pieces

Endive, torn in large pieces

Watercress, torn in large pieces

Tiny Italian cherry tomatoes

Whole, small, red radishes

Black olives

Cucumbers, thickly sliced

Young small scallions

Tuna fish or tiny shrimp

Rolled anchovies with capers

Artichoke hearts

Canned whole green beans, crisp and undercooked

Fresh dill, chopped

The greens in this salad can be any combination of 3-4, according to taste, but the success of the salad depends on the variety. The pieces in this salad should be large. Garnish top with scallions. Serve with dressing. *This is one of my favorites. I have used it for as many as 20 to 30 people for a buffet and for as few as 4 to 6 people as a first course at dinner. It has even become a great Sunday night supper.*

ITALIAN DRESSING

Oil

Vinegar

Garlic

Oregano

Parmesan cheese

Salt and pepper

Combine all ingredients according to taste.

Regina Resnik

ALL GREEN SALAD

1 can (1 lb.) whole green beans

French dressing

1 small head lettuce

2 cups spinach, shredded and uncooked

½ teaspoon curry powder (optional)

1 avocado, diced or sliced

1 cucumber, sliced

1 small can artichoke hearts

Drain liquid from can of green beans and fill can with French dressing. Return green beans to refrigerator to marinate 2 hours. Wash greens well, drain, and refrigerate. When chilled and crisp, tear lettuce and spinach into salad bowl. Drain green beans, saving the dressing. Add curry powder to dressing. Add green beans, avocado, cucumber and artichoke hearts. Toss. using only enough dressing to moisten. Serves 4-6.

Mrs. Robert E. Dever

COLD VEGETABLE SALAD

1 package frozen broccoli

1 package frozen, French-style, green beans

1 package frozen cut asparagus

2 packages frozen artichokes

1 green pepper, sliced

1 cucumber, thinly sliced

Cook frozen vegetables one-half the time prescribed on packages. Drain; chill. Add cucumber and green pepper.

DRESSING

½ cup light cream or half and half

3 tablespoons lemon juice

2 tablespoons garlic vinegar

1 cup mayonnaise

¼ cup onion, finely chopped

3 teaspoons anchovy paste

Salt and pepper to taste

Combine all ingredients and pour over salad. Refrigerate overnight. Serves 6-8.

Mrs. Robert J. Shoemaker

GREEK GREEN BEANS

2 cans Del Monte green beans

1 bunch green onions, chopped

1 can (3 oz.) mushrooms, drained and chopped

1 can (5 oz.) water chestnuts, chopped

1 small bottle stuffed green olives, sliced

1 can artichoke hearts, drained

2 tablespoons olive oil

1 teaspoon wine vinegar

2 tablespoons parsley flakes

1 tablespoon oregano

Juice of 2 lemons

Garlic salt to taste

Combine all ingredients, and marinate in refrigerator for at least 6 hours before serving. Serves 6-8.

Mrs. Don Malouf

VIENNESE SALAD BOWL

3 tomatoes, peeled and sliced

1 cup cooled green beans

1 head iceberg lettuce, broken

2 tablespoons parsley, chopped

1 hard-cooked egg, riced

½ cup small croûtons

Combine tomatoes, green beans, lettuce, parsley and egg in bowl, and top with warm dressing and croûtons.

DRESSING

¼ cup heavy cream

2 tablespoons olive oil

1 tablespoon prepared mustard

1 tablespoon white vinegar

1 tablespoon tarragon vinegar

Cook until thick and serve warm.

Helen Corbitt

OLD-FASHIONED LETTUCE SALAD

1 head lettuce, chopped

1 small onion, chopped

2-3 hard-boiled eggs, chopped or mashed

Mustard

Vinegar

Sugar

Bacon, fried crisp and chopped

Salt and pepper to taste

Hot grease from bacon

Mix lettuce with onion. Combine eggs and small quantities of mustard, vinegar and sugar. Toss salad with all ingredients just before serving. Serves 4.

Mrs. George N. Aldredge

GUACAMOLE SALAD

1 ripe avocado, mashed gently

1 tomato, peeled and finely diced

1 medium onion, finely chopped

Salt

Pepper

Dash of hot sauce

Combine all ingredients. Serve on lettuce leaf or tomato slice or dip with tostados.

Mrs. Raymond Stehr

CONFETTI SALAD

1 package (11-12 oz.) extra fine vermicelli

6 ounces Girard's Original French dressing

½ cup juice from crisp sweet pickles

2 cloves garlic, minced

Salt

Dash of cayenne pepper (optional)

1 tablespoon poppy seed

1 teaspoon celery seed

½ teaspoon caraway seed

1 cup hearts of celery and leaves, finely chopped

1 bunch green onions and some tops, finely chopped

6-8 large sprigs parsley, finely chopped

Cook vermicelli in boiling water with 1 teaspoon salt. Rinse and drain. Put in large bowl and coat well with Girard's dressing. Add the pickle juice, garlic, dash of salt, cayenne, poppy seed, celery seed and caraway seed. One hour before serving, add the hearts of celery, the onions and tops and parsley. Serve cold. This salad can be made the day before and kept refrigerated with the greens added 1 hour before serving. Serves 12. *I won a blue ribbon with this recipe in a 1965 food competition in Dallas.*

Mrs. Edward A. Mohns

TWENTY-FOUR HOUR SLAW

1 head cabbage

½ cup sugar

1 onion, chopped

1 green pepper, chopped

½ cup stuffed olives, sliced

¾ cup vinegar

1 teaspoon salt

1 teaspoon celery seed

½ teaspoon black pepper

1 teaspoon prepared mustard

½ cup salad oil

Shred cabbage into large salad bowl. Add sugar, onion, green pepper and olives. Combine vinegar, salt, celery seed, pepper, mustard and salad oil in a saucepan. Boil 3 minutes and pour hot over cabbage mixture. Cover and refrigerate for 24 hours. Serves 8.

Mrs. James D. Flickinger

MARINATED KRAUT SALAD

1 can (1 lb. 12 oz.) sauerkraut, drained and chopped

1 large bell pepper, chopped

1 large onion, chopped

1 cup celery, chopped

1 tablespoon prepared mustard

1 tablespoon horseradish mustard

1 cup cider vinegar

1 cup sugar

1 small jar pimentos

Mix all ingredients except vinegar and sugar. Bring sugar and vinegar to a boil, and boil a few minutes. Pour over first mixture. Place, covered, in refrigerator and marinate overnight before serving. Serves 6-8. *This is a good salad for a covered dish supper or a picnic.*

Mrs. William T. Townsend

POTATO SALAD

Potatoes

Tarragon vinegar

White wine

Celery, chopped

Salt and pepper to taste

Onion, thinly sliced

Lemon juice

Mayonnaise

Sour cream (optional)

Cook, cool and peel the amount of potatoes you need for your salad. Slice the potatoes thinly and begin to make layers in the container in which you are going to mix the salad. Sprinkle each layer with tarragon vinegar, white wine, celery and salt and pepper. Next, add onion and mask this with lemon-flavored mayonnaise or mix 1/2 mayonnaise and 1/2 sour cream. Repeat this process until all potatoes are used. Stir lightly. Let stand for several hours. Put into appropriate serving dish garnished with greens

Gerald Ramsey

NANA'S HOT GERMAN POTATO SALAD

4-5 medium red potatoes

Salt

1 bunch green onions, sliced

¼ cup flour

½ cup sugar

1 pound bacon, sliced into small pieces before frying

½ cup vinegar

1½ tablespoons celery seed

Cook potatoes with jackets, then cool and slice. Salt lightly. Add green onions, plus some of the tops, flour and sugar, and mix well. Brown bacon and add vinegar to frying pan; stir and remove from fire. Pour all contents of frying pan (bacon, grease and vinegar) over salad mixture, and toss gently. Sprinkle with celery seed. This salad should be kept warm until served and is best made in the morning and set inside the oven with just the pilot light on. It does not have to be baked; just warmed for serving. Serves 4. *Serve with thinly sliced ham, rye bread and relish tray*

Mrs. John J. Cadigan

HOT CITRUS FRUIT SALAD

½ jar citrus fruit, cut and drained (canned may be used)

1 cup black cherries, pitted

½ cup maraschino cherries

1 scant teaspoon curry powder

2 large, firm bananas, cut in large chunks

½ cup margarine, melted

½ cup brown sugar

2 tablespoons cornstarch

Mix citrus fruit, cherries, curry powder and bananas. Add margarine to fruit. Mix gently, then add sugar and cornstarch. Bake 40 minutes at 350°. Serves 12. *This salad is especially good for Thanksgiving and Christmas dinners. It is also an excellent accompaniment for beef.*

Mrs. Robert L. Johnson

HOT PINEAPPPLE SALAD

2½ cups chunk pineapple

⅓ cup sugar

½ cup flour

1 cup Cheddar cheese, grated

Butter

Put the pineapple, sugar and flour into a pan. Mix thoroughly. Add Cheddar cheese and dot with a little butter. Pour juice from pineapple over all and cook over low heat 15 minutes until thick. Do not cook too fast. Serves 4-6.

Mrs. Harry E. Bryan

ONE-CUP SALAD

1 cup small marshmallows
1 cup sour cream
1 cup coconut, fresh or toasted

1 cup pineapple
1 cup mandarin oranges
1 cup green grapes (optional)

Mix all ingredients together. Should be prepared in advance and stored in refrigerator for 24 hours. Serves 6. *This is a delicious and very simple salad.*

Ann Donaldson

MINTED FRUIT FREEZE

⅔ cup mint-flavored apple jelly
1 cup salad dressing
1 cup miniature marshmallows

1 cup diced pears
1⅓ cups pineapple tidbits, drained
1 cup heavy cream, whipped

Melt jelly over low heat. Gradually add salad dressing, mixing well. Add marshmallows and fruit. Fold in whipped cream. Pour into a 1½-quart mold; freeze. Unmold and garnish with additional dressing if desired. Serves 6-8.

Sue Herzog

APRICOT SALAD

1 can (7 oz.) apricots, chopped
1 large can crushed pineapple
2¼ cups water
1 large package orange Jello
1½ cups apricot juice, adding water to make 1½ cups, if necessary
1 cup miniature marshmallows
½ cup sugar

3 tablespoons flour
1 egg, beaten
2 tablespoons butter
Juice and rind of 1 lemon
1 envelope unflavored gelatin
1 cup pineapple juice
1 cup whipped cream

Drain apricots and pineapple. Pour 2 cups hot water over Jello; add apricot juice. Cool and fold in apricots, pineapple and marshmallows. Pour into mold. In a saucepan cook sugar, flour, egg, butter, lemon juice and rind, gelatin (dissolved in ¼ cup cold water) and pineapple juice. Stir constantly. Cool and fold in cream. Spread over congealed fruit mixture and refrigerate. Serves 8.

Elizabeth Patterson

CHERRY DELIGHT

1 large package black cherry Jello
1 can pitted black cherries

1 large package cream cheese, softened
3 teaspoons coffee cream

1 cup pecans, chopped

Prepare Jello as directed, using juice from cherries for liquid. Combine cream cheese with coffee cream, add nuts and form into balls. Drop cheese balls into Jello as it begins to set. Pour into 1½-quart square pan, and cut in squares when set; or pour into individual molds. Top with dressing.

DRESSING

1 can crushed pineapple, drained

1 cup sour cream

1 cup whipped cream

Combine ingredients and serve on salad. Serves 6-8.

Mrs. B. T. O'Malley

CRANBERRY SALAD

2 cups hot water
2 packages (3 oz.) cherry gelatin

1 can (1 lb.) whole cranberry sauce
1 pint sour cream

½ cup nuts, broken

Dissolve gelatin in hot water. Chill until it is about to thicken. Add cranberry sauce, mix well, and chill. When it is almost set, fold in sour cream and nuts. Let set several hours before serving. Serves 6-8.

Mrs. Melvin W. Jackson

GREEN GAGE PLUM SALAD

1 can (1 lb. 4 oz.) green gage plums and syrup
1 package lime Jello

2 packages (3 oz.) Philadelphia cream cheese
2 tablespoons almonds, chopped and toasted

2 drops of green coloring (optional)

Drain plums, reserving syrup (light syrup is best). Remove seeds from plums. Put ½ cup of syrup and ½ cup water in top of double boiler; bring to boil; add Jello. Place over double boiler, add cheese, whip, remove from fire. Add plums and almonds. Add green coloring. Pour in individual molds or 1½-quart mold. Serves 6.

Louise Kent Kane

MANGO SALAD

3 boxes (3 oz.) lemon Jello

4 cups water

1 package (8 oz.) cream cheese

2½ cups canned mangoes
with juice

Green grapes

Dissolve Jello in 4 cups of water. Soften cream cheese in blender, gradually adding mangoes and juice. Blend well. Add to Jello and put into 3-quart mold. Chill until firm. To serve, unmold onto platter and fill center with grapes. Serves 10-12.

John Druary

ORANGE JELLO MOLD

1 large package orange Jello

3 cups boiling water

2 cans Mandarin oranges
(drain and save juice)

1 small package orange Jello

1½ cups boiling juice and water

1 package (8 oz.) softened cream cheese

1 cup heavy cream, whipped

Dissolve large package Jello in boiling water and add oranges. Pour into 1½-2-quart greased mold. Place in refrigerator for about 1 hour or until congealed. Make second layer of Jello. Dissolve small package Jello in liquid. Place cream cheese in blender and pour the liquid into the blender. Blend until smooth. Combine cream cheese mixture and cream. Pour over fruit mixture in mold and refrigerate until firm and ready to serve. Serves 6-8.

Mrs. Sam B. Marcus

MARSHMALLOW CHEESE LUNCHEON SALAD

1 package lime gelatin

1 cup boiling water

1 cup minature marshmallows

1 package (8 oz.) cream cheese

¼ cup sugar

2 teaspoons lemon juice

Pinch of salt

1 can (9 oz.) crushed pineapple

½ cup pecans, chopped

½ pint heavy cream, whipped

Pour gelatin into boiling water, add marshmallows and stir well. Put into a 6-cup mold and refrigerate until almost firm. Thoroughly cream the cheese with sugar and add to the gelatin. Add lemon juice, salt, pineapple and nuts. Fold in cream. Chill until firm. Serves 8.

Mrs. Will Garonzik

STRAWBERRY SALAD MOLD

1 package (6 oz.) strawberry Jello

1½ cups boiling water

1 package (16 oz.) frozen strawberries

1 small can crushed pineapple, drained

½ cup nuts

½ pint sour cream

Dissolve the strawberry Jello in water. Add strawberries, pineapple and nuts. Frozen berries will cause the Jello to congeal quickly. Pour half the mixture into an 8 x 8-inch dish and freeze until congealed. Spread with sour cream and top with remainder of Jello. Serves 8.

Juanita Teal Peters

Have you ever wondered why so many colonial houses used the pineapple as a decorative motif? When the Spanish arrived in the West Indies they found that the Indians decorated their huts and villages with pineapples or pineapple tops to express their friendship and hospitality. Since that time it has remained a symbol of welcome.

ASPARAGUS MOLD

1 tablespoon gelatin

¼ cup cold water

1 can cut green asparagus

½ cup mayonnaise

½ cup cream, whipped

1 teaspoon salt

2 tablespoons lemon juice

1 cup blanched slivered almonds

Dissolve gelatin in water. Drain liquid from asparagus and add enough water to make 1 cup. Heat liquid and pour over gelatin. When partially set, fold in mayonnaise, cream, salt and lemon juice. Then add asparagus and almonds. Pour into mold, greased with mayonnaise, and chill. Serve with mayonnaise, whipped with lemon juice. Serves 6. *This is a recipe from my aunt, Mrs. Lera Drake Hancock, who was head of the Home Economics Department at the University of Texas in Arlington.*

Mrs. Jerry W. Peterman

CHEESE SALAD RING

2 teaspoons unflavored gelatin
¼ cup cold water
2 cups cottage cheese
¼ pound blue cheese, crumbled
2 tablespoons parsley, snipped

½ cup mayonnaise
1½ teaspoons Worcestershire sauce
¼ teaspoon seasoned salt
2 tablespoons onion, minced
½ cup heavy cream, whipped

Sprinkle gelatin over water to soften; stir over hot water until dissolved. Blend into cottage cheese and blue cheese; then add parsley, mayonnaise, Worcestershire sauce, salt and onion. Fold in cream. Turn into 1¼-quart ring mold. Refrigerate until set. At serving time, unmold on salad greens. Fill with your favorite fruit salad or cooked vegetable salad. Serves 6-8.

Mrs. Jack N. Cohen

GARDEN SALAD MOLD

2 packages (3 oz.) lime-flavored gelatin
2 cups boiling water
¾ cup cold water
½ cup white vinegar
½ teaspoon salt
2 cups cabbage, coarsely shredded

½ cup radishes, sliced
½ cup celery, finely chopped
½ cup carrot, finely shredded
½ cup green pepper, chopped
2 tablespoons onion, chopped
Salad greens

Place gelatin in bowl; pour boiling water over gelatin and stir until dissolved. Stir in cold water, vinegar and salt. Chill just until mixture begins to thicken. Meanwhile, toss together cabbage, radishes, celery, carrot, green pepper and onion; pack into 1¼-quart ring mold. Pour thickened gelatin over vegetables and chill in refrigerator until firm. Unmold on salad greens and fill center with seasoned cottage cheese. Serves 6-8.

SEASONED COTTAGE CHEESE

2 cups cottage cheese
2 teaspoons onion, grated
¼ teaspoon celery salt

Mix ingredients together and refrigerate. Makes 2 cups.

Mrs. I. C. Deal

JELLIED CUCUMBER SALAD

1 package (3 oz.) lemon Jello
1½ cups boiling water
Medium-sized cucumber, peeled and grated
2 tablespoons vinegar
Lettuce
Pinch of salt
Green pepper, chopped
Pimento, chopped
Mayonnaise or cottage cheese dressing

Dissolve Jello in boiling water; add cucumber, vinegar and salt. Pour into molds or a flat dish and refrigerate. Place on lettuce leaves and garnish with green pepper and pimento. Serve mayonnaise or cottage cheese dressing with it. Serves 4-6.

Aline Murray

TOMATO ASPIC

1 can (1 lb. 4 oz.) tomatoes
¾ cup cold water
1 teaspoon salt
2 teaspoons sugar
½ teaspoon Worcestershire sauce
½ teaspoon pepper
1 tablespoon onion, chopped
2 tablespoons celery, chopped
2 cloves
1 bay leaf
Generous dash of Tabasco
2 tablespoons gelatin
½ cup cold water
1 can undiluted tomato soup
1 tablespoon lemon juice
Small can imported caviar
6 hard-boiled eggs
Mayonnaise

Cook first 11 ingredients slowly for 30 minutes. Soak gelatin in ½ cup cold water for 15 minutes. Add tomato soup to the tomato mixture and stir while still over the fire. Strain mixture over the soaked gelatin and add lemon juice. Pour a small amount of the aspic into rinsed molds and let harden on ice. Split eggs in half lengthwise. Remove the yolks and mash with enough mayonnaise to make a smooth paste. Add caviar to this, mixing gently; place a stuffed egg (stuffed-side down) on top of the set aspic. Fill the molds with rest of mixture and let harden in the refrigerator. Serve unmolded on lettuce, topping with mayonnaise. Seafood, asparagus tips or mixed vegetables may be added instead of eggs. Serves 8-10.

Mrs. Alex F. Weisberg, Jr.

PINK TOMATO ASPIC

1 can tomato soup, diluted
1½ packages (3 oz.) cream cheese
1 tablespoon unflavored gelatin
¼ cup cold water

¾ cup celery, chopped
¾ cup spring onions, chopped
¾ cup green pepper, chopped
1 cup mayonnaise
½ teaspoon salt

Heat soup; remove from heat and beat in cheese. Add gelatin to water and steam by setting in pan of hot water; cool. Add vegetables, mayonnaise and salt. Pour in individual molds; chill. Unmold and serve on half a tomato, cottage cheese or lettuce, surrounded by crabmeat. Makes 8-15 molds.

Ann W. Garlichs

QUICK TOMATO ASPIC

2 cups V-8 juice
1 package (3 oz.) lemon Jello
Pinch of salt
1 small onion, shredded
Small amount of celery, chopped

Cottage cheese
Small amount of green onions and tops, chopped
Small amount of Philadelphia cream cheese
Dash of Worcestershire sauce

Mix 1 cup hot V-8 with Jello thoroughly, then add 1 cup cold V-8, mixing well. Add salt, onion and celery, and pour into individual ring molds or 1 large mold. Fill with combination of cottage cheese, green onions, cream cheese and Worcestershire sauce. Serves 6-8.

Mrs. J. Hub Hill

EXOTIC SYMPHONIC CHICKEN SALAD

3 cups cooked chicken or turkey, cut in large chunks
2 teaspoons onion, grated
2 cups celery, diced
1 cup slivered almonds or pecans, chopped
2 cups seedless green grapes
2 cans (6 oz.) water chestnuts, drained and chopped

2 cups apples, pared and diced
½ cup mayonnaise
⅓ cup wine
1 tablespoon salt
⅛ teaspoon pepper
3 avocados
Lemon juice

Combine chicken, onion, celery, almonds, grapes, water chestnuts and apples. Mix mayonnaise, wine, salt and pepper; toss with chicken mixture. Refrigerate until served. Cut avocados in half, seed and sprinkle with lemon juice just before serving. Serve salad in avocado halves, topped with a few grapes. Serves 6.

Mrs. Kenneth H. Parker

CHICKEN WALDORF SALAD

1½ cups cooked chicken, diced
⅔ cup whole green grapes
½ cup pecans, chopped
⅔ cup celery, chopped
½ teaspoon salt
⅔ cup mayonnaise

Mix all ingredients together and chill before serving. Serves 4.

Mrs. Preston Smith

HAM MOUSSE

½ cup cooked ham, finely ground
1 cup tomato juice
1 cup beef consommé
½ teaspoon paprika
4 tablespoons cold water
1 envelope gelatin
2 cups heavy cream, whipped
Salt to taste
Watercress

Mix ham, tomato juice, consommé and paprika together, and bring to a boil. Dissolve gelatin in water; add to ham mixture. Refrigerate and stir occasionally. When it begins to congeal slightly, fold in cream. Add salt. Pour into 1 large mold or individual molds. Let set in refrigerator until firm. Unmold, garnish with watercress. Serve with mayonnaise dressing. Serves 4-6.

MAYONNAISE DRESSING

Mayonnaise
Few drops of lemon juice
Small amount of heavy cream
Chives, finely chopped

Combine all ingredients and serve with ham mousse.

Mrs. Richard M. Nixon

HAM RING SUPREME

2 eggs, hard-cooked
1 envelope unflavored gelatin
¼ cup celery, chopped
1 small onion, grated
1 cup ground ham (crab or lobster may be used)
1 tablespoon lemon juice
1 teaspoon horseradish
2 tablespoons catsup
Dash of hot pepper sauce
2 teaspoons prepared mustard
Salt

½ cup mayonnaise

Slice 1 egg and arrange in oiled, 1-quart ring mold. Chop remaining egg. Soften gelatin in ½ cup water and dissolve over boiling water. Mix chopped egg, gelatin, celery, onion, ham, lemon juice, horseradish, catsup, hot pepper sauce and 1 teaspoon mustard. Add salt if needed and pack mixture into ring mold. Chill until set. Unmold and serve with mayonnaise seasoned with 1 teaspoon mustard. Serves 4.

Mrs. Asbury B. Greene

BOUILLABAISSE SALAD

1 head Boston lettuce	½ pound cooked shrimp
1 head romaine lettuce	2 peeled tomatoes, quartered
1 bunch watercress	½ cup celery, slivered
1 cup canned or fresh crabmeat	1 hard-cooked egg, chopped
	1 tablespoon chopped chives
1 lobster tail, cooked	

1 small onion, thinly sliced

Break greens in bowl. Arrange seafood, tomatoes and blanched and drained celery on top. Sprinkle with egg and chives. Heap onions on top. Toss with dressing. Serves 6-8.

CAVIAR DRESSING

½ cup sour cream	1 tablespoon horseradish
½ cup mayonnaise	2 tablespoons caviar

Mix sour cream, mayonnaise and horseradish together. Fold in caviar.

Helen Corbitt

CRABMEAT-ASPIC SALAD

1 envelope gelatin	3 hard-boiled eggs, chopped
¼ cup cold water	4 tablespoons sweet relish
¼ cup hot water	1 cup celery, chopped
½ pint whipping cream	1 can (8 oz.) crabmeat or
1 cup mayonnaise	1 cup fresh crabmeat
	1 package lemon Jello

2 cups tomato juice

Soften gelatin in cold water, then dissolve in hot water. Whip cream and add mayonnaise, chopped eggs, relish, celery and crabmeat. Mix with gelatin; put in mold and refrigerate until firm. When the mixture has set, dissolve Jello in 1 cup hot tomato juice, then add 1 cup cold tomato juice. When cool, ladle tomato mixture on top of crabmeat salad. When this has set, unmold entire salad and serve. This can be made the day before. Serves 8-10.

Mrs. H. Ross Perot

SALMON MOUSSE

1 can (1 lb.) red salmon
1 tablespoon plain gelatin
¼ cup cold water
2 tablespoons wine vinegar
¼ cup catsup
¼ cup onion, grated
¼ cup celery, finely minced
½ cup mayonnaise

Drain salmon, remove skin and bones, flake finely. Dissolve gelatin in water. Heat vinegar, add catsup and stir in gelatin. Mix and cool slightly. Stir in onions, salmon, celery and mayonnaise. Serve with cucumber dressing.

CUCUMBER DRESSING

1 cup sour cream
1 tablespoon wine vinegar
1 medium cucumber, peeled and chopped
Dash of Beau Monde

Blend all ingredients in electric blender until smooth. Chill. Serves 6. *This is nice for Sunday supper or a luncheon.*

Mrs. Lucian W. Spencer

TUNA OR CRAB SALAD

2 envelopes gelatin
1 can tomato soup
1 large package Philadelphia cream cheese
1 cup mayonnaise
1 cup celery, chopped
3 tablespoons pickle relish
1 can (6½ oz.) tuna or crab
Nuts (optional)

Stuffed olives, sliced

Dissolve gelatin in enough water to make ⅔ cup liquid. Add soup and melted cream cheese. Add mayonnaise, celery, relish, tuna or crab and nuts. Chill until set. Garnish with stuffed olives. Serves 6.

Mrs. George D. Clark

AVOCADO DRESSING

2 ripe avocados, peeled and quartered
Juice of 1½ lemons
¼ cup vegetable oil
⅛ cup olive oil
1 teaspoon salt
⅛ teaspoon pepper

1 tablespoon dried minced onion
2 tablespoons mayonnaise
2 heads romaine lettuce or iceberg lettuce, broken in bite-sized pieces
2 tablespoons sesame seed, toasted

Place avocados in blender and cover immediately with lemon juice to preserve color. Blend slightly. While beating, slowly add oils. Blend well, and add seasonings. Refrigerate until ready to serve on lettuce. Add sesame seeds. Makes 8 servings.

Mrs. George T. Nicolaou

BASIC BLENDER MAYONNAISE

1 egg
2 tablespoons cider vinegar
¾ teaspoon salt

½ teaspoon dry mustard
Dash of white pepper
1 cup olive oil or salad oil

Place all ingredients except oil in blender and blend at high speed for 5 seconds. Then add ¼ cup oil. Blend 5 seconds more at low speed. Then turn blender to high and add remaining oil in a steady stream. Makes 1⅓ cups.

Mrs. James C. Reid

The origin of mayonnaise is controversial to say the least. Garlic mixed with oil was used by the ancient Egyptians. The Romans brought this sauce to Europe and added eggs. This recipe was used throughout the Mediterranean. Finally in 1757, after the capture of Mahon, a city on the island of Minorca, the Duc de Richelieu discovered the sauce, removed the "horrible" garlic and took mayonnaise to France.

BOURBON SALAD DRESSING

½ cup vinegar

Scant ⅓ cup bourbon

1½ cups oil

1 teaspoon salt

2 tablespoons anchovy paste

1 teaspoon onion

1 teaspoon parsley

½ teaspoon salad herbs

Pepper

Mix and chill. Makes 3 cups.

The Cookbook Committee

CELERY SEED SALAD DRESSING

2¼ cups sugar

4½ teaspoons salt

4 teaspoons paprika

4 teaspoons celery seed

1 onion, chopped

1⅓ cups catsup

1⅝ cups cider vinegar

2 cups Wesson oil

Mix sugar, salt, paprika and celery seed. Add onion, catsup and vinegar. Add oil a little at a time, mixing well after each addition. This will keep indefinitely in the refrigerator. Makes 8 cups.

Mrs. Donald M. Edney

GREEN GODDESS DRESSING

1 cup mayonnaise

1 tablespoon lemon juice

2 tablespoons tarragon vinegar

2 tablespoons garlic vinegar

2 tablespoons shallot vinegar

1 rounded tablespoon anchovy paste

⅓ cup parsley flakes

2 tablespoons onion, grated

½ cup stuffed olives, drained

1 cup heavy cream

Mix all ingredients together adding cream last.

Mrs. Louis T. Kimple

GREEN SALAD DRESSING

1 egg

1 teaspoon salt

1½ teaspoons brown sugar

1 teaspoon dry mustard

½ teaspoon paprika

⅛ teaspoon powdered garlic

½ teaspoon Parmesan cheese

3 tablespoons wine vinegar

1½ cups cold corn oil

Break egg into blender. Add dry ingredients and vinegar; blend well. With blender on high speed, slowly add chilled oil until mixture is thick and well-blended. Chill before serving over tossed green salad. Makes 2 cups.

Peggy Frager Miller

LEMON DRESSING

⅔ cup fresh lemon juice

¼ teaspoon fresh cracked Java black pepper

¼ teaspoon MSG

1 teaspoon Beau Monde

1 teaspoon salt

4 tablespoons French vermouth

2 tablespoons cream sherry (Harvey's, Gordon's or Cresta Blanca Triple Cream)

1⅔ cups French olive oil (Old Monk or James Plagniol)

Finely grated rind of 1 lemon

Combine all ingredients and allow to set overnight for best flavor.

Mrs. Saul N. Hertz

ROQUEFORT DRESSING

½ cup green onions, chopped

½ cup parsley, chopped

2 cups mayonnaise

2 cloves garlic, peeled and halved

1 cup thick sour cream

½ cup wine vinegar

2 tablespoons lemon juice

½ pound Roquefort or blue cheese (may use less)

Salt and pepper to taste

2 tablespoons anchovy paste (optional)

Combine all ingredients in a blender or mixer and let stand overnight before serving. Makes 2½ cups. *This may be used for either green salads or potato salad.*

Mrs. Richard A. Erb

SPRING SALAD DRESSING

2 cups Hellman's mayonnaise

2 ounces parsley, chopped

3 ounces green onions and tops, chopped

2 hard-boiled eggs, chopped

2 tablespoons prepared mustard

2 teaspoons salt

3 tablespoons black pepper

3 tablespoons sugar

1 cup vinegar

2 tablespoons garlic powder or 1 teaspoon fresh garlic, finely chopped

2½ cups salad oil

Combine all ingredients. Makes 2 quarts dressing.

Mrs. Anthony Briggle

Pepper came from a small East Indian climbing shrub with bright red, highly-flavored berries. This expensive item helped to open trade routes by sea to the East. Royal gifts were made of this precious substance.

THOUSAND ISLAND DRESSING

½ cup catsup

½ cup mayonnaise

3 sweet pickles, chopped

2 strips bacon, fried and chopped

1 hard-boiled egg, chopped

1 teaspoon onion, grated

1½ teaspoons vinegar

Combine all ingredients and chill before serving. This may be kept in refrigerator for several days. Serves 8.

Mrs. Donald M. Edney

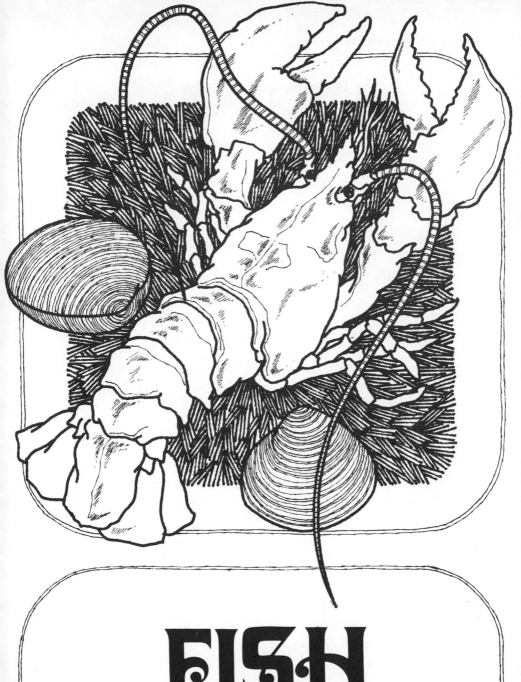

FISH
& SHELLFISH

HUNGARIAN GYPSY FISH
An Old Family Recipe

1 large potato per person, boiled in its skin, peeled and sliced

Butter

Salt and pepper to taste

Paprika

Sour cream

1 large fresh fish, good white meat, about 8 ounces per person

Bacon

Onion rings (1 large onion yields 3-4 portions)

Green pepper, sliced into rings

Tomatoes, sliced

Parsley, chopped

Butter a large Pyrex dish liberally, cover the bottom with a 2-inch layer of sliced potatoes, sprinkle with butter, salt, pepper, paprika and sour cream. Rub the cleaned fish inside and out with salt and butter, make holes on both sides about 2 inches apart and stuff with uncooked bacon. Place the fish over the potato "bed", and cover everything with sour cream, paprika, onion rings and pepper rings. Decorate with tomato slices, and sprinkle the entire dish with chopped parsley. Bake in a hot oven; allow 10-12 minutes per pound, depending on quality of fish. Serve with a mixed green salad with a lemon and olive oil dressing.

Antal Dorati

POMPANO BAKED IN WINE

1 whole (1½ lb.) pompano, split

2 tablespoons pimento, chopped

2 tablespoons onion, chopped

1 cup fresh mushrooms, sliced

2 tablespoons fresh parsley, chopped

2 tablespoons buttered crumbs

½ teaspoon salt

Freshly ground black pepper to taste

1 cup chicken stock

¼ cup dry white wine

Preheat oven to 375°. Place the fish, skin side down, on a greased heatproof platter. Mix the pimento, onion, mushrooms, parsley, buttered crumbs, salt and pepper, and spread over the fish. Mix the stock and wine, and pour around the fish. Bake, uncovered, about 25 minutes, basting occasionally with the wine and broth mixture. Serves 2.

John Browning

POMPANO IN PAPILLOTE

3 medium pompano, cut in halves and boned
3 cups water
1 tablespoon shallots, chopped
6 tablespoons butter
2¼ cups white wine
1 cup crab
1 cup diced shrimp, cooked

Salt and pepper
½ clove garlic, minced
1½ cups onion, chopped
Pinch of thyme
1 bay leaf
2 tablespoons flour
2 egg yolks
Parchment paper
Oil

Simmer heads, bones and water 45 minutes or until reduced to 2 cups. Strain. Sauté shallots and filets in 2 tablespoons butter. Add 2 cups wine. Cover, simmer 5 minutes. Sauté crab, shrimp and ½ the garlic in 1 tablespoon butter. Add onions, salt, pepper and rest of garlic. Cook 10 minutes. Add thyme, bay leaf and 1¾ cups fish stock. Simmer another 10 minutes. Blend flour and butter. Add other ¼ cup fish stock. Add to crab and shrimp mixture along with wine stock drained from the filets. Cook, stirring until thick. Beat yolks, add hot sauce to them slowly, and add ¼ cup wine. Mix. Place in refrigerator until firm. Oil 6 parchment hearts 8x12 inches. Place a spoonful of sauce on 1 side and filet on other. Fold and seal. Lay on an oiled baking sheet. Place in 450° oven for 15 minutes. Serve in bags, letting each person cut his own. The bags may pop in oven when done. Serves 6.

The Cookbook Committee

POACHED SALMON IN BOUILLON

3 pints water
1 bottle dry white wine
1 large onion, sliced
4 carrots, sliced
2 stalks celery, sliced
2 bay leaves

1 bouquet garni
Salt
1 whole (6 lb.) fresh salmon
Lemon slices
Watercress
Cucumber slices

Combine water, wine, onion, carrots, celery, bay leaves, bouquet garni and salt in a kettle large enough for the salmon, bring to a boil and let simmer for about 30 minutes, while skimming. Lower the salmon, wrapped in muslin, into the bouillon, adding water to cover the fish, if necessary, and simmer gently for about 45-50 minutes or until the fish flakes easily with a fork. Remove the fish from the bouillon, lifting in the muslin, and remove the skin. Arrange the salmon on a hot platter, garnished with lemon and cucumber slices and watercress. Serve with melted butter, cucumber salad and boiled peeled potatoes. Serves 10-12. *This is the way my mother used to poach fresh salmon. I was born in Norway on a farm outside of Oslo.*

Ingrid Bjoner

STUFFED EGGPLANT

1 pound steamed snapper
  or cooked shrimp

2 eggplants, halved

2 cups soft bread crumbs
  or buttered croûtons

1 small onion, minced

1 tablespoon parsley, minced

Salt and pepper to taste

1 tablespoon butter

Cook the fish. Steam the eggplant. Remove the pulp and mix with fish and other ingredients. Bake until heated through. Serves 4. *A Creole cook in New Orleans originated this recipe.*

Daisy C. Polk

The tomato traveled from Montezuma's table to Spain, but its tart taste was no more than a curiosity. Finally a clever chef at the Spanish court combined the puréed fruit with olive oil and onions thus creating the world's first tomato sauce.

BAKED RED SNAPPER PLAKI

1 stalk celery, cut into 2-inch
  pieces

½ bunch parsley

3 bunches fresh scallions,
  cut in pieces

2 garlic cloves, finely
  chopped (optional)

1 can tomatoes, crushed
  (optional)

Salt and pepper to taste

4-5 pound red snapper

1 cup cooking oil

2 lemons, thinly sliced

Mix all vegetables together except lemons. Put in bottom of pan. Salt and pepper vegetables. Cover with water. Salt and pepper red snapper. Pour oil over fish. Place lemon slices on top of fish. Bake at 350° for 1½ hours or until vegetables are cooked, basting fish every 15 minutes. Serve fish on a platter and arrange vegetables around fish. Serves 4-6.

Mrs. Gus J. Carras

FILET OF DOVER SOLE

3 filets of sole

¼-½ cup very dry
  white wine

Lemon juice

Flour

Butter or margarine

Heat butter or margarine in a 325° electric skillet. Flour fish and brown 5 minutes on each side. Add lemon juice and wine. Cover and cook 5 minutes. Serve at once. Serves 3.

Mrs. Gerald C. Mann

FILET OF SOLE OSTENDAISE

Butter

1 tablespoon shallots, chopped

½ cup dry white wine

2 double filets of sole

Salt and white pepper

1 cup cream

3 tablespoons San Francisco Bay shrimp, chopped; if not available use Gulf shrimp, chopped

1 tablespoon parsley, chopped

2 tablespoons Hollandaise sauce

Butter a baking dish; add shallots and wine. Flatten filets, season lightly with salt and pepper, and score slightly with a knife so that the filets will not curl. Fold filets in half lengthwise, and place in a pan. Cook on top of stove until the wine starts to simmer, then transfer to a 350° oven until filets are cooked, about 7-10 minutes. Remove filets from pan and keep warm. Return pan to stove, cook wine until nearly evaporated; add cream, evaporate slightly. Add shrimp and parsley. Remove from heat. Add Hollandaise sauce, and stir well. Pour sauce over fish. Serves 2. *This recipe comes from M. Coleux, chef-owner of Le Bayeux Restaurant, in the outskirts of Brussels, Belgium.*

Mrs. John P. Hall, Jr.

TROUT AMANDINE

4 (6-8 oz. each) filets of trout

Salt and pepper to taste

1 egg, beaten

1 cup milk

Flour

½ cup butter

½ teaspoon onion juice

1 tablespoon lemon juice

⅓ cup almonds, blanched and slivered

1 tablespoon parsley, chopped (optional)

Wash and dry fish. Salt and pepper the filets. Dip in batter of egg and milk. Drain. Dredge lightly in flour. In 9-inch skillet, melt ¼ cup butter and ¼ teaspoon onion juice, and sauté trout about 5-8 minutes until a light brown. Remove trout to a warm platter. Pour off the butter and onion juice left in the pan, and add remaining butter and onion juice to the same pan. Add the almonds, and brown slowly. Add lemon juice and parsley, and when the mixture foams, pour it over the fish. Serves 4.

Mrs. Jimmy T. Lontos

TROUT IN VERMOUTH BOUILLON
VERMOUTH BOUILLON

1 tablespoon butter	1 teaspoon parsley
¼ cup carrot, chopped	½ teaspoon salt
¼ cup celery, chopped	6 peppercorns, crushed
½ cup onion, chopped	1 cup dry vermouth

1 cup water or fish stock

Melt butter in saucepan. Add chopped vegetables, parsley, salt and peppercorns, and sauté lightly for 5 minutes. Add vermouth and water or stock. Simmer 15 minutes.

TROUT

8 small brook trout	2 whole cloves
1 quart Vermouth Bouillon	¼ teaspoon mace
1 bay leaf	1 egg yolk, beaten

1 tablespoon butter

Clean trout but do not scrape them. Cover trout with Vermouth Bouillon. Add bay leaf, cloves, mace. Let liquid come to boil, then lower heat and simmer fish about 15 minutes. Carefully lift trout out and remove to warm platter. Reduce remaining liquid to about 1 cup. Remove from heat and stir in egg yolk and butter. Let come to a boil, then pour over fish and serve immediately. Serves 4-6. *This recipe was given to me by Met soprano, Dorothy Kirsten, and she relates the following story about it: "This delicious fish was first served to me in the mountain village of Madonna di Campiglio in the Italian foothills."*

Mrs. Alex F. Weisberg, Jr.

TOPSY-TURVY TUNA LEMON PIE

1 lemon, unpeeled and sliced	2 tablespoons lemon juice
1 can (6½ oz. or 7 oz.) tuna	⅓ cup catsup
2 tablespoons onion, minced	1 egg, well-beaten
1 tablespoon green pepper, minced	¼ pound processed Cheddar cheese, sliced
¼ cup fresh bread crumbs	6 tablespoons milk
½ teaspoon dry mustard	1 cup packaged biscuit mix

Heat oven to 400°. Grease an 8-inch round shallow casserole. Arrange lemon slices in bottom of dish. Mix tuna, onion, green pepper, crumbs, mustard, lemon juice, catsup and egg; spread over lemon slices. Top with cheese slices. With a fork, stir milk into biscuit mix to make soft dough. Spread dough over cheese layer. Bake, uncovered, 15-20 minutes or until light brown. Loosen edges; quickly invert onto a serving dish; cut into wedges. Serve hot as is or with a thin white sauce. Serves 6-8.

Mrs. Paul D. Freeman

TUNA ITALIAN

½ cup onion, chopped

1 can condensed cream of mushroom soup

1 can (6 oz.) evaporated milk or ⅔ cup light cream

⅓ cup grated Parmesan cheese

1 can (7 oz. or 9¼ oz.) tuna, drained

1 can (3 oz.) broiled, sliced mushrooms, drained

6 ounces noodles, cooked and drained

½ cup ripe olives, chopped

2 tablespoons parsley, minced

2 teaspoons lemon juice

Paprika

Cook onion in small amount of hot fat until tender but not brown. Add soup, milk and cheese; heat and stir. Break tuna in chunks; add with remaining ingredients, except paprika. Pour into greased 2-quart casserole. Sprinkle with additional Parmesan cheese and paprika. Bake at 375° for 20-25 minutes. Top with parsley and olive slices. Serves 6.

Mrs. James L. Terry

FISH BALLS

3 pounds whitefish

1 pound carp

2 pounds pike

4 onions

2 raw eggs

½ teaspoon sugar

Salt and pepper to taste

2 teaspoons cracker meal

3 quarts fish stock

2 carrots, cut in ½-inch slices

Filet fish, but retain the heads and vertebrae. Salt the fish and refrigerate while you make the stock. Combine the fish heads and vertebrae with 2 chopped onions, a little salt and pepper, and cover with water. Bring stock to a boil and simmer gently for 15-20 minutes. Put the fish and 2 additional onions through a food chopper, and grind them finely. To this mixture add the eggs, sugar, salt and pepper. Add cracker meal, and chop until the mixture is thoroughly blended. Shape into balls 2-3 inches in diameter. Immerse the balls in the boiling stock (add water to cover if necessary) and cook, covered, for about 2½ hours, until the fish turns white and doubles in size. Add carrots to the pot 30 minutes before the fish balls are finished. Makes about 2 dozen.

Richard Tucker

FISH CASSEROLE

1 small onion, minced

2 tablespoons butter, melted

2 tablespoons flour

1 can (1 lb.) stewed tomatoes

½ cup processed American cheese, diced

1 carton (8 oz.) cottage cheese

Salt, pepper and garlic powder to taste

1 pound fresh or 1 package frozen haddock or cod, thawed

Soft bread crumbs, mixed with butter

Sauté onion in the butter 2 minutes. Blend in flour. Gradually add tomatoes and cook, stirring constantly, until thickened. Add American cheese and stir until melted. Remove from heat, add cottage cheese and seasonings. Cut fish into 2-inch pieces, and put in 1½-quart casserole. Season lightly with salt, and pour tomato mixture on top. Sprinkle with crumbs. Bake at 350° for 35-40 minutes. Serves 4.

Mrs. H. I. Patterson

POULPE À LA GRECQUE
Greek Octopus

1 octopus

4 ounces olive oil

4 ounces vinegar

8 ounces water

2-3 onions

1 clove

Pepper

Garlic

Usually the entire octopus is edible, except for the parrot-like beak. Beat the octopus by laying it on a rock or board, and hit it with a stick from the head down to the extreme ends of all tentacles to soften that big mussle which is called octopus. Then skin the octopus by scratching with a knife, or, as all fishermen do, rub with sand. Cut it in little parts, and put this in a tightly-covered pan. The best way is to seal the pan with a flour-water paste. Add olive oil, vinegar, onions, clove, some pepper and garlic but no salt. Cook for about 2 hours on a very slow fire. I cannot give an approximate cooking temperature since the fire varies from gas to a traditional drift wood fire. If the pan is not completely sealed, the octopus will be spoiled. It can be delicious by itself, or mixed with boiled potatoes or rice. *A true skindiver leaves an octopus alone unless he wants to eat it. Be sure to beat it, otherwise the octopus will be transformed into a product that can compete with the best tires on the market.*

Bernard Kruysen

CLAM PIE

2 cups canned clams, ground or minced, and drained, reserving juice

½ cup cracker crumbs

¼ cup clam juice

1 egg, well-beaten

1 tablespoon butter

1 cup milk

2 small stalks celery

1 small onion

Salt and pepper to taste

2 9-inch unbaked pie crusts

Grind celery and onion in blender with clam juice. Mix all ingredients. Pour into bottom pie shell, dot with butter. Cover top with second pie crust. Prick top crust. Bake at 350° for 1 hour. Serves 8. *This is fun as a hot hors d' oeuvre. I love to serve it during cocktails and tell my guests that they are having their dessert first. It is also a fine luncheon or buffet dish.*

Mrs. Morton Miller

A 4th century Greek writer warned that eating asparagus might cause blindness. The warning was obviously not taken seriously for this vegetable was a favorite with the Greeks. Judging from a recorded remark of the Emperor Augustus . . . that a certain task should be completed quicker than you would cook asparagus . . . the Romans liked their asparagus barely steamed.

CRABMEAT AND ASPARAGUS AU GRATIN

2 tablespoons butter

2 tablespoons flour

1⅔ cups milk

¼ cup sharp Cheddar cheese, grated

¼ cup Swiss cheese, grated

1 teaspoon salt

⅛ teaspoon white pepper

1 tablespoon dry sherry

24-30 asparagus spears, cooked

½ pound crabmeat, in big chunks

Grated Parmesan cheese

Melt butter, stir in flour and add milk gradually, stirring constantly to make a smooth sauce. Add cheese and stir occasionally until melted. Add seasonings and sherry. Simmer very slowly for 10 minutes or longer. Line each individual dish with 4-5 spears of asparagus, using fresh asparagus if possible, or use a 2-quart casserole. Sprinkle well with salt and pepper. Place a layer of crab over the asparagus and cover thoroughly with the sauce. Sprinkle heavily with Parmesan cheese. Bake at 375° for about 20 minutes, or until sauce is bubbly and top is golden. Serves 6. *The assembling of the dish may be done ahead of time, with only the actual heating left for the last minute. It is especially attractive served in individual gratin dishes.*

Mrs. Herbert Beutel

CRAB-STUFFED ARTICHOKES

5 medium artichokes
2 cans (6½ oz.) crabmeat
1 cup processed Swiss
cheese, cubed
⅓ cup green pepper, chopped

¼ cup onion, finely chopped
1 teaspoon salt
½ cup mayonnaise
2 teaspoons lemon juice

Cook artichokes. Be careful not to overcook; they should be firm enough to hold together. Drain crabmeat; break into chunks. Toss with cheese, green pepper, onion and salt. Add mayonnaise and lemon juice to crab mixture; toss lightly. Remove small center leaves and chokes from artichokes. Fill the cup of the artichoke with the crab salad. Place in large casserole. Pour hot water around artichokes to a depth of 1 inch. Cover and bake at 375° for about 35 minutes. Serves 5.

Mrs. James M. Copps

CRABMEAT AND ARTICHOKE CASSEROLE

3 tablespoons butter
3 tablespoons flour
1½ cups hot milk
1 teaspoon salt
⅛ teaspoon pepper
⅛ teaspoon dry mustard
½ teaspoon Tabasco

¼ teaspoon Worcestershire
sauce
⅔ cup grated Parmesan
cheese
4 hard-boiled eggs, quartered
1 can (1 lb.) artichoke hearts,
drained
2½ cups crabmeat

Melt butter, add flour and cook 2 minutes without browning. Whisk in milk and cook until thickened. Add salt, pepper, mustard, Tabasco, Worcestershire sauce and ⅓ cup Parmesan cheese. Add artichoke hearts. Mix eggs, artichoke hearts, sauce and crabmeat. Turn into 7 x 11-inch casserole. Sprinkle with ⅓ cup Parmesan cheese and bake at 350° for 30 minutes. Serves 8.

Mrs. T. Wayne Hensley

CRAB FLORENTINE CASSEROLE

2 packages frozen spinach, cooked and well-drained

1 can (8 oz.) tomato sauce

1 cup sour cream

1 cup cheese, grated

1 cup crabmeat, fresh or canned

1/2 teaspoon nutmeg

1/2 teaspoon Lawry's seasoned salt

1 tablespoon onion, grated

Place spinach in greased 9 x 13-inch casserole. Mix all other ingredients and pour over spinach. Bake at 350° for 25 minutes. Serves 6.

Mrs. Wesley W. Burgess

CRAB CASSEROLE

1 green onion with tops, chopped

1 green pepper, chopped

Margarine, melted

1 can crabmeat, boned and flaked

1 cup soft bread crumbs

3 hard-boiled eggs, chopped

1 can cream of mushroom or celery soup

1 cup mayonnaise (not salad dressing)

1/2 teaspoon salt

1/2 teaspoon pepper

1 tablespoon Worcestershire sauce

3-5 drops Tabasco (optional)

2 cups buttered bread crumbs

Brown onion and green pepper in margarine. Mix all ingredients together and put in 1/2-quart casserole. Sprinkle with bread crumbs. Bake 30 minutes at 350°. Serves 6-8.

Mrs. Howard M. Jarratt

CRABMEAT LUNCHEON DISH

1 can (6 1/2 oz.) crabmeat

3 hard-boiled eggs, diced

1/2 cup slivered almonds

1/2 cup mayonnaise

1/4 cup whipped cream

Sliced ripe olives

Bread crumbs

Mix crabmeat, eggs and almonds with mixture of mayonnaise and whipped cream. Put in individual baking shells or casserole. Sprinkle olives over top and cover with bread crumbs. Bake at 350° for 25 minutes. Serves 4.

Mrs. Robert F. Amundsen

CRABMEAT IMPERIAL CASSEROLE

1 large green pepper, diced

2 pimentos, diced

½ teaspoon salt

½ teaspoon white pepper, freshly ground

1 tablespoon dry mustard

3 tablespoons mayonnaise

2 eggs, lightly beaten

3 tablespoons sherry

2 pounds fresh back-fin lump crabmeat

Paprika

Mix the green pepper and pimentos. Add salt, pepper, mustard, mayonnaise, eggs and 2 tablespoons of sherry; mix. Carefully fold the crab into the pepper mixture so as not to break the lumps of crab. Add the remaining tablespoon of sherry and place in a buttered casserole. Coat the top of the casserole with a thin layer of mayonnaise and sprinkle with paprika. Bake at 350° for 15 minutes. Serves 6. *Most of the cooking in the Price home is done by her housekeeper, but Miss Price has a flair for the art. Friends say that she excels.*

Leontyne Price

CRAB PILAF

4 strips of bacon

2 medium sized onions, finely chopped

1 clove garlic, finely chopped

1 cup raw rice

2 cups white wine

¼ cup parsley, chopped

¼ cup Cognac

2 tomatoes, peeled, seeded and chopped

1 pound crabmeat, lump or back-fin

½ cup heavy or sour cream

Salt to taste

Freshly ground black pepper to taste

Place bacon in heavy, cold skillet, and heat slowly until crisp. Remove the bacon. Add onion, garlic and rice to the bacon fat. Cook until onion is transparent and rice is done. Add wine, parsley, bring to boil and cover. Turn heat down low, and cook for 15-20 minutes or until liquid is absorbed. Stir in the Cognac, tomatoes, crabmeat and bacon, and heat. Stir in the cream just before serving, and season to taste. This is best made with the fresh lump crabmeat, but the frozen king crab from the Pacific Coast will do, as will the canned. Serves 6-8.

Mrs. Robert R. Rember

CRABMEAT REMICH

1 tablespoon celery salt
1 tablespoon dry mustard
1/2 teaspoon paprika
1 quart mayonnaise

3/4 cup chili sauce
1/2 cup tarragon vinegar
1 1/2 pounds lump crabmeat
3 slices bacon, broiled

Combine celery salt, mustard, paprika and mayonnaise, and blend well. Add chili sauce and vinegar, mixing well after each addition. Place crabmeat in a 2-quart greased casserole and bake at 450° for 10 minutes. Arrange bacon halves on top. Add sauce. Broil for 5 minutes. Serves 6. *This recipe originated at Hotel Pontchartrain in New Orleans.*

Mrs. Robert E. Clements, Jr.

S.A.E. CRABMEAT

2 cups or 2 cans (6 1/2 oz.)
    crabmeat, flaked
2 cups sharp chese, shredded

4 tablespoons onion, minced
1/2 cup celery, diced

1 cup Hellman's mayonnaise

Mix all ingredients together. May be served in shells as an entrée or put on small biscuits or crackers and heated in the oven for an appetizer. If cooked in shells, bake at 350° for 10 minutes. Serves 8. *This is a favorite of the Sigma Alpha Epsilon Fraternity Mother's Club.*

Mrs. Roy R. Matthews

CRABMEAT QUICHE

1 1/2 cups white crabmeat
1 tablespoon celery, finely
    chopped
1 tablespoon onion, finely
    chopped
2 tablespoons parsley, finely
    chopped

2 tablespoons sherry
Pastry-lined tin
4 eggs, lightly beaten
2 cups half and half
1/8 teaspoon nutmeg
1/2 teaspoon salt

Mix and refrigerate crab, celery, onion, parsley and sherry. Place in pastry-lined tin. Mix eggs, half and half, nutmeg and salt, and add to crab. Bake at 450° for 15 minutes; reduce heat to 350° and bake until set. Serves 6.

Helen Corbitt

COQUILLES OF DEVILED CRAB

1 pound lump crabmeat,
    fresh, not frozen
8-10 slices day-old bread
    with crust
1 cup butter, melted
1 cup celery, finely chopped
1 cup parsley, finely chopped
4 hard-boiled eggs, finely
    chopped

1 raw egg
1 clove garlic (optional)
3 dashes Tabasco
1 tablespoon Worcestershire
    sauce
Beau Monde
MSG
Finely ground pepper
Cracker crumbs

Toast bread in oven for a few minutes to dry thoroughly. Soak bread in water; squeeze out all water. Place bread in 1/2 cup butter in large skillet, and turn with wooden utensil until brown and dry. Keep fluffy and do not pat. Remove from heat. Add celery, parsley, hard-boiled eggs, garlic, seasonings and crab. Add raw egg and mix well. Try not to break up the large pieces of crabmeat. Grease Pyrex dish and add rest of butter. Sprinkle cracker crumbs on top and add small pats of additional butter on top of cracker crumbs. Bake 45-60 minutes at 350° until cracker crumbs are brown. Serves 8-10.

Mrs. Maurice C. Kramer

CRAB SANDWICH

1 pound crabmeat, fresh or
    frozen
3/4 pound Swiss cheese,
    grated

1/2 cup Miracle Whip
2 tablespoons onion
Pinch of salt
1 tablespoon vinegar

Mix all ingredients together and put on a bun, open-faced. Let bake for 20 minutes at 350°. *Serve with a green salad for a bridge luncheon.*

Mrs. Miles McInnis

KING CRAB SANDWICH

6 English muffins, sliced and
    toasted
Butter
1 1/2 cups crabmeat

1 tablespoon Worcestershire
    sauce
1 teaspoon MSG
24 slices bacon, cooked
12 slices sharp Cheddar cheese

Butter muffins. Combine crabmeat, Worcestershire sauce and MSG. Spread 2 tablespoons of mixture on each muffin half. Criss-cross each with 2 slices bacon. Top with cheese slice. Broil until cheese is melted. Serve hot. Serves 6.

Mrs. Raymond A. Beall

DEVILED LOBSTER TROPICAL

6 small lobsters, or lobster tails or crayfish

6 ripe tomatoes

4 tablespoons butter

1 teaspoon Worcestershire sauce or other hot sauce

1 dessert spoon prepared mustard

4 tablespoons mango chutney

1 teaspoon tarragon vinegar

2 bay leaves

Juice of 1 small lime

1 tablespoon parsley, grated

4 tablespoons peanuts, finely chopped

1 dessert spoon Indian curry powder

Few cubes soft bread dipped into melted mild cheese

Small glass sherry

Grated Parmesan cheese

Plunge live lobsters into boiling water and cook for 20 minutes. Remove from pot, split shells lengthwise and remove dark vein along the back and the small sac behind the head. Remove the flesh and cut it into 1-inch cubes. Keep the shells in neat halves for use later. (Precooked lobster may be used.) Remove meat from the claws and add to rest. Scald and skin a ripe tomato for each lobster and chop coarsely. In a heavy pan melt butter; add Worcestershire sauce, mustard, chutney, tarragon vinegar, bay leaves, lime juice, parsley, peanuts and curry powder. Add the lobster cubes and tomatoes. Sauté slowly over a low fire. At the last minute add the bread cubes and the sherry. Rub the inside of the lobster shells with garlic and fill with the above mixture. Sprinkle lightly with Parmesan cheese and brown under the broiler. Serve at once. Everything up to adding the bread cubes and sherry and stuffing the shells can be done in advance, if desired. Serves 6. *It is a heavenly dish with the flavor of the most exotic curry you ever had, complete with condiments.*

Mrs. Fred M. Zeder

LOBSTER TAILS THERMIDOR

6 (8 oz.) rock lobster tails	Paprika
6 tablespoons butter	1 teaspoon salt
4 tablespoons flour	3 tablespoons sherry
1/8 teaspoon nutmeg	2 cups light cream

1/4 cup Cheddar cheese, grated

Boil unthawed lobster tails in boiling salted water, using 1 teaspoon salt per quart of water, and allowing 3 minutes longer than the ounce weight of largest tail (e.g. 11 minutes for 8-ounce tails.) Drain and cool. With scissors cut away thin underside membrane completely, and with fingers pull out meat. Snip lobster meat into chunks. Rinse shells and drain thoroughly. Refrigerate lobster meat and shells while preparing sauce. In a 2-quart double boiler melt butter; stir in flour, nutmeg, dash of paprika, salt and sherry. Slowly add cream, stirring constantly. Add lobster chunks. Cook over hot water, until just thickened. Heat broiler. Fill reserved shells with hot lobster mixture. Sprinkle each with grated cheese and sprinkle lightly with paprika. Arrange filled shells in foil-lined jelly-roll pan. Broil 6 inches from source of heat until sizzling and just golden on top. Serves 3-6.

Mrs. Stanley H. Boulas

LOBSTER MERMITAGE

1 cup butter	1 1/4 cups heavy cream
4 cups lobster meat	1/3 cup Hine 5 Star Cognac
Salt and pepper to taste	1/6 cup Mohawk anisette
Juice of 1 large lemon	1/4 teaspoon paprika

Heat butter and add lobster to pan. Heat until mixture is warm; do not allow butter to burn. Add salt, pepper and lemon juice. Keep stirring. Add cream and reduce heat. Add Cognac and anisette when ready to serve. Ignite and spoon into the center of a ring of cooked rice. Decorate with paprika. *Mr. Kriendler is the owner of Jack and Charlie's "21" in New York.*

Bob Kriendler

OYSTERS AND SHAD ROE IN CREAM

24 shucked oysters with their juice

12 mushrooms, cleaned and sliced

3 shallots, finely minced

1 sprig parsley, finely minced

1/2 cup white wine

3 pairs shad roe

Butter

2 tablespoons sour cream

1/4 cup heavy cream, whipped

Poach oysters in their own juices and transfer them to a warm place with just enough liquid to keep them moist, reserving the rest. Butter an ovenproof dish generously and add mushrooms, shallots, parsley, wine and shad roe, arranged side by side. Add reserved oyster juice and cover dish with buttered wax paper. Poach the roe at 350° for 10-15 minutes, or until tender. Put them on a heated platter and strain the liquid into a saucepan. Reduce the liquid by half and blend in sour cream and whipped cream. Arrange the poached oysters on the roe and brown them under the broiler. Serve with sauce. Serves 3-6.

The Cookbook Committee

BROILED SPANISH SHRIMP

2 pounds raw Spanish shrimp

4 tablespoons parsley, finely chopped

2 cloves garlic, finely minced

1 cup olive oil

Marinate shrimp overnight. Broil with only the oil that clings to them, about 3 minutes on each side. Sprinkle with fresh ground pepper and salt if needed, but remember seafood carries its own salt box. Serves 4-6.

Helen Corbitt

INDIAN BARBECUED SHRIMP

2 pounds shrimp, jumbo or prawns

1 cup olive oil

3 cloves garlic, minced

1 tablespoon fresh basil, chopped

1 tablespoon mint leaves, chopped

1 tablespoon turmeric

Salt and pepper to taste

Clean and devein shrimp. Mix remaining ingredients together for a marinade. Marinate overnight at least. Thread shrimp on skewers and broil about 10 minutes over hot coals, brushing with marinade. Serve with remaining marinade heated as a dip for the shrimp. Serves 3-4. *This recipe is one of which I am particularly fond. I normally do the broiling on the hibachi in our living room fireplace.*

Igor Kipnis

MARINATED SHRIMP

2 large onions, cut into rings
5 pounds shrimp, cooked
¾ cup sugar
¼ cup salad oil

½ teaspoon salt
2½ teaspoons celery seed
2½ tablespoons capers
2 bay leaves

Dash of Tabasco

Put a layer of onion rings and a layer of shrimp alternately in a bowl until all shrimp and onion are used. Beat sugar, salad oil, salt and celery seed with an egg beater. Add capers and bay leaves. Pour over shrimp. Marinate for 3 days, mixing twice a day. Pour off liquid and serve. Serves 18.

Mrs. Leon Rabin

SHRIMP PACIFIC

1 can (20 oz.) sliced pineapple
1 cup long grain rice
2 cups rich chicken stock or broth
1 teaspoon salt
¼ cup peanut or mild cooking oil
1 large garlic clove, minced or ¼ teaspoon garlic powder

1 onion, chopped
1 green pepper, cut in strips
1½ cups ham, diced
2 teaspoons curry powder
2 teaspoons soy sauce
2 tablespoons preserved ginger, chopped
1-1½ pounds shrimp, cleaned and cooked
2 green onions, sliced

Remove 2 slices from the can of pineapple and ⅓ cup of syrup. Chill the rest of the pineapple. Cook the rice with salt in the chicken stock until it is fluffy. Heat oil and mix in garlic, onion, green pepper and ham. Cook until vegetables are shiny looking but still crisp. Blend curry powder, soy sauce, ⅓ cup of pineapple syrup and ginger. Stir into mixture and heat through. Mix in rice, shrimp, green onions and 2 slices pineapple that you have cut into pieces. Mix and heat until well-mixed and thoroughly heated. Serve on warm platter with icy cold pineapple slices. Serves 6.

Mrs. James P. Neill

POLYNESIAN SWEET-SOUR SHRIMP

1 medium onion, chopped

1 green pepper, cut in 1-inch pieces

2 tablespoons salad oil

3 tablespoons vinegar

1 tablespoon soy sauce

2 tablespoons brown sugar

1/4 teaspoon salt

1/4 teaspoon garlic salt

1/8 teaspoon white pepper

1 can (13 1/2 oz.) pineapple tidbits, undrained

2 tablespoons cornstarch

1/4 cup water

1/2 pound shrimp, cooked, or 1 can (7 oz.) shrimp, drained

Sauté onion and pepper in oil until tender. Add seasonings, pineapple, cornstarch (mixed with water) and shrimp, and simmer, stirring until thickened. Serves 3-4. *Serve with rice, bean sprouts or Chinese noodles.*

Mrs. Barry A. Thompson

There is an old saying in India, "He who plants a coconut tree plants vessels and clothing, food and drink, a habitation for himself and a heritage for his children."

ALOHA CASSEROLE

2 cans cream of mushroom soup

1 cup sour cream

1 cup mushrooms, sliced

1/2 cup Parmesan cheese, grated

Dry mustard

2 cups shrimp, cooked

1 pound spinach, cooked

Toasted coconut

Combine soup, sour cream, mushrooms, Parmesan cheese and mustard. Heat; then stir in cooked shrimp. Layer in serving dish with cooked spinach. Garnish with toasted coconut. Serves 6.

Mrs. Robert A. Fanning

SHRIMP AND ARTICHOKE HEARTS CASSEROLE

1 can (20 oz.) artichoke hearts, drained

3/4 pound shrimp, cooked

1/4 pound fresh or canned mushrooms, drained

1 1/2 cups cream sauce

2 tablespoons butter

1 tablespoon Worcestershire sauce

1/4 cup dry sherry

1/4 cup Parmesan cheese, grated

Salt and pepper

Paprika

Arrange artichoke hearts in a buttered baking dish. Spread the shrimp over the artichokes. Sauté the mushrooms in butter for 6 minutes and add to the baking dish. Mix Worcestershire sauce with sherry and cream sauce, and pour into baking dish. Sprinkle top with Parmesan cheese and paprika. Bake for 30-40 minutes at 375°. Serve hot, garnished with parsley. Serves 4-5. *This recipe was found in a collection of souvenir recipes in the Adlai Stevenson family kitchen records. Mr. Stevenson served it at a luncheon for the late President Kennedy and Mr. U Thant.*

Roberta Peters

The avocado was a favorite with the inhabitants of Mexico long before the arrival of the Spanish conquistadors in the 16th century. The fruit was so honored that many of the native potters designed their ceramic jars in its pear-like shape.

AVOCADO BOMBAY

1 small white onion, chopped

1 small apple, peeled and chopped

2 tablespoons butter

2 cans cream of chicken soup

Pinch of salt

3-4 teaspoons curry powder

2 1/2 cups cooked shrimp or chicken

6 ripe avocados, peeled and halved

4-5 cups cooked rice

Sauté onion and apple in butter over low flame. Stir in chicken soup. Do not add water. Salt to taste and add curry powder. Heat over low flame until smooth. Add shrimp or chicken. Place avocado half on bed of rice on each plate and fill with curry mixture. Serve with condiments: raisins, crisp bacon pieces, chopped nuts, green pepper, toasted coconut and kumquats. Serves 6. *This is a great "one-dish" meal. Avocado Bombay is good with fresh fruit salad with poppy seed dressing, hot holls, white wine and lemon meringue pie for dessert.*

Mrs. William A. Kramer

AVOCADO WITH SHRIMP REMOULADE

¼ cup tarragon vinegar

2 tablespoons horseradish mustard

1 tablespoon catsup

1½ teaspoons paprika

¼ teaspoon cayenne

½ teaspoon salt

½ cup salad oil

¼ cup celery, minced

¼ cup green onions and tops, minced

2 pounds shrimp, cleaned and cooked

4 medium avocados

In a small bowl, combine vinegar, horseradish mustard, catsup, paprika, cayenne and salt. Slowly add oil, beating constantly. Stir in celery and onions. Pour sauce over shrimp; marinate in refrigerator about 5 hours. Halve and peel avocados. Lift shrimp out of sauce and arrange 5-6 shrimp on each avocado half. Can also be served with carrot strips, hard-boiled egg halves, asparagus spears on lettuce leaves for luncheon meal. Serves 8.

Norman Treigle

SHRIMP CREOLE

1 pound raw shrimp, unshelled

2 tablespoons salt

2 bay leaves

¼ teaspoon thyme

¼ teaspoon marjoram

1 small red pepper

1 cup onion, minced

½ cup green pepper, minced

½ cup shortening

1 cup tomatoes, chopped

1 cup celery, minced

1 tablespoon parsley, minced

1 clove garlic

¼ cup flour

Wash shrimp 3-4 times in water. Place shrimp in a pan. Add enough water to cover. Add salt, bay leaves, thyme, marjoram and red pepper. Boil approximately 8 minutes. When cool enough to handle comfortably, shell and devein shrimp. Save the liquid to use later. Set shrimp and liquid aside. In a skillet, sauté onion and green pepper in ¼ cup shortening until slightly browned, add tomatoes, no water. Cook on a slow fire for 5-8 minutes. Add celery, parsley and garlic. Cook 5-8 minutes. Set aside. In a fresh skillet, brown flour in remaining ¼ cup shortening. Add shrimp liquid or water until a satisfactory gravy consistency is reached. Add all vegetables and cook slowly about 10 minutes. Stir often. Add cooked shrimp last. Serves 3-4. *This is a favorite New Orleans dish.*

Mrs. W. Fred Buchanan

SHRIMP À LA GRECQUE

6 tablespoons olive oil

1 medium onion, chopped

1 clove garlic, peeled

1 can (1 lb. 12 oz.) whole peeled tomatoes

Salt and pepper

1/4 teaspoon sugar

2 tablespoons butter

2 pounds shrimp, shelled and deveined

2 tablespoons Cognac

2 tablespoons Ouzo

1/4 pound feta cheese, diced

2 tablespoons parsley, chopped

French bread

Heat 4 tablespoons oil in a heavy skillet; add onion and garlic, and cook until lightly browned. Add tomatoes, salt, pepper and sugar. Cook over moderate heat until thickened, about 30 minutes. Melt butter and remaining oil in a skillet. Add shrimp and sauté until they lose their transparency. Add Cognac and Ouzo. Heat and flame the shrimp. Place shrimp in a casserole, cover with tomato sauce and cheese, then sprinkle with parsley. Bake 15 minutes at 425°. Serve over crisp, toasted French bread in large, shallow bowls. Serves 4. *This is a hearty, strongly-flavored dish good served with a robust red wine and a green salad with black olives. The Ouzo, an anise-flavored Greek liqueur, and the Greek goat cheese, feta, are absolutely necessary for the success of this dish.*

Bill Goldsmith

COLD CURRIED SHRIMP WITH COLD RICE AND CHUTNEY

3 pounds shrimp

1 pound long grain rice

4 medium-sized apples, peeled, cored and sliced

2 large onions, chopped

6 stalks celery, chopped

1/2 cup butter

4 tablespoons flour

4 tablespoons curry powder

4 cups hot chicken broth

1/2 cup light cream

1 jar chutney

Boil shrimp. Shell, devein and refrigerate. Cook rice until fluffy and cool. Cook apples, onions and celery in 6 tablespoons butter until soft and brown, about 10-15 minutes. Add 2 tablespoons butter and 4 tablespoons flour mixed with curry powder. Stir in hot chicken broth and simmer for 30 minutes. Cool. Place mixture in a blender a little at a time until mixture is completely liquified. Chill. Add cream and stir well. Place rice on luncheon plates or dinner plates, and pile with shrimp. Pour sauce over shrimp, reserving part for a sauce boat. Accompany with chutney. Serves 8.

Mrs. Robert H. Mitchell

SHRIMP JAMBALAYA

2 packages (6 oz.) Spanish rice mix

2 slices boiled ham, ¾ inch thick, cut into ½-inch cubes

3 tablespoons butter, melted

2 cups celery, chopped

½ cup scallions, snipped

2 cups green peppers, coarsely chopped

1½ pounds shrimp, cooked and deveined

2 teaspoons seasoned salt

¼ teaspoon seasoned pepper

1 can (1 lb.) whole tomatoes, drained

Cook rice as directed. Sauté celery and green pepper in 2 tablespoons butter until tender. Add scallions and ham. Sauté a few minutes longer. Add remaining 1 tablespoon butter and shrimp. Add seasoned salt and seasoned pepper. Cook, tossing often, until shrimp are heated through. Add tomatoes and heat. Add shrimp-vegetable mixture to rice and toss lightly. Serves 8-10.

Mrs. Richard I. Allen

SHRIMP PILAU

4 strips bacon

¼ cup green pepper, chopped

¼ cup celery, chopped

¾ cup rice, uncooked

1 clove garlic, minced

½ cup water

2 tablespoons onion, chopped

1 can (1 lb. 12 oz.) tomatoes

1 teaspoon salt

¼ teaspoon pepper

Tabasco to taste

2 cups shrimp, cooked, shelled and deveined

Fry bacon until crisp. Remove, drain and reserve. Add green pepper, celery, rice, garlic and onion to fat in pan. Cook slowly until rice is golden brown. Stir in water, tomatoes and seasonings. Blend well. Stir in shrimp. Pour in 3-quart casserole. This may all be done ahead of time. Bake at 300° until rice is tender and liquid is almost absorbed, about 45 minutes. Toss in crumbled bacon prior to serving. Serves 4.

Mrs. Arthur E. Hewett

SHRIMP CASSEROLE

1½ cups cooked rice

1½ cups cooked shrimp, halved

1 can mushroom soup

1 teaspoon parsley, chopped

Juice of ½ lemon

½ teaspoon salt

Small amount of blue cheese

2 tablespoons butter, melted

2 tablespoons celery, chopped

½ bell pepper, chopped

2 tablespoons onion, chopped

Juice of ½ clove garlic

1 cup Swiss cheese, grated

Paprika

Combine rice, shrimp, soup, parsley, lemon juice, salt and blue cheese. Sauté celery, pepper, garlic and onion in butter. Add to shrimp mixture. Place in greased casserole and cover with Swiss cheese and paprika. Cook at 350° for 40 minutes. Serves 4.

Mrs. Cecil M. Higginbotham

ARROZ DE GAMBAS VARANDA DO CHANCELER
Rice with Shrimp from Portugal

1½ pounds raw shrimp

3 tablespoons butter

1 cup fresh tomato purée

¼ cup heavy cream

2½ cups rice, cooked

Salt and pepper to taste

Shell and devein shrimp. Sauté shrimp in butter for about 5 minutes or until they are bright pink. Add tomato purée and cream; stir well. Cook the shrimp gently in the sauce until heated through. Combine shrimp mixture with rice, and season with salt and pepper. Turn shrimp and rice into a buttered casserole and bake at 350° for 10 minutes. Serves 4.

Alvin Kerr

UNCLE VICTOR'S BOUILLABAISSE

1 pound green shrimp

12 cloves

1/2 pound fresh mushrooms

2 large onions, cut in small pieces

2 cloves garlic, mashed

2 tablespoons chicken fat, olive oil or butter

1 can tomato soup

3 bay leaves

1 1/2 teaspoons imported curry powder

1 cup American cheese, diced

1/2 cup sherry or 1/2 beer and 1/2 whiskey

Salt to taste

Dash of ground pepper

2 pounds fish filets (haddock, flounder, etc.)

1 pound lobster meat (canned may be used)

1 pound scallops

2 dozen oysters

Boil shrimp and 4 cloves in 1 1/2-quarts water and 1 level teaspoon salt for 6 minutes. Remove shrimp with straining spoon leaving water in pot to be used later for fish. Remove shells from shrimp and slit in half lengthwise. Cut mushrooms in 1/4-inch slices and let stand with shrimp until needed. Put chicken fat in a large frying pan. Fry onion and garlic until golden and add soup and 1 soup can water. Add 4 cloves, bay leaves, curry powder, cheese, 1/4 cup sherry, and allow mixture to simmer 30 minutes. Season with salt and pepper to taste. As soon as this mixture is started, bring the shrimp water to the boiling point, turn heat to very low and add fish, scallops, remaining 4 cloves and 1/4 cup sherry. Allow to simmer until fish is tender. The water must not actually boil or the fish will break up. After fish has simmered 15 minutes, turn off heat so it will remain hot but not cook. When mixture in frying pan has simmered 1/2 hour, turn off heat if you are not ready to serve. Allow to stand. If you are ready to serve, add shrimp, mushrooms, 2 tablespoons of a thickening mixture (made by mixing 1 egg white with 1/2 cup milk and 2 tablespoons of flour beaten together until smooth) and allow to cook 5 minutes, stirring constantly. The mushrooms should not cook more than 5 minutes. The lobster meat and oysters should be added the last 2 minutes of cooking. (If fresh lobster is used, it should be boiled first, meat removed and added last.) To serve, strain water from fish. Place fish on a large hot serving platter and gently break it up distributing it over the platter. Remove bay leaves from frying pan mixture and pour over the fish. Serves 10. *This is nice for buffet with fried rice, green vegetables and green salad.*

Mrs. H. Neil Mallon

GUMBO

½ cup bacon grease or cooking oil

2 green peppers, minced

4 medium onions, minced

8 stalks celery, minced

4 tablespoons flour

5 packages frozen cut okra, defrosted

3 cans (1 lb.) tomatoes

Salt and pepper

2 tablespoons Worcestershire sauce

2 tablespoons Tabasco

2 tablespoons Kitchen Bouquet

2 tablespoons vinegar

1 tablespoon gumbo filé

4 quarts water

3 pounds shrimp

2 pounds crabmeat

2 cans clams with juice

1 quart oysters (optional)

Heat bacon grease and cook green pepper slowly until tender. Add onions and celery, and cook until tender and brown, stirring. Add flour and blend. Remove from heat. In a separate pot cook okra until no longer stringy and brown at edges. Drain tomatoes thoroughly, put through a food grinder and add to okra. Cook and stir for 15 minutes. Combine vegetable and flour roux with okra mixture, juices from tomatoes, salt, pepper, Worcestershire sauce and Tabasco to taste. Add Kitchen Bouquet, vinegar, gumbo filé and 1 quart water. Cook uncovered for 1 hour. Add 3 quarts water and simmer 3 hours. Add shrimp, crab, clams and oysters. Heat and serve. Serves 24.

Mrs. Christiaan J. D. Rote

POULTRY

KURINAYA OTBIVNAYA COTLETTA

1 chicken breast, split and
   deboned

Salt and pepper to taste

Tarragon (optional)

Flour

1 egg, separated

Butter

Oil

Place chicken breast between 2 pieces of waxed paper. Pound well and season with salt, pepper and tarragon. Dip in flour. Beat egg white stiffly. Beat egg yolk and fold into egg white. Season with salt, pepper and tarragon. Dip chicken breast in egg mixture, and fry immediately in preheated skillet with half butter and half oil for approximately 5 minutes on each side. Serve immediately. Serves 2.

Mstislav Rostropovich

CHICKEN SUPREME

6 chicken breasts, boned,
   skinned and halved

1 can mushroom soup

1/4 pound dried beef

1/2 pint sour cream

12 strips bacon

Soak dried beef to remove some of the saltiness. Then chop it and place it in the bottom of a casserole large enough to hold the chicken. Roll chicken breasts and wrap each with a strip of bacon. Place in casserole. Mix mushroom soup with sour cream, pour over chicken breasts and marinate for at least 3 hours in refrigerator. Bake at 275° for about 3 hours. Serves 12.

Rose E. Bampton

CHICKEN MOMI

STUFFING

¼ cup light cream	½ pound ground pork
1 cup soft bread crumbs	1 egg
⅓ cup onion, finely chopped	1 tablespoon soy sauce
1 can (5 oz.) water chestnuts, drained and minced	1 teaspoon fresh ginger, grated
2 tablespoons butter	⅛ teaspoon MSG
¼ pound ground veal	⅛ teaspoon cayenne

Pour cream over bread crumbs. Sauté onion and chestnuts in butter. Mix onion mixture with softened bread, veal, pork and seasonings.

CHICKEN

6 whole chicken breasts, boned	2 tablespoons honey
	1 tablespoon soy sauce
Salt	1 tablespoon sesame seed
2 tablespoons soft butter	

Papaya and lime slices

Pound inside of chicken breasts to flatten slightly, sprinkle with salt. Top each with a scant ½ cup of stuffing. Tuck corners of the chicken over the stuffing and fasten with skewers or wooden picks. Place skin side up in a greased baking pan. Cream butter with honey; slowly beat in soy sauce. Spoon mixture over chicken. Bake in a 325° oven about 45 minutes, basting occasionally with pan drippings, until chicken is tender. Sprinkle with sesame seed, increase temperature to 450°, and continue baking about 10 minutes longer or until well-browned. Garnish with papaya and lime slices before serving. Serves 6.

Dr. Robert E. Gaylord

ROLLED CHICKEN

½ cup fresh mushrooms, finely chopped, or 1 can (3 oz.) broiled chopped mushrooms, drained

2 tablespoons butter

2 tablespoons flour

½ cup light cream

¼ teaspoon salt

Dash of cayenne

1¼ cups sharp Cheddar cheese, shredded

6-7 whole chicken breasts, boned

Flour

2 eggs, slightly beaten

¾ cup dry bread crumbs

For cheese filling, cook mushrooms in butter for about 5 minutes. Blend in flour; stir in cream. Add salt and cayenne. Cook and stir until mixture becomes very thick. Stir in cheese and cook over very low heat, stirring constantly, until cheese is melted. Turn mixture into pie plate. Cover, chill thoroughly, for about 1 hour. Cut the firm cheese mixture into 6-7 equal portions. Shape it into short sticks. Remove skin from chicken. Place each piece, boned side up, between 2 pieces of waxed paper. Over-lap meat where chicken breast is split. Working out from the center, pound with mallet to form cutlets not quite ¼ inch thick. Peel off paper. Sprinkle with salt. Place a cheese stick in each chicken breast. Tucking in the sides, roll chicken as for jelly roll. Press to seal well. Dust the chicken rolls with flour; dip in eggs, then roll in fine bread crumbs. Cover and chill chicken rolls for at least 1 hour. About 1 hour before serving time, fry rolls in deep, hot fat for 5 minutes or until crisp and golden brown; drain on paper towels. Place in shallow baking dish and bake at 325° about 30-45 minutes. Serve with your favorite sauce. Serves 4.

Mrs. Mitchell T. Peters

In Homer's day, the Greek women's kitchen duties were to grind cereal, bake bread and prepare soups . . . but the men did all the serious cooking.

SUPREMES DE VOLAILLE À LA MILANAISE

4 supremes (chicken breasts, boned)

¼ teaspoon salt

Big pinch of pepper

1 cup flour

1 egg, beaten

⅛ teaspoon salt

½ teaspoon olive oil

½ cup freshly grated Parmesan cheese

½ cup fresh white bread crumbs

Season the supremes with salt and pepper. One at a time, roll them in the flour and shake off excess. Mix egg, salt and olive oil; dip supremes in olive oil mixture. Then roll in the cheese and bread crumbs, patting them in place with the flat of a knife. Lay the supremes on waxed paper and allow cheese and bread crumbs to set 10-15 minutes or several hours if preparing ahead of time. Sauté on both sides in Clarified Butter until resilient to the pressure of your finger. Serve with Brown Butter Sauce poured over the supremes. Serves 6-8.

CLARIFIED BUTTER (BEURRE CLARIFE)

When ordinary butter is heated until it liquifies, a milky residue sinks to the bottom of the saucepan. The clear yellow liquid above it is clarified butter. To clarify butter, cut it into pieces and place it in a saucepan over moderate heat. When the butter has melted, skim off foam and strain the clear yellow liquid into a jar leaving the milky residue in the bottom of the pan.

BROWN BUTTER SAUCE (BEURRE NOISETTE)

4 tablespoons clarified butter

3 tablespoons fresh parsley, minced

1 tablespoon lemon juice

Add Clarified Butter to butter in which supremes were sautéed. Cook over moderately high heat until the butter has turned a very light golden brown, for 1-2 minutes. Immediately remove from heat, stir in parsley and lemon juice and taste for seasoning. Pour over the supremes and serve.

Frank Porretta

CHICKEN ANTOINETTE

3 chicken breasts, boned, skinned and cut in half
½ cup butter
1 tablespoon onion, minced
½ tablespoon salt
½ tablespoon crushed black pepper

2 cups heavy cream
1 pound fresh mushrooms, sliced and sautéed
4 tablespoons brandy
4 tablespoons sherry or Madeira
8 ounces wild rice

Sauté chicken in butter. Add seasonings, then cream and mushrooms. Before serving, add brandy and sherry or Madeira. Serve chicken and sauce on bed of wild rice. Serves 6.

Mrs. Harold C. Howard

CHICKEN RICHELIEU

6 chicken breasts, boned
Salt, pepper, celery salt, garlic salt, Accent, flour, paprika
6 tablespoons butter

1 can cream of mushroom soup
¼ cup sherry
1 can (3 oz.) sliced mushrooms
2 teaspoons bell pepper flakes

1 can chicken broth, or 2 chicken bouillon cubes dissolved in 1 can (10½ oz.) water

Season chicken on both sides with salt, pepper, celery salt, garlic salt and Accent. Roll in flour, then sprinkle paprika generously on both sides and place, skin side down, in baking pan in which the butter has been melted. Brown for 20 minutes in 450° oven, turn chicken, and reduce oven temperature to 350°. Add soup, sherry and broth, combined with mushrooms and bell pepper flakes, and continue cooking until tender, basting occasionally, if liquid does not cover. When ready to serve, place chicken on serving dish, and use liquid for gravy or sauce. Serves 6-12, depending on size of chicken breasts.

Mrs. Ben R. Buford

CHICKEN DIVINE

3 pounds chicken breasts, boned

1 stalk celery

1 large onion

2 packages frozen broccoli

In a pot of hot water sufficient to cover the contents, place the chicken breasts, celery and onion. Cook about 30 minutes over medium heat. Remove the chicken but save the broth. Slice the cooled chicken into thin pieces. Cook broccoli until almost done, but still firm. Slice thinly.

SAUCE

⅓ cup plus 2 tablespoons butter

½ cup flour

Pepper to taste

1¼ cups chicken broth

1 cup whipping cream

1¼ teaspoons salt

Grated Parmesan cheese

1 can (4½ oz.) mushrooms, sliced

Melt ⅓ cup butter in saucepan and add flour. Gradually add broth, cream and salt. Cook slowly until thickened. Butter an oblong Pyrex roasting dish. Arrange broccoli in the dish and sprinkle with salt and pepper. Cover with ½ of the sauce. Sprinkle lightly with cheese. Add mushrooms and chicken slices. Pour remaining sauce over the chicken. Sprinkle with cheese. Pour 2 tablespoons melted butter over the top. Bake at 350° for 30 minutes. Serves 8.

Claire Campbell

CHICKEN BREASTS À LA MADEIRA

¼ cup sherry

½ cup Madeira

1 can cream of chicken soup

1 can cream of celery soup

8 chicken breasts

Cheddar cheese, grated

Paprika

Add wines to soups and pour over chicken breasts in shallow baking dish. Sprinkle with cheese and paprika. Bake at 275° for 2½-3 hours.

Jean Madeira

BREAST OF CHICKEN PAPILLOTE À LA PAILLARD

4 large chicken breasts

Salt and pepper to taste

6 ounces pâté de foie gras

Flour

3 tablespoons butter

2 tablespoons oil

½ pound small mushrooms

½ pound small cooked carrots

3-4 tablespoons butter

4 large mushroom caps

4 sheets parchment paper or Kraft paper

1 cup Marsala

2 cups demi-glacé

1 truffle

Salt and pepper the breasts, spread the pâté on the meaty side. Dredge with flour and pat with hands to distribute evenly. Sauté slowly in butter and oil for approximately 15 minutes on each side. Meantime, sauté mushrooms and carrots together in butter. Reserve and keep warm. Sauté the mushroom caps and keep warm. Place breasts on oiled parchment paper. Drain oil and butter from chicken pan and deglaze with Marsala. Then add demi-glacé, salt and pepper. Garnish with the small mushrooms and carrots for each breast. Add slice of truffle to each and julienne remainder to decorate. Top with sautéed mushroom caps. Spread each breast with 1½ teaspoons sauce. Fold paper to form papillote and 1 minute before serving place in 450° oven. The paper may pop when ready to serve. To form papillote, place square of paper with one point up, one down, and one on each side. Place chicken in lower center. Fold up bottom point over chicken, then fold in each side. Fold bottom up and over towards top leaving enough top paper to make a flap. Tuck flap in bottom half. Serves 4.

The Cookbook Committee

CHICKEN PARISIENNE

4 large or 6 medium chicken breasts

1 can cream of mushroom soup

1 can (3 oz.) mushrooms

1 cup sour cream

½ cup cooking sherry

Salt and pepper to taste

Paprika

Place chicken breasts, skin side up, in an 11½x7½x1½-inch baking dish. Combine remaining ingredients; pour over chicken. Sprinkle generously with paprika. Bake at 350° for 1-1¼ hours. Serve with hot fluffy rice. Serves 4-6.

Mrs. William J. Alexander

CHICKEN MARILYNNE

¼ cup butter
10 chicken breasts
2 cans cream of chicken soup
1 can (4 oz.) mushrooms, sliced

1 can (5 oz.) water chestnuts, sliced
½ cup white wine
½ cup toasted almonds, diced
Salt, pepper and paprika

Place chicken in baking dish. Season lightly with salt, pepper and paprika. Top with dabs of butter. Bake in 350° oven for 1-1¼ hours until lightly browned. Mix together soup, mushrooms, water chestnuts and wine. Pour over baked chicken. Sprinkle almonds on top and heat in 300° oven for 45 minutes. Serves 6-8.

Mrs. J. Ronald Horowitz

CHICKEN IN WINE

4 large chicken breasts, halved
1½ cups Vin Rosé
¼ cup Wesson oil
¼ cup soy sauce
2 tablespoons brown sugar

½ teaspoon oregano
2 teaspoons powdered ginger
1 can (8½ oz.) pineapple chunks
1 can (2 oz.) mushroom pieces
1 tablespoon flour

1 package (2½ oz.) almonds

Arrange chicken breasts in roaster or baking dish. For wine sauce mix wine, Wesson oil, soy sauce, brown sugar, oregano and ginger. Pour sauce over chicken. Cover and bake at 325° for 1½-2 hours or until tender. Last ½ hour, add pineapple chunks and mushrooms to sauce. Remove chicken and keep warm. Dissolve flour in water to form a paste, and add to sauce. Cook to thicken. Pour sauce over chicken breasts. Top with almonds. Serves 8.

Mrs. William H. Clingman

BREAST OF CHICKEN SAUTÉ

6 whole chicken breasts   ⅓ cup Cognac
½ cup butter   1 cup flour
¾ cup beef consommé   1 teaspoon salt
½ teaspoon paprika

Skin chicken; dredge in seasoned flour. Shake off any excess. Melt butter in skillet. Sauté chicken until golden brown on all sides. Remove. Deglaze skillet with consommé. Add Cognac and ignite. Return chicken to pan. Cover and simmer for 5 minutes. Baste chicken. Serve on asparagus. Serves 6.

ASPARAGUS SAUTÉ

18 stalks asparagus   ¼ cup butter
Grated lemon peel

Cut asparagus slanty-eyed. Place in skillet with butter. Cover and cook about 3 minutes. Shake to prevent sticking. Sprinkle with grated lemon peel.

Helen Corbitt

CHICKEN ORANGE

6 chicken breasts   1 package onion soup mix
1 small can frozen orange juice

Preheat oven to 350°. Clean and dry chicken. Place in baking dish; sprinkle with soup mix. Spoon orange juice on top of chicken. Place in oven for 1½ hours. Keep container covered with foil for 1 hour; then remove for last 30 minutes. Serves 6.

Mrs. Marvin G. Kramer

BREAST OF CHICKEN VERONIQUE

3 tablespoons butter

1 large chicken breast, halved

6 medium mushroom caps, quartered

1 tablespoon flour

½ cup seedless grapes

½ cup light cream

2 tablespoons dry white wine

⅓ cup ham, diced

Salt and white pepper

Melt 2 tablespoons butter in heavy pan. Brown skinned chicken over medium heat and transfer to casserole. Melt remaining butter in skillet and sauté mushrooms 3 minutes over high heat. Remove them and scatter over chicken. Reduce heat and stir flour into skillet. Cook 1 minute. Add cream and wine. Add ham. Cook 2 minutes. Season and pour sauce over chicken. Bake, covered, at 350° for 35-40 minutes. Uncover casserole, scatter the grapes on top and bake 10 minutes more. May be made ahead, refrigerated, and reheated, but grapes should not be added and cooked until 10 minutes before serving. Serves 2.

Mrs. Herbert Beutel

CHICKEN CELESTE

8 chicken breasts

Flour, seasoned with salt and pepper

2 tablespoons corn oil

2 tablespoons butter or margarine

½ teaspoon Accent

½ cup green onions, chopped (part of tops included)

1 cup sherry

1 cup mayonnaise

2 tablespoons parsley, minced

Paprika

Salt to taste

Shake chicken in a paper bag with the flour. Melt butter and oil together in a heavy skillet; brown chicken on all sides. Add Accent, onion and sherry. Cover and simmer gently for about 45 minutes until chicken is tender, turning and basting occasionally. Remove to platter and keep warm. Add mayonnaise to juices in the skillet and blend thoroughly until smooth, using a rotary beater if necessary. Add parsley and salt. Serve chicken and gravy (which may be thinned with additional sherry if desired) over rice, topping with a dash of paprika. Serves 4-6.

Mrs. Thomas W. Massey

TRUFFLED CHICKEN

4 chicken breasts
¼ cup butter, melted
1 small can truffles
2 cups light cream sauce
¼ cup port wine
Pepper and salt to taste

½ cup imported Swiss cheese, grated
1 can (3 oz.) mushrooms, sliced
½ cup dry bread crumbs
2 tablespoons Parmesan cheese, grated

Sauté the skinned chicken breasts in butter for 20 minutes. Meanwhile, slice truffles thinly, add liquid to cream sauce, and cook truffles 2 minutes over medium heat in small pan with port wine. Place the sautéed chicken pieces in a buttered casserole and season. Sprinkle with half of the Swiss cheese. Add mushroom liquid to cream sauce. Top chicken with mushrooms and sprinkle with rest of cheese. Finish with sliced truffles, then pour sauce over all. Sprinkle with bread crumbs and cheese mixture, dot with butter, and bake at 350° for 40 minutes (first 20 minutes covered; second 20 minutes uncovered). Serves 4. *Are you entertaining next week's guest soloist for the symphony? Serve him something elegant for dinner — truffled chicken with brown rice, Brussels sprouts with green grapes and crème de menthe parfait.*

Mrs. S. Morris Evans, Jr.

BROILED CHICKEN WITH MUSHROOMS

¼ broiler per person
Fresh lemon
¾ cup melted butter
2 garlic cloves
8 large mushrooms, chopped

2 teaspoons marjoram
½ teaspoon salt
Pinch of nutmeg
2 tablespoons soy sauce
½ cup brandy

Rub all sides of broiler pieces with lemon juice. In saucepan, melt 6-8 tablespoons of the butter; add garlic. Lay chicken, skin side down, on rack in 450° oven. Brush with garlic butter. Broil 12 minutes, turn and broil for 15 minutes. Meanwhile, melt 4 tablespoons butter in small skillet; add mushrooms, marjoram, salt, nutmeg and soy sauce. Cook 5 minutes. When chickens are golden brown, remove to pan. Pour mushroom mixture over and bake at 300° for 20 minutes. Pour warm brandy over and ignite. Let flames die before serving. Serves 4.

Mrs. James F. Rose

CHICKEN LUCETTE

2 chickens (3 lbs. each)
1½ cups sherry
½ cup butter
4 tablespoons cooking oil
½ can (8 oz.) tomato sauce
2 teaspoons flour

Salt and pepper to taste
Herbs (parsley, 2 bay leaves, pinch of thyme)
12-18 medium-sized mushrooms
1 pint heavy cream

1-2 medium-sized truffles

Cut the chicken into 8 pieces. Reserve chicken livers. Pour sherry over chicken pieces and let marinate 2-3 hours, turning pieces from time to time. Dry chicken with paper towels and sauté until golden brown in a skillet with butter and oil; add sherry in which chicken has been soaked, tomato sauce, salt, pepper and herbs. Cook until almost done, about 40 minutes. Add mushroom stems and the 2 chicken livers. Cook 7 minutes more. Remove chicken pieces to warm platter; keep warm. Reserve mushroom stems and chicken livers for garnish. Blend the flour into juices and stir in cream gradually. Taste for seasoning. Pour strained sauces over chicken. In preparing stuffed mushroom caps, sauté the mushroom caps lightly in frying pan with another piece of butter and some oil. Fill them with a stuffing made of the cooked chicken livers, mushroom stems and truffles, all finely chopped together, and sautéed in butter 3-4 minutes. Surround chicken with stuffed mushrooms. Serves 6-8.

Maurice Abravanel

CHICKEN PARMESAN

1 chicken, cut in pieces
1 can (4 oz.) Parmesan cheese
½ cup butter

Place chicken, skin side down, on broiling pan. Sprinkle heavily with cheese. Dot tops with butter. Broil about 25 minutes. Turn pieces skin side up, and again sprinkle heavily with cheese, and dot with butter. Cook for 7-10 minutes until crispy brown. Serves 4.

Mrs. Walter M. Kilgo

CHICKEN ROSEMARY

1 (2¼ lb.) chicken
1 medium onion, chopped
1 garlic clove, crushed
¼ cup butter
2 teaspoons rosemary, crushed

1 teaspoon lemon-pepper seasoning
1 cup flour
1 teaspoon salt
8 ounces sauterne or Chablis
½ pint half and half

Lightly brown onion and garlic in butter. Mix rosemary, lemon-pepper seasoning, flour and salt in large bowl. Dredge the disjointed chicken pieces in dry ingredients. Brown with the onion and garlic. Sprinkle about 2 tablespoons of dry ingredients on chicken pieces as they are browning. Add wine and cook covered at 300° for 1 hour or until tender. Remove chicken to hot platter. Add cream to sauce in skillet; heat and pour over chicken. Serves 4.

Mrs. Thomas J. Dean

CHICKEN IN SAUTERNE

3 pounds frying chicken
Salt and pepper to taste
Seasoned flour
6 tablespoons butter
6 green onions, finely chopped

4 tablespoons parsley, finely chopped
Dash of thyme
Dash of basil
2½ cups sauterne
18 mushrooms, sliced

Salt and pepper chicken. Dust chicken with flour. Sauté chicken in butter until golden brown. Add onions, parsley, thyme, basil and sauterne. Gently simmer chicken until tender. Cover while cooking. If chicken seems dry, add a little more wine as it cooks. However, heat the wine before adding to chicken. Add mushrooms the last 15 minutes of cooking. Simmer 1 hour. Serve with rice. Serves 6.

Alice Mary Creegan

CHICKEN VERONIQUE

1 (3 lb.) chicken, cut in pieces	½ cup sauterne
½ lemon	⅔ cup Swanson chicken broth
Salt to taste	1 cup seedless green grapes
⅓ cup butter or margarine	Paprika

Rub chicken well with cut side of lemon. Sprinkle with salt. Let dry on rack for 15 minutes. Heat butter in skillet until bubbly. Brown chicken in butter, about 10-15 minutes, turning with tongs. Pour in sauterne and broth; spoon over chicken. Cover and simmer until chicken is tender, 35-45 minutes. About 3 minutes before it has finished cooking, add grapes. Dash generously with paprika. Serves 4.

Mrs. Edwin R. Daniels

UNSALTED BAKED CHICKEN WITH GRAPES

2½ pounds broiler chicken, cut in pieces	Salt (optional)
1 cup water	⅛ teaspoon garlic, finely chopped
2 tablespoons onion, finely chopped	4 teaspoons cornstarch
¾ teaspoon ground thyme	4 teaspoons water
¼ teaspoon ground black pepper	1 cup white seedless grapes
	1 tablespoon cooking sherry

Place chicken pieces in 15½x10½x2¼-inch baking dish. Add water. Combine onion, thyme, black pepper and garlic; add to chicken. Bake, uncovered, in preheated 350° oven, 1½ hours or until chicken is tender. Remove chicken to serving dish. Thicken liquid in a pan with cornstarch mixed with water. Add grapes and cooking sherry. Serve hot with gravy. Serves 4. *This is delicious without salt for those on low sodium diets, but it is more delicious with salt for others.*

Mrs. Frank W. Wozencraft

HONEY FRIED CHICKEN

1 (2½ lb.) frying chicken,
  cut in pieces
1½ cups sherry (optional)
½ teaspoon salt
½ teaspoon pepper
½ teaspoon poultry seasoning

1½ cups bread crumbs
1½ cups flour
2 eggs, well-beaten
½ cup honey
Oil for frying

Marinate chicken in sherry for 45 minutes. Mix seasonings in bread crumbs. Dredge chicken in flour, dip into eggs, then into crumb mixture. Fry in shallow oil at 300° until brown. Brush with honey, then bake in 350° oven for 30 minutes longer. Serve with almond rice. Serves 4.

The Cookbook Committee

CHICKEN IMPERIAL

2 broiler-fryer chickens,
  halved (about 2½ lbs.
  each)
1 teaspoon salt
¾ cup butter, melted
2 teaspoons Worcestershire
  sauce

1 teaspoon curry powder
1 teaspoon oregano
½ teaspoon dry mustard
½ teaspoon garlic powder
¼ teaspoon paprika
2-3 dashes of Tabasco
⅓ cup dry sherry or vermouth

Season chickens with salt. Place halves, skin down, in shallow baking pan. Blend remaining ingredients and brush generously with sauce. Bake at 350°, turning and basting with pan drippings several times. Bake until chicken is fork tender and drumstick twists easily out of thigh joint, 1-1½ hours. Temperature may be increased during last 15 minutes to crisp chicken, if desired. Serve on a warm platter. Smaller portions (quarters rather than halves) will make 8 servings of the two chickens. Serves 4.

Mrs. Ted F. Pancerz

PARTY PERFECT CHICKEN WITH CURRY GLAZE

2 broiler-fryers, quartered	1 teaspoon ground ginger
6 tablespoons flour	6 tablespoons butter
1½ teaspoons salt	Hot buttered rice

Cut away backbones and any small rib bones from chickens. Pull off skin, if desired. Shake chicken pieces in mixture of flour, salt and ginger in paper bag to coat well. Melt butter in large, shallow baking or roasting pan. Roll chicken in melted butter to coat well, then arrange, skin side up, in single layer in pan. Bake, uncovered, at 400° for 20 minutes, or until chicken begins to turn golden. Spoon about half of Curry Glaze on top of chicken to make a thick coating; bake 20 minutes. Spoon on remaining glaze; bake 20 minutes longer, or until tender and richly browned. Arrange chicken around a mound of hot, buttered rice on serving platter. Serves 8.

CURRY GLAZE

½ cup onion, chopped	1 can condensed beef broth
6 slices bacon, finely diced	2 tablespoons flaked coconut
2 tablespoons flour	2 tablespoons applesauce
1 tablespoon curry powder	2 tablespoons catsup
1 tablespoon sugar	2 tablespoons lemon juice

Combine all ingredients in medium-sized saucepan. Heat to boiling, stirring constantly, then simmer 15 minutes, stirring often until thickened. Makes about 2 cups.

Mrs. Dayne W. Ramey

CHICKEN DELIGHT

1 fryer, cut in pieces	1 can mushroom soup
1 cup butter	½ soup can milk or cream

½ soup can sherry

Brown chicken in butter. Remove to casserole. In a bowl, mix soup, milk or cream, and sherry. Stir well; add to skillet. Let cook until boiling point is reached. Pour over chicken and put into preheated 350° oven. Cook, covered, for 30 minutes; uncover, and continue to cook 30 minutes more. Serve on brown or white rice. Serves 4. *This is very impressive for unexpected company.*

Mrs. W. Arnold Diffey

The French ladies of New Orleans fell in love with a strange powder (of sassafras) that was used for cooking by the Indians of that area. The Indians called this fragrant herb, filé. Their one important secret in using filé was it must be added to the liquid after removal from the fire or the stew would become lumpy and strong. It is still an important rule in cooking gumbo.

CHICKEN WITH CABBAGE

1 broiler

Salt and pepper to taste

1 head of cabbage

Butter, melted

Marjoram

1½ cups coffee cream

Lard

Disjoint broiler, season with salt and pepper, brown on both sides. Cover pan and steam until tender. Shred cabbage, boil in plain water 6 minutes. Drain and season with salt, butter and lots of marjoram. Add coffee cream to cabbage, and add to chicken and simmer for 5 minutes. Serves 4.

Mrs. Morton Miller

CHICKEN-IN-THE-POT

2 broilers, disjointed

4 carrots, diced

1 package frozen peas or

   1 pound fresh peas

10 small onions

1 stalk celery, diced

2 teaspoons salt

½ teaspoon seasoned salt

1 clove garlic, minced

6 cups water

Boil water with 1 teaspoon salt. Add onions, carrots and celery. Season chicken with salt, seasoned salt and garlic. Add to boiling water: onions, carrots and celery. Cook over low flame for 45 minutes. Add frozen or fresh peas. Remove from flame in another 30 minutes, or when chicken is tender. Skim fat from broth before serving. Serve in individual covered casseroles with a generous portion of chicken, some carrots, peas and celery. Garnish with a piece of parsley. The broth and chicken should be served with the vegetables. Serves 6.

Jan Peerce

To make one ounce of saffron, it takes about four thousand crocus flower blooms.

CHICKEN PORTUGUESE

1 (3 lb.) chicken
2 tablespoons olive oil (Old Monk or James Plagniol)
½ cup butter
Salt and pepper to taste
1 cup rice
1 cup chicken stock base (Spice Island's)
Saffron

1 large onion, chopped
1 clove garlic, crushed
4 tomatoes, halved
2 sweet green peppers, cut in squares
½ cup pitted green olives
½ cup small mushroom caps
Fresh parsley, chopped
½ cup dry white wine
½ cup fresh coffee cream

Cut chicken into 6-8 portions and brown lightly in the combined mixture of hot oil and butter about 10 minutes. Salt and pepper to taste. Cover and bake at 325°-350° for 30 minutes. Meanwhile, cook the rice by double boiler method using chicken stock base to which you add a generous pinch of saffron. Mix well. This makes the most beautiful golden yellow rice. Remove the chicken from the oven and add the onion, garlic, tomatoes, peppers, olives, mushroom caps and a little parsley. Replace, uncovered, in 375° oven for another 10 minutes. Have a hot serving dish ready. Arrange the pieces of chicken in the center and make a ring of the golden rice around the chicken. Garnish with the vegetables. Pour the white wine into the cooking pan. Correct the seasoning. Bring to the boiling point and remove from the fire. Combine with the fresh cream and pour over the chicken. Serve at once. Serves 4.

The Cookbook Committee

ALMOND RICE CHICKEN

1 tablespoon onion, chopped
3 tablespoons butter
¼ cup flour
1 cup chicken stock
½ cup milk
½ cup light cream

1 cup cooked chicken, diced
¾ cup blanched almonds
1 teaspoon salt
Dash of pepper
Grated cheese
2 cups boiled rice

Sauté onion in butter until lightly browned. Stir in flour, add stock and milk gradually, and cook, stirring until thickened. Add cream, chicken, almonds, salt and pepper, and bring to a boil. Mix with boiled rice. Turn into a greased casserole or individual baking dishes and cover with grated cheese. Bake at 400° about 20 minutes or until browned. Serves 6.

Mrs. Dan C. Williams

CHICKEN GUMBO FILÉ

6 tablespoons shortening
6 tablespoons flour
1 onion, minced
¼ cup celery, diced
1 chicken, cut in pieces

6 cups hot water
2 tablespoons salt
2 teaspoons black pepper
1 green pepper, chopped
½ cup parsley

½ teaspoon gumbo filé

Heat shortening on high heat. Add flour, stirring constantly until flour is dark brown. Add onion and celery, and stir until vegetables are slightly wilted; add chicken. Add the hot water and mix well to dissolve all of the roux. Season with salt and pepper. Cover with a tight-fitting lid and bring to a steaming point on high heat. Reduce heat to simmer and cook until chicken is tender, about 1½-2 hours. Add green pepper and parsley to gumbo 5 minutes before removing from heat. Then add gumbo filé. Do not cook after filé has been added. Serve with hot fluffy rice. Serves 8-10. *Variation: Add 2 dozen oysters or shrimp to gumbo 15 minutes before removing from heat.*

Mrs. Walter F. Smith, Jr.

POULET FAÇON BAYEUX

1 chicken, quartered
Salt and white pepper
Butter, melted
1 tablespoon shallots, chopped
2-6 tablespoons dry white wine

1 cup cream
½ tablespoon beurre manie (kneaded butter and flour)
1 large tomato, peeled, chopped and seeded
1 teaspoon tarragon

2 tablespoons Hollandaise sauce

Season chicken with salt and pepper. Brown chicken in butter in ovenproof kettle on top of stove. Place in moderate oven and cook until tender. Remove chicken and keep warm. Pour off most of the butter and chicken fat. Add shallots and return to stove. Deglaze with white wine, add cream, beurre manie and tomato. Cook over medium low heat until sauce has thickened and tomato is well mixed. Take off heat; add tarragon and Hollandaise sauce. Pour over chicken. Serves 2. *This is a recipe of M. Coleux, chef-owner of Le Bayeux, a restaurant on the outskirts of Brussels, Belgium.*

Mrs. John P. Hall, Jr.

COUNTRY CAPTAIN

1 frying-size chicken, cut in pieces
1 cup flour

Salt and pepper to taste
½ cup shortening

Dredge chicken with seasoned flour and fry in shortening until slightly brown but not completely done. Remove chicken from fat and place in baking pan.

SAUCE

1 large onion, chopped
1 garlic clove, crushed
1 large green pepper, chopped
1 tablespoon Worcestershire sauce
1 teaspoon curry powder
1 teaspoon thyme

1 teaspoon salt
1 teaspoon black pepper, freshly ground
1 cup canned tomatoes
½ cup tomato purée
1 can (4 oz.) mushrooms
½ cup currants or raisins

¼ pound blanched and toasted almonds

Fry onion, garlic, green pepper in chicken drippings until tender but not brown. Add all seasonings and tomatoes. Stir over low flame until well-blended. Pour sauce over chicken pieces, adding mushrooms and cook at 350° for 1 hour. Fifteen minutes before serving, add currants and toasted almonds over top. When ready to serve, pour chicken over hot cooked rice. Serves 6.

Mrs. Joe L. Bergin

PARTY CHICKEN AND CRABMEAT

6 tablespoons margarine
6 tablespoons flour
1½ cups chicken broth
1½ teaspoons salt
Dash of pepper
¾ teaspoon paprika
1 small clove garlic, crushed

¼ teaspoon nutmeg
2¼ cups sour cream
3 cups cooked hen, in bite-sized pieces
2 cups crabmeat (2 6½ oz. cans), tendons removed
8 slices bacon, fried crisp and crumbled

2 packages (10 oz.) frozen peas

Make a sauce in double boiler by melting margarine. Add flour and broth. Stir and cook until thickened. Add salt, pepper, paprika, garlic and nutmeg. Cook 10 minutes. Add sour cream, chicken, crabmeat and bacon. Reduce heat to simmer in double boiler. Cook peas. Serve chicken-crabmeat in center of large platter with peas around it. Garnish with parsley. May be served in pastry shells. Serves 10. *This is an easy chicken dish for buffet suppers.*

Mrs. George D. Blaylock

BRUNSWICK STEW

2 onions, finely chopped
1 pint tomatoes, chopped
3 slices bacon
1 hen or 2 small chickens
1 quart boiling water
1 can (1 lb. 4 oz.) corn

2 cups rich chicken stock
1 cup fine bread crumbs
½ teaspoon brown sugar
1 teaspoon salt
½ teaspoon white pepper
½ pod red pepper

1 teaspoon Worcestershire sauce

Place onions, tomatoes, bacon and disjointed chicken into large soup pot. Add water and let mixture simmer until tender. Remove chicken from the liquid. When cool enough to handle, cut meat from bone and cut in small pieces. Return to kettle, add corn, and boil 20 minutes. Add stock, bread crumbs, sugar, salt, peppers and Worcestershire sauce. Simmer 10 minutes more. Serve hot. Serves 10-12. *This is a particular favorite in the deep South, especially after hunting.*

Mrs. William M. Lamont

COTLETKI TOUREL

3 chicken breasts, cooked
1 pound roast loin of pork, cooked
2 eggs
2 slices white bread, trimmed and soaked in milk
1 medium onion

Salt and pepper to taste
1 scant teaspoon fresh dill, chopped
Bread crumbs
1½ tablespoons oil
1½ tablespoons margarine

Skin and bone the chicken breasts and cut the pork into small pieces. Grind both together or chop them very fine. Add the eggs, bread, onion, salt and pepper to the chicken and pork. Add the chopped dill and blend all ingredients to a semi-moist mixture. Shape the mixture into cutlets or croquettes and roll lightly in the bread crumbs. Melt margarine with oil in a hot skillet and fry the cotletkis until very well done. They will be a golden brown on the outside. The cotletkis are sometimes served with a mushroom sauce in Russia. Serves 4.

Jennie Tourel

CHICKEN WITH PEPPERS

1 (1½ lb.) fryer or broiler, boned and cut in ½-inch cubes

2 egg whites, slightly beaten

1½ tablespoons cornstarch

2 tablespoons oil

1 tablespoon sherry

2 tablespoons soy sauce or 1 teaspoon salt

1 teaspoon sugar

½ teaspoon Tabasco

½ cup green peppers, seeded and diced

½ cup red peppers, seeded and diced

Dip chicken in egg whites to which cornstarch has been added. Heat oil thoroughly and stir in chicken. Sauté for 2-3 minutes. Add sherry. When skillet is very hot again, add soy sauce, sugar and Tabasco. Stir constantly for about 5 minutes, or until the chicken is almost done and juices are bubbling. Add peppers and cook for about 4 more minutes. Serves 4. *A very fine dish if properly cooked. The peppers must be crisp, the chicken tender and the sauce rich and hot. Both red and green peppers are used for their color.*

Danny Kaye

CHICKEN MOUSSE

1 large hen

Chicken stock

¼ pound blanched almonds

1 tablespoon gelatin

¼ cup cold water

½ pint cream, whipped

Mayonnaise

Boil the chicken until thoroughly tender. Any desired seasoning may be used. Cool; remove meat from bones and put meat and almonds through food chopper. Cool stock; remove all fat and reduce to 3 cups. Soak gelatin in water and dissolve in hot chicken stock. Add the chicken and almonds to stock and as it starts to thicken, fold in whipped cream. Refrigerate. When firm, slice and serve on lettuce. Top with mayonnaise. Serves 8.

Mrs. Henry M. Robinson

CHICKEN TORTILLA CASSEROLE

4-6 large meaty chicken
   pieces (breasts or thighs)
Salt and pepper to taste
3-4 onions
Bay leaf

1 can mushroom soup
1 can chicken soup
1 package tostados or large-
   sized corn chips
1 can Ro-Tel tomatoes and
   juice

1 pound Cheddar or sharp cheese, grated

Stew chicken pieces with salt, pepper, 1 onion and bay leaf. Reserve broth, and bone chicken. Shred into bite-sized pieces. In a 2-quart casserole alternate layers of chicken, soups, tostados, tomatoes, cheese and 2-3 chopped onions, ending with a topping of cheese. Use broth for more liquid, if necessary. Bake at 350° for 1 hour or until the casserole is bubbly and the cheese topping is toasted. *This is good served with a green salad, hot French bread, a good white or red wine and strawberries for dessert.*

James F. Gilbert

CHICKEN CURRY

2 tablespoons butter, melted
1½ cups apples, chopped
   and pared
½ cup celery, chopped
1 cup onion, chopped
½ cup green pepper, chopped

1 clove garlic, minced
2 tablespoons all-purpose
   flour
2-3 teaspoons curry powder
1 teaspoon salt
2 cups milk

2 or more cups cooked chicken, cubed

Sauté apples, celery, onions, green pepper and garlic in butter for 5 minutes. Stir in flour, curry powder and salt. Slowly blend in milk. Cook and stir until thick. Add chicken and heat thoroughly. Serve with rice and condiments. Serves 4.

Mrs. Dale E. Selzer

CREPES CORELLI*

1 breast of capon	½ pint Curry Sauce
Consommé	8 crêpes
6 mushroom caps, diced	½ pint Béchamel Sauce
Butter	Salt and pepper to taste

Dice capon, which has been poached in a good consommé. Simmer mushroom caps in butter. Add capon and Curry Sauce. Allow to cook for 5 minutes. Remove from fire. Put 2 tablespoons capon mixture in each crêpe and roll up. Set crêpes in serving dish. Pour Béchamel Sauce over crêpes and glaze under a hot broiler. Serves 4.

CURRY SAUCE

2 tablespoons curry powder   Cold milk

1 cup Cream Sauce

Dilute curry powder in small amount of milk and add to hot Cream Sauce. The curry powder may be varied to taste.

CREAM SAUCE

2 tablespoons butter	1 cup milk or cream, scalded
2 tablespoons flour	Salt and pepper to taste

Melt butter in a saucepan and add flour gradually. Stir continually over low heat for 4-5 minutes. Pour milk or cream in gradually, stirring constantly. Add salt and pepper, and continue to cook over hot water until thick.

BÉCHAMEL SAUCE

2 tablespoons butter	3 egg yolks
1½-2 tablespoons flour	Salt to taste
½ cup milk	Paprika to taste
½ cup meat or vegetable stock	1 cup heavy cream, stiffly beaten

Melt butter, blend in flour, and slowly add milk and stock, stirring constantly. Cook sauce, stirring until smooth and boiling. Beat a small amount of sauce into 1 egg yolk, which is at room temperature; then add mixture to rest of sauce. Place over very low heat until sauce thickens slightly, being careful not to let sauce boil. Add salt and paprika. Remove from heat and add remaining egg yolks and cream.

Quo Vadis Restaurant

*From *Bel Canto Cookbook*, by Peter Gravina
Published by Doubleday and Company

Some fine advice once given by Machon and quoted by Athenaeus: "He who wishes not to spoil the dishes served up to others should be pleased himself. For he who rightly cares for his own eating will not be a bad cook . . . Often taste your dishes while you are boiling them. Do they want salt? Add some. Is any other seasoning needed? Add it and taste again, till you've arrived at harmony of flavor; like a man who tunes a lyre until it rightly sounds."

POULET À LA CHAMPENOISE

Barding pork or blanched bacon
1 (3 lb.) chicken
¼ pound bacon
1 small onion, finely chopped

2 shallots, finely chopped
2 carrots, finely chopped
1 stalk celery, finely chopped
½ calf's foot (optional)
½ bottle champagne

Truss and bard (cover with strips of bacon) chicken, then stuff it with Champenoise Stuffing. In an oven-proof saucepan brown a few lumps of bacon and the vegetables. Add the chicken and calf's foot. Begin the cooking in a 425° oven. When all ingredients are well-browned, add the champagne, then cover and cook until done at 325°. Skim fat. Serves 2-4.

CHAMPENOISE STUFFING

1 medium onion, finely minced
1 clove garlic, finely minced
1 shallot, finely minced
2 tablespoons butter

Large glass "crude" champagne
1 pound sausage, cooked
1 chicken liver, cooked
¼ cup parsley, finely minced

Salt, pepper and spices to taste

Sauté onion, garlic and shallot in butter until golden. Drain; place in small saucepan. Deglaze with the champagne and cook until liquid is reduced to half. Add sausage, chicken liver, parsley, salt, pepper and spices. Grind to mincemeat; press through a sieve.

Philippe Entremont

STUFFED CHICKEN

1 broiler, boned
Oil
Reconstituted frozen
    orange juice
1 tablespoon soy sauce
½ cup butter
Shallots, chopped
Celery, chopped
Water chestnuts

½ pound chicken livers
¼ pound sweet Italian
    sausage
½ cup bread crumbs
1 egg, beaten
Salt
Freshly ground pepper
Thyme
1 tablespoon Cognac

Marinate the chicken overnight in the oil, orange juice and soy sauce. For stuffing, sauté the shallots, celery and chestnuts in ¼ cup butter. Add livers that have been simmered until barely cooked. Mash with a fork and reserve half of the mixture for use in the sauce. Add remaining livers to sausage which has been cooked and drained of fat. Add bread crumbs, remaining butter, egg, salt, pepper, thyme and Cognac. Mix well and stuff this into the chicken. Pat the chicken into shape and skewer and tie as necessary so that it is securely closed. Place breast side down in a heavy roaster which has been lightly greased. Bake at 400° for 10 minutes. Baste with marinade and in another 10 minutes turn breast side up. Roast 10 minutes and baste again. Repeat, turning and basting until all skin is brown about 40-50 minutes. When done remove skewers and thread. Add pan juices to reserved chicken livers. Return chicken to oven for at least 30 minutes.

SAUCE

Reserved chicken livers
1 tablespoon cornstarch

1 cup chicken stock
2 tablespoons Cognac

Purée chicken livers and pan juices, and add cornstarch and stock. Simmer until thickened and add Cognac. Correct seasonings, cook a few minutes longer and serve over chicken. Serves 4.

Gary Graffman

131

BAKED CHICKEN

1 (2½ lb.) whole fryer
¼ cup butter
Lawry's seasoning salt
Garlic powder

Lemon-pepper marinade
Salt
Pepper
1 small onion, peeled

Wash chicken and pat dry, then rub completely with butter, placing large chunk of butter in cavity. Pack outside with Lawry's seasoning salt, covering completely. Add garlic powder, lemon-pepper marinade, salt and pepper. Place onion in cavity. Put chicken, breast side up, in shallow, uncovered pan and bake in preheated 400° oven for 10 minutes. Reduce heat to 325°. Bake for about 45 minutes. Then with a long fork in cavity gently turn chicken over so back side may brown. Cook another 30-45 minutes. Turn chicken back over so that breast skin may brown for 10 minutes. Remove chicken to platter. Deglaze pan with a small quantity water, and pour gravy over chicken. *This is one of the simplest entrées because it takes 5-10 minutes to prepare for baking.*

Mrs. David Donosky

CHICKEN LIVERS WITH RICE

1 large onion, sliced
Shortening
1 can (3 oz.) mushrooms (if possible, 3-4 sliced fresh mushrooms would be better)

1 teaspoon garlic powder
½ teaspoon oregano
7-8 chicken livers
1 can (8 oz.) tomato sauce
Salt and pepper to taste

2 cups cooked Uncle Ben's rice

Sauté onions in small amount of shortening until golden brown. Add mushrooms, garlic powder and oregano about 5 minutes before onions are brown. Then place chicken livers into pan, and mix them gently with the onions and mushrooms; and sauté until livers are done. Add the tomato sauce and stir again. Heat all ingredients until tomato sauce bubbles. Add salt and pepper. Serve livers on a bed of cooked rice. Serves 2-4.

Mrs. Charles Blackman

CHICKEN LIVERS

¼ cup butter

½ cup onions, chopped

½ pound chicken livers, floured

1 cup consommé, or 1 cup hot water and 1 teaspoon BV liquid, or 1 cup broth

1 tablespoon Worcestershire sauce

Sauté onions in butter until clear. Remove with slotted spoon. Add floured chicken livers to butter. Brown lightly. Reduce heat, add consommé and Worcestershire sauce; return onions to pan. Cover. Simmer for 10 minutes. If sauce is thin, thicken with small amount of cornstarch and water, mixed together. Stir until clear. Serve with wild rice, steamed rice or noodles. Serves 3-4.

Mrs. E. C. Dicken

TURKEY DRESSING

½ cup butter

1 large onion, finely chopped

2 pounds lean round steak, ground

1 tablespoon salt

¼ teaspoon pepper

2 cups chicken broth

½ cup Uncle Ben's rice

2 cups celery hearts, chopped

2 cups raisins

2 cups pecans

½ pint light cream

Melt butter in 3-quart saucepan. Add onions and sauté until soft. Add ground beef, salt and pepper, and brown. Add broth. Stir, and when mixture is very hot, add rice. Cook, covered, over slow fire for 15 minutes or until rice is soft. Add celery and cook, covered, for 15-20 more minutes. Remove from heat. Add raisins, pecans and light cream. If dressing becomes too dry, add more cream. Stir all ingredients together. The dressing is now prepared to stuff a 10-14 pound turkey. Any surplus dressing may be cooked in a buttered casserole for approximately 30 minutes at 350°.

Mrs. Tom D. Lontos

DUCKLING AS IN EGER

1 duck

4 tablespoons butter, melted

Neck, gizzard and wings of duck

2 pieces beef filet

2 onions, cut in large pieces

2 carrots, cut in large pieces

1 stalk celery

1 tablespoon flour

2 cups Egri Bikaver (Hungarian red wine)

2 cups beef broth

Salt and pepper to taste

2 garlic cloves, pressed

Parsley

Thyme

1 glass sherry

2 tablespoons Swiss cheese, grated

Mushrooms

For the sauce, cook the neck, gizzard, wings and beef filets for a few minutes in the butter. Add onions, carrots and celery. Thicken with flour. Allow to brown. Add Egri Bikaver, or a full-bodied dry red wine, and beef broth. Salt carefully, add pepper, garlic cloves, parsley and thyme. Bring to boil and simmer 3 hours. Roast well-seasoned garlic-rubbed duck about 1½ hours at 350° or until done. Cut in pieces. Take out most of the carcass and keep warm. Crush the carcass and put it in roasting pan after removing fat. Add sherry and pour sauce into pan. Cook for 15 minutes. Strain sauce. Crush vegetables and add again to sauce and boil for a few minutes. Finish sauce by filtering through fine cheese cloth. Place duck pieces in baking dish on a layer of sautéed mushrooms, cover with sauce, sprinkle with Swiss cheese and place under broiler a few minutes. Serves 2-4, depending on size of duck. *This dish originated in the city of Eger, Hungary, and uses the famous Bull's-Blood wine of the country.*

Mrs. Janos Starker

ROAST DUCK

2 ducks (5-6 lbs.), Long Island ducks recommended

Onion salt

1 clove garlic, minced

6 oranges, quartered crosswise

⅓ cup butter

1 medium onion, chopped

1 can (17 oz.) purple plums

1 can (6 oz.) frozen lemonade

⅓ cup chili sauce

¼ cup soy sauce

1 teaspoon Worcestershire sauce

1 teaspoon ginger, dry or chopped crystalized

2 teaspoons prepared mustard

2 drops of Tabasco

¼ cup Grand Marnier (optional)

Sprinkle ducks with onion salt and garlic. Place orange quarters in bottom of roasting pan. Set ducks, breast up, on orange slices. Roast at 325° for 2 hours. Use no water and it is not necessary to baste while roasting. Prick the skin at ½-inch intervals along the back, the thighs, and the lower part of the breast to let the fat drain out. Pour off the excess fat as the ducks bake. While the ducks are roasting, melt butter in a large skillet; add onion and simmer until tender. Pour plums and juice into sieve over a bowl, pit and purée plums. Add purée to onion and blend in lemonade, chili sauce, soy sauce, Worcestershire sauce, ginger, Tabasco and mustard. Simmer for 12 minutes. After the ducks have baked for about 1½ hours, remove oranges from baking pan, brush ducks with plum sauce and return to oven. Baste often with sauce for next 30 minutes. Add Grand Marnier to remaining sauce and baste frequently for the next 25 minutes; then remove the well-glazed ducks from the oven. Serves 8.

Louise E. Finley

SHADY OAKS WILD DUCK

4 wild ducks

Salt

Pepper

Evangeline hot sauce

2 cups celery, finely chopped

2 cups onion, finely chopped

½ cup green pepper, finely chopped

4 bay leaves

4 small tart apples, peeled

Cooking oil

1 cup water

½ cup sherry

Clean ducks well. Make incisions crosswise with small, sharp knife just below neck on either side of breast bone. Insert teaspoon with back up and work back and forth to loosen flesh from carcass thereby forming 2 small pockets. Rub inside of ducks with salt and pepper and a dash or two of hot sauce. Stuff the breast pockets as well as the main cavity of the ducks with celery, onion, and green peppers, plus 1 bay leaf mixed together. Close main cavity with apple. Truss if necessary. Salt and pepper ducks, coat lightly with oil, sprinkle with a few drops of hot sauce for each bird. Place in a roaster after coating bottom of the roaster ¼ inch deep with cooking oil. (Wild ducks are not greasy like domestic ducks.) Add water. Cover pan and roast at 350° for 2-3 hours, depending on size and age of birds. Baste frequently, adding a small amount of water if needed. About ½ hour before ducks are done, add sherry and continue basting. Serve on a bed of wild rice. Use natural gravy. Ducks may be cut in half with poultry shears when done.

Mrs. Morton Marr

LONG ISLAND DUCKLING, BLACK CHERRY SAUCE

1 Long Island duckling,
    quartered
1½ teaspoons salt

1 teaspoon pepper
2 teaspoons poultry seasoning

2 teaspoons paprika

Rub seasonings into duckling, place in dry skillet, skin side down, and cover tightly. Cook at 350° in electric skillet or over medium heat on range for 1 hour, turning at 20 minute intervals. Do not pour off fat during cooking.

SAUCE

½ cup port wine
1 whole clove
Pinch of nutmeg
Pinch of thyme
Pinch of allspice
¼ teaspoon orange peel,
    grated

½ cup brown sauce
½ cup currant jelly
½ cup canned pitted black
    cherries
Juice of ½ orange
1 tablespoon butter

Combine the wine, clove, nutmeg, thyme, allspice and orange peel, and cook over moderate heat until volume is reduced to half. Heat brown sauce and add. Blend well and add jelly. When jelly is dissolved, add cherries, orange juice and butter. Serve very hot over the duckling. Serves 4. *This is one of Mrs. Nelson Rockefeller's favorite recipes.*

Mrs. D. B. Denney

ROCK CORNISH HENS

4 Rock Cornish hens
2 tablespoons butter

Salt
¼ cup peach juice

¼ cup Triple Sec

Rub hens with butter and salt. Roast breast down for 30 minutes at 375°. Baste with peach juice. Turn, continue roasting until brown and tender, basting with the peach juice. Add Triple Sec, ignite, and serve with hot juices. Serves 4.

Helen Corbitt

CORNISH GAME HENS WITH ORANGE SAUCE

4 Cornish game hens,   2 teaspoons salt
   completely thawed

2 teaspoons poultry seasoning

Season each bird with ½ teaspoon salt and ½ teaspoon poultry seasoning. Allow to stand 1 hour at room temperature before putting in oven.

DRESSING

8 slices stale bread   1 cup onion, chopped
2 cups chicken broth   4 tablespoons chicken fat or
   (Spice Island base)   butter
1 cup celery, chopped   1 cup mushrooms, chopped

Soak bread in chicken broth. Sauté celery and onions to transparent stage in chicken fat. When tender mix with bread and add mushrooms. Fill bird cavity loosely and close with poultry pins. Place birds in deep casserole dish.

SAUCE

2 oranges, thinly sliced   1 teaspoon mace or cinnamon
1 tablespoon brown sugar   1 cup dry white wine

Arrange oranges in bottom of 10-12-inch skillet. Sprinkle with brown sugar and mace. Cover with wine and simmer 5 minutes. Pour sauce over birds, including orange slices. Place in 350° oven and baste birds every 10 minutes for 40 minutes. Turn oven to 500° for an additional 7-10 minutes to turn birds to a golden brown. Serve garnished with the orange slices and sprigs of fresh parsley. Serves 4.

Mrs. Saul N. Hertz

CORNISH HENS

½ cup butter   Salt and pepper to taste
Juice of 1 lemon   4 Cornish hens

Melt butter in a saucepan along with lemon juice. Salt and pepper hens and place them in a shallow roasting pan. Bake, uncovered, at 350° for 1½ hours, basting every 15 minutes with lemon-butter sauce until hens are golden brown. Serve with wild rice. Serves 4.

Mrs. Arthur L. Sarris

PHEASANT IN SOUR CREAM

6 pheasant breasts

Salt and pepper

½ cup butter

2 tablespoons onion, grated

1 pound mushrooms, sliced

1 cup chicken bouillon or broth

4 tablespoons brandy

2 tablespoons dry sherry

1 cup thick sour cream

1 tablespoon caraway seeds (optional)

Season pheasants with salt and pepper. Sauté in butter until golden brown. Remove pheasants from skillet and sauté onions and mushrooms in the same butter for 3-4 minutes. Return pheasants to the pan with the onions and mushrooms. Add the chicken broth and simmer, covered, for 45 minutes. Remove pheasants and keep warm. Add brandy and sherry to the pan and simmer for 5 minutes. Remove pan from heat and stir in the sour cream and caraway seeds. Return pan to heat and simmer very gently for 2 minutes, stirring constantly. Pour sauce over pheasants and serve. *This is my very favorite recipe. My family raised pheasants commercially for years and I have eaten them many ways, but this is the best!*

Mrs. Matthew Murphy

ROAST PHEASANT

1 (2-3 lb.) young pheasant

Salt and pepper

1 bay leaf

3 celery tops

1 slice lemon

1 onion, sliced

4 bacon slices

½ cup chicken bouillon

½ cup Madeira or sherry

Sprinkle pheasant inside with salt and pepper. Place bay leaf, celery tops, lemon slice and onion slices in pheasant's cavity. Tie legs. Turn wings under. Place in roasting pan. Cover bird with bacon strips. Mix bouillon and wine and pour gently over bird. Roast at 350° for 25-30 minutes per pound. Baste frequently, as bird tends to be dry. Remove bird from roasting pan. Untie the legs and remove the vegetables inside the cavity. Serve with nutted rice in orange cups. Serves 4.

Mrs. Robert H. Mitchell

BAKED QUAIL

6 slices bacon or 12 1-inch cubes salt pork

12 quail

Salt and pepper to taste

1 cup butter

2 medium onions, chopped

2 cups Sauterne

2 cups chicken bouillon

Salt and pepper each bird and put ½ slice of bacon or 1-inch cube of salt pork in each cavity. If using skinned quail, wrap birds entirely in bacon rather than stuffing them; this keeps them from becoming too dry. Truss and fry in butter until brown. Transfer to a baking dish. Add onions, Sauterne and bouillon to skillet. Bring to a boil and pour over quail. Bake at 325° for about 2 hours or until tender, depending on age of birds. Serves 12.

Mrs. George W. Beams

STUFFED QUAIL

Quail

¼ cup butter

½ cup green onions, finely chopped

½ cup celery, finely chopped

3 cups cornbread crumbs

3 cups day-old biscuits, crumbled

Salt and pepper to taste

1 can Swanson chicken broth

½-1 cup sherry (optional)

Flour

Sauté the onions and celery in butter. Add cornbread and biscuit crumbs. Season with salt and pepper. Moisten with ¾ can chicken broth. Mix together. Flour and brown quail in a skillet. Stuff quail (allowing 1 cup of dressing to 1 pound of dressed bird). Put quail in a roaster in 1 inch of water. Cover and cook slowly at 275°-300° for 2 hours. Baste with remaining chicken broth and sherry, if desired.

Mrs. Samuel A. McKnight

QUAIL À LA GENE

Flour

Salt

Garlic powder

Lemon-pepper marinade

Paprika

2 quail per person

½ cup butter

2 tablespoons oil

1 cup Sauterne or other dry white wine

1 tablespoon parsley flakes

1 tablespoon Spice Island fines herbes

1 teaspoon dill weed

¼ teaspoon curry powder

Salt and pepper to taste

2 tablespoons Cognac

1 cup skim yogurt or sour cream

Mix flour, salt, garlic powder, lemon-pepper and paprika together and dredge quail with mixture. Brown quail well in heavy skillet in butter and oil. While quail are browning, mix the wine, parsley, fines herbes, dill, curry, salt and pepper together. When quail are browned, pour this mixture over them, cover and simmer on low heat for 20-25 minutes, spooning sauce in pan over them once or twice. Do not overcook. Remove quail and keep warm. Add Cognac and yogurt or sour cream. Blend and heat thoroughly. More wine may be added if the sauce cooks down too much. Pour sauce over the quail, saving some for a gravy boat if desired.

Mrs. Gene H. Bishop

History records that King François I was suffering from an intestinal ailment and had tried every known medicinal ingredient to correct it, but to no avail. A Jewish doctor from Constantinople had a reputation for many miraculous cures and was called to Paris to care for this royal patient. And come he did — with a flock of sheep to prepare a secret concoction later revealed to be yogurt. The King was indeed cured by the treatment.

QUAIL MADEIRA SUR CANAPÉS

6 slices homemade-type white bread, ¼ inch thick

½ cup clarified butter

6 quail livers or 2-3 tablespoons foie gras

3 tablespoons bacon

¼ teaspoon salt

Pinch of pepper

1 tablespoon Rainwater Madeira

6 quail or other game hens

½ tablespoon salt

2 tablespoons shallots, finely minced

½ teaspoon dried tarragon

4 tablespoons butter

6 strips of bacon, blanched

3 tablespoons butter

1 tablespoon oil

½ tablespoon salt

For the canapé, remove crust from bread and cut into rectangles 2x3½ inches. Sauté bread in butter until lightly browned. Chop livers very fine, almost into a purée. Simmer bacon for 10 minutes in water, rinse, and dry to remove extra salty flavor. Add the bacon to purée. Blend with seasonings, Madeira and foie gras. Season quail cavities with salt, shallots, tarragon and 1 teaspoon butter each. Rub with butter. Cut bacon in half and criss-cross over breasts. Place in roasting pan and set in middle of 400° oven. Baste with butter and oil and turn every 5-7 minutes for 30 minutes or until done. When quail are done, remove and sprinkle with ½ tablespoon salt.

SAUCE

1 tablespoon shallots, minced

1½ cups brown stock or canned bouillon mixed with meat glaze

¼ cup Madeira

2 tablespoons softened butter

Remove all but 2 tablespoons fat from roaster. Stir in shallots and cook slowly 1 minute. Add stock and wine and boil rapidly, scraping up juices and reduce to half. Remove from heat and butter just before serving.

MUSHROOMS

1½ pounds fresh mushrooms, washed and dried

2 tablespoons butter

1 tablespoon oil

1 tablespoon shallots, minced

½ clove garlic, minced

¼ teaspoon salt

Pinch of pepper

Sauté mushrooms for 5 minutes in butter and oil in large enameled skillet. Stir in shallots, garlic, salt and pepper. Place quail on a canapé spread with liver mixture. Surround with sautéed mushrooms. Spoon sauce over the birds. Serves 3-6.

The Cookbook Committee

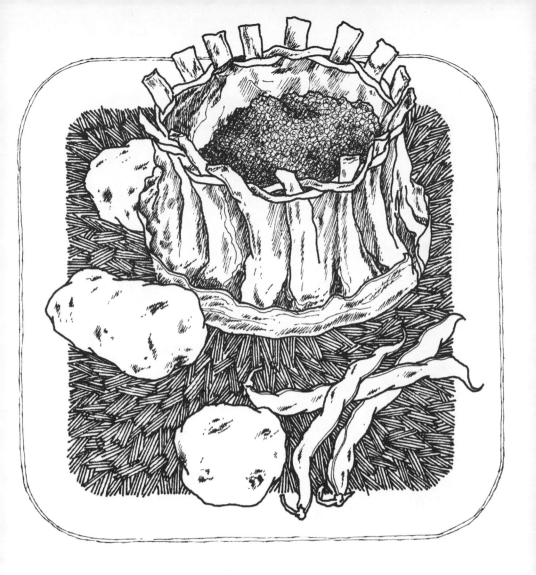

MEATS

LONDON BROIL

4 ounces filet of beef, cut
    into 2 slices

2 slices bacon

½ tomato

Julienne potatoes

1 slice of toast

Broil beef, bacon and tomato. Serve filet on toast; garnish with tomato at one end of the plate and potatoes at the other end. Arrange the bacon in a figure X over the filets. Serves 1. *This recipe comes from the Savoy Hotel in London.*

Mrs. Hubert G. Foster

FILETS OF BEEF VARANDA DO CHANCELER

¼ cup butter

4 (6 oz. each) filets of beef

3 tablespoons Cognac

½ cup dry Madeira

½ cup cream

½ cup brown sauce or canned
    beef gravy

3 tablespoons butter

1 tablespoon catsup

½ teaspoon dry mustard

½ teaspoon Worcestershire
    sauce

½ pound ham

½ pound mushrooms

Heat butter in the blazer of a chafing dish until it bubbles. Sear the filets in this, browning meat lightly on both sides. Pour warm Cognac over this and set it aflame. Remove the filets to a heated serving plate and keep them warm. Deglaze the pan by stirring the Madeira into it. Add cream, brown sauce, butter, catsup, mustard and Worcestershire sauce. Cut the ham into fine julienne strips; trim and finely chop the mushrooms. Add them to the pan and simmer for 3-4 minutes. Return the filets to the pan and let them heat through. Serve the filets immediately with sautéed potatoes. Serves 4. *Mr. Kerr, the Associate Editor of Gourmet Magazine, included this recipe in his recent publication on Portugal.*

Alvin Kerr

FILET OF BEEF WELLINGTON

5 pound filet of prime beef

1 teaspoon dry English mustard

Larding pork

4 tablespoons butter

½ pound mushrooms, finely minced

¼ pound cooked ham, finely minced

3 shallots, minced

¼ teaspoon salt

⅓ cup Madeira

4 chicken livers

1 tablespoon oil

1 tablespoon tomato purée

1 tablespoon meat extract

3 truffles, finely chopped

Puff paste

1 egg yolk

1 teaspoon water

Spread filet with mustard, tie larding pork over it. Roast in 400° oven for 25 minutes. Remove and cool. Remove pork, skim pan juices, and reserve them. In 2 tablespoons butter, sauté mushrooms, ham and shallots for 5 minutes. Add salt and Madeira. Sauté chicken livers in 2 tablespoons butter and oil until done. Chop and add to mushroom mixture. Add tomato purée, meat extract and truffles. Mix well, and remove from heat. Roll out puff paste. Lay the cold filet in the center and pile the ham and mushroom mixture on and around it. Carefully wrap the filet in pastry, turning in ends, and press all seams together firmly. Lay it, seam side down, on a baking sheet and brush with dorure (egg yolk beaten with water). Cut decorative shapes from the trimmings of the pastry. Brush them with dorure and fix them to the top of the wrapped filet. Bake in a preheated 425° oven for 35-40 minutes or until pastry is cooked through. Arrange filet on a heated serving platter and carefully slice it, keeping the crust intact around each slice. Serve with the sauce and a good red Bordeaux wine. It is possible to roast the filet the day before and to mix up the pastry ahead, then do the sauce, and assemble the day of the party. Serves 10.

MADEIRA SAUCE

½ cup good beef stock

½ cup Madeira

1 tablespoon tarragon, chopped

2 tablespoons butter

To the reserved pan juices, add the beef stock, Madeira and tarragon. Heat for 5 minutes. Reduce heat and swirl in butter.

Mrs. Jack W. Lively

TOURNEDOS

Pepper, freshly ground

4 (6 oz. each) tournedos

6 tablespoons butter

2 tablespoons olive oil

4 rounds of bread, about 3 inches in diameter

Sprinkle pepper on beef. Put 4 tablespoons of butter and olive oil in skillet, and cook tournedos over high heat for about 5 minutes on each side so meat will be brown on outside and rare inside. Transfer to warm serving dish. Pour off fat in pan. Sauté bread in remaining butter untill golden, then drain on absorbent paper. Place a tournedo on a bread round, and spoon a sauce, such as Madeira over. Serves 4.

MADEIRA SAUCE

½ cup Madeira

½ cup beef stock

2 tablespoons truffles or mushrooms, finely chopped

2 tablespoons butter

Add Madeira to pan and cook until reduced about half. Add beef stock and truffles. Add butter and mix well. Serve over the tournedos. *This is an impressive company dish.*

Dorothy Sinz

TENDERLOIN OF BEEF

Tenderloin of beef, preferably heavy

8 boxes table salt

4 cups butter

Garlic to taste

Empty the salt into a large pan. Start your fire so that by the time the following operation is complete, the coals are hot and red. Put a piece of brown wrapping paper, large enough to wrap around meat twice, on the table or work area. Place meat on the paper. Dampen the hands lightly with water, too much moisture will dissolve salt, and mold a salt casing around the entire tenderloin an inch or more thick. Wrap the salt encased meat with brown paper, and moisten the whole sufficiently to hold in place. Put the prepared package on the grate over the hot fire. Set a 1-quart pan near the fire and drop in the butter. Let melt, but not brown. Add garlic. Prepare a board and knife for slicing. Let the meat cook for approximately 45 minutes in its own juice within the hard salt shell. You can judge the time by the paper which will become dark and brittle. Strange as it may seem, the meat will not absorb the taste of salt. When ready, break open with a hammer. Slice the tenderloin into 1½-inch slices, and drop them into the warm butter. Serve on a warm plate with condiments to suite taste. *This recipe is designed for open cooking on a grate over hot coals either indoors or out. You will have the tenderest and juiciest steak you have ever eaten.*

Eugene Conley

GINGERED BEEF

1 rib eye of beef, oven-ready   ¼ cup fresh ginger, slivered
2 tablespoons soy sauce   1 cup sherry

Rub meat with soy sauce and cover with ginger. Roast uncovered at 350° for 1 hour, or longer if you wish. You allow 10 minutes per pound for rare meat. Baste with sherry. Use pan juices with ginger for sauce.

GREEN NOODLES

1 package (8 oz.) green   1 teaspoon salt
   noodles   Cracked pepper
1 cup sour cream

Cook in boiling water until tender. Drain, but do not wash. Add sour cream. Season with salt and a little cracked pepper.

Helen Corbitt

PRIME RIB

10 pound prime rib   Lawry's seasoning salt
Garlic   Salt and pepper
       2 small onions, sliced

Rub garlic over roast. Pack Lawry's salt into fat on top and meat on sides. Cover completely with lots of Lawry's salt. Season with salt and pepper. In shallow pan place sliced onions. Lay roast on top. Do not put water in pan while cooking. Place in 400° preheated oven, uncovered, for 20-30 minutes. This sears the outside. Reduce heat to 325°, and bake 15 minutes per pound. This will give you a rare or medium rare roast. Do not overcook. When desired doneness is reached, remove roast from oven and let stand on platter. To prepare gravy, put pan over medium heat and deglaze with water. Simmer a few minutes and serve. Leave onions in gravy as they add to the flavor. Serves 10.

Mrs. Henry S. Miller, Jr.

ENGLISH YORKSHIRE PUDDING

½ pound flour   2 eggs
Salt   1 pint milk
     1 cup fat from roast beef

Put the flour and good pinch of salt into a basin, make a well in the center and break in the eggs. Stir gradually, mixing in the flour from the sides and add milk by degrees until a smooth batter is formed. Beat well for 10 minutes and then add remainder of milk. Allow to stand for at least 1 hour. Put the fat in heated baking dish. Pour in batter and cook at 450° for 40-45 minutes. Cut in 2x4-inch pieces and serve with a prime rib roast. Serves 6.

Mrs. W. Clark Spruce

SIRLOIN ROAST

1 heavy beef sirloin steak,   Salt
   cut 3 inches thick
                               Pepper
Accent

Sprinkle both sides liberally with Accent, salt and pepper. Put on rack in open pan at 300° for 2 hours. Medium well, medium rare and rare slices may be cut from this roast. Serves 8-10.

Mrs. Charles R. Ferguson

BRISKET

6-7 pound beef brisket   Celery salt

Garlic salt   ½ bottle liquid smoke

Onion salt   ½ bottle Worcestershire sauce

Salt and pepper

Line baking pan with enough aluminum foil to cover and seal the brisket. Put fat side down and sprinkle garlic salt, onion salt and celery salt generously over all of the brisket. Add liquid smoke, cover with the foil and refrigerate overnight. The next morning, add Worcestershire sauce, salt and pepper, again sprinkling over all of the brisket. Bake at 275° for 5-6 hours. Take out of oven and let cool before slicing. Serves 8. *Variation: Cover the meat with Hickory Smoked Barbecue Sauce and bake, uncovered, for 1 more hour.*

Mrs. James W. Hixon

GOURMET CORNED BEEF

4-5 pound corned brisket of   2 stalks celery
   beef (or rump)
                               2 bay leaves

2½ quarts water   1 small orange, sliced

2 cups white table wine   1 stick cinnamon

½ cup onion, finely chopped   3 whole cloves

⅛ teaspoon garlic powder   3 drops Tabasco

1 teaspoon dried dill

Cover corned beef completely with cold water in a large saucepan, bring to a boil, and simmer for ½ hour. Discard this cooking water. Cover beef again with 2½ quarts of water and add all remaining ingredients. Cover and simmer until meat is tender, about 3 hours. Allow beef to cool in liquid, if not to be served immediately after cooking. Place weight on top of cooling beef for better slice conformity. This freezes well. Serves 10.

Mrs. R. F. Schermerhorn

SAUERBRATEN WITH POTATO DUMPLINGS

3 pound round steak
(2½-3 inches thick)
1 tablespoon salt
½ teaspoon pepper
2 onions, sliced
1 carrot, sliced
1 stalk celery, chopped
4 cloves
4 peppercorns

½ cup red wine vinegar
2 bay leaves
3½ cups water
2 tablespoons kidney fat
4 tablespoons butter
3 tablespoons flour
1 tablespoon sugar
5 gingersnaps

Wipe round steak with a damp cloth. Sprinkle with salt and pepper. Place meat in an earthenware, glass, or enamel bowl. Add salt, pepper, onions, carrot, celery, cloves, peppercorns, vinegar, bay leaves and water to cover meat. Cover container and refrigerate for 4 days. On the fifth day, drain meat and pat dry with paper towels. Strain and reserve the marinade. In heavy casserole or Dutch oven, heat and melt kidney fat and 1 tablespoon butter. Add round steak and cook over high heat until well-browned. Turn and brown other side. Add the marinade, bring to a boil, cover and cook over low heat at just the simmering point for 3 hours. In small skillet melt 3 tablespoons butter and stir in flour and sugar; and cook, stirring, until this roux becomes a dark color, about the color of dark brown sugar. Add to simmering meat liquid, cover, and continue to simmer for 1 hour longer. Remove meat to warm serving platter. Add crushed gingersnaps to gravy. Cook, stirring, until sauce is smooth and thickened. Strain into sauce boat, and serve with meat and potato dumplings. Serves 8.

POTATO DUMPLINGS

3 pounds potatoes
3 egg yolks, beaten
3 tablespoons cornstarch
3 tablespoons raw farina

½ teaspoon pepper
1 teaspoon salt
¼ teaspoon nutmeg, grated
2 slices white bread, diced

2 tablespoons butter

Peel potatoes and cook in boiling salted water for about 30 minutes or until soft enough to mash. Drain and mash thoroughly. Beat in egg yolks, cornstarch, farina, pepper, salt and nutmeg. Sauté bread in hot butter until golden brown. Drain croûtons on a paper towel. Shape the potato mixture into dumplings the size of a golf ball, with a few croûtons in the center of each. Roll each dumpling lightly in flour. In a large skillet bring 1½ quarts salted water to a rapid boil. Reduce heat to simmer and gently lower dumplings into the water. Cover skillet and poach dumplings for 15-20 minutes without allowing the water to boil. Remove cooked dumplings with slotted spoon and serve hot around platter of sauerbraten. Makes 16 dumplings.

Mrs. Ronald L. Kuhn

BENGAL CURRY WITH PINEAPPLE RICE

¼ cup shortening or
  cooking oil
4 pounds chuck or sirloin,
  cut in 1-inch cubes
1 cup onions, sliced
2 tablespoons curry powder
2 teaspoons salt
¼ teaspoon pepper
¼ teaspoon ground cloves

½ teaspoon ground ginger
2 tablespoons fresh mint
  leaves or 1 teaspoon
  dried mint
¼ cup unsifted all-purpose
  flour
3 cans beef bouillon
1 cup flaked coconut
¼ cup lime juice

1 cup light cream

Brown the meat in oil or shortening approximately 20 minutes. Remove meat from skillet. Sauté onions, spices and mint until onions are soft. Remove pan from heat and add flour, bouillon and browned meat. Simmer until tender, approximately 1½-2 hours. Ten minutes before serving, stir in coconut, lime juice and light cream. Heat 5 minutes. Turn into chafing dish and serve with pineapple rice. Serves 8.

PINEAPPLE RICE

2½ cups raw long-grain rice
1 quart cold water
2½ teaspoons salt

2½ tablespoons butter
1 cup (8½ oz.) crushed
  pineapple, drained

Combine rice with cold water and salt. Bring to boil, stirring. Reduce heat and simmer, covered, according to package directions. Add butter and pineapple, tossing with fork to mix.

Mrs. Robert J. Shoemaker

FONDUE BOURGUIGNONNE

Tenderloin of beef, cubed or
  sliced thinly

Olive oil or ½ butter,
  ½ oil

Place beef on a wooden tray or board, either place on table or pass for guests to help themselves. Spear with a long-tined fondue fork. Place meat in hot oil in fondue pot or chafing dish to desired doneness. Serve with an array of sauces to "dress" the beef. Serve with raw relishes, spiced fruits and anything else you desire.

Helen Corbitt

BEEF BOURGUIGNONNE

6 slices bacon
4 pounds trimmed lean
  sirloin
2 cloves garlic, crushed
2 pounds mushrooms, sliced
2 bay leaves, crushed
1 teaspoon thyme

2 tablespoons parsley,
  chopped
1 teaspoon salt
1/8 teaspoon pepper
1/4 cup flour
1/2 cup butter
13 ounces consommé

14 ounces Burgundy wine

Cut bacon into small pieces and fry in Dutch oven. Cut sirloin into strips, 1/4-1/2 inch by 2 inches with the grain. Remove bacon and sauté the sirloin in the bacon drippings until beef is evenly browned. Add garlic, mushrooms, bay leaves, thyme, parsley, salt and pepper. Add the bacon and remove the mixture from the heat. In another pan make a roux of the flour and butter, cooking and stirring until it is lightly browned. Add consommé and Burgundy, stirring and cooking until it is slightly thickened. Pour over the meat and stir. Cover and simmer 1 1/2 hours or until beef is tender. This may be made ahead and reheated in casserole. Serve it over noodles or rice. Serves 8-10.

Mrs. Donald Johanos

BEEF BURGUNDY

2 pounds beef
2 tablespoons butter
2 tablespoons hot sherry
24 small whole silver-skin
  onions
12 firm mushrooms, quartered
1 teaspoon tomato paste or
  1 large fresh tomato,
  peeled and strained

2 tablespoons consommé
3 tablespoons flour
1 cup stock
1 1/4 cups red wine
Salt and pepper
1 carrot, halved
1 bay leaf
Sprig of parsley
Celery stalk

Fresh thyme

Cut beef in squares. Brown meat in butter. Add hot sherry. Remove meat from pan. Place onions in pan and cook 3-4 minutes. Then cook mushrooms 2 minutes with onions. Add tomato paste or fresh tomato. Add consommé mixed with flour in a cup. Stir and pour stock on mixture. Stir carefully with fork until it boils. Add meat, 1/4 cup wine, salt and pepper. Add bouquet garni (carrot, bay leaf, parsley, celery stalk, fresh thyme, put in cheese cloth). Cook with entire mixture slowly until meat is tender. During last hour, slowly add 1 cup red wine. Remove garni before serving. Serves 4-6.

Mrs. John Tower

HUNGARIAN GOULASH

1½-2 pounds lean round
   steak

1 large onion

1 clove garlic, chopped

1 tablespoon butter

¾ tablespoon paprika

Salt and pepper to taste

Flour

Cut fat off and cube the meat. Brown onion and garlic in butter in a large skillet. Mix cubed meat with browned onion and garlic. After thoroughly brown, add paprika, salt and a little pepper. Mix ingredients well. Then begin adding boiling water. Keep meat just covered with water and cook for 2-3 hours, or until meat is tender, always making sure that the meat is covered by enough juices (otherwise add more water). When finished, add small amount of flour to juice to make gravy somewhat thicker.

Arthur Fiedler

STROGANOFF SULLIVAN-STYLE

3 onions, sliced

3 tablespoons bacon fat

2 pounds round steak, cut
   into thin slices

1 pound mushrooms, sliced

1 can condensed tomato soup

1 can (6 oz.) tomato paste

1 tablespoon Worcestershire
   sauce

1 cup sour cream

Salt and pepper to taste

Cook onions in fat slowly for 20 minutes. Add meat and mushrooms, and brown. Add soup, tomato paste and Worcestershire sauce. Simmer for 1 hour until meat is tender. Check seasonings. Add sour cream, and slowly reheat. Serve over rice or noodles. Serves 6.

Brian Sullivan

BEEF STROGANOFF

1 cup rice	1 tablespoon Worcestershire
Beef consommé	sauce
Water	½ bell pepper, diced
2 pounds lean beef cubes, diced into 1-inch squares	1 clove garlic, diced
1 cup butter	1 tablespoon garlic salt
1 onion, diced	1 cup sour cream
1 cup mushrooms	1 cup heavy cream
Dash of Tabasco	3 tablespoons wine vinegar
	2 tablespoons flour

Boil rice in one part beef consommé and one part water, following package directions, until golden brown. Sauté beef cubes in butter until brown. After meat begins to brown, add onions, mushrooms, Tabasco, Worcestershire sauce, bell pepper, garlic clove and garlic salt. When these ingredients begin to soften, add sour cream, heavy cream and wine vinegar. Now add the flour. Let this mixture continue to simmer for 1 hour or until meat cubes are completely tender. Serve over rice, and garnish. Serves 4. *Newspaper columnists and radio-T.V. interviewers across the country are constantly inquiring as to my very favorite recipe. This recipe I commandeered in the middle European countries approximately ten years ago and worked up several years adjusting the trappings and balance of the recipe to emulate the middle European flavors, yet utilizing ingredients from American stores. This recipe for Beef Stroganoff has to be my favorite. Bon Appétit!*

David Wade

Rice has always been the staff of life in the Orient and it was here that rice probably had its beginning. Some believe it was originally much like our American wild rice and through cultivation evolved into the long-grained variety of today. There is a wealth of mythology surrounding this grain, in the Orient there was the belief that a soul lay within each grain of rice.

MARINATED SIRLOIN TIPS

2 pounds loin tips, cut into 1-1½-inch cubes

Adolph's Instant Meat Tenderizer

½ cup olive oil

2 tablespoons lemon juice

¼ teaspoon thyme

2 tablespoons vinegar

1 teaspoon dry mustard

2 teaspoons salt

3 cloves garlic

¼ teaspoon oregano

½ cup onion, chopped

1 teaspoon rosemary

2 teaspoons catsup

½ teaspoon marjoram

1 tablespoon Worcestershire sauce

1 teaspoon chili powder

1 tablespoon Lawry's seasoning

¼ teaspoon mace

2 cans (4 oz.) button mushrooms

1 carton cherry tomatoes

2 green peppers, cut into 1-inch squares

Wash beef carefully, and sprinkle heavily with meat tenderizer. Puncture each cube several times with a fork. Stir the olive oil, lemon juice, thyme, vinegar, mustard, salt, garlic, oregano, onion, rosemary, catsup, marjoram, Worcestershire sauce, chili powder, Lawry's seasoning and mace together in a saucepan. Bring marinade to a boil, reduce heat, and boil for 5 minutes. Pour over meat, and allow to marinate for 6 or more hours before broiling. Place marinated meat and green peppers into 10x14-inch baking pan and cover with marinade. Place under hot broiler for about 15 minutes or until brown on top. Remove from broiler and turn meat. Add mushrooms and cherry tomatoes and cover with marinade as much as possible, and return to broiler. Broil approximately 15 minutes more or until done. Serves 6.

Mrs. Jimmy T. Lontos

It has been said that the onion is the oldest known vegetable in the world. The biennial plant is a native of Asia. The vegetable was so highly thought of in Egypt that it was worshipped and included among their foodstuffs in the pyramids.

ROLLED SLICES OF BEEF IN CREAM

¼ pound anchovies

3 parsley sprigs

1 medium-sized onion

1 clove garlic

1½ pounds filet of beef, cut into 4 slices

4 tablespoons butter

2 cups hot veal stock or beef stock

½ teaspoon pepper

¾ cup cream

1 tablespoon lemon juice

Bone anchovies (use less if boned anchovies are used). Chop the parsley and onion very fine and crush the garlic clove. Mash these ingredients to a paste. Spread the anchovy mixture on beef slices. Roll these slices and tie together. Put butter into iron pot over medium heat. When hot, place the rolled slices of beef in the pot. Brown lightly on all sides, add the hot veal or beef stock, add pepper, and simmer over low flame for 1 hour. After 45 minutes, add cream mixed with lemon juice. Cook 15 minutes longer. Remove the strings, and serve. Serves 4.

André Previn

BEEF IN BEER

1 pound round steak or leftover beef, cut in julienne pieces

2 tablespoons butter

1 can beer

½ teaspoon basil

½ teaspoon salt

⅛ teaspoon pepper

1 package mushroom gravy mix

Brown beef in butter in skillet. Add beer, basil, salt and pepper. Cover and simmer 30-45 minutes or until tender. Stir in gravy mix, and cook 5-7 minutes. Serve with hot rice or noodles. Serves 4.

Mrs. Matthew Murphy

BEEF DILL BIRDS

2 pounds round steak, cut
   ½ inch thick

¼ cup flour

3 medium dill pickles, cut
   lengthwise

¼ cup water

1 bay leaf

1 teaspoon salt

⅛ teaspoon pepper

3 slices bacon, cut in half

2 tablespoons fat

¼ cup liquid from dill pickles

Cut steak into 6 servings. Combine salt, pepper, and flour, and pound into steak until it is ¼ inch thick. Place ½ slice of bacon on each piece. Roll beef and bacon around pickle slice. Fasten with toothpicks. Brown rolls in fat in a large skillet. Pour off fat. Add water, liquid from pickles and bay leaf. Cover tightly and cook slowly 1½ hours or until tender. Should liquid mixture cook out, add another ¼ cup of water and ¼ cup of liquid from dill pickles. Remove rolls from pan to heated serving platter. Spoon any liquid left in pan over the rolls. Serves 6. *An unusual recipe with a tart flavor that goes quite well with white or wild rice.*

Mrs. Robert M. Greenberg

MELITZANES PAPOUTZAKIA
Greek, Stuffed Eggplants

8 small eggplants

2 onions, finely chopped

4 tablespoons butter

1 pound ground beef

1½ teaspoons salt

¼ teaspoon black pepper

1 egg

¼ cup milk

½ cup grated Parmesan cheese

Cut eggplants lengthwise. Scoop out pulp from center. Sauté onions in butter in skillet. Add eggplant pulp, beef, salt and pepper. Cook, stirring occasionally, for 10 minutes. Stuff eggplant shells with mixture. Place in shallow casserole and bake at 250° for 35 minutes. Beat egg and milk together; add grated cheese. Remove eggplants from oven. Top each with cheese mixture; place under broiler. Heat until browned. Serves 8.

Christine Louis

MOUSAKA À LA GRECQUE

1 large and 1 medium egg-
   plant, cut in ¼-inch slices
2 tablespoons salt
Flour
Oil for frying
2 medium onions, finely
   chopped
8 tablespoons butter
1½ pounds lean ground beef
½ cup dry red wine

1 can (8 oz.) tomato sauce
Pinch of sugar
½ cup water
1½ teaspoons parsley, minced
Salt and pepper to taste
Fine bread crumbs
½ cup freshly grated
   Parmesan cheese
2 egg whites

Place eggplant slices in a long flat pan; cover with salted water. Cover top of eggplant with a plate, and let stand for 30 minutes or longer. Remove eggplant from water; drain thoroughly. Coat each slice with flour, and fry in hot oil until golden brown; drain well. In a large skillet, sauté onions in 4 tablespoons butter until limp and golden brown; add ground meat. Continue to sauté until meat is brown, not thoroughly cooked. Add wine, tomato sauce with sugar, water, parsley, salt and pepper. Stir well; bring mixture to a boil, lower heat to a simmer, and continue to cook for 1 hour or more, if necessary, as there should be no liquid in the meat sauce. Remove from heat; uncover, and cool. Grease the bottom and sides of a 9x13-inch baking pan with melted butter. Sprinkle bottom and sides with bread crumbs. Line bottom of pan with eggplant slices. Stir 6 tablespoons cheese, 2 tablespoons bread crumbs and the egg whites into the cool meat mixture. Mix gently. Spread all the meat evenly over the eggplant; cover meat with remaining eggplant. Now pour Béchamel Sauce over eggplant and spread evenly, smoothing top and covering all corners and edges. Sprinkle top with remaining cheese, 1 tablespoon bread crumbs and 3-4 tablespoons melted butter. Bake at 350° for 40 minutes. Allow to stand before cutting into desired portions. Serve hot. Serves 20-24.

BÉCHAMEL SAUCE

3 cups milk
6 tablespoons butter
7 tablespoons flour

2 egg yolks, beaten
⅛ teaspoon nutmeg
Salt and pepper

First bring milk to a boil and keep warm. In another saucepan over low heat, melt butter and blend in (use a whisk) flour. (Do not permit mixture to brown.) Then add hot milk gradually, stirring until the sauce is smooth and free from lumps. Add salt, pepper and nutmeg, and continue stirring until mixture thickens and comes to a boil. Remove pan from heat, add egg yolks, mix, and return to heat. Do not boil.

Evelyn Semos

PASTITSIO

Greek Macaroni and Beef Casserole

3 tablespoons butter or margarine

3 tablespoons flour

1½ cups milk

¾ cup grated Parmesan cheese

1 egg, beaten

⅓ cup vegetable oil

1½ cups onions, chopped

1 pound ground beef

2 tomatoes, peeled and chopped

1½ teaspoons salt

¼ teaspoon freshly ground black pepper

1 pound macaroni, cooked and drained

Melt the butter or margarine in a saucepan. Blend in the flour until smooth. Gradually add the milk, stirring constantly, to the boiling point. Mix in ¼ cup of the cheese, and cook over low heat 5 minutes. Gradually add the hot sauce to the egg, beating constantly, to prevent curdling. Taste for seasoning. Sauté the onions in oil until soft. Add beef and brown, then add tomatoes and cook over low heat 15 minutes. Blend in the remaining cheese. Spread half of the macaroni on the bottom of a greased 3-quart casserole. Pour the meat mixture over it, and cover with the remaining macaroni. Pour the sauce over the top. Bake at 375° for 35 minutes. Cut into diamond-shaped portions. Serves 4-6.

Charles Treger

Cinnamon is derived from the inner bark of a small laurel tree originally found in Ceylon. Historically, it has been used in rituals of worship as an ingredient in incense, as "holy oil" to be used by the priests, and in the making of candles for religious purposes.

PASTITSIO

1 medium onion, chopped	1 teaspoon cinnamon
1 clove garlic, minced	Salt and pepper to taste
1 pound butter	1 pound Romano cheese, grated
3 pounds ground meat, beef or lamb	12 eggs
½ can tomato paste	6 tablespoons flour, sifted
1 teaspoon sugar	1 quart milk
2 tablespoons water	1½ pounds macaroni

Bread crumbs

Sauté onion and garlic in small amount of butter; add a little water and cook until soft. Add meat, sauté until browned, then add tomato paste and sugar (diluted with water), cinnamon, salt and pepper. Keep mixing and cook at least 10 minutes longer over slow heat. Allow mixture to cool. Add about 3 tablespoons Romano and 1 beaten egg. To prepare cream sauce, melt ¼ pound butter in pan, add flour slowly and brown, stirring constantly. Heat milk and add slowly to flour mixture, stirring constantly. Cook over low heat. When mixture boils, remove from heat. Cool. Add remainder of cheese reserving at least 5 heaping tablespoons for macaroni. Add 7 beaten eggs, mixing well. Boil macaroni according to package directions. Strain; rinse well in cold water and drain. Melt ¼ pound butter, add to macaroni; then add 4 eggs, beaten well. Add the reserved Romano. Mix all ingredients well. To assemble casserole, melt remaining butter and distribute alternately in arranging the layers in an 18x12x2-inch pan. Butter the pan, using a pastry brush, bottom and sides. Sprinkle bottom with bread crumbs. Place ½ of the macaroni in pan; dribble some butter over this layer, plus a couple of ladles of cream sauce; add meat mixture, spreading evenly. Dribble a little butter on this layer; add remaining maccaroni, dribble remainder of butter. Pour cream sauce evenly over entire mixture. Bake in preheated 400° oven for 10 minutes. Reduce heat to 325° and bake 40-50 minutes longer or until nicely browned and set. Cut into squares and serve warm. Serves 30 generously.

Mrs. Pepecha Booziotis

HAMBURGER CHEESE BAKE

1 pound ground beef

½ cup onion, chopped

2 cans (8 oz.) tomato sauce

1 teaspoon sugar

¾ teaspoon salt

¼ teaspoon garlic salt

¼ teaspoon pepper

4 cups medium noodles, uncooked

1 cup cream-style cottage cheese

1 package (8 oz.) cream cheese, softened

¼ cup dairy sour cream

⅓ cup green onion, sliced

¼ cup green pepper, chopped

¼ cup Parmesan cheese, shredded

Brown ground beef and onion in a skillet. Stir in tomato sauce, sugar, salt, garlic salt and pepper. Remove from heat. Meanwhile, cook noodles according to package directions and drain. Combine cottage cheese, cream cheese, sour cream, green onion and green pepper. Spread half the noodles in 11x7x1½-inch baking dish, and top with a little meat sauce. Cover with the cream mixture. Add remaining noodles and remaining meat sauce, and sprinkle with Parmesan. Bake at 350° for 30 minutes. Serves 8-10. *This is a quick and hearty supper dish.*

Mrs. John D. Arnold

JOHNNY BOZZINI

1 pound ground beef

1 large onion, chopped

1 tablespoon butter

1 can tomato soup

1 can whole grain corn

1 green pepper, chopped

1 package medium-sized noodles, cooked

1 can mushrooms

½ pound grated cheese

1 small bottle stuffed olives

1 small package almonds

3 tablespoons Worcestershire sauce

Sear beef and onion in butter. Add remaining ingredients and bake at 350° for 40 minutes. Serves 6.

Mrs. O. P. Corley

BACHELOR'S QUICK DINNER

1 medium onion, finely
  chopped
2 tablespoons bacon grease
1 pound hamburger
1 can tomato soup

1 cup water
2 cups uncooked noodles
Salt and pepper
1 can pitted ripe olives

1 cup grated Parmesan or Romano cheese

Brown onion in bacon drippings. Mix in hamburger and continue cooking until the meat is brown. Drain off any excess fat. Stir in tomato soup and water. Mix in noodles and continue cooking until the noodles are tender. Add more water if necessary. Season to taste. Add ripe olives. Pour into a buttered casserole and cover with grated cheese. Cook at 350° for about 45 minutes. Serves 6.

David A. Stretch

HAMBURGER STROGANOFF

½ cup green onions, sliced
2 cloves garlic, minced
½ cup butter
4 cans (4 oz.) mushrooms,
  sliced
2 pounds ground round

6 tablespoons lemon juice
6 tablespoons Burgundy
2 cans beef consommé
2 tablespoons salt
1 package (10 oz.) medium
  noodles

2 cups commercial sour cream

Sauté onions and garlic in butter. Add mushrooms and beef and cook until redness is gone. Stir in lemon juice, wine, soup and salt. Simmer, uncovered, for 15 minutes. Stir in uncooked noodles. Cook, covered, for 10 minutes. Just before serving add sour cream, being careful not to let it boil as it will curdle. Serves 8-10.

Mrs. Ray B. Moore

ITALIAN PANCAKE CASSEROLE

1 pound lean ground beef	¾ teaspoon garlic salt
1 can (6 oz.) tomato paste	1 teaspoon oregano
2 tablespoons instant onion	½ teaspoon salt
1 teaspoon basil	½ teaspoon pepper

Brown beef in skillet. Add tomato paste, onion, basil, garlic salt, oregano, salt and pepper. Simmer while preparing pancakes.

PANCAKES

2 eggs	¼ teaspoon salt
⅔ cup milk	1 cup creamed cottage cheese
½ cup Pillsbury self-rising flour	2 cups (½ lb.) shredded Mozzarella cheese

¼ cup grated Parmesan cheese

Combine eggs and milk in medium mixing bowl with rotary beater. Add flour and salt. Beat until smooth. Heat a 9-inch skillet over medium high heat. Grease lightly before baking each pancake. Pour batter, ⅓ cup at a time, into skillet, tilting pan to spread evenly over bottom. When pancake is light brown and set, turn to brown other side. Prepare 4 9-inch pancakes. Place pancake on bottom of 10-inch pie pan. Spread with ¼ cup cottage cheese, ¼ meat mixture, ½ cup Mozzarella cheese and 1 tablespoon grated Parmesan cheese. Repeat layers with remaining pancakes ending with cheese. To serve, cut in wedges. Serves 4-6.

Mrs. James E. Williams

CORNED BEEF SOUFFLÉ

2 tablespoons butter	⅛ teaspoon cayenne
1 slice garlic	⅛ teaspoon nutmeg
1 large onion, chopped	½ cup milk
Parsley	3 egg yolks
2 tablespoons flour	3 egg whites
1 tablespoon lemon juice	1 can corned beef, shredded

Melt butter, add the garlic, onion, parsley, flour, lemon juice and seasonings. When blended, add the milk. Cook together; when thick and smooth, add egg yolks and corned beef. Fold in the stiffly-beaten egg whites and bake in a greased casserole 30 minutes at 350°. Serves 4.

Mrs. Hubert B. Braden

LATVIAN PANCAKES

1 beef brisket	Stalk of celery with leaves
2 quarts cold water	Salt to taste
3 carrots	5 peppercorns
Parsley	1 bay leaf

Slowly cook beef brisket in 2 quarts cold water, with carrots, parsley, celery, salt, peppercorns and bay leaf. When meat is tender remove from heat. Keep liquid and meat in refrigerator overnight. The next day take out meat, grind it up to make 2½ cups.

STUFFING

1 tablespoon butter	Salt and pepper to taste
1 large onion, chopped	½ cup sour cream
2½ cups ground brisket, cooked	¼ cup beef stock

Cook onion in butter. Add to onion the ground meat, salt, pepper, sour cream and stock from day before.

PANCAKES

½ teaspoon salt	3 large eggs, beaten
1 teaspoon sugar	1½ cups milk
3 tablespoons butter, melted	1 cup flour

Add salt, sugar and butter to eggs. Then add milk. Blend into flour slowly. Fry the pancakes in a heavy 7-8-inch skillet, browning one side only in butter. Put pancakes on wax paper with the cooked side up. Place stuffing in center, folding sides in. Then fold top and bottom in as with an envelope. Return stuffed pancake to frying pan, brown on all exposed sides. For each helping serve 1 cup hot broth, reserved from cooking of brisket, and cranberry sauce. This can also be served cold. *These pancakes, similar to crêpes, are often served in Latvia for the main Sunday meal because they can be prepared in advance.*

Margaret Gulbis

CHAFING DISH MEATBALLS

1½ pounds ground chuck
½ cup bread crumbs
1 teaspoon salt
½ teaspoon pepper
1 egg
½ cup milk
¼ cup shortening

2 cups canned tomato juice
2 tablespoons flour
¾ cup bottled barbecue sauce
¼ cup water
1 can (1 lb. 4½ oz.) pineapple chunks, drained
Stuffed olives

Early on day of serving, combine ground chuck, bread crumbs, salt, pepper, egg and milk until well-blended. Shape mixture into ¾-inch balls. Put in shallow pan with shortening and refrigerate. In saucepan, combine tomato juice and flour until smooth. Add barbecue sauce and water. Blend well. Later in the day, bake meatballs at 350° for 30 minutes. Drain excess fat from browned meatballs. Pour on tomato sauce and bake 45 minutes longer. To serve, spoon meatballs into chafing dish. Place pineapple chunks and olives here and there and spoon sauce over all. Makes about 48 meatballs.

Mrs. Ernest T. Lontos

HIBBYBURGERS FOR BACHELORS

2 pounds ground meat
2 eggs
2 tablespoons English bread crumbs
Onion, chopped
Green pepper, chopped

1 can (3 oz.) mushrooms, drained
Salt and pepper
Garlic salt
Worcestershire sauce
Lawry's seasoned salt

1 ounce Gallo straight sherry

Add eggs to ground meat. Add onion, green pepper and bread crumbs to mixture. Knead in. Add mushrooms. Add seasonings and spices to taste. Add sherry. Mix well together. Have charcoals red hot. Initially sear hamburgers slightly on each side to keep juices from escaping. Make sure the grill is far enough away from the coals so the hamburgers do not burn. Grill hamburgers for 5 minutes, turn and cook the other side. Serves 6. *This is a hamburger recipe for experimental hamburger lovers. Ingredients can be added at the chef's discretion.*

Martin Cohen

JOAN CRAWFORD'S MEAT LOAF

2 pounds ground sirloin

1 pound ground veal

1 pound Jones bulk pork sausage

3 raw eggs

1 large Bermuda onion, finely chopped

2 green peppers, finely chopped

3 tablespoons Lawry's seasoned salt

3 tablespoons Worcestershire sauce

3 teaspoons A-1 steak sauce

4 hard-boiled eggs

1 cup water

Combine meats, raw eggs, onion, peppers, 1 tablespoon Lawry's seasoned salt, 1 tablespoon Worcestershire sauce and 1 teaspoon A-1 sauce. Mix thoroughly. Shape mixture into oval loaf form in shallow baking pan. Gently press whole hard-boiled eggs into loaf. Sprinkle remaining Lawry's seasoned salt, Worcestershire sauce and A-1 sauce on top of loaf as a crust. Pour water in base of pan. Bake in preheated 350° oven for 30 minutes. Turn oven down to 300° and bake for 30 minutes. Turn oven down to 250° and bake for 45 minutes to 60 minutes, basting frequently with pan juices. Serves 10. *This tasty dish was prepared for me by Miss Crawford on one of my visits to New York.*

Charles Sharp

GERMAN MEAT LOAF

1 pound ground beef

1 pound sausage meat

1/4 cup dry bread crumbs

1/4 cup onion, minced

1 tablespoon parsley, minced

1 egg yolk, beaten

1 1/2 teaspoons salt

1/2 teaspoon freshly ground black pepper

1/4 teaspoon nutmeg

3/4 cup beer

Mix beef, sausage, bread crumbs, onions, parsley, egg yolk, salt, pepper, nutmeg and beer together. Shape into a loaf and place on a greased baking pan. Bake at 350° for 1 1/4 hours.

GLAZE

1 cup brown sugar

2 teaspoons prepared mustard

1/4 cup beer

While the meat is baking, prepare the glaze. Mix brown sugar, mustard and beer. Cook over high heat 5 minutes. Pour over the loaf at the end of 1 hour. Bake 15 minutes longer, basting frequently. Serves 4-6.

Mrs. Fred F. Johnston

HUNGARIAN STUFFED CABBAGE

1 head cabbage	1 pound spareribs
2 pounds hamburger	2 cans (1 lb.) sauerkraut
1 egg	2 onions, sliced
Salt and pepper to taste	1 can (1 lb. 13 oz.) tomatoes
½ cup rice	1 cup water

Sour cream

Pour boiling water over cabbage to soften leaves. Drain and fill separated leaves with following meat mixture. Mix hamburger with egg, salt, pepper and uncooked rice. Brown spareribs in skillet and set aside. Line a large pot with sauerkraut; add onions, a layer of spareribs, filled cabbage leaves and tomatoes in that order. Add another layer of sauerkraut and 1 cup water. Simmer on top of the stove for about 3 hours. When done put sour cream on top and serve. Serves 6.

Eileen Farrell

STUFFED PEPPERS

6 green peppers	2 tablespoons Worcestershire sauce
1 pound ground chuck	
⅓ cup onion, chopped	1 tablespoon brown sugar
1 tablespoon fat	Salt and pepper to taste
1 (1 lb.) can tomatoes	1 cup sharp Cheddar cheese, shredded
¾ cup precooked rice	

Remove tops, clean and wash peppers. Parboil peppers. Cook onion in fat until tender. Brown meat. Add tomatoes, rice, Worcestershire sauce, brown sugar, salt and pepper. Simmer until rice is tender. Add cheese, reserving a little for top of peppers. When cheese is melted, stuff peppers, sprinkle cheese on top and bake in 350° oven for 25 minutes. Serves 6.

Mrs. C. E. Davidson

BEAN DISH

5 strips bacon
1½ pounds ground sirloin
2 medium onions, chopped
2 medium green peppers, chopped
½ cup catsup
2 teaspoons French's mustard
1 teaspoon salt
½ teaspoon pepper

3 tablespoons vinegar
3 tablespoons brown sugar
1 can (20 oz.) red kidney beans
1 can (20 oz.) garbanzos (chick peas)
1 can (20 oz.) Boston-style baked beans
1 cup Cheddar cheese, grated

Fry bacon until crisp, and set aside on paper. Use bacon grease for browning ground sirloin with onions and peppers. In a separate bowl combine catsup, mustard, salt, pepper, vinegar and brown sugar. Add this combination to meat mixture. Now carefully add beans with a little juice from cans. (Too much mixing will mash them.) Put in a 4-quart casserole and bake uncovered 30-40 minutes at 350°. When done sprinkle grated cheese and crumbled bacon all over top and return to the oven for a couple of minutes until cheese melts. Serves 6. *I love this for after concert suppers. Served with green salad and garlic bread, it's a real winner! Finger desserts are all that you need to top it off.*

Marilyn Horne

CHILI

2 tablespoons shortening
1 medium onion, chopped
2 garlic cloves, minced
1 pound ground beef
1 tablespoon chili powder

½ teaspoon salt
¼ teaspoon cayenne pepper
⅛ teaspoon black pepper
2 cans tomato soup
1 can kidney beans

Melt shortening in a large skillet. Add onion, garlic and beef; brown slightly. Add remaining ingredients. Cover and simmer 30 minutes, stirring occasionally. Serves 6-8.

Laraine Jones

YOU ASKED FOR IT

1 loaf French bread, unsliced
1½ pounds ground round steak

Salt and pepper
1 small onion, finely chopped
Catsup
Cheese, grated

Slice bread lengthwise. Separate and spread steak evenly over each half. Salt and pepper to taste. Sprinkle onion over meat. Spread catsup covering each section. Bake at 350° for 20-25 minutes or until desired degree of rareness. Sprinkle with cheese. Turn on broiler until brown on top. Serves 8.

Mrs. J. Erik Jonsson

CORNISH PASTIES

3 cups flour
1 teaspoon baking powder

1 cup shortening
1 teaspoon salt

Ice water

Mix flour, baking powder, shortening and salt, and moisten with ice water. Divide into halves for 2 large pasties or into smaller amounts for small pasties.

FILLING

1 pound round steak, diced
2 medium potatoes, diced

1 small bunch green onions, diced
1 cup parsley, scissored

Mix steak, potatoes, onions and parsley together. Roll out dough. Place equal amounts of filling in the dough. Fold dough over into half-circles and crimp edges. Bake at 300° for 1 hour. *This is a recipe from Mr. Shaw's maternal Grandmother, handed down from her Cornish ancestors. Pasties were an all-in-one lunch carried by miners.*

Robert Shaw

WORSTEN BROODJES

1 pound chopped beef
½ pound chopped veal
½ pound chopped pork
1 medium onion, chopped
1 teaspoon salt
½ teaspoon pepper

½ teaspoon garlic salt
1 egg, beaten
3 packages pie crust mix
Burgundy
3 tablespoons parsley, chopped

Combine meat in a mixing bowl, add onion, seasoning and egg, and mix well. Mix pastry, following directions on package but substituting wine for water and adding parsley. Roll out, on a floured surface, a long strip of pastry about 8 inches wide and as thin as possible. Shape meat into rolls about 5 inches long and ½ inch in diameter. Wrap a meat roll in a section of the pastry allowing about a 1-inch overlap. Cut and press ends together with a fork to seal the meat inside. Place on cookie sheet seam-side down, and prick across the top of crust 3 or 4 times with fork. Bake at 375° until golden brown and flaky, about 35 minutes. Serves 16. *Variation: These may be made in small sizes about 2 inches long and served as hot canapés.*

Mrs. Lynn Brown

L'OSSO BUCO
Italian Veal Stew

2-3 pounds knuckle of veal or veal chops

3-4 carrots

1-2 stalks of celery

Butter

Salt and pepper

1 tablespoon flour

1 bay leaf

1 cup tomato pulp

1 cup white wine

Veal stock or water

Strip of lemon peel, finely chopped

A sprig of thyme

Parsley, chopped

The knuckle of veal must be sawed in 2-inch lengths, not chopped, as the marrow must remain inside the bone. Chop the vegetables very fine and put them in a saucepan with a good lump of butter. Add the meat and season highly with salt and pepper. When the vegetables and meat are well-browned, add a little butter worked with flour. Then add the tomato pulp, wine and sufficient stock or water to barely cover the meat. Add the herbs, tied together. Simmer very gently for 1-1½ hours. Ten minutes before serving, take the meat from the saucepan and strain the sauce, removing the herb bouquet. Then place both meat and sauce in a clean saucepan; and just before serving, sprinkle with lemon and parsley. Serves 4. *I first learned of this way of preparing veal when I studied opera in Italy. The simplicity of this recipe immediately appealed to me, and ever since it has been one of the regulars in my kitchen.*

Dorothy Kirsten

HECCA

1½ pounds veal

1½ pounds beef sirloin

½ cup oil

2 garlic cloves, finely crushed

2 tablespoons sugar

2 jiggers bourbon

1 small bottle soy sauce

6 bunches young scallions

1 large red onion

2 cups rice

Cut veal and beef into 1-inch strips, trim off all fat. Marinate all day (or at least 3 hours if pressed for time) in the oil with crushed garlic. Season with salt and pepper. At the end of the day, brown the meat in the marinade, heating in a big copper skillet for 5 minutes. When meat is browned, add sugar, bourbon and soy sauce. Trim scallions to 3-inch lengths and lay on top of meat with slices of red onion. Cover tightly and steam slowly until onions are tender, about 5-7 minutes. Serve on cooked rice with a tossed salad and hard rolls. Serves 6.

Brian Sullivan

VEAL AND SAUSAGE BROCHETTE

¾ pound fine quality link pork sausages

Water

2 pounds boneless veal for scallopine, pounded very thin

½ cup flour

½ teaspoon salt

¼ teaspoon pepper

Olive oil

1 bunch green onions, white part only, thinly sliced

3 stalks celery, finely chopped

½ cup fresh parsley, chopped

4 small cloves garlic, crushed

½ teaspoon commercially packaged mixed Italian dry herbs

⅛ teaspoon celery salt

⅛ teaspoon coarsely ground black pepper

¼ cup olive oil

2 cups dry white wine

1 pound fresh mushrooms, thickly sliced

1 cup sour cream

1 tablespoon chives, chopped

Hot steamed rice

Cover sausages with cold water, slowly bring just to boiling point, remove from heat, let cool in water, drain, and chill thoroughly. Cut each sausage into thirds or about 1¼-inch pieces. Cut veal into strips as wide as sausage pieces, and wrap each veal strip around a sausage piece; secure with a toothpick. Shake veal rolls in flour seasoned with salt and pepper in paper bag. In a large frying pan, brown veal rolls well on all sides in olive oil. Transfer rolls to a 3-quart kettle with cover. Sprinkle rolls with onions, celery, parsley, garlic, dry herbs, celery salt and black pepper. Add olive oil and the wine. Add mushrooms. Cover tightly and simmer slowly for 30 minutes or until done. Just before serving, stir in sour cream and chives. Taste and correct seasoning. Heat thoroughly. Serve over rice. Serves 6.

The Cookbook Committee

PAUPIETTES COPENHAGEN — CORDON BLEU

4 large thin slices of veal

Mustard

4 slices of ham

4 slices of cheese

1 egg, beaten

Bread crumbs

Salt and pepper

Butter

Hammer veal flat and spread mustard on both sides. Roll the ham around the cheese and then fold the veal around the ham. Dip in egg, then in bread crumbs seasoned with salt and pepper, and fry in butter until pale brown. Serve with green salad and buttered noodles. Serves 3-4.

Serge Fournier

ESCALOPE DE VEAU A LA NORMANDE

4 veal cutlets

8 tablespoons butter

1 tablespoon flour

Salt to taste

3 tablespoons shallots, finely chopped

6-8 small button mushrooms

1 cup fresh cream

Few drops of wine

Parsley or watercress

Melt butter in skillet (preferably electric). Sprinkle veal cutlets with flour and salt. Brown veal in butter. At same time add shallots, slightly brown, and add mushrooms. Add cream at intervals. Let meat simmer in skillet, covered, for 45-60 minutes. Then add a few drops of wine. Immediately place each cutlet, topped with sauce, on a hot serving platter. Garnish with parsley or watercress. Serves 4. *This is a delicious and attractive French recipe.*

Mrs. Melvin M. Garrett

PAPRIKA WIENER SCHNITZEL

1½ pounds veal steak

1 medium onion, thinly sliced

1 clove garlic

2 tablespoons fat

¼ cup enriched flour

1 teaspoon salt

¼ teaspoon pepper

1 tablespoon paprika

1 cup sour cream

⅓ cup consommé

Cut meat in serving pieces. Pound until double in area. Cook onion and garlic in hot fat until tender, but not brown. Remove from skillet, dip veal in flour, seasoned with salt and pepper, brown on both sides in hot fat. Add cooked onion and garlic to meat in skillet. Cover and cook slowly 15 minutes or until meat is tender. Combine paprika, sour cream and consommé, and pour over meat. Cover tightly and simmer 10-15 minutes. Serves 4.

Gregor Piatigorsky

VEAL SCALLOPINE

2 pounds veal cutlets

Salt, pepper and flour

1/4 cup butter

1/2 pound fresh mushrooms, sliced

1 cup dry white wine

1 large onion, sliced

1 tablespoon sugar

1 parsley sprig

1/4 teaspoon rosemary

1/4 teaspoon marjoram

1/4 teaspoon peppercorns

Season veal with salt and pepper and dip in flour. Brown quickly in butter. Add mushrooms and set aside. Liquify all remaining ingredients 5 seconds in blender at high speed. Pour over meat in skillet. Cover and simmer 15 minutes or until meat is tender. Serve with rice or plain spaghetti. Serves 6.

Linda J. Gerhard

COLD VEAL WITH SAUCE MIRAMARE

2 cloves garlic

3 spoonfuls olive oil

4 anchovies

2 pounds loin or round milk-fed veal

1/2 cup carrots

1/2 cup celery

1/2 cup onions

2 bay leaves

2 tablespoons wheat meal

1 cup dry white wine

2 cups water

Let garlic brown in olive oil. Add anchovies and cook a few minutes. Add veal. Slice vegetables and add with bay leaves; remove from heat. In the meanwhile, let wheat meal dissolve in wine and water, and pour it on the meat. Return to heat, and continue cooking for 30 minutes. Remove from heat; place all ingredients into a tureen and let cool. Thinly slice meat, and cover with sauce.

SAUCE

8 ounces tuna, shredded

3 1/2 tablespoons anchovies, chopped

3 1/2 tablespoons pickles, chopped

3 1/2 tablespoons mushrooms, chopped

Juice of 2 lemons

1 1/2 cups mayonnaise

Meat sauce

Crush all ingredients and combine with mayonnaise and meat sauce. Serves 4-6.

Giorgio Tozzi

ROAST PORK LOIN

1 pork rib roast	2 teaspoons rosemary leaves
2 Polish or summer sausages	2 cups Sauterne
Salt and pepper	Arrowroot or cornstarch

Allow approximately two ribs per person. Take a long sharp knife and punch a hole all the way through roast, end to end. Insert sausage in this opening. Place in a roast pan. Salt and pepper lightly and sprinkle with rosemary leaves. Add Sauterne to pan. Cover with aluminum foil and roast about 1 hour at 350°. Remove foil and continue roasting about 1 more hour, basting frequently. Add more Sauterne and water to make sufficient broth for gravy. Strain broth and thicken with arrowroot. *Sweet and sour red cabbage is a good accompaniment for this — or maybe you prefer sauerkraut flavored with caraway seeds.*

Gerald Ramsey

LOIN OF PORK À LA BOULANGERE

4½ pounds loin of pork	1 teaspoon parsley, chopped
1 tablespoon salt	Pepper
8 potatoes, peeled and sliced	2 tablespoons butter
1 onion, chopped	½ cup water

Season pork with salt. Place in large roasting pan; roast at 425° for 1 hour, turning several times to brown all over. Remove pork from pan and pour off surplus fat. Make the gravy by deglazing the pan with a small quantity of water. Remove gravy from pan and set aside. Mix potatoes with onions, parsley and remaining salt and pepper. Put potato mixture in the pan; dot with butter, and lay meat on top. Add enough water to almost cover potatoes. Bring to a boil. Return to oven. Reduce heat to 400°, and cook about 1½ hours longer or until done. Reheat gravy to serve with the meat. Serves 8.

Mrs. Marshall S. Cloyd

LUAU RIBS

1 can (13½ oz.) crushed pineapple

¼ cup molasses

¼ cup Dijon-style mustard

1 teaspoon MSG

3 tablespoons lemon juice

3 tablespoons soy sauce

2 tablespoons Worcestershire sauce

Dash of pepper

4 pounds spareribs or loin back ribs

For glaze combine all ingredients except spareribs and set aside. Salt ribs; place bone side down on grill over slow coals. Keep an eye on heat, as ribs tend to dry out and char with too much heat. Grill about 20 minutes, turn meat side down and grill until browned, about 10 minutes. Turn meat side up, and brush with the pineapple glaze. Continue grilling without turning for 30-45 minutes or until meat is well done. Loin back ribs will take longer. Slide a piece of foil under thinner end of ribs if done before thicker end. Serves 4-6.

Mrs. Thomas S. Barnes

PORK CHOPS WITH APPLES

4 pork chops

Salt and pepper to taste

2 apples, thickly sliced and cored

Brown sugar

1 pint half and half

Trim fat off pork chops. Render the fat in a 10-inch skillet. Salt and pepper the chops, and brown in skillet. Cover with apples. Sprinkle heavily with brown sugar, covering chops. Pour in half and half. Turn heat to low, cover pan tightly, and cook until apples are soft and chops are tender. Serves 4. *This is delicious served with sweet potatoes, green salad and hot rolls.*

Mrs. Julius Dorsey

PORK CHOPS WITH CAPER SAUCE

6 rib or loin pork chops,
   1 inch thick

5 tablespoons flour

3 tablespoons butter

1 teaspoon salt

½ teaspoon freshly ground
   black pepper

½ cup beef stock or broth

⅓ cup onion, chopped

2 teaspoons prepared mustard

2 tablespoons capers

⅓ cup water

¾ cup sour cream

Dredge chops in 3 tablespoons flour, and brown in butter. Pour off butter, and season chops with salt and pepper. Add beef stock, onion, mustard and capers to chops; cover tightly, and simmer 45-60 minutes or until done. Remove chops to warm platter. Blend remaining flour with water. Add to drippings in pan and cook, stirring constantly, until thickened. Fold in sour cream and cook until heated through. Do not boil. Serve sauce over chops. Serves 3-4.

Mrs. Ross W. Powell

PORK CHOPS MADEIRA

4 loin pork chops

⅓ cup sour cream

3 tablespoons Madeira

Salt and pepper to taste

Brown pork chops in an electric skillet. When tender, and a nice brown, remove them from the pan. If there is an excess of fat in the pan, pour it off. Add Madeira and sour cream, stirring well into the gravy, and scraping the pan to loosen any particles of meat that may adhere. Now return the pork chops to the pan and cook for another 5-10 minutes, frequently basting the chops. Add salt and pepper. Serves 2.

Mrs. Claude R. Wilson

PORK CHOP AND RICE CASSEROLE

4-6 pork chops

Finely ground pepper

Paprika

Hickory-smoked salt

Beau Monde

1 onion, chopped

1 tablespoon green pepper, chopped

1 cup Minute rice or ¾ cup regular long-grain rice

1 carrot, chopped (optional)

1 can Swanson clear chicken broth

Trim excess fat from pork chops and use to grease skillet. Remove pieces of fat before browning chops. Sprinkle chops with seasonings. Brown chops on both sides. Add onion, green pepper, rice, carrot and chicken broth. Cover and cook at 325° for 1 hour. Serves 4. *This is my husband's favorite dish. I enjoy serving it with spiced apple rings and a green salad full of artichokes, avocados, etc.*

Mrs. William W. Lynch, Jr.

LEONE'S PORK CHOPS WITH SPAGHETTI

3 tablespoons olive oil

½ cup butter, melted

2 large garlic cloves, mashed

⅓ teaspoon freshly ground black pepper

Pinch of crushed red pepper

4 lean pork chops, 1 inch thick

1 teaspoon crumbled dried rosemary

½ teaspoon salt

4 medium-sized ripe tomatoes or 2 cups canned plum tomatoes, chopped

10 fresh parsley sprigs, chopped

¾ pound spaghetti

¼ cup grated Parmesan cheese

Heat olive oil and ¼ cup butter in a large heavy-bottomed skillet. Add garlic and black and red pepper and cook slowly for 2 minutes. Add pork chops; sprinkle with rosemary and brown on each side for 5 minutes. Lower heat to medium and add salt, tomatoes and parsley. Cover and cook slowly for 20 minutes. Uncover and cook slowly for 20 minutes longer or until done. Taste for salt. Place spaghetti in a pot of boiling salted water. Cook for about 10 minutes. Taste 1 strand. If as desired, drain well. Place back in the pot in which it was cooked. Add remaining butter and mix well. Add the grated cheese and a little sauce and mix. Place spaghetti on a hot plate with the chops and pour sauce over both. Serve with green salad and a Bardolino wine. Serves 4. *This recipe is from Leone's Restaurant in New York.*

Mrs. Spencer C. Relyea

SAUERKRAUT AND SMOKED PORK CHOPS

1 large onion, sliced
3 tablespoons butter
1 can (8½ oz.) crushed
    pineapple
1 can (1 lb.) applesauce

1 teaspoon caraway seeds
2 bouillon cubes
1½ cups water
1 can (1 lb. 11 oz.) sauerkraut

4 or more smoked Hormel center-cut pork chops

Sauté onion in butter until brown. Add pineapple and apple-sauce. Stir well. Add sauerkraut, caraway seeds, bouillon cubes and water. Cover and cook on high heat for 30 minutes. Then reduce to medium heat for 1 hour. Add the chops, turn to low and simmer 30 minutes longer. Serves 4.

Mrs. Robert L. Presley

SPANISH PORK WITH RICE

1 clove garlic, crushed
1 teaspoon salt
¾ teaspoon Tabasco
½ teaspoon paprika
⅛ teaspoon ground cloves
⅓ cup salad oil
6 boned pork chops or steaks,
    1 inch thick

Flour
1 onion, minced
1 cup water
2 tablespoons vinegar
¼ teaspoon saffron (optional)
1 can (8 oz.) Mexican-style
    corn
4 cups hot cooked rice

In a large shallow dish, combine garlic, salt, ½ teaspoon Tabasco, paprika and cloves; stir in oil. Add pork chops. Marinate 8 hours or overnight in refrigerator. Drain marinade into a large skillet; dust chops with flour; brown on both sides in heated marinade. Add onion, water, vinegar and saffron; simmer about 30 minutes, or until chops are fork tender. Heat corn, add ¼ teaspoon Tabasco, and toss with rice to serve as pork accompaniment.

Walter Carringer

CHOUCROUTE GARNIE

2 cans (1 lb. 12 oz.) sauerkraut

1 large onion

2 carrots

1 large sweet apple

Butter

10 peppercorns

6 juniper berries

8 ounces thin-sliced smoked ham, proscuitto or Polish-type

1 bay leaf

1 can consommé

1 cup beer

Knockwurst

Polish sausage

Potatoes

Salt to taste

Wash sauerkraut well in several changes of water. Drain, pressing to remove water. Chop onion fine. Slice carrots crosswise. Pare, core and slice the apple. Rub bottom of casserole with butter. Spread a layer of half of sauerkraut on bottom. Sprinkle over it half of onion, carrots, apple, peppercorns and juniper berries. Cover with half of ham. Add bay leaf, the remaining sauerkraut and apple, onions, carrots and the remaining ham slices. Dot well with butter. Pour consommé and beer over all. Cover casserole tightly. Place in 350° oven for about 3½-4 hours. Add knockwurst, Polish sausage and potatoes for the last hour of cooking only. Count 1 knockwurst, ½ Polish sausage and 1 potato per person. Serves 6.

Mrs. David A. Stretch

Historically some of the fortunes of Europe's greatest families were founded on the peppercorn. Ancient merchants trading their spices became very wealthy men because a pound of ginger was the price of one sheep, a pound of cloves would pay for a cow, and a whole sack of pepper could even buy a man!

CRÊPES FLORENTINE
CRÊPES

1 cup flour

½ teaspoon salt

1¾ cups milk

1 teaspoon sugar

2 eggs, beaten

Sift together flour, salt and sugar. Gradually add eggs and milk. Stir to make a smooth batter the consistency of heavy cream and strain it through a fine sieve. Let the batter stand 2 hours before cooking the crêpes. Brush a 5-6-inch seasoned hot skillet with melted butter. Pour a generous tablespoon of batter into the pan and tip the pan to coat it with a thin layer of batter. When the crêpe is brown on the bottom, turn it and brown the other side.

FILLING

2 pork link sausages

¼ cup onion, chopped

1 tablespoon olive oil

1 egg, slightly beaten

½ cup spinach, cooked and well-drained

½ cup fine soft bread crumbs

¼ teaspoon salt

⅛ teaspoon rosemary

⅛ teaspoon thyme

⅛ teaspoon pepper

2 tablespoons grated Parmesan cheese

Remove casing from sausages and break up meat. Add onion and sauté in oil. Add egg, spinach, bread crumbs, salt, rosemary, thyme, pepper and Parmesan cheese. Blend well. Divide into 8 portions and roll each in a crêpe. Place seam-side down in a buttered baking dish. Tightly cover. Bake at 350° for 20-25 minutes.

FROMAGE SAUCE

½ teaspoon cornstarch

½ cup half and half or light cream

¾ cup Swiss cheese, shredded

Dash of salt

Dash of pepper

Dash of cayenne

1 teaspoon parsley, chopped

In a small saucepan combine cornstarch and cream. Cook and stir constantly until it boils thoroughly and is thickened. Add cheese, salt, pepper, cayenne and parsley. Keep warm over hot water until needed. Arrange 2 crêpes on each plate and cover with Fromage Sauce. Serves 4.

Mrs. Richard E. Lohr

HAM WITH BURGUNDY WINE AND BLACK CHERRIES

3 pounds center-cut ham

Black pepper

¾ cup canned black cherries, reserve juice

2 thin slices of lemon

1 bay leaf

6 thin slices of onion

2 tablespoons mushrooms, chopped

1 cup Burgundy wine

1 tablespoon creamed butter

1 tablespoon flour

Rub both sides of ham with black pepper. Broil quickly on both sides. Remove to baking dish, add ½ cup of strained cherry juice, lemon, bay leaf, onion and mushrooms. Pour Burgundy over this, cover and bake at 250° for 1½ hours. Remove ham to platter. Strain gravy from baking dish into saucepan. Stir in butter and flour, bring to boil, then stir in cherries. Pour ½ sauce over ham and serve remainder in sauce bowl. Serves 6.

Mrs. Vera Hartt Martin

HAM LOAF

1 pound ground ham

2 pounds ground fresh pork

2 eggs

1 cup milk

1 cup corn flakes

Beat eggs, add milk and corn flakes. Add meat and mix well. Bake in a buttered meat loaf pan for 1 hour at 350°. Serve with the following sauce.

SAUCE

1 cup mayonnaise

1 cup heavy cream, whipped

6 sweet pickles, chopped

2-3 teaspoons horseradish

Mix together the mayonnaise, cream, pickles and horseradish. Serves 8.

Mrs. A. Ray Edsel

HAM LOAF WITH MUSTARD SAUCE

3 pounds ground ham

2½ pounds ground pork loin

3 cups soft bread crumbs

1 cup onions, chopped

4 eggs, beaten

1 cup undiluted Carnation milk

Combine ingredients and mix thoroughly. Press lightly into oiled 6½-cup ring mold. Refrigerate overnight. Turn out onto shallow pan. Bake 1¼ hours at 350°. After baking for 10 minutes, brush loaf with Sweet and Sour Glaze.

SWEET AND SOUR GLAZE

1 cup brown sugar

2 tablespoons dry mustard

4 tablespoons vinegar

2 teaspoons water

Mix sugar and mustard. Stir in vinegar and water.

MUSTARD SAUCE

1 cup dry mustard

1 cup vinegar

2 eggs

⅔ cup sugar

Dash of salt

Mayonnaise

Mix mustard and vinegar, and let stand overnight. In top of double boiler, beat eggs. Stir in sugar, salt and mustard mixture. Cook over hot water and stir constantly until thick. Cool. Before serving, add an equal amount of mayonnaise to Mustard Sauce. Serves 26.

Mrs. Frank Pearcy

SPAMROLLA

1 package bake and serve rolls (Pepperidge Farm small oblong rolls, or equivalent)

1 can Spam

3 hard-boiled eggs

1 dill pickle

½ pound sharp cheese

1 small onion

½ green pepper

2 tablespoons catsup

½ teaspoon MSG

Mayonnaise

Cut or scoop out rolls after they are chilled or frozen. (They are easier to handle, if frozen.) Grind Spam, eggs, pickle, cheese, onion and pepper. Add catsup, MSG and mayonnaise to spreading consistency. Mound filling into rolls and top with paprika or cheese. Bake at 325° for 10-15 minutes. *These are excellent luncheon finger sandwiches.*

Mrs. Howard W. Dunham, Jr.

GIGOT D 'AGNEAU EN CROÛTE

3 small lamb kidneys
(Do not use beef.)

5 tablespoons butter

⅓ cup Madeira

4 mushrooms, coarsely
chopped

⅛ teaspoon thyme

⅛ teaspoon rosemary

¼ teaspoon tarragon

Salt to taste

Leg of baby lamb (2-2½
pounds), leg bone removed,
shank bone left in

Butter

1 pound rough puff pastry
(See index.)

1 egg, beaten

2 tablespoons cream

Cut kidneys into small pieces and toss in hot butter until lightly browned. Rinse the pan with Madeira. Add the mushrooms and herbs and season with salt. Stuff the boned part of the leg with this mixture. Reform the gigot and secure it with a skewer. Rub the outside with butter and roast in a 450° oven for 10 minutes. Reduce the heat to 375° and roast for 10 minutes longer. Remove from oven and cool. Roll out the puff paste (or a pie pastry) ½ inch thick and envelop the leg, leaving the shank bone exposed. Cut out small pastry leaves and decorate the top with them. Brush with egg and cream. Bake at 375° until pastry is brown and crisp, about 20-25 minutes. Serve with gratin potatoes. Serves 4-6. *We first had this lamb in a world-renowned French country restaurant surrounded by flowers. The baby lamb and delicate lamb kidneys combine into a beautiful selection for a dinner party. To be most successful you need to use baby lamb; therefore, fix 2 to 3 smaller ones rather than a larger one for a party.*

Mrs. Jack W. Lively

Potatoes come from a small wild plant from Peru, not from Ireland as we have been led to believe. Possibly they were accidently thrown into an Indian campfire and their delicious taste enjoyed by all. They were then introduced into Europe by Spanish and English explorers of the 16th century. Only in 1621 was the potato brought to North America to the Virginia colony.

ROAST LAMB

½ pint olive oil
2 tablespoons lemon juice
Salt and pepper
Accent
½ teaspoon sweet basil
1 teaspoon oregano

4 sprigs rosemary
4 cloves garlic
3-4 pound leg or shoulder of lamb
6 large potatoes, peeled and quartered

½ pint water

Put olive oil, lemon juice, salt, pepper, Accent, basil, oregano, rosemary and garlic in blender, and blend. Marinate the lamb with mixture at least 12 hours before cooking. Place the meat in a roasting pan, surrounded by potatoes. Pour balance of marinade and water over lamb. Cook in 325° oven, adding more water if necessary until the meat is ready and potatoes are nicely browned. Serves 6-8. *Variation: Use 3 pounds chestnuts to replace the potatoes and omit the oregano and garlic. Chestnuts should be parboiled and peeled before putting with the meat.*

Mrs. Frank Nick

BRIDE'S ROAST LAMB

1 teaspoon salt
¼ teaspoon pepper
1 teaspoon paprika

¼ teaspoon rosemary
¼ teaspoon garlic powder
2 teaspoons lemon juice

Shank half of a leg of lamb (about 3 lbs.)

Mix the salt, pepper, paprika, rosemary, garlic powder and lemon juice together, and spread over surface of lamb. Roast lamb on a rack at 325°-350° to desired doneness, approximately 25 minutes per pound for medium well. Serves 6.

Mrs. James B. Francis

ROAST LEG OF LAMB IN PASTE

1 leg of lamb
1 clove garlic
1 tablespoon salt
1 tablespoon black pepper, ground
2 tablespoons flour

2 tablespoons cider vinegar
1 tablespoon A-1 sauce
1 teaspoon dry mustard
1 teaspoon Lea and Perrins Worcestershire sauce
2 tablespoons butter or margarine

Cut garlic clove and rub over leg of lamb. Mix all of the paste ingredients together; chop garlic clove very fine and add to paste. Rub lamb with paste before cooking. Roast at 325° for 35 minutes per pound.

Mrs. Ralph B. Rogers

RACK OF LAMB WITH CRUMBS AND PARSLEY

1 rack of lamb
Salt and pepper
2 tablespoons onion, finely chopped
2 tablespoons celery, finely chopped
1 teaspoon rosemary

¼ cup butter
⅓ cup parsley, chopped
4 shallots
½ cup white bread crumbs
¾ cup white wine
½ cup consommé
2 teaspoons currant jelly

Salt and pepper lamb. Roast 30 minutes at 350°. Remove from oven and cover with vegetables, butter, seasonings and crumbs. Roast 30 more minutes. Remove. Add wine and consommé to pan. Cook 10 minutes. Add jelly and strain. Allow 2 ribs per person.

Helen Corbitt

LAMB SHANKS WITH DRIED FRUITS

4 lamb shanks
Salt and pepper
Flour
2 tablespoons butter
2 large cloves garlic, minced
2 cups mixed dried fruits: peaches, apricots, pears and prunes

½ cup sugar
1 teaspoon cinnamon
½ teaspoon allspice
½ teaspoon ground cloves
¼ cup tarragon vinegar
3½ cups water

Dust the lamb shanks with salt, pepper and flour. Brown with the garlic in the butter. Put in a large casserole with the dried fruits, sugar, cinnamon, allspice, cloves, vinegar and water. Add more water if necessary to keep moist. Cover tightly and bake at 350° about 3 hours or until the lamb shanks are tender. Serves 4-6. *Serve with nut and currant pilaf, rice cooked in chicken broth with currants and sprinkled with slivered almonds.*

David A. Stretch

LAMB CASSEROLE

2 cups leftover roast lamb, cubed
1 can (20 oz.) tomatoes, drain and save juice
1 medium onion, grated
¼ green pepper, chopped
2 teaspoons salt

⅛ teaspoon black pepper
3 cups liquid (tomato juice and leftover gravy)
1 tablespoon A-1 sauce
½ pound fresh mushrooms, sliced, or 2 small cans (4 oz.) sliced mushrooms

½ cup uncooked rice

Mix together and heat ingredients. Pour into 2-quart casserole and bake for 1½ hours at 350°. Stir several times while casserole is baking. Serves 6-8.

Mrs. Ralph B. Rogers

LAMB SHANKS IN CAPER SAUCE

4 lamb shanks	Sprig of parsley
Celery leaves	1 bay leaf
1 carrot, sliced	Thyme
¼ onion	Salt

Freshly ground peppercorns

Have butcher crack and trim fat from lamb shanks. Put in pot and cover with cold water, bring to boil and skim. Add a few celery leaves, carrot, onion, parsley, bay leaf, a sprinkle of thyme, salt and freshly ground peppercorns. Bring to boil, lower heat, and simmer covered until shanks are tender. This can be done in morning. Remove meat and put in casserole. Strain broth and pour a little of it over the lamb shanks to keep them moist until they are warmed later. Serve with Caper Sauce.

CAPER SAUCE

2 tablespoons butter	1 cup light cream
2 tablespoons flour	Salt and pepper to taste
1½ cups lamb broth	½ cup capers, drained

Melt butter and stir in flour. Add lamb broth slowly, stirring constantly. Cook and stir until reduced to 1 cup. Add cream and simmer, stirring for 5 minutes. Season to taste with salt and freshly ground black pepper. Add capers.

Mrs. Ted F. Pancerz

SHISH KEBAB

1 leg of lamb, cubed	4 ounces tomato sauce
1 large onion, chopped	1 tablespoon salt

1 teaspoon pepper

Be sure that lamb cubes are larger than bite size, but not too large as they will not cook. Place in bowl, mix in onion, tomato sauce, salt and pepper. Let stand in refrigerator for 24 hours. Place on skewers. Place over a charcoal fire, and cook until done, not over 10 minutes. Serves 8.

V. Y. Rejebian

Until the 13th century, merchants would not disclose the secrets of their spice sources. Marco Polo finally changed all of that when he visited the Orient and wrote about his voyages. Vasco da Gama sailed around the continent of Africa to seek the rich sources of spices; and Magellan, after two hard, adventurous years, finally reached the Spice Islands of New Guinea where in abundance cloves, nutmeg, cinnamon, pepper and other spices were growing.

LAMB CURRY

2 teaspoons curry

3 tablespoons butter

4 large onions, diced

4 large apples, diced

Flour

1½ pounds lamb, cubed

Bacon grease

1 can beef consommé

Raisins (optional)

Salt and pepper to taste

Brown curry in butter. Add onions and cook until transparent. Add apples and cook until soft. Add lamb that has been floured and browned in bacon grease. Cover and simmer 4 hours or until apples and onions are reduced to thick sauce and lamb is very tender. While cooking add consommé. Add raisins last ½ hour of cooking if desired. Increase curry to 1 tablespoon if you like hot curry. Serves 4.

Mrs. David C. Tyrrell

KIBBEE SINEYE

Baked Ground Lamb with Burghul

2 pounds ground lean lamb

2 cups fine burghul or medium wheat

1 onion, grated

Salt and pepper to taste

Cinnamon to taste

Butter

Wash burghul several times and drain. Mix with ground meat, onion, salt, pepper and cinnamon. Add cold water and knead to soften. Butter a 9x13-inch baking dish or pan. Divide kibbee mixture in half. Moisten hands with cold water. Using half of kibbee, spread bottom layer evenly.

FILLING

1 pound lamb, coarsely ground

¼ cup pine nuts (snoobar)

Salt and pepper to taste

¼ cup butter

1 tablespoon oil

Brown lamb, pine nuts, salt and pepper in skillet. Spread filling on bottom layer. With remaining kibbee pat out small portions and place over filling. Moisten hands and smooth top layer. Cut in diamond shapes. Dot top with butter and oil. Bake in preheated 450° oven for 30-40 minutes. Serve hot. Serves 6. *Variation: Use ½ lamb and ½ beef in kibbee mixture.*

Rosalind Elias

CALVES LIVER EN CASSEROLE

2 pounds calves liver,
   thinly sliced
Flour
Salt, pepper, cayenne to taste
4 tablespoons cooking oil,
   Crisco or fat

1 green pepper, chopped
1 large onion, chopped
3 stalks celery, chopped
1 can button mushrooms and
   juice

1 can tomato purée

Cut liver in 2-inch squares. Dredge in seasoned flour and brown quickly in melted fat. Set aside. Sauté pepper, onion and celery in fat. Add mushrooms. Combine with meat and moisten with juice reserved from mushrooms. Add tomato purée. Check for seasoning and cook together for 5 minutes. Turn into buttered casserole, cover, and bake for 1 hour in 350° oven. Delicious with spoon bread or rice. Serves 4.

Mrs. Morton Marr

THYME TONGUE

1 fresh beef tongue
1 cup brown sugar
1 tablespoon salt
2 onions, sliced
1 clove garlic, sliced

1 tablespoon thyme
1 tablespoon mustard
1 cup red wine
2 cups vinegar
Flour and water paste

Wash, dry tongue and remove roots. Prick all over. Soak in marinade of sugar, salt, onions, garlic, thyme, mustard, wine and vinegar for 3 days, turning frequently. Drain, wipe, and put in roaster. Cover with thick paste of flour and water. Pour marinade over tongue and bake at 300° for 4 hours or until tender. Remove paste, skin and serve hot or cold. Drain marinade and thicken for sauce. Serves 4.

Mrs. Kenneth Tunnell

VEAL KIDNEYS PORTO

2 tablespoons olive oil

4 tablespoons onions, chopped

3 tomatoes, skinned and sliced

5 tablespoons fresh mushrooms, sliced

1 teaspoon fresh or dried tarragon, chopped

1 teaspoon fresh or dried thyme, chopped

3 veal kidneys, very thinly sliced

Garlic salt

1¾ cups port wine

Brown onions, tomatoes and mushrooms in hot oil. Add tarragon and thyme. After 2 minutes add kidney slices, lightly salted with garlic salt, and let stand 5 minutes. Add port wine and bring to a boil. Serves 3. *Serve with ioasted Italian bread and mixed endive and tomato salad for a perfect meal.*

Serge Fournier

VEAL KIDNEY STEW

1 kidney per person

Flour

Butter

Salt and pepper

½ teaspoon Worcestershire sauce

1 tablespoon sherry

Soak kidneys for 1 hour in salt water. Trim off most of the fat and any white cords or strings. Cut into thin slices, roll in flour. Sauté in butter. When brown, cover with water and simmer 10 minutes. Season with salt, pepper, Worcestershire sauce and sherry. *Serve with Little Corn Cakes.*

Mrs. H. Neil Mallon

VENISON IN RICH SAUCE

1 haunch of venison
(young deer)

Vinegar

2 onions, sliced

4 carrots, sliced

4 parsley roots

¼ celery root

5 laurel leaves

10 peppercorns

Salt

¼ pound bacon

2 tablespoons flour

½ cup sour cream

Put water in a deep bowl, adding enough vinegar to flavor it. Add onions, carrots, parsley roots, celery root, laurel leaves, peppercorns and salt. Put the haunch of venison with bone already cut off into the bowl so it is completely covered by vinegar mixture. Marinate for 3-7 days. Then take venison out and cook it with all the roots and onions in a pressure cooker, with very little water added, for about 25 minutes. Take meat out separately and press the cooked roots through a sieve. Then fry the bacon until all the grease is in the pan and add the sauce to it. In the meantime, add flour to the sour cream. Mix well and add to the sauce while stirring. Season to taste with either salt or a little sugar, and then add meat. *Serve with cranberries, noodles or boiled potatoes.*

Teresa Stich-Randall

ANTELOPE STROGANOFF

2½ pounds lean antelope
meat

Meat tenderizer

Flour

Oil

1 cup celery, chopped

1 cup onions, chopped

1 cup potatoes, chopped

1 cup Burgundy wine

1 cup orange juice

½ cup water

1 tablespoon Kitchen Bouquet

Salt and pepper

½ pint sour cream

Cut meat into thin strips. Put tenderizer on strips and dust with flour. Brown lightly in small amount of oil. After meat has browned, add rest of ingredients, except sour cream. Cover and simmer 3-4 hours, stir occasionally, add more liquid if needed. The vegetables should cook to mush and the sauce should be medium thick. Thicken with a little flour, if necessary. Add sour cream about 2 minutes before removing from heat. Serve with peppered rice. Serves 6-8.

Mrs. Jerry W. Peterman

STIFATHO
Greek Deer Stew

2 pounds deer meat	⅓ cup olive oil
2 teaspoons salt	½ teaspoon cumin
7 teaspoons vinegar	6 cloves garlic
2 bay leaves	½ teaspoon pepper
Pinch of rosemary	½ can tomato paste
12 whole allspice	24 medium onions

Soak meat in cold water overnight with 1 teaspoon salt and 1 teaspoon vinegar. Next day wash well, cut into medium-sized pieces and boil 5 minutes. Empty water. Put 2 cups fresh water in pot. Add a garni of bay leaves, rosemary and allspice. Next add olive oil, cumin, garlic, pepper, remaining salt and vinegar and tomato paste. Boil in covered pan over medium heat until meat is half-cooked. Add onions and finish cooking. Add more water if needed, but there should be little water left when the stew is completed. Remove spice garni before serving.

Mrs. Gus J. Carras

CHEESE, EGGS, RICE AND PASTA

QUICHE LORRAINE

Unbaked 9-inch pie shell
½ pound sliced bacon
1½ cups (6 oz.) natural Swiss cheese, grated
3 eggs

1½ cups light cream
¾ teaspoon salt
Dash of nutmeg
Dash of cayenne
Dash of pepper

Prepare pie shell. Refrigerate until ready to use. Preheat the oven to 375°. Fry bacon until crisp; drain on paper towels, crumble bacon into bits and sprinkle over bottom of pie shell. Then sprinkle with Swiss cheese. In medium bowl, with rotary beater, beat eggs with cream, salt, nutmeg, cayenne and pepper until well-combined but not frothy. Pour into pie shell. Bake 35-40 minutes, or until the top is golden and the center seems firm when gently shaken. Let cool on a wire rack for 10 minutes before serving. Makes 6 servings or 12 hors d'oeuvres servings.

Mrs. John D. Murchison

QUICHE LORRAINE

CRUST

1 cup flour
½ cup butter
1 package (3 oz.) cream cheese

Combine flour, butter and cream cheese for crust. Form into ball. Wrap in wax paper and chill at least 30 minutes.

FILLING

1 pint light cream
½ cup Cheddar cheese, grated

2 eggs
¼ pound bacon, fried

Salt and pepper to taste

Scald cream. Add grated cheese, eggs, bacon, salt and pepper. Take out the crust and roll into thin, flat form. Bake in round pie pan for 10 minutes at 450°. Then put in filling, and bake for approximately 30 minutes or until the quiche is firm and can be cut into slices. Serves 4-6.

Jaime Laredo

CHEESE RAMEKINS

2 cups Swiss cheese, grated ¼ teaspoon salt
1 cup coffee cream ¼ teaspoon dry mustard
2 eggs Pinch of cayenne pepper
Tart shells

Mix and pour into shells lined with pastry. Bake at 400° for 15 minutes. Serves 6.

Helen Corbitt

SOUFFLÉ FOR ONE

¼ cup milk 1 egg yolk, slightly beaten
1 tablespoon butter ⅓ cup cheese, grated
1 tablespoon flour ⅛ teaspoon salt
Few drops of liquid or dry pepper

Place majority of milk in saucepan with butter; heat, being careful not to scorch. Place flour in a jar with a lid with enough very cold milk to dissolve it. Shake until lump free. Pour into hot mixture all at once, and stir constantly with whisk until sauce comes to a boil. Beat in a small amount of sauce with egg yolk, repeat once or twice until warmed. Then stir yolk into main mixture. Add cheese, salt and pepper. Cover container. This may be made several hours ahead of time.

LEAVENING

1 egg white Pinch of salt
⅛ teaspoon cream of tartar or cornstarch

Beat egg whites, salt and cream of tartar until soft curved peaks are formed when beater is withdrawn. Gently fold sauce into egg whites immediately. The unbaked mixture may stand about 30 minutes; fill a pottery container ¾ full and bake in preheated 350° oven about 20 minutes for 1-4 eggs (50 minutes for more than 4 eggs) until well-browned.

Mrs. Barron U. Kidd

FANTASTIC SOUFFLÉ SANDWICH

4 slices white bread

2 slices Kraft Old English
  cheese

1 egg

1 scant cup milk

1 can mushroom soup

Trim crust from bread. Put cheese between bread and place in flat baking dish. Beat egg into milk. Pour over bread. Soak 4 hours. Bake in 325° oven for 45-60 minutes. Heat undiluted soup and pour over baked sandwich. Serves 2.

Mrs. Benjamin F. Irby

CHEESE SOUFFLÉ

3 teaspoons minute tapioca

1 teaspoon salt

1 cup milk

1 cup sharp cheese, grated

3 egg yolks

3 egg whites

Place tapioca, salt and milk in double boiler. Cook 5 minutes after it reaches the scalding point. (It will be very thick.) Remove from water, add cheese and set aside. Beat egg yolks, until very thick or lemon-colored. Blend yolks into milk mixture. Carefully fold in whites, beaten stiffly. Pour into buttered, 2-quart baking dish. Place in pan of hot water. Bake at 350° for about 50 minutes or until brown and crinkly. (For individual baking dishes, bake 30 minutes.) Serve at once. Serves 4.

Mrs. Cecil H. Green

CHEESE AND MUSHROOM SOUFFLÉ

1 can condensed mushroom
  soup

4 egg yolks, beaten

1 package (8 oz.) nippy
  spreading cheese, diced

½ teaspoon salt

Dash of white pepper

4 egg whites, stiffly beaten

¼ cup slivered blanched
  almonds

Heat soup in double boiler. Add small amount of hot soup to egg yolks, add to remaining hot mixture. Cook 2 minutes. Add cheese. Stir to melt. Season to taste. Fold in egg whites. Pour into ungreased 1½-quart baking dish. Sprinkle with almonds. Bake in 325° oven until inserted knife comes out clean, about 1 hour. Serves 8.

Mrs. Paschal Lee Garth

SHARPLEIGHT LUNCHEON CHEESE

3 slices stale bread
Butter
2 eggs
¾ cup thin cream or milk
1 tablespoon butter

1 teaspoon salt
½ teaspoon mustard
¼ teaspoon paprika
Few grains cayenne

½ pound mild or sharp cheese, diced

Cut bread into ⅓-inch slices. Remove crusts and spread with butter. Slice into finger-shaped pieces. Arrange around sides of a buttered baking dish, having bread extend about 1 inch above dish. Line bottom of dish. Beat eggs slightly, add cream, butter, salt, mustard, paprika, cayenne and cheese. Bake at 350° for 30 minutes. Serves 4.

Mrs. Charles D. Briner

ROQUEFORT TORTE

2 cups Roquefort cheese
2 packages (3 oz.) cream cheese
4 tablespoons butter
¼ cup sherry wine

¼ teaspoon salt
¼ teaspoon paprika
1½ cups heavy cream, whipped
Baked pie shell

Chopped chives

Beat cheeses, butter and wine until light, and add salt and paprika. Fold in cream, pile into pie shell and cover with chives. Refrigerate, and serve with a green salad for lunch or as an hors d'oeuvre. Serves 4-6.

Helen Corbitt

TOASTED CHEESE SANDWICH

Bread, sliced
Sharp cheese, sliced

Fresh tomatoes, sliced
Bacon

Place slices of bread on cookie sheet. On each slice of bread layer cheese, then tomato; top with bacon. Bake at 350° until cheese is melted. Broil until bacon is brown. Serve immediately.

Mrs. J. Erik Jonsson

FAVORITE WELSH RAREBIT

1 tablespoon butter	1/2 teaspoon salt
1 pound American cheese, finely cut	1/4 teaspoon dry mustard
	Dash of pepper
1 cup cream	1 egg, beaten

Toast or crackers

Put butter and cheese into pan, and let melt together over slow heat. Add cream gradually, stirring constantly until smooth. Mix salt, mustard and pepper; add to egg. Pour into the top of a double boiler, pour in the melted cheese, still stirring and let thicken over the hot water. Pour over toast or crackers before serving. Serves 4.

Clifford Curzon

FONDUE

1 1/2 cups bread, cubed	1 tablespoon Kirsch
4 tablespoons butter	3/4 cup Sauterne
3/4 cup Longhorn cheese, finely shredded	1 tablespoon paprika
	1/2 teaspoon pepper
1/4 cup Gouda cheese, finely shredded	1/2 teaspoon salt
	1 sprinkle chili powder
1/4 cup Swiss cheese, finely shredded	Dash of ground lemon peel

Grease fondue dish or 5-inch deep saucepan lightly with Crisco. Melt butter in dish over a low fire. Slowly mix in the various cheeses. The flavor is better if the cheeses blend together as you are putting them in the pan. Stir constantly and add more butter if needed. Add Kirsch and stir for a few seconds to let it blend completely. Slowly pour in Sauterne, stirring constantly. Still stirring, add the paprika, pepper, chili powder and ground lemon peel. Each ingredient must be blended in the mixture completely to give the best flavor. Serves 4-6.

Mrs. Robert G. Spickelmier

SWISS FONDUE

Crusty French bread

2 tablespoons cornstarch

3 tablespoons Kirsch

1 clove garlic, peeled and crushed

2 cups dry white wine

Dash of pepper

Dash of nutmeg

3 cups (¾ lb.) Gruyère cheese, finely grated

About 30 minutes before serving, cut French bread into small cubes, then heap in bread basket. Stir together cornstarch and Kirsch until smooth; set aside. Rub inside of earthenware casserole with garlic. Pour in wine, then heat until just below boiling; add pepper and nutmeg. Gradually add small amounts of cheese, while stirring constantly with a fork. Then add cornstarch mixture, and stir until smooth and bubbling. Place over alcohol burner, warm enough to keep it bubbling slightly. Each person heaps some bread cubes on his plate; then with fork, he dips them, one by one into fondue, being careful not to lose a piece, because that means he must donate 1 bottle of wine for the next fondue party. Serves 3-4. *This recipe comes from a Swiss chef in New Glarus, Wisconsin, a delightful "old-country" village which is still predominately Swiss in character and ancestry.*

Mrs. Richard J. Goebel

SWISS CHEESE FONDUE

1 cup dry white wine

1½ pounds imported process Gruyère cheese

1 cup Kirsch

1 loaf French bread, in 1-inch cubes

Using earthenware fondue pot, heat wine on stove until almost to boiling point. Do not let wine boil. Add the grated cheese, a little at a time, stirring constantly with a wooden fork. Add more cheese as the mixture takes on a creamy blend. Be certain to stir the mixture constantly. When all cheese has been blended, add Kirsch. Mix in and remove fondue pot to an alcohol burner on low heat and stir as the mixture gradually thickens. Spear bread cubes with fondue fork and dip into the cheese mixture. Serves 4-8.

Brad Manson

FRESH RICOTTA

1 gallon grade A milk	2-3 tablespoons sugar
1 quart half and half	2 pinches of salt

2 quarts buttermilk

Heat milk, half and half, sugar and salt in 8-quart container to boiling point, stirring constantly. It has reached the proper temperature (180°) when it has the "cooked milk smell". Pour some of the buttermilk into the center and then some around the edge. Do not stir after you add the buttermilk. When curds are rising and forming, lift them out gently with a slotted spoon, being careful not to disturb the rest. Place in colander resting in a pan. After removing the curds, pour the whey which has drained from the colander back into the milk. Wait a few moments, then pour some more buttermilk around the edge only. (After the first addition of buttermilk, the rest is added only around the edge.) Continue this process until all buttermilk has been added and there are no more curds. If the curds do not seem to be setting because of lack of acidity (milk should be green), add a small quantity of vinegar. This ricotta may be frozen, but only when it is to be used for cooking, not for cannoli. Makes about 3 cups.

Victor Alessandro

RICOTTA BALLS

2 cloves garlic	1 cup Parmesan cheese
1 can (8 oz.) tomato purée	4 eggs
6 cups (3 lb. tin) Italian ricotta	Parsley
	Black pepper
2 cups bread crumbs	½ teaspoon salt

Make a sauce by frying garlic and adding tomato purée. Cook for 30 minutes over low heat, adding water if too thick. Heat ½ inch of oil in a skillet. Drain water out of ricotta by putting into a dish towel for an hour. Mix the ricotta, crumbs, cheese, eggs, parsley, pepper and salt together. Roll into balls and fry. As the balls are fried, drop gently into the sauce. Simmer 30 minutes. Serves 10.

Ezio Flagello

EGGS HUSSARDE

6 Holland Rusks

6 slices grilled ham or Canadian bacon

1 cup Marchand du Vin sauce

6 slices grilled fresh tomato

6 soft-cooked poached eggs

1-2 cups Hollandaise sauce

On a Holland Rusk base, place a slice of ham. Top with Marchand du Vin sauce. Next place a slice of tomato and top it with 1 poached egg. Cover with Hollandaise sauce and serve immediately. Serves 3.

The Cookbook Committee

Basil was once so precious that only a sovereign was allowed to cut it and only then, so the legend goes, with a golden sickle.

EGGS OMAR PASHA

Chopped onion

Butter

Eggs

Grated Parmesan cheese

Chopped parsley (optional)

Sauté 1 tablespoon onion per person in butter until tender. Line each individual casserole with onion, then break 1 egg over onion and sprinkle with 1 teaspoon cheese. Put in 400° oven and let eggs cook until firm, but not hard. Take out and pour tomato sauce over. Sprinkle with chopped parsley and serve.

TOMATO SAUCE

3 slices bacon

1 onion, chopped

2 tablespoons carrots, chopped

1 can (1 lb. 4 oz.) tomatoes

Bay leaf, crumbled

Pinch of thyme

Pinch of marjoram

Pinch of basil

Pinch of summer savory

4 peppercorns, slightly bruised

½ clove garlic, crushed

¼ teaspoon sugar

1 tablespoon flour

¼ cup consommé

2 ounces sherry

1 tablespoon butter

Chop bacon and brown slightly; add onion and carrots. When onion is tender add tomatoes, bay leaf, thyme, marjoram, basil, summer savory, peppercorns, garlic, sugar, flour mixed with consommé and sherry. Simmer for about 45 minutes. Strain sauce into another saucepan, rubbing vegetables through sieve. Heat and add butter. Serves 4. *This is a good Friday or Sunday night supper recipe.*

Mrs. Ted F. Pancerz

EGGS ST. DENIS

6 Holland Rusks

6 slices grilled ham or
  Canadian bacon

6 eggs

2 cups Marchand du Vin
  sauce

On a base of rusk, place a slice of ham. Add an egg that has been fried in deep fat. Cover all with sauce. Serve immediately. Serves 3.

Joseph D. Zimmerman

EGGS SARDOU

1-2 cups creamed spinach

6 artichoke bottoms

6 eggs

1-2 cups Hollandaise sauce

On a base of creamed spinach, place artichoke bottoms. Fill these with poached eggs and cover all with Hollandaise sauce. Serve immediately. Serves 3.

The Cookbook Committee

BLUE CHEESE EGG BAKE

7 tablespoons butter

6 tablespoons flour

1 teaspoon salt

3 cups milk

⅓ cup blue cheese,
  crumbled

½ cup celery, chopped

¼ cup pimento, chopped

Salt and pepper to taste

12 hard-cooked eggs,
  quartered lengthwise

9 saltine crackers, finely
  crushed

In a saucepan, melt 6 tablespoons butter over low heat, blend in flour and salt. Add milk. Cook and stir until mixture thickens and bubbles. Stir in blue cheese, celery and pimento. Add salt and pepper. Place eggs in 12x7x2-inch baking dish. Top with cream sauce. Toss cracker crumbs with 1 tablespoon melted butter. Sprinkle around edge of casserole. Bake at 325° for 45-50 minutes or until bubbly and top is slightly browned. Serves 8.

Mrs. William R. Newsom, III

TART NORMANDY

6 eggs

1 tablespoon flour

2 tablespoons butter, melted

1 cup milk

½ teaspoon salt

6 bacon slices

Unbaked pie shell

Mix eggs, flour and butter. Add milk and salt. Fry bacon slices until crisp. Crumble into the mixture. Put ingredients into pie shell. Bake slowly at 350° until firm. Serves 6-8. *This is an old English dish served for supper, Sunday morning breakfast or brunch.*

Mrs. Franklin Martin

OMELETTE À LA ROSE

1½ tablespoons butter

1 tablespoon dry bread crumbs

1 tablespoon Parmesan cheese, freshly grated

1 teaspoon Schilling's Salad Supreme seasoning

¼ teaspoon oregano

2 eggs, beaten

4 heaping tablespoons Cheddar cheese, freshly grated

Heat butter in pan. Add bread crumbs, Parmesan cheese, seasoning and oregano to eggs. Pour into pan over medium heat. Lift sides of omelette to let liquid run down. When almost cooked, add Cheddar cheese over half of omelette, and fold over. Continue cooking for 3 minutes until cheese melts. Serve immediately. Serves 1.

Leonard Pennario

OMELET WITH HAM AND SOUR CREAM

5 egg yolks

1 cup sour cream

¼ teaspoon salt

5 egg whites, stiffly beaten

1 cup cooked ham, finely diced

2 tablespoons butter

Beat egg yolks until thick and lemon-colored; beat in half of the sour cream and the salt. Fold in the egg whites and ham. Heat butter in 10-inch skillet; pour in omelet mixture, leveling gently. Cook over low heat until lightly browned on bottom, about 5 minutes. Finish cooking in 325° oven until top is golden brown, about 12 minutes. Finish by loosening omelet; slide onto warm plate. Frost with remaining sour cream. Cut into wedges with two forks. Serves 4.

Mrs. Anthony Briggle

STUFFED EGGS AU GRATIN

8 hard-cooked eggs, halved lengthwise

Onion salt

½ teaspoon Worcestershire sauce

1 can (2¼ oz.) deviled ham
2 tablespoons mayonnaise

2 packages (10 oz.) frozen French-style green beans

1 can (10 oz.) condensed cream of celery soup

⅔ cup milk

1 package (8 oz.) American cheese, shredded

Remove yolks and mash with onion salt, Worcestershire sauce, deviled ham and mayonnaise. Fill cavities in egg whites with yolk mixture. Cook green beans as directed on package. Drain. Place in 8x8x2-inch baking dish. Arrange stuffed eggs on beans. Mix soup, milk and half the cheese. Pour into baking dish around the eggs. Sprinkle top of casserole with remaining cheese. Bake at 350° for 30 minutes. Serves 8. *This is an unusual and tasty supper dish.*

Mrs. I. C. Deal

EGGS 'N ONION

Butter

Onions, chopped

1 dozen eggs

Salt and pepper

Paprika

In a large iron skillet, sauté a 1½-inch layer of onions in butter until clear. Break eggs into the onions and season with salt, pepper and paprika. Bake or cook on top of the stove, covered tightly, until eggs are done. This can be cooked outside for a real ranch breakfast. Serves 6.

James F. Gilbert

GREEN RICE

1 cup long-grain rice

2 cups boiling water

3 teaspoons Spice Island chicken-seasoned stock base

½ cup butter

1 bunch celery (tops included), finely chopped

1 bunch green onions (tops included), finely chopped

1 bunch parsley, snipped

½ teaspoon Spice Island Beau Monde seasoning

½ teaspoon oregano

¼ teaspoon ground cumin

¼ teaspoon pepper

Cook rice in boiling water with chicken stock base; set aside. In large heavy skillet, melt butter; add celery, onions, parsley, Beau Monde, oregano, cumin and pepper. Mix well, cover and cook slowly until onion is soft and celery is still somewhat crisp. Toss cooked rice with vegetables; place in casserole. Cover and heat through at 275°. This may be made a day ahead (this is better as flavors blend) and warmed at 275°. If this is done, sprinkle about 2 tablespoons of water on top before warming, for additional moisture. Serves 6. *This is wonderful with steak or broiled chicken.*

Ruth Tears

SOUTHERN RICE

1 teaspoon salt

3 cups water

1 cup regular rice (not instant)

1 cup milk

Bring salted water to a boil, slowly add rice, stirring constantly, and let boil about 20 minutes, uncovered. Drain rice and return to pan. Add milk and simmer until all milk is absorbed. Serve as a vegetable with butter, or as a cereal with sugar and butter.

Mrs. Clay Burnett

RICE AND MUSHROOM CASSEROLE

3 onions, sliced

2 cups sliced mushrooms, fresh or canned

½ cup butter

1 cup consommé

1 cup water

1 cup rice

Salt and pepper to taste

Sauté onions and mushrooms in butter. Add consommé and water. Mix well with thoroughly washed uncooked rice. Season. Bake in greased casserole at 350° for 45-60 minutes. Serves 8-10.

Mrs. William L. Groth, Jr.

PILAF

4 cups chicken stock

2 cups long-grain rice, not processed rice

½ cup butter, not margarine

1 large twist of vermicelli, crumbled in the palm of the hand

Bring stock to a boil. Use a heavy vessel and keep it covered as the rice steams. Add the rice which has been washed well and drained. Bring to a boil and reduce to very low heat. While this is steaming, melt butter in a separate pan and brown the vermicelli until golden brown. Add to steaming rice, folding it in thoroughly and carefully. Steam 20-30 minutes until rice is thoroughly cooked. Serves 8. *Shish kebab and pilaf go together as do bacon and eggs.*

Mrs. V. Y. Rejebian

RICE SUPREME

1 green pepper, diced

1 large onion, diced

4 tablespoons margarine

4 cups cooked rice

1 teaspoon salt

2 eggs, beaten

¼ teaspoon black pepper

1 carrot, grated

1 can turkey soup

1 cup grated cheese

Sauté green pepper and onion in margarine. Then add rice, salt, eggs, pepper, carrots and soup. Pour into greased baking dish. Sprinkle cheese on top of mixture. Bake 30 minutes at 350°. Serves 4.

Mrs. Lester A. Russell

HAWAIIAN RICE

2 medium onions, chopped

2 tablespoons bacon drippings

1 pound ground round steak

1¼ cups long-grain Uncle Ben's regular rice

2 cans beef consommé

1 can mushrooms

3 teaspoons curry powder

Butter

Salt and pepper to taste

1-2 cartons sour cream

Cook onions slowly in bacon drippings until they begin to wilt, then add meat and sear. Butter a large Pyrex dish and mix all ingredients except sour cream. Cover with foil and bake at 325° for 1 hour. At mid-point of cooking, stir gently but completely. When done, stir lightly, dish up and place generous portion of sour cream on each serving. Better still, let each guest add their own sour cream. If some is left over, add a little water when reheating. Serves 8.

Mrs. M. E. Van Hemert

WILD RICE SOUFFLÉ

½ cup salad oil

1 cup fresh parsley, snipped

1 large onion

1 clove garlic, minced

2 cups wild rice, boiled

1 large can Carnation milk or dairy milk

¼ teaspoon salt

½ pound sharp Cheddar cheese

Pepper

Dash of ground cayenne

½ teaspoon marjoram

2 eggs, beaten

Place salad oil in heavy skillet over low heat; add parsley, onion and garlic; sauté until soft, but not browned. Add rice, milk, salt, cheese, pepper, cayenne, marjoram and eggs. Pour into well-greased casserole; bake at 350° for 30 minutes. Serves 8.

Louise E. Finley

WILD RICE CASSEROLE

2 eggs

½ cup cooking oil

1 onion, finely chopped

1 cup parsley, chopped

1¾ cups Cheddar cheese, grated

1½ cups wild rice, cooked, or Uncle Ben's long-grain and wild rice combination

1 cup milk

Salt to taste

1 tablespoon paprika

Beat eggs well. Gradually add oil, then onions and parsley. Stir in cheese, and add rice, milk and salt. Pour into greased casserole. Top with paprika. Bake at 325° for 45 minutes. Serves 6. *Serve with fowl or game.*

Mrs. William R. Newsom, III

Macaroni, spaghetti and similar "pastes" are considered by the general public as a typical and peculiarly Italian food and Italy is probably entitled to the credit for her early appreciation and dedication to the pastes (or pastas). History, however, must credit the Chinese with their invention. (This is disputed by the Japanese who claim priority, their product being rice instead of wheat.) From China the pastes traveled to Germany for a brief stay but by the 14th century, the Italians were the only Europeans who knew the secret methods of manufacturing macaroni. This secret was well guarded for over a hundred years.

LASAGNE

1 pound ground beef, pork sausage or Italian sausage

1 tablespoon olive oil

1 clove garlic, minced

1 tablespoon parsley flakes

1 tablespoon basil

2 teaspoons salt

2½ cups canned tomatoes

1 can (6 oz.) tomato paste

1 package (10 oz.) lasagne noodles

2 cartons (12 oz.) large curd, cream-style cottage cheese

2 eggs, beaten

½ teaspoon pepper

2 tablespoons parsley flakes

½ cup grated Parmesan cheese

1 pound Mozzarella cheese, thinly sliced

Brown the meat in olive oil with garlic, parsley flakes, basil and salt. Add tomatoes and tomato paste. Simmer for 1 hour. Cook noodles until tender, rinse in cold water. Combine cottage cheese with beaten eggs, pepper, parsley flakes and Parmesan cheese. Place half the noodles in a 13x9x2-inch baking dish; spread half of the cottage cheese mixture over; add half of the Mozzarella cheese and half of the meat mixture. Repeat layers and bake at 375° for 30 minutes. Serves 12.

Mrs. George T. Nicolaou

LASAGNE PASTICCIATE

Baked Lasagne with Meat and Cream Sauces

6-8 quarts water

1 tablespoon salt

½ pound lasagne

Cook lasagne as per package directions, but be sure not to overcook — noodles should have a little resiliency. Set pot under cold running water for a few moments to cool pasta. Lift strips out and spread side by side on paper towels to drain.

BESCIAMELLA FOR LASAGNE

3 tablespoons butter

6 tablespoons flour

2 cups milk

1 cup heavy cream

Pinch of ground nutmeg

1 teaspoon salt

In a heavy 2-3-quart saucepan, melt butter over moderate heat and stir in flour. Remove pan from heat, pour in milk and cream all at once, beating with a wire whisk until the flour is partially dissolved. Return the pan to high heat and cook, stirring constantly with whisk. When sauce comes to a boil and thickens to a smooth cream, reduce heat and simmer, still stirring, for 2-3 minutes. Remove from heat, and add nutmeg and salt.

RAGU BOLOGNESE
North Italian Meat Sauce
for Lasagne Pasticciate

¼ pound (1 cup) smoked ham, coarsely chopped

1 cup onions, coarsely chopped

¼ cup carrots, coarsely chopped

½ cup celery, coarsely chopped

2 tablespoons butter

2 tablespoons olive oil

1 pound round steak, ground twice

¼ pound lean pork, ground twice

½ cup dry white wine

2 cups beef stock, fresh or canned

1 can (6 oz.) tomato paste

1 cup heavy cream

Pinch of ground nutmeg

Salt and pepper to taste

½ cup imported Parmesan cheese, freshly grated

Combine ham, onions, carrots and celery on a cutting board and chop them together into small pieces. Melt butter in a heavy 10-12-inch skillet over moderate heat. When the foam subsides, add chopped mixture, cook for about 10 minutes, stirring frequently. Transfer this mixture to a heavy 3-4-quart saucepan. Heat olive oil in the same skillet and lightly brown the ground round and pork, stirring to break up any lumps. Then pour in the wine, increase the heat and boil briskly, still stirring constantly, until almost all of the liquid in the skillet has cooked away. Add the meat to the mixture in the saucepan, and stir in the stock and the tomato paste. Bring to a boil over high heat, then reduce to a simmer. Partially cover the pan, and simmer for 45 minutes, stirring occasionally. Then stir in the cream, taste the Ragu and then season with nutmeg, salt and pepper. To assemble casserole, spread a layer of Ragu Bolognese evenly about ¼ inch deep over the bottom of a generously buttered 9x12x3-inch casserole. Spread over it about 1 cup of Besciamella sauce. Lay ⅓ of the lasagne on the Besciamella, overlapping the strips slightly. Repeat the layers of Ragu, Besciamella, and lasagne 2 more times, then top with the rest of the Ragu and a masking of Besciamella. Sprinkle with cheese. Bake at 350° for 30 minutes or until the sauce is bubbling hot. Serves 8-10.

Mrs. Dale E. Selzer

LASAGNE VERDE

4 tablespoons shallots, diced

½ cup olive oil

½ pound top round beef, ground

1 can (6 oz.) tomato paste

1 can (1 lb.) tomatoes, peeled

2 bay leaves

Pinch of oregano

Freshly ground black pepper

1 teaspoon salt

½ teaspoon sugar

½ cup dry red wine

1 pound lasagne verde

½ pint ricotta

1 pound Mozzarella

Sauté shallots in olive oil until transparent. Add ground beef. Brown. Add tomato paste with equal part water and simmer. Add tomatoes with spices. Simmer over low heat for 1 hour. Add wine. Simmer for 1 hour. Add small amounts of water if sauce becomes too thick. (It should never be watery.) Cook lasagne in rapidly boiling salted water. Check with fork (al dente is good, i.e., not too soft.) Rinse. While lasagne boils, prepare casserole. Put layer of sauce on bottom, then quickly place in alternate layers lasagne, ricotta, Mozzarella in strips and sauce until all has been used up. Cover casserole with aluminum foil and bake until done. Serves 6-8. *I discovered this dish in a tiny but magnificent "Trattoria" in Bologna, Italy while on tour there some years ago. It has been a favorite ever since.*

Abbey Simon

MACARONI SUPREME

1 package (8 oz.) short elbow macaroni

½ cup mayonnaise

¼ cup green pepper, chopped

¼ cup pimento, chopped

1 small onion, grated

1 can mushroom soup

1 cup sharp cheese, diced

1 teaspoon salt

½ cup milk

Cook macaroni and drain. Add mayonnaise, green pepper, pimento, onion, mushroom soup, cheese, salt and milk. (You may wish to sprinkle some of the cheese on top.) Bake at 275° for about 30-40 minutes, until bubbly. Serves 8.

Mrs. John B. McCullough

DUTCH MACARONI AND CHEESE

8 ounces macaroni

½ pound boiled ham, ground

1 package (3 oz.) cream cheese

2 tablespoons butter

½ teaspoon salt

Dash of pepper

⅛ teaspoon nutmeg

1½ teaspoons lemon rind, grated

4 eggs, slightly beaten

1½ cups milk

Cook macaroni in boiling, salted water for 8-10 minutes or until tender. Drain; add ground meat, cream cheese, butter and seasoning to hot macaroni and toss together lightly until cheese and butter melt. Turn mixture into greased 1½-2-quart casserole. Combine eggs and milk; pour over macaroni. Place casserole in pan of warm water and bake at 350° for 35-40 minutes, or until silver knife inserted near edge comes out clean. Serves 6-8.

Mrs. William M. Lamont

MACARONI-MEAT CASSEROLE

1 large package Kraft's macaroni and cheese dinner

1-1½ pounds ground meat

1 medium onion, chopped

Salt and pepper to taste

1 large can tomato sauce

Boil macaroni according to package directions. While macaroni is cooking, brown the ground meat in sautéed onions. Add salt and pepper to meat. Drain macaroni and mix together in casserole with meat, cheese and tomato sauce. Cover and bake 30 minutes at 350°. Serves 6. *This simple dish has been a life-saver for me. With the addition of Jello, you have a wholesome and enjoyable meal for children.*

Mrs. David Donosky

MACARONI WITH MEAT SAUCE

MEAT SAUCE

1/2 pound salt pork, diced

1/4 cup olive oil

1/4 cup butter

3/4 pound onions, peeled and diced

1 3/4 pounds lean beef, cut into 1/2-inch cubes

4 chicken livers, finely chopped (optional)

2 bay leaves, crumbled

5 garlic cloves, mashed

1 tablespoon fresh rosemary

1/2 teaspoon ground allspice

1 teaspoon freshly ground black pepper

5 pounds ripe fresh tomatoes or 6 cans (1 lb. each) peeled plum tomatoes, finely chopped

1/4 pound carrots, scraped and minced

1/4 pound celery, minced

1 1/2 teaspoons salt

7 ounces tomato paste

Combine salt pork, olive oil and butter in a large saucepan; heat. Add onions and sauté to medium brown. Add beef, chicken livers and bay leaves; stir. Cook slowly, uncovered, for 30 minutes. Chop garlic and rosemary together and add to sauce with allspice and pepper. Stir well, and continue to cook over low heat for 20 minutes. Cook, covered, for 5 minutes. Add tomatoes, carrots, celery and salt. Simmer slowly for 1 1/2 hours, stirring occasionally. Cool; strain sauce. Put remains in strainer through a food mill and return to sauce. Add tomato paste, stir well, and bring to a boil. Makes 3 1/2 quarts.

MACARONI

3/4 pound ziti or other large macaroni

3 quarts water

1 tablespoon salt

Butter

Grated fresh Parmesan cheese

Cook macaroni in boiling salted water for 20-25 minutes. Drain well and place in a warm bowl. Add bits of butter and sprinkle generously with cheese. Mix well. The meat sauce and macaroni may be served separately or combined. Serves 6.

Gina Bachauer

HUNGARIAN NOODLE BAKE

4 ounces fine noodles
1 cup cream-style cottage cheese
1 cup dairy sour cream
1/4 cup onion, finely chopped
1 clove garlic, minced

1 tablespoon Worcestershire sauce
Dash of Tabasco
1 tablespoon poppy seeds
1/2 teaspoon salt
Dash of pepper
Paprika

Parmesan cheese, grated

Cook noodles in boiling, salted water until tender; drain. Combine noodles with remaining ingredients, except paprika and Parmesan cheese. Bake in greased 10x6x1½-inch baking dish at 350° for 25-30 minutes. Sprinkle with paprika. Serve with Parmesan cheese. Serves 6.

Mrs. Dan Hughes, Jr.

SPICY BEEF AND NOODLE CASSEROLE

1½ pounds hamburger
1 can (8 oz.) tomato sauce
1 can (10 oz.) Ro-Tel tomatoes
1 teaspoon sugar
1 teaspoon salt
1/4 teaspoon chili powder
1/4 teaspoon dried basil

1 package (8 oz.) wide noodles
1 cup sour cream
2 teaspoons chives, chopped
1 package (3 oz.) cream cheese
1/2 cup Cheddar cheese, grated

Brown meat and pour off fat. Add the tomato sauce, Ro-Tel tomatoes, sugar, salt, chili powder and basil. Cover and cook 20 minutes. Cook noodles and drain. Line bottom of a 2-quart casserole with 1/3 of noodles. Mix chives with sour cream and cream cheese. Spread 1/3 of mixture over noodles. Cover with meat sauce. Repeat layers twice. Bake at 350° for 20 minutes. Sprinkle with Cheddar cheese and return to oven until cheese melts. Serves 6-8.

Mrs. Robert E. Peterson

SOUR CREAM NOODLE RING

4 ounces broad egg noodles   2 eggs

1 cup cottage cheese   ½ teaspoon salt

1 cup sour cream   ⅛ teaspoon pepper

¼ cup butter, melted

Cook noodles according to directions on package, rinse and drain. Add other ingredients and mix well. Bake at 300° for 1½ hours in a buttered ring mold. Turn onto platter. Serves 6. *This dish is attractive and good when filled with chopped spinach seasoned with butter and lemon juice.*

Mrs. William R. Guffey

STUFFED SHELLS À LA MILNES

1 pound ground sirloin or   1 pound box large pasta
   chuck   shells

Olive oil   Ricotta cheese

1 large jar prepared seasoned   Mozzarella cheese
   spaghetti sauce

Brown sirloin or chuck in olive oil in a large skillet. Add spaghetti sauce and simmer. Boil pasta shells until al dente. Drain shells and put back into the pot. Stir ricotta into shells, add the meat, stirring it also into the shells. Pour the mixture into a casserole and top with slices of Mozzarella cheese. Bake at 350° for about 20 minutes. Serves 3-6. *Baritone Sherrill Milnes by his own admission is not much of a cook. "Actually, I prefer to eat," he admits candidly. "But there are times when I like to have a few friends in, so I concocted a dish which affords me the maximum of time with my guests and the minimum of time in the kitchen."*

Sherrill Milnes

BOILING POT SPAGHETTI

Grease from 6 strips of bacon
½ cup fresh parsley, snipped
1 garlic clove, pressed
1½ teaspoons salt
1 teaspoon ground pepper

Spaghetti (not too thin, but not macaroni)
2½ tablespoons clear olive oil
1½ cups butter

Sauté parsley and garlic in bacon grease and season. Boil spaghetti decently (any sauce is secondary). The length of boiling time is the essential matter. Stir often and refrain from putting salt in water, this only sours the pasta. The water, of course, must be boiling fortissimo before depositing the spaghetti. Drain in colander and pour into an oven-proof dish (perferably crockery). The bowl must be very hot and previously filled with the oil and butter. Mix bacon mixture into spaghetti along with already-existent butter and oil. Mix well. *This variation of spaghetti was invented when none of the "right" ingredients could be found, late at night, in the kitchen. It avoids the confusion of tomato sauces which only chefs from Naples can do properly anyway! If you resist eating meat after this sublime spaghetti, you will lose weight not gain it. Share it with a good salad, wash everything down with a coffee, Dallas-style, and you've got it made! Good luck!*

Thomas Schippers

CHICKEN SPAGHETTI

1 (4 lb.) chicken, boiled and diced
2 packages (8 oz.) spaghetti
1 cup celery, diced
1 package (6 oz.) American cheese, grated

1 package (1¼ oz.) blue cheese, diced
1 large green pepper, diced
1 large onion, diced
1 can (12 oz.) tomatoes
1 can (8 oz.) mushrooms
1 can mushroom soup

Garlic powder to taste

Cook spaghetti in chicken stock and drain. Combine spaghetti with remaining ingredients and put in 3-quart casserole. Cook 1½ hours at 350°. Serves 8.

Mrs. Raymond D. Nasher

CHILI SPAGHETTI CASSEROLE

1 package (1 lb.) spaghetti
2 cans (20 oz.) chili without beans
2 cans (20 oz.) tomatoes
2 cans tomato soup
1 tablespoon Tabasco
1 tablespoon Worcestershire sauce
1 teaspoon salt

1 pound Longhorn cheese, grated

Cook spaghetti as directed on package. Mix chili, tomatoes, soup, cooked spaghetti and seasonings in a large bowl. In a 4-quart casserole alternate layers of spaghetti mix and cheese, ending with layer of cheese. Bake at 350° for 1-1½ hours. Serves 4-8. *This is good as a side dish with barbecued chicken or as a main dish with salad and garlic bread.*

Mrs. Martin B. Cohen

PARTY CHICKEN À LA DOROTHEA
SAUCE

¼ pound butter
1 cup flour
4 cups whole milk
4 cans mushroom soup
2 pounds Velveeta cheese, cubed
8 ounces sharp cheese, grated
1 can beer
1 cup dry sherry
2 large green peppers, cubed
2 cans (7 oz.) mushroom stems and pieces
2 cans (7 oz.) cut pimentos
Salt and pepper to taste

Melt butter. Add flour, stirring constantly until smooth. Add milk slowly, stirring constantly. Add mushroom soup and mix well. Add Velveeta cheese and grated sharp cheese. Stir constantly until all cheese is entirely melted; add salt and pepper. Add beer, a little at a time, beating well. Add sherry gradually. Sauté green peppers in butter until soft, but still bright green. Add to sauce along with mushrooms and pimentos.

CHICKEN AND SPAGHETTI

12 pounds stewing hens
3 packages (10 oz.) cut spaghetti
Parmesan cheese

Boil chickens until tender. Save broth. Cool and cube meat to make 12 cups (1 pound usually makes 1 cup). Cook spaghetti in reserved broth. Butter two 2-quart casseroles. Alternate layers of chicken, spaghetti and sauce, sprinkling each layer with Parmesan cheese. Bake at 350° until hot. Reserve chicken broth in case sauce needs thinning. May be frozen. Serves 30. *This dish with a salad and light dessert is easy to serve to a small crowd and men really go for it.*

Mrs. Frank Schoeneman

EASY SPAGHETTI BAKE

1/2 pound bacon
2 onions, chopped
1 clove garlic, minced
1 pound ground beef
1 1/2 teaspoons salt
1 1/2 teaspoons pepper
1 teaspoon chili powder

2 cans (8 oz.) tomato sauce
1 can (6 oz.) tomato paste
2 1/2 cups water
1/2 cup ripe olives, sliced
1 pound spaghetti
1 cup Cheddar cheese, grated or cheese of your own choice

Fry bacon, remove from pan and crumble. Add onions and garlic to bacon grease and sauté. Add ground beef cooking until almost brown. Stir in seasonings, sauces and water. Cover and simmer 1 1/2 hours. Stir in olives and bacon. Break half of the uncooked spaghetti into greased 2-quart casserole. Cover with half of the sauce and half of the cheese. Repeat layers ending with sauce. Cover and bake 30 minutes at 350°; uncover, and bake 15 minutes longer. Can be frozen after cooking. Serves 4.

Mrs. Raymond A. Beall

The Chinese were the first to value peas as a green vegetable. Dried peas had been eaten by the Persians, Romans, and Greeks. During the famine in 1555, the English finally took notice of their "pease" and during the 17th century "petits pois" became the rage of Louis XIV's court.

SPAGHETTI CASSEROLE

1 small onion, chopped
1/2 green pepper, chopped
1 tablespoon butter
1-1 1/2 pounds lean ground round or chuck
1 can (15 oz.) tomato sauce
Salt and pepper to taste
Pinch of chili powder
1/2 teaspoon oregano

1/2 teaspoon sweet basil
2 sprigs of parsley, chopped
1 can (3 oz.) button mushrooms
1 can (8 oz.) green peas, drained
1 can (8 oz.) asparagus pieces, drained
1 package (7 oz.) thin spaghetti, broken in half

1 cup Cheddar cheese, grated

Brown onion and green pepper in butter until golden. Add ground meat and brown lightly. Add tomato sauce and seasonings, and simmer briefly. Meanwhile, boil spaghetti according to package directions and drain. Add mushrooms, peas and asparagus to meat sauce. Gently mix together spaghetti, cheese and sauce. Place in casserole. Bake 1 hour at 350°. Grated Parmesan cheese may be sprinkled on top. Serves 6.

Mrs. Lawrence S. Pollock, Jr.

SPAGHETTI À LA VONGOLE
Spaghetti in Clam Sauce

5 tablespoons olive oil

1-2 garlic cloves, sliced

2 cups parsley, chopped

1 large can (28 oz.) peeled tomatoes

4 (7½ oz.) cans clams in natural juice

3 pounds long Italian spaghetti

Heat oil, put in garlic and parsley, and sauté over low fire until garlic is lightly browned. Add clams with their natural juices and tomatoes. Season to taste with salt and pepper. Cook over low fire at least 1 hour. Cook the spaghetti in plenty of bubbling hot water with a tablespoon of salt added for about 8 minutes (be sure it is al dente or slightly firm, not too soft) then drain very well. Pour half of the sauce over the spaghetti and mix well over low fire. Arrange on a large serving platter and pour rest of the sauce into center of spaghetti. Garnish with sprigs of parsley. No Parmesan, please! Serves 6-8.

Antal Dorati

TURKEY SPAGHETTI CASSEROLE

1 large white onion, chopped

1 tablespoon bacon fat

1 can cream of tomato soup plus 1 soup can water

1 can (6 oz.) tomato paste plus 1 can water

¼ pound American or mild Cheddar cheese, grated

1 cup turkey stock or 3 chicken bouillon cubes in 1 cup water

Salt and pepper to taste

1 can (4 oz.) mushrooms and stems, drained

2½ cups turkey breast, diced in 1-inch pieces

1½ packages (7½ oz.) long spaghetti, broken in thirds and cooked

1 large can dried green peas (optional)

Sauté onion in bacon fat until tender but not brown. Add soup, tomato paste, water, cheese, stock, salt, pepper, mushrooms and turkey. Mix with spaghetti. If desired, green peas may be added. Put in long, shallow casserole and leave in refrigerator overnight to mellow. Reheat for 1 hour at 250°. If mixture seems dry, pour on 1 cup mild stock, salted. Sprinkle with Parmesan cheese when serving. Serves 8.

Mrs. William Dow Hamm

VEGETABLES

ARTICHOKE HEARTS AND SPINACH

1 can (1 lb.) artichoke hearts
1 clove garlic
1/4 teaspoon salt
1 1/2 cups water
1 cup French dressing

1 package frozen chopped spinach, cooked
Medium cream sauce
1/2 cup grated Parmesan cheese

Heat artichoke hearts with garlic. Drain well and marinate in French dressing 1/2 hour. To spinach, add cream sauce about equal to amount of spinach (about 1 1/2 cups). Add Parmesan, reserving enough to cover top of casserole. Cover bottom of greased 1 1/2-quart casserole with artichoke hearts, cover with creamed spinach. Sprinkle top with Parmesan. Bake at 350° until bubbling hot, about 15-20 minutes. Serves 8.

Mrs. Robert S. Addison

Vegetables were slow to gain enthusiasm from the Europeans. In 1847, the first vegetarian society was begun based on the belief that . . . "meat-eating begets ferocious dispositions, a callousness . . . but a vegetarian diet develops the gentler affections".

MAURICE'S ARTICHOKES

1/2 cup margarine, melted
1/4-1/2 cup dry minced onion

2 cans (17 oz.) artichoke hearts, drained
1/3-1/2 cup dry sherry

Sauté onion in margarine until brown. Add artichoke hearts and sherry. Simmer until liquid is absorbed, about 45-60 minutes, in a 2-quart pan. Serves 6. *This is one of my favorite accompaniments for steaks.*

Mrs. Oscar W. Ponder

STUFFED ARTICHOKES AMELIA

16 artichokes

Lemon slices

Garlic clove

4 tablespoons butter

2 tablespoons flour

Salt and pepper

Pinch of nutmeg

¾ cup milk

Juice of ½ lemon

2 egg yolks

Cook artichokes in boiling water with lemon and garlic. Invert and cool until they can be handled. Before beginning sauce, remove leaves from each artichoke. Using a spoon, scrape pulp from inner sides of leaves as they are removed. Cut out the tough chokes from each vegetable and discard along with scraped leaves. Carefully scoop out heart but leave enough to make a container for the stuffing. Chop up the artichoke bottoms, and add to the pulp from inner sides of leaves, mashing until smooth. Melt the butter. Add flour and let the roux cook 2-3 minutes without browning. Add seasonings and hot milk and cook until thick. Add lemon juice. Beat egg yolks and add a little of the hot mixture to them. Then pour into sauce. Add sauce to the pulp, mixing well. Mound stuffing into artichoke hearts. Place in buttered baking dish and bake at 325° for 25 minutes. Serves 8. *This takes time. Plan to prepare 1-2 days before. I named this for my dear friend, Amelia Martin, who could live on artichokes.*

Mrs. Gene H. Bishop

ASPARAGUS AND PEAS CASSEROLE

2 cans (15 oz.) green asparagus tips

1 can (1 lb.) petite peas

1 can mushroom soup

¾ cup sharp Cheddar cheese, grated

1 cup soft white bread crumbs

2 tablespoons margarine, melted

Chill asparagus; drain well. Arrange half of asparagus in buttered 2-quart casserole dish. Gently mix drained peas, soup and cheese. Spoon half of mixture over asparagus, add remaining asparagus. Top with rest of soup mixture. Sprinkle buttered crumbs on top. Bake at 350° for 30 minutes or until brown. Serves 8-10.

Mrs. Carroll Wynn Phillips

CARCIOFI ALLA GIUDIA

Fresh artichokes

2-4 cups olive oil, or ½ olive oil mixed with ½ vegetable oil

Juice of 2 lemons

1 teaspoon salt

½ teaspoon pepper

Allow 1 large or 2 small per person. Peel stalks and cut off tips of artichokes. Remove all tough outer leaves and spread remaining ones open by pressing artichoke down and holding by stem. Remove spiny choke from center with a small, sharp knife. Wash artichokes in water to which lemon juice has been added. Drain. Sprinkle inside leaves with salt and pepper. Place oil in deep saucepan to cover artichokes. Fry artichokes one at a time over medium heat, for 8-10 minutes, turning occasionally. Remove artichoke to absorbent paper. Let artichoke stand for at least ½ hour (even as long as 3 hours) before continuing preparation. Then reheat oil in pan and, when hot, hold each artichoke by the stalk and dip it in. The artichoke will open, its leaves will curl and become a dark golden color. Remove to absorbent paper, sprinkle lightly with salt and serve hot. Each leaf should be golden and as crisp as a potato chip. *Anyone who has been served this dish in Rome has known utter rapture. To prepare it at home is to recapture everything wonderful about Rome.*

Mrs. James R. Pratt

VERY GREEN ASPARAGUS

1 pound fresh asparagus

¾ cup chicken bouillon

Juice of ½ large lemon

¼ cup butter

¼ teaspoon nutmeg

Salt and pepper to taste

1 tablespoon dry white wine (optional)

Rinse asparagus thoroughly; break, do not cut, tough ends. Lay in heavy, deep skillet. Cover with bouillon and lemon juice and bring to simmer. Add butter, nutmeg, salt and pepper. Simmer slowly for 10-12 minutes. Add wine during last 5 minutes for flavor. Slow open cooking keeps green vegetables green.

Mrs. Saul N. Hertz

GREEN BEAN CASSEROLE

1 onion, chopped
1/4 cup butter
2 cans French-cut beans
1/4 cup flour
1 1/2 cups milk
1/2 pound Velveeta cheese

1 can water chestnuts
Dash of Tabasco
2 teaspoons soy sauce
1/2 teaspoon black pepper
1/4 teaspoon Accent
2 small cans mushroom pieces

Slivered almonds

Sauté onion in butter and add all ingredients except almonds. Mix well and pour into well-greased casserole; top with almonds. Bake at 325° for 30-40 minutes. Serves 8.

Mrs. W. H. Goldsmith

SPICED BEANS

2 cups sugar
4 tablespoons Wesson oil
1 cup vinegar
Few whole cloves

4 cans Del Monte Blue Lake beans
1 large onion, sliced
4 pimento strips

Make a syrup of sugar, oil, vinegar and cloves; and boil. Put beans, onions and pimento strips in alternate layers in crock. Pour hot sauce over them. Heat in oven when ready to serve. This is also good cold. Lift beans very carefully when serving. Serves 8.

Mrs. Hawkins Golden

GLAZED SWEET AND SOUR BEANS

1 cup sugar
1 cup salad oil

3/4 cup vinegar
2 cans French-cut beans, drained

1 can bean sprouts, drained

Dissolve sugar into oil and vinegar. Pour over beans and bean sprouts. Marinate all ingredients overnight. Serve hot as a vegetable or cold as a salad. Serves 8.

Mrs. Timothy H. Carroll

MUSTARD BEANS

1 cup sugar

½ cup vinegar

3 tablespoons prepared mustard

½ cup instant minced onion

½ teaspoon salt

1 can (1 lb.) yellow wax beans

Combine all ingredients except beans. Bring to boiling point, stirring until sugar is dissolved. Add beans, simmer, uncovered, for 5 minutes. Cool. Refrigerate in covered jar or bowl overnight. Serves 6. *This is delicious for a patio supper.*

Mrs. Agnes Muller

ZIPPY FIRESIDE BEANS

1 jar (1 lb. 11 oz.) B&M beans

½ cup dark Karo syrup

1 tablespoon onion, grated or instant minced onion

1 teaspoon ground ginger

½ pound Canadian bacon, sliced (optional)

Mix beans, syrup, onion and ginger in 2-quart, oven-proof casserole. Arrange slices of bacon on top. Bake at 400° about 1 hour, basting bacon 3-4 times to glaze. Serves 4.

Mrs. William W. Lynch, Jr.

MARY'S BEET SOUFFLÉ

6 egg whites

1 teaspoon cream of tartar

4 egg yolks

½ teaspoon salt

4 tablespoons butter

4 tablespoons flour

½ cup milk

½ cup beet juice

2 cans beets, chopped coarsely in blender with remainder of juice

4 tablespoons dry minced onion

Beat egg whites dry but not stiff with cream of tartar. Using the. same beater, beat egg yolks with salt. In heavy skillet, add flour to melted butter, stirring constantly. Over low heat, stir in milk and beet juice. Set cream sauce aside to cool slightly. Add beets and egg yolks to sauce. This is important; fold the egg whites into the cream sauce-beet mixture, up and down and over until all is blended. Pour into greased 6-8-cup casserole perferably with straight sides. Sprinkle with onion. Bake for 30-35 minutes at 350°. These soufflés usually rise an inch or more above the rim of the baking dish. Serve at once. Serves 4. *Our cook invented this soufflé, and it is the best-flavored one I have eaten.*

Izler Solomon

SPICED BEETS

2 cups water (use beet juice water)

3 cups cider vinegar

3 cups sugar

2-3 tablespoons whole allspice

1 gallon cooked sliced beets

Bring water, vinegar and sugar to a boil; add allspice. Pour over beets and let stand several hours. Can be served hot or cold. Keeps well for at least 2 weeks in refrigerator. *This is a favorite recipe of all who eat it.*

Mrs. Frank Pearcy

BROCCOLI CASSEROLE

¼ cup onion, finely chopped

6 tablespoons butter

2 tablespoons flour

½ cup water

3 eggs, slightly beaten

1 jar (8 oz.) pasteurized cheese spread (Cheese Whiz)

2 packages (10 oz.) frozen chopped broccoli, defrosted

½ cup cracker crumbs

Sauté onions in 4 tablespoons butter until soft. Stir in flour. Add water. Cook over low heat until mixture thickens. Blend in cheese. Combine this sauce with broccoli and eggs. Turn into greased 1½-quart casserole. Cover with cracker crumbs. Dot with remaining butter. Bake at 350° for 30 minutes. Serves 8.

Mrs. Louis F. Dolch

BROCCOLI PUFF

3 packages (10 oz.) chopped broccoli

3 cans cream of mushroom soup

3 teaspoons onion, grated

1½ cups sharp processed cheese, grated

¾ cup milk

¾ cup mayonnaise

3 eggs, well-beaten

¾ cup fine, dry, bread crumbs

3 tablespoons butter, melted

Cook broccoli, omitting salt. Drain well and place in baking dish. Mix soup, onion and cheese. Gradually add milk, mayonnaise and beaten eggs. Blend well and pour mixture over broccoli. Add melted butter to bread crumbs and sprinkle over top. Bake at 350° for 45 minutes. Serves 12.

Mrs. William H. Clingman

YOUNG CABBAGE WITH CARAWAY

1 small cabbage, shredded	½ teaspoon marjoram
1 cup water	1 teaspoon salt.
1 teaspoon caraway seed	3 tablespoons butter

Cook cabbage with water, and seasonings until tender, but still crisp. Add butter at the last, before serving. Serves 4.

The Cookbook Committee

Honey was used in place of sugar in Europe from ancient times up until the 18th century.

CARROT SOUFFLÉ

1½ cups puréed carrots	½ cup butter
Pinch of cloves	6 tablespoons flour
2 tablespoons honey	1½ cups cream
1 teaspoon salt	6 egg yolks
8 egg whites, stiffly beaten	

Season carrots with cloves, honey and salt. Butter soufflé dish with some of the butter. Melt remaining butter; add flour and cook 1 minute. Add cream and cook until thick. Add egg yolks and carrots. Cool. Fold in egg whites. Bake at 350° for 35 minutes.

Helen Corbitt

MINTED GLAZED CARROTS

½ cup sugar	2 tablespoons mint, chopped, or ½ tablespoon dried mint flakes
¼ cup butter	
1 can (1 lb.) baby carrots, drained	

Melt sugar and butter. Add carrots. Cook slowly until glazed, but do not brown. Sprinkle with mint when almost ready to serve. Serves 6.

Mrs. Robert Wilmans, Jr.

CREAMY CORN

1 package (3 oz.) cream
    cheese, softened
¼ cup milk
1 tablespoon butter

½ teaspoon onion salt
1 can (1 lb.) whole kernel
    corn, drained
Parsley or paprika

In saucepan combine cream cheese, milk, butter and onion salt. Stir over low heat until cheese melts. Add corn, heat thoroughly and serve. Garnish with parsley or sprinkle with paprika. Serves 6.

Mrs. Roland Cazes

HATTIE MAE'S CORN SAUTÉ

10 ears fresh corn
2 teaspoons salt

½ teaspoon fine black pepper
¼ cup water

½ cup butter

Cut corn off cob and be sure to scrape off all the milk. Add salt, pepper and water. Melt ¼ cup butter in skillet. Add corn mixture. Cook on medium heat for 15 minutes; lower heat and cook for 5 minutes. Use remaining butter to prevent sticking. Serves 6.

Mrs. Robert D. Stecker

ROAST CORN ON THE COB

1 bushel of last month's old
    newspapers

1 bushel of friends gathered
    outdoors under any old
    tree or on lake shore

1 bushel fresh corn, unshucked

Soak newspapers until good and sopping; start large bonfire and let burn down to a bed of very hot coals. Wrap ears of corn in about ¼ inch of wet newspaper much the same as a tamale is wrapped by shucks. Put corn wrapped in wet newspapers on top of coals and let cook until outside newspapers appear dry and begin to scorch or burn. Gloves are helpful in the process of removing corn ears from fire. Remove corn, shuck, sprinkle with salt and start eating. Butter is optional.

Herc Ficklen

EGGPLANT CASSEROLE

3 medium eggplants
½ cup onions, minced
3 teaspoons salt
4 eggs, slightly beaten

Dash of pepper
4 tablespoons butter
2 tablespoons cream
1 cup buttered bread crumbs

1 cup sharp cheese, grated

Pare eggplant, cut in cubes, soak in salt water 20 minutes, drain. Boil, covered, eggplant with onion and 2 teaspoons salt in 2½ cups boiling water until tender but not mushy, about 10 minutes. Drain. Add eggs, 1 teaspoon salt, pepper, butter and cream. Pour into buttered 10x6x2-inch Pyrex baking dish. Cover with bread crumbs and cheese. Bake, uncovered, at 350° for 45 minutes. Serves 6-8. *Variation: Add 1 cup fresh or frozen oysters, drained, with cream.*

Mrs. Kenneth H. Parker

EGGPLANT AND RICE

8 large mushrooms
1 tablespoon butter
1 shallot, chopped
1 teaspoon flour
½ cup coffee cream
1 eggplant, peeled and cut into ½-inch thick slices

8 thick slices of tomato, peeled
Milk
Flour
Salt and pepper
1½ cups olive oil or salad oil
2 cups cooked rice

Sauté mushrooms and shallot in butter. Add flour, cook until bubbly. Add cream; cook until thick. Dip eggplant and tomatoes in milk, then seasoned flour. Sauté in oil. Arrange overlapping around rice on a shallow platter or casserole. Pour mushroom sauce over. Serve at once. Serves 4-6.

Helen Corbitt

CREAMED MUSHROOMS AND CHESTNUTS

5 tablespoons butter, melted
2 tablespoons flour
½ teaspoon salt
Pepper to taste

1½ cups half and half
3 cans (5 oz.) chestnuts, sliced
3 cans (3 oz.) mushrooms

1 tablespoon parsley, chopped (optional)

Add flour, salt and pepper to butter. Blend to make sauce. Add cream and mix, then add chestnuts and mushrooms. Cook for 3-4 minutes or until done. If too thick, add a little more cream. Garnish with parsley. Serves 8. *This is a delicious, different vegetable dish or sauce for meat.*

Mrs. Bill R. Jones

STUFFED MUSHROOMS WITH BACON

24 large mushrooms
Lemon juice
3 shallots, chopped
4 tablespoons butter

2 cups soft bread crumbs
Dash of Worcestershire sauce
Salt and pepper to taste
3-4 slices bacon, cooked and
  crumbled

Trim stems of mushrooms. Sprinkle caps with lemon juice. Chop stems finely. Sauté stems and shallots in butter until shallots are golden. Add bread crumbs, Worcestershire sauce, salt, pepper and bacon. Fill mushroom caps with the mixture. Arrange caps on a buttered baking dish. Bake at 350° for about 20 minutes. Serves 6-8. *Variation: Combine the mushroom mixture, minus bread crumbs, with frozen creamed spinach, cooked as directed, and stuff mushroom caps.*

Mrs. Garry A. Weber

BAKED ONIONS

6 yellow onions, thinly sliced
1 bag (3¾ oz.) potato chips,
  crushed
½ pound Wisconsin mild
  cheese, grated

2 cans cream of mushroom
  soup
1 cup milk
⅛ teaspoon cayenne

Place alternate layers of onions, potato chips and cheese in a buttered casserole. Pour mushroom soup mixed with milk over all. Sprinkle cayenne over the top and bake at 350° for 1 hour. Serves 6. *This is good with ham or barbecue.*

Mrs. Robert D. Crowell, III

BURGUNDY ONION RINGS AND KIDNEY BEANS

6 large yellow onions, sliced
  ¼ inch thick
3 tablespoons butter

1 cup Burgundy wine
2 cups red kidney beans,
  drained

Separate onions into rings. Sauté in butter until well-coated and golden. Add wine and simmer until tender. Add beans and heat. Serves 12.

Helen Corbitt

CREAMED PEANUTS

1 tablespoon butter
1 tablespoon flour
1 cup light cream
Pinch of soda

1 small can mushrooms, chopped
1 cup salted peanuts, skins removed

Put butter in saucepan. Add flour and light cream. Do not use high heat. Cook until mixture begins to thicken. Add peanuts and cook until about like a custard. Remove from heat. Drain mushrooms well, add soda, and mix well. Add to peanut mixture. This will keep several days in the refrigerator, but should be served hot. If it thickens, thin with cream. Serves 4. *I have never served this to anyone who had any idea what it was, but all loved it.*

Mrs. Walter W. Lechner

The peanut plant was cultivated by the Pre-Incan races thousands of years ago. Many varieties are found buried with ancient mummies in the Pre-Incan and Incan graves and tombs. The value of the nut is impossible to exaggerate. A pound of peanuts contains more proteins than a pound of the best sirloin steak, as much carbohydrates as a pound of potatoes and one-third as much fat as a pound of pure butter.

GINGERED PEAS WITH WATER CHESTNUTS

2 packages (10 oz.) frozen peas
2 tablespoons butter
1 can (5 oz.) water chestnuts, thinly sliced

1 tablespoon chicken-seasoned stock base
$\frac{1}{2}$ teaspoon ginger
$\frac{1}{4}$ teaspoon nutmeg
1 teaspoon cornstarch

1 tablespoon water

Break up peas; place in saucepan with butter. Add water chestnut liquid, stock base, ginger and nutmeg. Simmer, covered, over low heat until peas are bubbling hot. Blend cornstarch and water; stir into peas. Cook slowly, stirring constantly, until liquid thickens and boils. Add water chestnuts. Simmer 2-3 minutes longer. Serves 8.

Mrs. Ronald Reagan

CASEROLE POTATOES

6 large potatoes
½ cup butter
2 cups sharp cheese, grated
⅔ cup green onions, chopped
(use green part)

1 cup milk
2 cups sour cream
Salt and pepper to taste

Boil potatoes in their jackets. Chill. (This may be done the day before preparing.) Grate or shred potatoes. Melt butter in double boiler and put in cheese, a small amount at a time. Add onions, sour cream and milk. Combine this sauce with potatoes; season. Put in a buttered 2½-quart casserole and bake at 325° for 1 hour. Serves 12.

Mrs. Harry R. Shawyer, Jr.

CRISP POTATO RINGS

Unpeeled Idaho potatoes,
thinly sliced

Butter
Salt and pepper to taste

Sprinkle potatoes with salt, pepper and butter. Bake at 375° until crisp and brown.

Helen Corbitt

WHIPPED POTATO CASSEROLE

4 medium potatoes
5 tablespoons butter
¼ cup cream

1 large onion, chopped
Salt and pepper to taste
2 eggs, separated

Grated Parmesan cheese

Cook potatoes in boiling salted water until tender. Drain and pare. Mash potatoes with electric mixer or potato masher. Gradually beat in 3 tablespoons of butter and the cream to make potatoes light and fluffy. Melt remaining butter in a skillet. Add onion and sauté until tender. Add to whipped potatoes. Season with salt and pepper. Cool. Beat egg yolks into cooled potatoes. Beat egg whites until stiff but not dry. Fold into potatoes. Generously grease a casserole, and spoon in potato mixture. Sprinkle top with cheese. Bake, uncovered, for 15-20 minutes in preheated 350° oven. Place under broiler for a few minutes to crisp the top. Serve immediately. Serves 4.

Mrs. James W. Hixon

GLAZED SWEET POTATOES

1 can (1 lb. 13 oz.) sweet
   potatoes
1 cup fresh orange juice
1 cup white sugar
½ cup flour

1 teaspoon nutmeg
1 cup water
1 cup brown sugar
2 tablespoons butter

Dip sweet potatoes in orange juice, then roll in a mixture of flour, ½ cup white sugar and nutmeg. Place in greased casserole. Combine ½ cup white sugar, water, brown sugar and butter, and bring to a boil. Pour over the potatoes. Add remaining orange juice and bake for 30 minutes at 350°. Serves 6.

Mrs. Ronald Reagan

CREAMED SPINACH

3 packages chopped frozen
   spinach
1 package (3 oz.) cream
   cheese
1 container (8 oz.) sour cream

2 cans artichoke hearts,
   sautéed
½ package slivered almonds
Salt, pepper and onion salt
   to taste

Cook and drain spinach. Add cream cheese and sour cream. Mix well and put in buttered casserole. Bake at 350° for 30 minutes. Place artichoke hearts and almonds on top and broil 10 minutes. Serves 8.

Mrs. Ted Strauss

CREAMED SPINACH NELSON

2 packages frozen chopped
   spinach
1 cup water
1 teaspoon salt

⅓ cup mayonnaise
Juice of ½ lemon
2 hard-boiled eggs

Cook the spinach in boiling, salted water until completely thawed and tender. Remove from fire. Drain well in colander. Return spinch to saucepan, but do not put back on fire. Add mayonnaise and lemon juice to the drained spinach and stir until well-blended. Grate eggs into the creamed spinach. Can be kept warm at simmering temperature on stove or on a hot tray. Serves 6. *Children love spinach prepared this way.*

Mrs. Neal T. Lacey

GREEN CASSEROLE WITH CRUNCH

4 cups eggplant, peeled and diced into 1-inch cubes

1/4 cup water

2 garlic cloves

1 package (1 lb.) fresh spinach

2 eggs, beaten

1 can mushroom soup

Freshly ground black pepper to taste

3 slices buttered bread, cubed

Cook eggplant in water with 1 garlic clove in pressure cooker until first hiss of full pressure. Reduce heat immediately. Drain and reserve liquid. Wash spinach, removing coarse stems. Cook spinach with 1 clove garlic under pressure until first hiss of full pressure. Drain and reserve liquid. Combine eggs with mushroom soup, pepper and a soup can of reserved liquid. Place eggplant in bottom of buttered casserole, and cover with half the sauce. Distribute spinach and cover with remainder of sauce. Ease the sauce into the spinach with a fork. Sprinkle top of mixture with a pattern of bread cubes. Bake at 350° until bubbly. Be careful not to overcook. Serves 9. *This dish was invented for Christmas buffet to which each member of the Beasley family brings a contribution.*

Mrs. Hermes Nye

SPINACH ROCKEFELLER

1 pound fresh spinach or 2 packages frozen chopped spinach

1/2 cup butter

3/4 cup fine dry bread crumbs

2 onions, finely chopped

2 eggs

Pinch of thyme

2 pinches of Accent

1 teaspoon garlic powder

Dash of Tabasco

1/2 teaspoon black pepper

1/4 cup Parmesan cheese

Salt to taste

Tomato slices, 1/2 inch thick

Cook spinach and drain well. Add the rest of the ingredients except tomato slices and bake at 350° for 25 minutes. Ten minutes before the spinach is done, put tomato slices in flat pan in same oven. This heats them thoroughly but does not cook them enough to cause them to fall apart. Serve by putting ice cream scoops of the spinach mixture on top of each tomato slice. Serves 6-8.

Mrs. Merlyn D. Sampels

SPANAKOPITA

2 pounds spinach

1 cup butter

1 bunch small green onions

3 tablespoons parsley

Salt and pepper to taste

6-7 eggs, beaten

1 cup feta cheese, crumbled coarsely to size of green peas

½ pound filo (pastry sheets)

Clean and chop spinach and either let drain or dry with paper towels. In a large bowl, mix together spinach, ½ cup melted butter, onions, parsley, salt and pepper. Add eggs and feta cheese and mix all ingredients together. Grease 10x14-inch pan with butter. Melt remaining butter. Place first sheet of filo in bottom of pan and brush with melted butter. Place the second sheet of filo in pan and do not brush with butter. Brushing butter over every other sheet of filo, place 8 sheets altogether in the pan before adding the filling. Spread spinach filling evenly in pan, and cover with 7 sheets of filo, buttering every other one. Then, butter top sheet very generously. Cut the top layers of filo into squares and sprinkle the pie surface lightly with water. Bake at 350° for 40 minutes or until filo is golden brown. Remove from oven and cut pieces through to bottom of pan. Serves 16-20.

The Cookbook Committee

SPINACH PATTIES

1 can (15 oz.) spinach

1 cup dry bread crumbs

2 tablespoons evaporated milk

1 onion, finely chopped

Salt and pepper to taste

1 egg, slightly beaten

Bread crumbs

Drain spinach thoroughly. Moisten bread crumbs with milk and combine with spinach, onion and seasoning. Let stand for 10 minutes. Make into patties, dip in egg and then in bread crumbs. Sauté until golden brown. Garnish with parsley. Serves 6.

Mrs. Robert J. Shoemaker

STUFFED ACORN SQUASH

3 medium acorn squash

2 tablespoons dry sherry

2 tablespoons brown sugar

6 tablespoons butter

½ cup crushed pineapple, drained

¼ teaspoon ground nutmeg

1 teaspoon salt

Cut squash in half. Scoop out seeds and fibers, and place in a baking dish. Put a teaspoon of each of the following in center of each: sherry, brown sugar and butter. Cover and bake for 45 minutes at 400°. Scoop out cooked squash, sherry, butter and sugar, leaving a ¼-inch shell. Mash the squash mixture and add remaining butter, pineapple, nutmeg and salt. Fill only 4 halves. Return to oven and heat for 35 minutes in 325° oven. Serves 4.

Mrs. Joseph F. McKinney

MARLENE'S SQUASH

8 small yellow crookneck squash

3 scallions, chopped, green and white parts

About 1 cup water

2 bacon slices

¼ cup sugar

Salt and pepper to taste

Boil squash and onions in water until tender. Meanwhile, fry bacon until crisp, and drain. Pour off all but 1 tablespoon of the drippings. Mash squash; place in skillet with drippings, sugar, salt and pepper. Cook until all water is gone and squash begins to brown and caramelize. Serves 4.

Mrs. Clay Burnett

SQUASH CASSEROLE

¾ cup onion, minced

½-1 green pepper, chopped

3 banana peppers, chopped

Butter

2 cups squash, stewed, drained and mashed

2 eggs, beaten

Salt and pepper to taste

1½ cups cracker crumbs

Sauté onion, green pepper and banana peppers in butter until soft; combine with squash. Add eggs, salt and pepper. Place in casserole and cover with thin layer of cracker crumbs. Dot with butter and cook at 375° for about 25 minutes. Serves 4.

Mrs. Willis E. Morgan

SPINACH-STUFFED ZUCCHINI

6 whole well-formed zucchini, scrubbed and trimmed

1 package (10 oz.) frozen chopped spinach, cooked

3 tablespoons butter

1 tablespoon onion, finely minced

3 tablespoons flour

1 cup half and half

3 eggs, separated

Salt, freshly ground black pepper, and nutmeg to taste

Grated Parmesan cheese

Simmer the zucchini in a little water, salted, until barely tender, 8-10 minutes. Drain and cool. Cut in half, lengthwise and carefully scoop out pulp and seeds, leaving an even shell. Invert on paper towels and allow to drain thoroughly. Drain the cooked spinach very thoroughly and reserve. Melt the butter in a large skillet and lightly sauté the onion. Blend in the flour and slowly add the half and half, stirring constantly. Cook until smooth and thickened. Reduce heat. Beat the egg yolks; gradually stir in a little of the half and half mixture into them. Return this egg mixture to cream sauce and cook 1 minute, stirring constantly. Add the spinach, and season with salt, pepper and nutmeg. Remove mixture from heat. Beat egg whites until stiff. Carefully fold into spinach mixture. Pile zucchini shells high. Sprinkle with Parmesan cheese. Arrange on lightly buttered baking dish. Bake in a preheated 350° oven 35-40 minutes or until spinach is set and zucchini is tender. Makes 12 "boats". *Variation: This may be served as a delicious soufflé by pouring the spinach mixture directly into a buttered 7-inch ring mold and baking in a hot water bath in a preheated 350° oven for 30-40 minutes. Serves 6.*

Mrs. Stanley H. Boulas

ZUCCHINI SQUASH WITH CURRY

Zucchini

Butter

Cherry tomatoes, halved

Curry powder to taste

Toasted sesame seeds (optional)

Water chestnuts (optional)

Wash the zucchini thoroughly and cut off stem end. Do not peel. Slice zucchini in circles approximately ¼ inch thick or larger. Cook in slightly salted water until tender. While these are cooking, melt butter to sauté enough cherry tomatoes to equal half the zucchini you are using. Cook just long enough to heat tomatoes through. Season with curry powder. Drain zucchini. Pour the hot tomatoes over the zucchini. Mix gently and serve at once. Garnish with sesame seeds or add a few water chestnuts for added color and texture.

Gerald Ramsey

ZUCCHINI CASSEROLE

2 pounds zucchini

⅔ cup ripe olives, coarsely chopped

2 eggs, slightly beaten

½ cup milk

1 teaspoon salt

Pepper to taste

1 cup American cheese, grated

1 cup soft bread crumbs

1 tablespoon butter, melted

Slice zucchini and cook in small amount of water until tender, drain, and mash. Stir in olives, eggs, milk, salt, pepper and cheese. Turn into 2-quart casserole. Blend crumbs with butter and sprinkle over top. Bake at 350° for 1 hour or until set in center. Serves 4-6.

Mrs. Maurice J. Bates

CREOLE TOMATOES

6 large, ripe tomatoes
1/4 cup butter
3 small onions, grated
1/2 green pepper, minced
2 stalks celery, minced
2 tablespoons deviled ham
1 can (2 oz.) mushrooms

1 teaspoon Worcestershire sauce
Dash of Tabasco
Salt, sugar and pepper to taste
2 cups cooked rice
Buttered crumbs
Paprika

Cut off tops of tomatoes and scrape out pulp. Melt butter in pan. Add onion, green pepper, celery and ham. Cook a few minutes, stirring. Dry mushrooms on a cloth and add to mixture. Add seasonings. Add tomato pulp and cook down for about 10 minutes. Stir in rice. Cook 5 minutes. Stuff tomatoes. Dot tops with buttered crumbs and paprika. Bake at 450° for 15 minutes. Serves 6.

Mrs. L. Rumsey Strickland

TOMATO CASSEROLE

Bread crumbs
Canned tomatoes, strained
Onion, diced

Sharp American cheese, grated

In deep baking dish, alternate layers of bread crumbs, tomatoes, onion and cheese. Repeat as necessary, ending with layer of cheese. Bake at 350° for approximately 1 hour.

Perle Mesta

TOMATO PUDDING

2 cans (10 oz.) tomato purée
1/2 cup boiling water
1 cup brown sugar

1/2 teaspoon salt
2 1/2 cups fresh white bread, cut in 1-inch squares

1 cup melted butter

Boil tomato purée, water, brown sugar and salt for 10 minutes. Put bread in casserole. Pour butter over squares of bread. Then pour tomato mixture over buttered bread in casserole. Bake in covered dish at 350° for 1 hour. Serves 6. *Tomato pudding is excellent served with beef.*

Mrs. Edwin H. Howell

LARGE VEGETABLE CASSEROLE

2 packages frozen chopped
spinach

1 package frozen chopped
broccoli

1 package frozen artichoke
hearts

1 package frozen zucchini

1 package grated Parmesan
cheese

½ pound fresh mushrooms or
1 can (3 oz.) mushrooms,
sautéed

Salt and pepper to taste

Onion salt to taste

Oregano to taste

Garlic salt to taste

9 eggs, beaten

Cook vegetables only until they defrost; then drain. Add rest of ingredients except eggs. This can be done ahead of time. Mix eggs with vegetables; taste for seasoning, and bake at 350° for about 40 minutes. Serves 12-16.

Mrs. H. I. Patterson

VEGETABLE MEDLEY

2 packages frozen asparagus

2 packages frozen baby lima
beans

2 cans whole kernel corn
with peppers

White cream sauce

1 cup Cheddar cheese, grated

Fried onion rings

Adding a pinch of sugar and salt, cook asparagus and limas separately according to package directions. Drain asparagus, limas and corn. Place alternate layers of vegetables in a casserole, saving most of asparagus for the top. Make a rich cream sauce. Add cheese and blend into cream sauce. Pour over vegetables, and place in 350° oven until bubbly, about 20-30 minutes. Top with a generous amount of fried onion rings. Bake for an additional 5 minutes. Serves 8-12.

Mrs. Samuel A. McKnight

SAUCES

SAUCES

BARBECUE SAUCE

1/4 cup butter

1/4 cup lemon juice

1/4 cup vinegar

1/4 cup catsup

1/4 cup Worcestershire sauce

Salt and pepper to taste

Tabasco to taste

Red pepper to taste

Garlic or onion (optional)

Melt butter in a sauce pan; add lemon juice, vinegar, catsup, Worcestershire sauce, salt, pepper, Tabasco and red pepper. Bring to a boil, and pour over meat to be barbecued. If barbecuing chicken, cut chicken in quarters; wash, drain, salt and pepper, and place in pan large enough not to have any chicken on top of each other. Place under flame and brown to a golden brown on both sides. Add barbecue sauce and cook, uncovered, in oven for about 1 hour or until nice and tender. Baste often.

Mrs. Lyndon B. Johnson

BARBECUE SAUCE

5 tablespoons vinegar

4 tablespoons catsup

2 tablespoons Worcestershire sauce

3 bay leaves

1 clove garlic, minced

2 tablespoons onion, chopped

1 cup canned tomatoes

3 ribs celery and leaves, chopped

1/2 lemon, thinly sliced

1 1/2 cups water

1/2 cup butter

Few drops of liquid hot pepper sauce (optional)

Simmer all ingredients, except butter, for 15 minutes. Strain and add butter. For those who wish a hot sauce, add liquid hot pepper sauce. Makes 2 1/4 cups sauce. *This is the barbecue sauce recipe which was given years ago on a CBS nationally broadcasted program out of New York called, "The Second Mrs. Burton", with Patsy Campbell. The program featured, once a month, an outstanding food suggestion or recipe. Nino, the famous maitre d'hotel of New York's Drake Hotel, prepared it and gave his approval. The requests for this recipe out-distanced any other recipes given on this program which was on the air for many years.*

Dorothy Sinz

BÉARNAISE SAUCE

2 tablespoons shallots, chopped

1 tablespoon tarragon, chopped

1 teaspoon chervil, coarsely chopped

4 peppercorns, crushed

Pinch of salt

¼ cup tarragon vinegar

5 egg yolks

¾ cup butter, melted

Pinch of cayenne

2 tablespoons mixed tarragon and chervil, minced

Simmer shallots, tarragon, chervil, peppercorns and salt in the vinegar over low heat until the vinegar has been reduced by ⅔. Cool to lukewarm. Add egg yolks, and beat briskly with wire whisk. Place over low heat, and gradually add butter. Whisk until sauce thickens. Strain. Season with cayenne, and stir in minced tarragon and chervil. Makes 1½ cups.

Mrs. Robert Miller

BROWN SAUCE

2-3 pounds browned bones with meat adhering

⅓ cup fat (beef or veal) or butter

1 onion, chopped

1 carrot, diced

⅓ cup flour

3 cups brown stock (utilizing leftover gravy and pan juices from roast)

1 cup canned or 3 fresh tomatoes

1 stalk celery

2 sprigs parsley

1 bay leaf

Pinch of thyme

1 clove garlic

½ teaspoon salt

3-4 peppercorns

To brown the bones, put them in a shallow pan in a hot oven, and cook until they have taken on a good, brown color. Prepare stock by cooking browned bones. Melt fat; add onion and carrot, and cook until golden brown. Add flour and cook until a good deep brown. Add stock and tomatoes and boil, stirring constantly, until flour and fat are combined with the liquid. Add celery, parsley, herbs, garlic, salt and peppercorns; and cook gently, skimming when necessary, for about 2 hours, when there should be about 2 cups of sauce left. Strain, let cool, and use as needed. This sauce is marvelous added to stews, leftover dishes and to other sauces. It thickens them, and gives full rich flavor. After sauce cools, it can be frozen in ice cube trays. When frozen, cubes can be stored in plastic bag in freezer, and a few cubes used in cooking as needed.

Mrs. William B. Glover, III

CURRY SAUCE

3 tablespoons butter, melted
¼ cup onion, finely chopped
¾ cup apple, peeled, cored, and grated
2 tablespoons flour

1 tablespoon curry powder
1 cup scalded milk
½ teaspoon salt
2 tablespoons peanut butter

Melt butter. Sauté onion and apple until tender. Sprinkle with a mixture of flour and curry powder. Blend well. Add milk gradually. Add salt and peanut butter. Cook over low heat, stirring constantly, until sauce is smooth and thickened. Serves 6-8. *Serve with fondue bourguignonne.*

Mrs. Gary D. Ketron

HAZEL BRUNER'S HOLLANDAISE SAUCE

5 egg yolks
10 tablespoons butter
Juice of 1 large lemon
Dash of Lawry's seasoned salt

Big dash of salt
½ teaspoon sugar
Dash of paprika
Dash of Beau Monde

Put yolks, butter, lemon juice, salts, sugar, paprika and Beau Monde into top of double boiler, 30-35 minutes before serving time. Butter should be cut into small pieces. Turn stove on warm. Water in lower double boiler must not boil. Stir once or twice gently during the cooking. If it begins to separate, put in an ice cube and stir. If it continues to separate, add another egg yolk, and stir in to reconstitute it. Makes 2 cups.

Mrs. Enslie O. Oglesby Jr.

QUICK HOLLANDAISE SAUCE

2 egg yolks
Pinch of salt

Juice of ½ lemon
½ cup butter, melted

Place egg yolks, salt and lemon juice in electric blender; whip for 1 minute. Turn blender on low speed, and slowly add butter. Mixture will thicken quickly. Makes ½ cup.

Mrs. Morris I. Jaffe

HORSERADISH CREAM SAUCE

3 tablespoons mayonnaise
½ cup heavy cream, whipped
1 tablespoon tarragon vinegar

1 teaspoon prepared mustard
½ teaspoon salt
Dash of cayenne

2 tablespoons bottled horseradish, drained

Fold mayonnaise into cream, then slowly add remaining ingredients. Serve very cold. This is good with roast beef or as a vegetable dip. Makes 1½ cups.

Mrs. Thomas J. Dean

MARCHAND DU VIN SAUCE

1 cup mushrooms, sliced	½ cup hot beef stock
1 cup ham, finely diced	1 cup brown sauce
1 small onion, finely chopped	½ cup dry red wine
2 shallots, finely chopped	Dash of lemon juice
4 tablespoons butter	Salt and pepper to taste

Sauté mushrooms, ham, onion and shallots in butter. Add hot beef stock, and simmer for 10 minutes. Add the brown sauce and red wine. Simmer for 20 minutes or until the desired consistency is obtained. Add lemon juice, salt and pepper. Makes about 2 cups. *This is a New Orleans version, used on Eggs St. Denis.*

Mrs. Joseph D. Zimmerman

MEAT SAUCE TUCCI

½ pound bulk pork sausage	2 cans (8 oz.) tomato sauce
½ pound ground chuck	1½ cups dry red wine
2 medium onions, finely chopped	1 teaspoon salt
2 large garlic cloves, minced or mashed	2 teaspoons coarsely ground black pepper
⅓ cup fresh parsley, chopped	2 teaspoons sage
1 ounce dried mushrooms; soaked, squeezed dry and finely chopped or ¼ pound fresh mushrooms, thinly sliced	2 teaspoons poultry seasoning
	2 teaspoons dried rosemary, crumbled

In a large casserole, slowly brown sausage; add chuck and brown. Add onions, and sauté until limp. Add garlic, parsley and mushrooms, and stir to coat with meat drippings. Stir in remaining ingredients. Cover loosely, and simmer, stirring occasionally, about 2 hours. The recipe makes about 1½ quarts, enough for 4 generous helpings. *For late suppers after performances at the Metropolitan Opera, I enjoy eating and serving this piquant sauce to friends and colleagues who drop in casually. Equally good over lasagne, manicotti or ravioli, the sauce is simple to make and can be frozen, together with pasta, until needed. It should be served with a leafy salad dressed with oil and fresh lemon juice, not vinegar.*

Gabriella Tucci

SPAGHETTI SAUCE ABRUZZI

1 ounce dry Italian mushrooms

⅔ cup water

1 medium onion, chopped

1 tablespoon salad oil

2 cloves garlic, minced

1 can (1 lb. 12 oz.) Italian-style peeled whole tomatoes

1 can (6 oz.) tomato paste

1 teaspoon sugar

1 ounce salt pork, cut into very small pieces

2 pounds spicy fresh Italian link sausages

1½ pounds ground chuck

¼ pound imported Romano cheese, freshly grated

1 egg

⅔ cup fresh parsley, chopped

¾ teaspoon salt

Freshly ground black pepper

Soak mushrooms in ⅓ cup water until tender, squeeze dry and slice thinly, reserving water. In a large kettle, sauté onions in salad oil until limp, stir in garlic, tomatoes, tomato paste, ⅓ cup water, water from soaking mushrooms, mushrooms and sugar. Cover loosely, and place over low heat. Meanwhile, in a 10-inch skillet, brown salt pork and add, with drippings, to the tomato sauce. Brown sausages, pouring off excess fat as it accumulates; add sausages to tomato sauce. Mix together ground chuck, cheese, egg, parsley, salt and black pepper. Form into meat balls the size of a walnut. Brown on all sides, and add to tomato sauce. Cover sauce loosely, and simmer, stirring frequently for 2-3 hours, until cooked down to a rich sauce. Skim off excess fat. Serve over hot cooked spaghetti. Pass freshly grated Romano cheese. Serves 8.

Orline Woodward

MUSTARD MAYONNAISE

1 can (3 oz.) Coleman's dry mustard

1 cup vinegar

⅔ cup sugar

1 egg

1 pint Hellman's mayonnaise

Mix mustard and vinegar, and let stand overnight. Beat egg, and mix with sugar. Add vinegar and mustard; cook over low heat until thick. Let cool. Mix with mayonnaise. Makes 3 cups. *This makes a good sandwich spread.*

Mrs. Joe C. Darrow

MUSTARD SAUCE FOR HAM

3 tablespoons dry mustard   1½ cups cream
3 tablespoons flour   2 egg yolks
½ cup sugar   ½ cup vinegar

Moisten dry ingredients with part of the cream. Put rest of cream in double boiler, and allow to warm. Add egg yolks to flour mixture, blending well. Add to warm cream, and cook until thick. Then add vinegar slowly, stirring until smooth. Makes about 1¼ pints. *This is also a delicious accompaniment for tongue, cold sliced beef or seafood.*

Mrs. Joseph J. Paige

In the 18th century, sugar was indeed quite rare and was sold by the ounce through apothecaries, who considered it to be an indispensable medicine.

RAISIN SAUCE FOR HAM

¾ cup seedless raisins   1 tablespoon cornstarch
1 cup water   ¼ teaspoon salt
4 whole cloves   Dash of pepper
¾ cup brown sugar   1 tablespoon butter
1 tablespoon lemon juice

Cover the raisins with water, add cloves, and simmer for 10 minutes. Mix brown sugar, cornstarch, salt and pepper; stir into raisin mixture. Cook, stirring constantly, until slightly thick. Add butter and lemon juice. Simmer a few minutes longer. Serve hot. Makes 1¾ cups.

Mrs. Glenn W. Blaylock

SOUR CREAM SUBSTITUTE

⅔ cup cottage cheese

¼ cup water

¼ teaspoon salt (optional)

1 teaspoon lemon juice

Combine ingredients in blender, and blend until free of lumps. Vary amount of water depending on desired thickness. Makes 1 cup.

Mrs. Robert Mitz

VINAIGRETTE SAUCE

⅓ cup pimento, finely chopped

¼ cup scallions, finely chopped

¼ cup raw carrot, finely chopped

¼ cup capers

1 tablespoon sour gherkins, finely chopped

1 tablespoon sweet gherkins, finely chopped

1 small clove garlic

2 teaspoons salt

½ teaspoon pepper

½ teaspoon dill

½ teaspoon tarragon

1¾ cups olive oil

1⅛ cups wine vinegar

Parsley, snipped

Hard-boiled egg, chopped

Mix ingredients together thoroughly, and store in covered glass jar in refrigerator. Before serving, add to each ¾ cup of sauce 2 tablespoons parsley and ½ hard-boiled egg. Makes about 3 cups.

Dr. Sue L. Nickey

CAKE TOPPING

1 cup sugar	½ teaspoon vanilla
½ teaspoon soda	1 cup buttermilk
	½ cup butter

Mix the sugar and soda in a saucepan. Add vanilla, buttermilk and butter. Cook 5 minutes to almost a soft-boil stage. Pour over cake or serve warm over cake slices. Makes 2½ cups.

Mrs. Joe F. Balisteri

FOAM SAUCE

2 eggs	2-3 tablespoons brandy
4 tablespoons sugar	1 cup cream, whipped
	Nutmeg or cinnamon

Stir two yolks with sugar to a soufflé mixture. Add brandy to the mixture. Carefully fold this mixture into the whipped cream. Fold in beaten egg whites. Sprinkle with nutmeg or cinnamon. Serves 8. *Serve over brownies, gingerbread or fruit cake.*

Mrs. C. Wesley Goyer, Jr.

HOLIDAY HARD SAUCE

½ cup butter, softened	2-3 tablespoons brandy
1½ cups sifted confectioners' sugar	¼ cup almonds, blanched and grated
	Dash of salt

Cream butter until light; gradually beat in sugar and brandy. Stir in almonds and salt. Chill well. Serve with steamed puddings or warm cake. Makes 2 cups.

The Cookbook Committee

SAUCES

MANDARIN ORANGE SAUCE

1 cup orange juice   2 teaspoons lemon juice
3/4 cup sugar   1 tablespoon sherry
1 tablespoon cornstarch   1 can Mandarin oranges
2 tablespoons butter   1 cup pecans
1 small bottle maraschino cherries

In a small saucepan, heat orange juice, sugar and cornstarch until boiling. When thick add butter, lemon juice, sherry, oranges, pecans and cherries. Do not include liquid from oranges and cherries in the sauce. Serve over a moist yellow cake or cupcakes. Serves 6-8.

Mrs. Thomas S. Davidson

SABAYON SAUCE

8 egg yolks   Juice of 1/2 lemon
1/8 teaspoon salt   1 cup sherry
1 cup sugar   2 tablespoons brandy
1 cup cream, whipped

Beat egg yolks, salt, sugar and lemon juice until light. Cook in a double boiler, stirring constantly until thick. Gradually add the sherry and brandy. Cool, then fold in cream. Serves 8. *This sauce is excellent with heated canned pears, fresh peaches or strawberries.*

Mrs. Stephen S. Kahn

SOUR CREAM AND ORANGE SAUCE

3 tablespoons butter   1 cup sour cream
3/4 cup confectioners' sugar   1 teaspoon orange rind, grated
3 tablespoons orange juice

Cream butter and confectioners' sugar until the mixture is very light and fluffy. Add sour cream, orange rind and orange juice. Mix together well, and serve cold with warm cake or hot pudding.

Mrs. Dan Hughes, Jr.

SOUR SAUCE

½ cup butter
1 cup sugar
1 tablespoon flour

2 cups boiling water
2 tablespoons cider vinegar
1 teaspoon vanilla

Cream butter, sugar and flour together. Add boiling water and cook about 15 minutes, stirring occasionally. Remove from fire, and add vinegar and vanilla. It may be stored in the refrigerator and reheated. Makes 3 cups. *This was my grandmother's recipe for sauce to serve with steamed pudding. It is a pleasant change from hard sauce.*

Mrs. Joseph D. Zimmerman

BUTTERSCOTCH SAUCE

1 egg yolk
4 tablespoons water

⅔ cup brown sugar
⅓ cup light Karo syrup

5 tablespoons butter

Beat yolks and water in top of double boiler with fork. Add sugar, syrup and butter. Cook directly over burner until boiling. Then put over boiling water, and let simmer for 30-60 minutes. Keep refrigerated. Makes 1¼ cups.

Mrs. James R. Hannay

Ice cream was introduced into Europe over eight centuries ago as an orange ice, which was brought back by Richard the Lion-Hearted on his return from the Crusades. The recipe was given to him by the great warrior Sultan of Egypt and Syria.

HOT FUDGE SAUCE

4 squares unsweetened
   chocolate
½ cup butter

3 cups sugar
Dash of salt

1 can (15 oz.) evaporated milk

Melt chocolate and butter in top of double boiler. Add sugar and salt; then add milk gradually. Stir and cook until smooth, about 5 minutes. This sauce will keep about 10 days in refrigerator. Take amount desired and heat again, then pour over ice cream. Makes 6 cups.

Gloria Stroud

PIER 66 DESSERT SAUCE

2 packages (6 oz.) Hershey
   chocolate bits
4 tablespoons butter

¼ cup white Crème de
   Menthe
1 teaspoon Curaçao

Brandy

Melt chocolate bits with butter, stirring constantly, until smooth and creamy. Add Crème de Menthe, a little at a time, stirring constantly. Add Curaçao. Stir until blended. Flame the brandy, and stir into hot chocolate sauce. Serve at once over vanilla ice cream. Serves 4-6.

Mrs. William L. Groth, Jr.

WINE CHOCOLATE SAUCE

2 squares unsweetened
   chocolate
1 tablespoon butter
½ cup cream
1 cup sugar

¼ teaspoon salt
2 tablespoons white corn
   syrup
¼ cup sherry
½ teaspoon vanilla

Melt chocolate and butter in top of double boiler, add cream, sugar, salt and syrup. Cook over medium heat for 5 minutes or longer to get desired thickness. Stir, if necessary, to prevent burning. Remove from heat; add sherry and vanilla. This sauce keeps well in refrigerator for 2 weeks or longer. Makes 1¼ cups.

Mrs. Stephen S. Kahn

BREADS

APRICOT NUT BREAD

½ cup dried apricots, diced
1 egg
1 cup sugar
2 tablespoons butter, melted
2 cups sifted flour

3 teaspoons baking powder
¼ teaspoon soda
¾ teaspoon salt
½ cup orange juice, strained
¼ cup water

1 cup walnut pieces, broken

Soak, drain and grind apricots. Beat egg, stir in sugar and butter. Mix well. Sift flour with baking powder, soda and salt. Add alternately with the juice and water to the sugar mixture. Add apricots and nuts. Mix well. Bake in a loaf pan at 350° for 1½ hours or until firm when tested.

Mrs. Richard M. Nixon

HOLLAND CARROT BREAD

2 cups sifted flour
2 teaspoons baking soda
2 teaspoons cinnamon
1½ cups sugar

1½ cups oil
3 eggs
2 teaspoons vanilla
2 cups carrots, grated

1 cup nutmeats or raisins (optional)

With an electric mixer beat all ingredients except carrots until well-blended; then fold in carrots. Add nutmeats. Turn the mixture into 2 well-greased and floured 9x5x3-inch loaf pans. Bake at 300° for 1 hour or until done. Freezes well. Makes 2 loaves.

Mrs. A. J. Tyler

HOLLAND DUTCH CARROT BREAD

2 cups sifted flour
2 teaspoons baking soda
2 teaspoons cinnamon
½ teaspoon salt
1½ cups sugar

1½ cups cooking oil
3 eggs
2 teaspoons vanilla
2 cups carrots, grated
1 cup nutmeats, broken

Sift flour, baking soda, cinnamon and salt together in a large bowl. Make a well in the center, and put sugar, oil, eggs and vanilla into it. With an electric mixer, beat at medium speed until well-blended. Fold in carrots and nutmeats. Turn the mixture into 2 well-greased and floured 9x5x3-inch loaf pans, and bake at 300° for 1 hour or until done. Makes 2 loaves. *This bread is moist and delicious, and the carrot cannot be detected.*

Mrs. M. E. Van Hemert

DATE NUT BREAD

¾ cup walnuts, chopped

1 cup dates, pitted and chopped

1½ teaspoons soda

½ teaspoon salt

3 tablespoons shortening

¾ cup boiling water

2 eggs, beaten slightly

1 teaspoon vanilla

1 cup sugar

1½ cups flour, sifted

Mix walnuts, dates, soda and salt with fork. Add shortening and water. Heat oven to 350°. Add eggs, vanilla, then sugar and flour, beating with fork. Add date mixture and blend. Pour into greased and floured loaf pan. Bake 1 hour or until done. Chill. Makes 1 loaf. *I was thrilled to be invited to sing Tosca and Mimi in the Caracas Opera Festival. However, being a Gringo, I was concerned about my adjustment to the change of food. Before leaving the United States, I made a large loaf of Date Nut Bread (it travels and keeps well), and my diet in Caracas for 3 days was Date Nut Bread and tea with sugar for breakfast, 2 fried eggs and wonderful Caracas beer for lunch, and cold roast beef sandwiches and coffee for dinner. The combination worked well. The only bad moment came after 4 days, on the flight home, when the airline served cold roast beef sandwiches for lunch.*

Jean Fenn

ORANGE BREAD

3 large orange rinds, chopped

1 teaspoon soda

2 cups water

1½ cups sugar

⅓ cup shortening

2 eggs, beaten

1 cup milk

3½ cups flour

3½ teaspoons baking powder

½ teaspoon salt

1 cup pecans

Put soda and 1 cup of water over orange rinds. Cook over high or medium heat until mixture comes to a boil, approximately 5 minutes. Pour off liquid. Add 1 cup of sugar and remaining water. Cook, do not boil, to a texture resembling preserves. Cream shortening and remaining sugar. Combine eggs and milk; blend with shortening and sugar mixture. Sift together flour, baking powder and salt, and add pecans. Combine dry ingredients with the creamed mixture, and blend in rind mixture carefully. Grease and flour a large tube pan, and fill with batter. Cook at 350° for approximately 35-45 minutes.

Mrs. Joseph T. Nance

PUMPKIN SPICED BREAD

3¼ cups flour

1 teaspoon cinnamon

1 teaspoon baking powder

3 cups sugar

1½ teaspoons salt

1 teaspoon nutmeg

2 teaspoons soda

4 eggs, well-beaten

1 cup Wesson oil

1½ cups nuts, chopped

1 can (1 lb. 4 oz.) pumpkin

1 cup None-Such mincemeat

Combine dry ingredients. Blend in eggs, oil, nuts, pumpkin and mincemeat. Pour into greased and floured 3½x7½-inch bread pans. Bake at 350° for 50 minutes. Cool in pans on racks for 30 minutes. Keep 24 hours before slicing. Can be frozen. Makes 5 loaves.

Mrs. Edward E. Shelton

The pumpkin is truly all-American. The Indians of the Northwest did not originate the pumpkin pie or the jack-o'-lantern, but they used pumpkins in making soup, boiling, baking and even making fried cakes. The Incans placed pumpkin seeds in the graves to provide the dead with the required sustenance on their long journey to Incan heaven. In many areas of South America roasted pumpkin seeds are as popular as peanuts are in this country.

PUMPKIN BREAD

4 cups sugar

1 cup vegetable oil

1 can (1 lb. 13 oz.) pumpkin

1 egg

5 cups flour

4 teaspoons soda

1 tablespoon cinnamon

1 tablespoon cloves

1 tablespoon salt

1 cup raisins

2 cups nuts

In large mixing bowl mix ingredients as given. Bake in pre-heated 350° oven for 1 hour. Makes 3 regular loaves.

Milton Katims

BATTER BREAD

2 eggs

2 cups buttermilk

2 cups water-ground corn meal

1 teaspoon salt

1 teaspoon soda

2 tablespoons bacon fat or shortening heated in the skillet

Mix all ingredients except the hot fat into a batter. Pour hot fat into the batter; stir. Then pour batter into hot iron skillet. Bake at 550° for 30-35 minutes.

Paul and Kitty Baker

BANANA BREAD

⅓ cup butter
1 cup sugar
2 eggs, well-beaten
3 tablespoons buttermilk
1 teaspoon soda

1 teaspoon baking powder
½ teaspoon salt
2 cups sifted flour
1 cup bananas, mashed
1 cup nuts

Cream butter with sugar in electric mixer on low speed. Add eggs, buttermilk, soda, baking powder, salt and flour, a little at a time until blended. Add bananas to the batter along with the nuts. Pour into an 8x5x3-inch bread pan which has been lined with foil. Bake at 350° for 1 hour or until done. Freezes nicely. Serves 12-16.

Mrs. John L. Burke, Jr.

ANADAMA BREAD

½ cup corn meal
2 cups boiling water
3 teaspoons salt
½ cup molasses

2 tablespoons Crisco
2 yeast cakes
⅓ cup water
8 cups flour

Sprinkle corn meal over boiling water, and cook to mush. Add salt, molasses and Crisco. Let cool. Add yeast softened in water and flour, and mix well. Let rise until double in size. Work dough again and knead well, then mold into 3 loaves. Put in greased 9x5x3-inch loaf pans, and let rise again. Bake at 350° until brown. Makes 3 loaves.

Rosa Rodriguez

BROWN SODA BREAD

¾ cup white flour
½ teaspoon salt

¾ teaspoon baking soda
1⅛-1¼ cups whole meal flour

1 cup sour milk or buttermilk

Sift white flour, salt and soda into a bowl. Add the whole meal flour. Make a well in the center of the flour, and pour in all the milk. Mix to a loose dough, adding more milk if necessary. Turn onto a floured board, and knead until the side next to the board is smooth. Turn the smooth side up, flatten out, and cut a cross on top with a floured knife. Place on a lightly floured tin. Bake at 300° for about 45 minutes. Serves 6.

Mrs. Stanley W. Blanchard

DILL CASSEROLE BREAD

1 package active dry yeast	2 teaspoons dill seeds
1/4 cup warm water	1 teaspoon salt
1 cup creamed cottage cheese	1/4 teaspoon soda
2 tablespoons sugar	1 egg
1 tablespoon instant minced onion	2 1/4-2 1/2 cups sifted all-purpose flour
1 tablespoon butter, melted	Salt

Soften yeast in water. In mixing bowl combine cottage cheese, heated to lukewarm, sugar, onion, butter, dill seeds, salt, soda, egg and yeast. Add flour to form stiff dough, beating well after each addition. Cover. Let rise in warm place for 50-60 minutes until doubled in size. Stir dough down. Turn into well-greased 8-inch round casserole. Let rise in warm place for 30-40 minutes. Bake at 350° for 40-50 minutes, or until golden brown. Brush with soft butter, and sprinkle with salt. *This makes a lovely round loaf of bread and is easy enough for the beginning cook.*

Mrs. Fred F. Johnston

A lazy Egyptian slave is given credit for the discovery of raising bread. It seems he had let the fire go out in the process of making flat cakes made from flour and water. In the morning he saw to his surprise that the dough had risen to a large size. He proceeded to put it in the oven to bake, and thus gave birth to bread as we know it.

WHOLE WHEAT BREAD

1 package or cake of yeast	1/2 cup hot water
1 1/2 cups lukewarm water	1/4 cup brown sugar, firmly packed
2 scant cups flour	
2 tablespoons sugar	3 tablespoons shortening
1 tablespoon salt	4 cups whole wheat flour

Soften yeast in lukewarm water; add flour, sugar and salt. Beat with spoon or on low speed of mixer until smooth. Let rise in warm place until light and bubbly. Combine hot water, brown sugar and shortening. Cool to lukewarm; add to yeast mixture. Add half of whole wheat flour; add rest as needed to make stiff dough. Turn out on lightly floured board, adding more flour as needed, to keep dough from sticking to board. Knead until smooth and bouncy. Place in greased bowl, and let rise in warm place until double in bulk. Divide into 2 balls. Cover, and let rest 10 minutes. Shape loaves, and place in greased pans. Let rise until dough is well above pans, and is nicely rounded. Bake at 350° for 50 minutes or until the loaf is brown and has a hollow sound when tapped. Remove from pans at once, cool, then wrap. Makes 2 loaves. *This won the grand champion ribbon at the 1964 State Fair of Texas.*

Mrs. M. G. O'Dell

WHOLE WHEAT BREAD

1/2 yeast cake
2 tablespoons warm water
Scant teaspoon sugar
1 1/8 cups whole wheat flour

2 cups white flour
1 1/2 teaspoons salt
1 tablespoon lard, melted
1 1/2 cups water

1 tablespoon molasses

Dissolve yeast in warm water. Add sugar. Mix whole wheat and white flour, salt and lard. Stir in water, yeast and molasses. Let rise 1 1/2 hours to double. Put in greased and floured pan about 1 hour to rise again. Bake 45 minutes at 350°. Makes 1 loaf. Serves 8.

Mrs. C. Wesley Goyer, Jr.

HOMEMADE BREAD

1 package dry yeast
3/4 cup warm milk
1 1/4 teaspoons salt

1/4-1/3 cup oil
6 tablespoons sugar
3/4 cup warm water

5 1/4 cups flour

Put yeast and warm milk in large bowl. Let set until yeast dissolves, about 2-3 minutes. Add salt, oil, sugar and water, then flour, and mix. Knead thoroughly until elastic on floured paper or board. Put back into bowl, and let rise until double in size, about 2 hours. Divide in half, and knead again. Then put half the dough into greased 9 1/2x5x3-inch bread pan. Repeat with other half of dough. Let rise until double in size. Bake at 400° for 20 minutes. Makes 2 loaves.

Mrs. James M. Spellings

OATMEAL BREAD

1 yeast cake
1/2 cup warm water
2 cups boiling water
2 cups oatmeal

1/2 cup brown sugar
3 tablespoons butter
1 teaspoon salt
5-6 cups white flour

Dissolve yeast in water. Scald oatmeal in boiling water, add sugar, salt and butter to this mixture. Let cool. When cool, add yeast. Mix in enough white flour so it can be removed to a bread board for kneading. Knead for 10 minutes. Place back into large bowl. Cover, and let rise to twice its bulk. Flour bread board, and put dough on board for second kneading. Add remainder of flour or a little more if necessary. Knead for 10 minutes. Form into 2 loaves. Place in greased 9x5x3-inch bread pans. Cover, and let rise again to twice its bulk. Bake at 400° for 15 minutes, then reduce to 350° for 30 minutes more. Cool on rack, and butter top crust slightly.

Mrs. Jerry Bywaters

LITTLE CORN CAKES

1 cup white corn meal	1 teaspoon sugar
2 tablespoons butter	2 eggs
1 cup boiling water	Milk
Pinch of salt	1 teaspoon baking powder

Scald corn meal and butter by pouring boiling water over it. Add salt and sugar. Break eggs into mixture and beat. Add enough milk to make batter very soft. Add baking powder. Drop by tablespoons into buttered frying pan to make each small corn cake. Makes 18. *Serve with Veal Kidney Stew.*

Mrs. H. Neil Mallon

FRENCH BREAKFAST PUFFS

1/3 cup shortening	1/2 teaspoon salt
1 cup sugar	1/4 teaspoon nutmeg
1 egg	1/2 cup milk
1 1/2 cups flour	6 tablespoons butter, melted
1 1/2 teaspoons baking powder	1 teaspoon vanilla
	1 teaspoon cinnamon

Mix together shortening, 1/2 cup sugar and egg. Sift flour, baking powder, salt and nutmeg together. Stir dry ingredients into creamed mixture alternately with milk. Fill greased muffin tins 2/3 full. Bake at 350° for 20-25 minutes or until golden brown. Roll immediately in butter and then in a mixture of 1/2 cup sugar and cinnamon. Makes 12 medium puffs.

Mrs. James H. Clark

A recent discovery by an archaeologist was the uncovering of a 6,700 year old Iraq village, in which two kinds of wheat, similar to the kind we grow today, were found. Chinese records show that they were using wheat 4,700 years ago, and even further back historians record wheat as a food 10,000 to 15,000 years before Christ.

QUICK MUFFINS

4 tablespoons flour

1 tablespoon whole wheat germ or Petti Johns Breakfast Food

1 teaspoon baking powder

Dash of salt

Milk

1 egg

4 tablespoons peanut oil

Put flour and wheat germ into a bowl. Add baking powder and salt, and stir thoroughly. Add milk to make loose batter and stir; add egg, and stir. Add oil and mix, but do not overbeat. Put 1 teaspoon peanut oil in each ring of a 6-ring muffin pan, and fill with batter. Bake 20 minutes at 400°. Makes 6 muffins. *This recipe is perfect for waffles or pancakes. Just add a little more liquid to the batter.*

Josephine Travis

BLUEBERRY MUFFINS

1 cup sugar

⅓ cup margarine

2 eggs, beaten

4 cups flour, sifted

2 tablespoons baking powder

1 teaspoon salt

2 cups sweet milk

1 can (14 oz.) blueberries, drained

Cream sugar and margarine. Add eggs. Sift flour, baking powder and salt. Add dry ingredients and milk to creamed mixture. Add blueberries. Butter and flour muffin tins; fill ⅔ full. Bake at 400° for 20-25 minutes. Makes 24.

Mrs. Jerry P. Jones

ORANGE MARMALADE MUFFINS

1 package Betty Crocker orange cake mix

½-1 cup nuts, chopped

½-1 cup white raisins

Orange marmalade

Prepare muffins according to package directions. Then add nuts and raisins. Bake in greased small muffin tins. Coat tops with marmalade while still hot.

Mrs. John D. Williamson

ORANGE MUFFINS

½ cup shortening

1 cup brown sugar, firmly packed

4 eggs

2 cups sifted flour

½ teaspoon salt

1 teaspoon soda

1 cup buttermilk

1 pound dates, finely chopped

¾ cup pecans, chopped

1 tablespoon orange rind, grated

Cream shortening, and add brown sugar; blend thoroughly. Add eggs, 1 at a time. Sift flour and salt together. Add soda to buttermilk. Add flour and buttermilk alternately to the creamed mixture. Then add the dates, pecans and orange rind. Bake for 15 minutes at 350°. Remove from oven, and while hot, dip in the orange juice mixture. Drain, and place on wax paper. Makes 96 bite-sized muffins.

DIP

3 cups sugar

1½ cups orange juice

Some grated orange rind

Combine all ingredients. Heat, do not boil.

Mrs. Rolland R. Anfin

POPOVERS RUBY

⅔ cup sifted flour

⅓ teaspoon salt

2 small eggs

⅔ cup milk

Sift flour and salt together. Make a hollow in the center, and pour in eggs beaten with half the milk. Mix until smooth, gradually adding remaining milk, then beat hard for 2 minutes. Pour into sizzling hot, well-greased, heavy gem pan. Bake at 375° for about 35 minutes. Makes 8.

Mrs. Lawson Goggans

NEVER-FAIL POPOVERS

1 cup flour	2 eggs, slightly beaten
¼ teaspoon salt	1 cup milk

1 teaspoon butter, melted

Sift flour with salt. Mix eggs, milk and butter together. Add the liquid to the flour, and stir until well-mixed and smooth. Fill cold (have in refrigerator 1-2 hours) well-greased custard cups ½ full of batter. Place cups on a cookie sheet, and place in a cold oven. Bake at 400° for 45-60 minutes. Makes 6 popovers. *The secret of the unfailing success of these popovers lies in having the custard cups and oven cold when baking starts.*

Mrs. David A. Stretch

BUTTER BISCUITS

2 cups sifted all-purpose flour	2 teaspoons sugar
4 teaspoons baking powder	½ cup shortening
½ teaspoon salt	1½ teaspoons Adam's butter flavor
½ teaspoon cream of tartar	⅔ cup milk

Sift together flour, baking powder, salt, cream of tartar and sugar; cut in shortening until mixture resembles coarse crumbs. Add butter flavor to milk, and then add all at once; stir only until dough follows fork around bowl. Turn out on lightly floured surface; knead gently ½ minute. Pat or roll ½ inch thick; cut with biscuit cutter. Bake on ungreased cookie sheet at 450° for 10-12 minutes. Makes 16 medium biscuits. *They taste like real butter biscuits!*

Mrs. John G. Adams

CORN MEAL BISCUITS

1½ cups flour	½ teaspoon soda
¾ cup corn meal	2 tablespoons Crisco
1 teaspoon salt	1 egg, well-beaten
3 teaspoons baking powder	¾ cup sweet milk
Melted butter	

Mix dry ingredients, and cut in shortening until well-blended. Add egg and enough milk to hold mixture together. Sprinkle corn meal on board, and roll dough ½ inch thick. Cut with biscuit cutter, and brush with butter. Fold over. Place on greased baking sheet, and bake at 400° for approximately 15 minutes. Makes 2 dozen.

Mrs. Dan C. Williams

ORANGE-SUGAR BISCUITS

1 can biscuits	Small sugar lumps
Melted butter	Orange juice

Preheat oven to 450°. Place biscuits in pie pan, brush tops with butter. Dip sugar lumps in orange juice, and press 1 into top of each biscuit. Bake for 7-9 minutes. *This is a blessing for wives and mothers who have enough trouble getting out of bed each morning; much less coming up with a good tasting, attractive breakfast. My family has never grown tried of Orange-Sugar Biscuits, and I can even prepare them before that first cup of coffee.*

Mrs. Robert M. Greenberg

CHEESE BISCUITS

1 package (6 oz.) biscuit mix	¾ cup sharp Cheddar cheese, grated

Combine cheese with dry biscuit mix first, and then add liquid, according to package directions. Bake according to package directions. *Variation: For appetizer, add 2 dashes of cayenne pepper, or Spice Island green onion flakes or crisply fried bacon, crumbled.*

Mrs. Lynn Brown

FRENCH BRIOCHES

1 package yeast
⅓ cup lukewarm water
3 tablespoons sugar
Approximately 4 cups sifted
    flour or unsifted instant
    flour

1 cup soft butter
1 teaspoon salt
7 eggs, slightly beaten
½ cup milk, scalded and
    cooled

A mixer with a dough hook is convenient, but not necessary. All steps can be done in the largest mixer bowl or in a 4-quart bowl. Soften yeast in the water. Add 1 teaspoon of sugar and 1 cup of flour. Mix thoroughly, and then knead until smooth. Form dough into a compact ball, and put it back in the bowl. Cover with lukewarm water. The ball will rise, expand and float in the water. This takes 15-60 minutes. It is very important when taking the ball out of the water to squeeze as much water out of the dough as possible. If the dough retains too much moisture at this point it is so sticky that it is extremely difficult to knead. Empty water out of bowl, and wipe dry. Put in remaining flour and salt. Add the ball of dough, ½ the butter and 2 eggs. Mix well, with fingers or dough hook, adding enough milk to make a soft nonsticky dough. Knead with hook or turn out on lightly floured board, and knead until smooth. Work in the remaining butter and 2 more eggs. Repeat the kneading. Lift the dough, and slap or bang it on the table until it is very smooth. Add 2 more eggs, work them into the dough, and repeat the kneading and banging on the table. Shape the dough into a ball, and place it in a greased bowl. Cover, and let rise in a warm place, 80°-85°, until double in bulk. Punch and stir the dough down. Shape into a ball, place in a clean greased bowl, cover tightly with Saran wrap, and chill overnight or slightly longer. To shape the brioches turn the dough on a floured board. Cut off about 1/6, and reserve for topknots of buns. Divide remainder of the dough into 18-24 portions, and shape each into a smooth ball. Place in greased brioche pans or 2¾x1¼-inch muffin tins. Cut reserved dough into the same number of small balls. Dampen a finger slightly, and make a depression in the center of each large ball. Place a small ball in the depression. Let rise in a warm place until double in bulk, about 1 hour or more. Preheat oven to 450°. Lightly beat 1 egg, and brush over the tops of the brioches. Bake until well-browned, or about 15 minutes. Serve warm with sweet butter and marmalade. Makes 18-24.

Mrs. James R. Pratt

BUTTER CREAM CRESCENTS

1 yeast cake

3 tablespoons sugar

1 egg, slightly beaten

3 tablespoons butter, broken into bits

1⅓ cups flour

⅓ teaspoon salt

⅓ cup warm milk

Mash yeast, and add 1 tablespoon sugar. Let set until liquified. Add remaining 2 tablespoons sugar, egg and butter. Add flour and salt alternately with milk. Mix with a knife, and set aside to double in bulk. Punch down and knead slightly, adding more flour if necessary. Roll to ¼-inch thickness and as nearly round as possible. Cut into 12 pie-shaped wedges. Starting at the broad end of the triangle, roll each piece down to the point. Place on a slightly greased tin, cover, and allow to rise. Bake at 400° for 20 minutes. Serve hot. Makes 12 crescents.

Mrs. James N. Michie

HOT ROLLS

1 cake compressed yeast or 1 package dry yeast

2 eggs, beaten

½ cup sugar

½ cup shortening

1 teaspoon salt

4 cups flour, sifted

Dissolve yeast in 3 tablespoons warm water, and set aside. Mix eggs, sugar, shortening and salt well, and stir in 1 cup warm water. Stir in yeast mixture and add flour. Mix well; cover bowl, and place in refrigerator overnight, or if to be used the same day, set aside at room temperature. About 2-3 hours before baking, roll circles to ¼-inch thickness; spread with butter. Cut into wedges, and roll from wide edge to point. Let rise 2-3 hours. Bake at 425° for approximately 6 minutes. Makes approximately 20 rolls.

Mrs. R. J. Byrd

CHOCOLATE TOAST

3 heaping teaspoons sugar

¼ teaspoon cocoa

Bread slices, buttered

Mix sugar and cocoa. Sprinkle over buttered bread, and toast under broiler. *The sugar and cocoa mixture can be made up in vast quantities and is always ready to use; just like cinnamon-sugar mixture.*

Mrs. Robert M. Greenberg

GOUGÈRE

2 cups milk
½ cup butter, cut up
2 teaspoons salt

Dash of ground pepper
2 cups sifted flour
8 eggs

6 ounces plus 4 tablespoons Gruyère cheese in fine cubes

Scald and cool milk. Strain into a large saucepan, and add butter, salt and pepper. Bring to a boil, and add flour all at once. Cook on low heat, stirring until a ball forms. Remove from heat. Beat in eggs, 1 at a time. When paste is shiny and smooth, add cheese. With tablespoon form a ring of dough on a buttered cookie sheet. Top with smaller balls made with a teaspoon. Brush with milk, and sprinkle with 4 tablespoons diced cheese. Bake at 375° for approximately 45 minutes or until puffed and golden. Serves 6-12. *Gougère makes a marvelous hot hors d'oeuvre for 12 people or with a salad a very nice lunch dish for 6.*

Bill Goldsmith

BLITZ KUCHEN COFFEE CAKE

1½ cups sugar
⅓ cup plus 2 tablespoons butter
3 eggs, separated
¾ cup milk

1½ cups flour
2 teaspoons baking powder
Cinnamon and sugar
½ cup almonds, grated (optional)

Cream sugar and ⅓ cup butter. Add well-beaten egg yolks. Add milk and dry ingredients alternately. Fold in beaten egg whites. Place in greased and floured 13x9x2⅝-inch pan. Melt remaining butter, and pour over top of batter. Sprinkle with sugar, cinnamon and almonds. Bake at 375° for 30 minutes. Serves 10-12.

Mrs. Aubrey C. Swygard

CHERRY RING

1 cup milk

½ cup sugar

1 teaspoon salt

½ cup butter

1 package active dry yeast

¼ cup warm water

1 egg

4½ cups unsifted flour

1 can (1 lb.) red, tart, pitted cherries

½ cup brown sugar

½ cup flour

½ cup pecans, chopped

Scald milk; add sugar, salt and butter. Cool to lukewarm. Dissolve yeast in water. Add lukewarm milk mixture, egg and 2 cups flour. Beat until smooth. Stir in 2 cups flour to make stiff batter. Cover tightly. Refrigerate 2 hours (or up to 2 days). On floured board, roll dough into two 14x7-inch oblongs. Spread with cherries and mixture of brown sugar, ½ cup flour and pecans. Roll lengthwise, seal edges. Form 2 rings, sealed edge down, on greased baking sheets. Seal ends. Cut two-thirds through rings at 1-inch intervals. Twist each section sideways. Cover; let rise in warm place until double, approximately 1 hour. Bake at 375° for about 25 minutes. Frost with confectioners' sugar icing while still warm. Makes 2 large rings.

Mrs. Mitchell T. Peters

Strange as it may seem, the rose family supplies us with a greater number of important, edible fruits than does any other one group of plants. The apple, pear, plum, cherry, almond, peach, apricot and many of the most important berries are all members of the rose family.

SOUR CREAM COFFEE CAKE

½ cup butter
1½ cups sugar
2 eggs
1 teaspoon vanilla
2 cups sifted flour

1 teaspoon baking powder
1 teaspoon soda
¼ teaspoon salt
1 cup sour cream
½ cup pecans, chopped

2 teaspoons cinnamon

Cream butter and 1 cup sugar, add eggs, vanilla, and beat well. Sift together flour, baking powder, soda and salt. Add sifted dry ingredients and sour cream alternately. Beat well. Mix nuts, ½ cup sugar and cinnamon. Put half of batter into lightly greased 10-inch tube pan. Sprinkle half of nut mixture over top. Add rest of batter, then last of nut mixture. Bake at 350° for 45 minutes. *This recipe was given to me, as a new, naval bride, by a retired, naval architect's wife. It is not only one of my favorite Christmas gifts to friends, but my husband enjoys it, sliced and heated with butter, for breakfast or for dessert on deer hunting trips.*

Mrs. John A. Pierce

SOUR CREAM COFFEE CAKE

1 box Duncan Hines yellow
  cake mix
1 package Jello vanilla
  instant pudding
1 pint sour cream

½ cup Wesson oil
4 eggs
½ cup pecans, chopped
¼ cup cinnamon
½ cup sugar

2 tablespoons cocoa

Combine cake mix, pudding, sour cream, Wesson oil and eggs. Beat for 7 minutes. Mix pecans, cinnamon, sugar and cocoa. Sprinkle small amount of pecan mixture in bottom of greased angel food pan. Pour half of batter over pecan mixture. Sprinkle pecan mixture over batter, reserving a little for the top. Pour in other half of batter, and cover with remaining pecan mixture. Swirl with a knife. Bake approximately 1 hour and 20 minutes in preheated 325° oven. Cake should pass straw test. Serves 10.

Mrs. Earle Cabell

BASIC CRÊPE RECIPE

7 tablespoons flour   1 pint milk

2 eggs   ½ teaspoon salt

1 tablespoon butter, melted

Mix flour and eggs with wire whisk. Add milk, salt and butter. Brush heated 4-6-inch skillet with butter; pour in 1 tablespoon batter. Tilt pan to cover bottom, and cook quickly on both sides.

Helen Corbitt

PANCAKES

¼ cup sugar   1 cup flour

3 tablespoons Wesson oil   2 teaspoons baking powder

2 eggs   ½ teaspoon salt

½ cup milk

Mix sugar, oil and eggs. Beat hard with rotary egg beater. Sift dry ingredients together, and add alternately with milk. Drop 1 spoonful per pancake on hot (390°) ungreased griddle. When bubbles begin to pop, turn to brown other side. Makes about twenty 2½-inch pancakes.

Mrs. James S. Robertson, Jr.

COTTAGE CHEESE PANCAKES

1 cup cottage cheese   ¾ cup flour

1 cup sour cream   1 tablespoon sugar

4 eggs   ¾ teaspoon salt

Butter

Combine cheese and sour cream; add eggs. Sift together flour, sugar and salt, and add to cheese mixture. Beat until well-mixed. Fry in butter. Makes 24 pancakes.

Mrs. Edward R. Genecov

CHEESE PANCAKES

1 pound cottage cheese	1 tablespoon flour
3 eggs	1/2 teaspoon salt
1/2 cup matzo meal	Sugar
Sour cream	Cinnamon
	Oil

Mix cottage cheese, eggs, matzo meal, 1 heaping tablespoon sour cream, flour, salt and 1 tablespoon sugar. Fry in oil like regular pancakes, 2-3 minutes per side. Serve with a cinnamon-sugar mixture and sour cream. If preferred, cinnamon may be mixed in with other dry ingredients. Serves 4.

Robert Merrill

PANCAKE NONPAREIL

1/2 cup flour	Pinch of nutmeg
1/2 cup milk	1/4 cup butter
2 eggs, slightly beaten	2 tablespoons confectioners' sugar
	Juice of 1/2 lemon

Preheat oven to 425°. In a mixing bowl combine flour, milk, eggs and nutmeg. Beat lightly. Leave the batter a little lumpy. Melt butter in a 12-inch skillet with heat-proof handle. When very hot, pour in batter. Bake 15-20 minutes or until golden brown. Sprinkle with sugar, and return briefly to oven. Sprinkle with lemon juice, then serve with jelly, jam or marmalade. Serves 4-6. *This pancake is as elegant and rich as it is easy to prepare. Serve it for breakfast, brunch or dessert.*

Mrs. Jack N. Greenman, III

SWEDISH PANCAKES

1 cup flour   1/4 teaspoon salt
2 tablespoons sugar   3 eggs
                      3 cups milk

Sift flour, add sugar and salt. Then add eggs and milk gradually, stirring until well-blended. Let stand 2 hours. Beat well before baking. Heat griddle to 400° (or pancake griddle until hot). Grease with salad oil. Pour on batter and tip griddle until batter covers it thinly. Let bake until brown on one side. Turn and bake lightly. Cut in 3 sections and roll up each one. Keep warm in oven until ready to serve with hot maple syrup (butter melted in it).

Mrs. O. P. Corley

THIN BUTTER PANCAKES

2½ cups flour   3 teaspoons baking powder
4 eggs   3 tablespoons sugar
3 cups half and half   1 teaspoon salt
                      1 cup butter, melted

Mix all ingredients except butter, and beat well. Stir in butter. Pour on a hot greased griddle in small amounts to make thin pancakes. Brown lightly on both sides.

Mrs. Arthur S. Baron

WAFFLES

2 cups flour   1 teaspoon salt
3 teaspoons baking powder   2 cups buttermilk
1 teaspoon soda   4 eggs, well-beaten
                      1 cup butter, melted

Sift dry ingredients together. Combine buttermilk and eggs. Add dry ingredients. Beat with hand or electric beater. Stir in butter.

Mrs. Alvin M. Owsley

DESSERTS

ANGELFOOD DELIGHT

1 medium-sized angel-
food cake

½ cup Kahlua liqueur

¾ cup heavy cream, whipped

5 small almond Hershey bars,
crushed

Make 24 small holes in cake. Fill holes with Kahlua and pour remainder over cake. Whip cream. Place Hershey bars in refrigerator so that the candy is as brittle as possible. Add crushed Hershey bars to whipped cream, and ice cake with cream mixture. Chill. Serves 10-12.

Mrs. William W. Lynch

APPLE PAN NUT CAKE

1 can apple pie filling

2 cups flour

1 cup sugar

1½ teaspoons soda

1 teaspoon salt

2 eggs, beaten

1 teaspoon vanilla

⅔ cup oil

½ cup pecans, chopped

Spread pie filling in bottom of a 9x13-inch pan. Combine flour, sugar, soda, salt, and sprinkle over pie filling. In a bowl, combine eggs, vanilla, oil and nuts; mix well. Pour over ingredients in pan; then stir until blended. Do not beat. Bake 45 minutes at 350°. Serves 12.

Mrs. Charles H. Chapman

FRESH APPLE CAKE

2 cups unsifted all-purpose
flour

2 cups granulated sugar

2 teaspoons baking soda

1 teaspoon cinnamon

½ teaspoon nutmeg

½ teaspoon salt

4 cups tart apples, pared and
finely diced

½ cup walnuts, chopped

½ cup soft butter

2 eggs

Confectioners' sugar

Preheat oven to 325° and grease a 13x9x2-inch baking pan. Into large bowl, sift flour with granulated sugar, soda, cinnamon, nutmeg and salt. Add apples, nuts, butter and eggs. Beat until just combined. Turn into prepared pan, and bake 50 minutes, or until top springs back when lightly touched. Cool slightly in pan on wire rack. Sprinkle with confectioners' sugar. Serve warm, cut into squares. Top with whipped cream or ice cream. Serves 10-12.

Mrs. James D. Carpenter

CAKE SQUARES

1 box brown sugar	Dash of nutmeg (optional)
1½ cups flour	4 eggs, beaten
1 teaspoon cinnamon	1 tablespoon vanilla

2 cups pecans, chopped

Mix brown sugar, flour, cinnamon and nutmeg, and add to eggs. Mix thoroughly, and add vanilla and pecans. Place in oblong cake pan in a 325°-350° oven and bake for 45 minutes. Cool, then cut into squares. The squares may be rolled in powdered sugar. Decorate with half a maraschino cherry on each square.

Mrs. Abe Bernard Gertz

You might be surprised to know that cheesecake was a very special treat even in the days of Socrates. Cheesecake was given as a prize in Pan-Hellenic contests, and used as an offering to the deities . . . as well as a wife's gift to capture her husband's heart.

CHEESECAKE

CRUMB CRUST

18 graham crackers, crushed   2 tablespoons sugar

6 tablespoons butter, melted

Mix together, and line spring mold.

FILLING

3 packages (8 oz.) cream cheese	4 eggs
1 cup sugar	2 teaspoons vanilla

Cream cheese in mixer to fluffy consistency. Add sugar slowly. Add eggs one at a time. Add vanilla, and beat thoroughly. (Total mixing time should be approximately 25 minutes.) Pour filling into crumb-lined pan. Bake at 350° for 35 minutes. Remove from oven and add topping.

TOPPING

1 pint heavy sour cream   2 teaspoons sugar

1 teaspoon vanilla

Mix well, and spread on top of cheese cake. Bake at 450° for 7 minutes. Serves 8-10.

Mrs. Morton H. Meyerson

BLUEBERRY DESSERT

1 large graham cracker crust

1 package (8 oz.) cream cheese

½ cup sugar

Pinch of salt

2 eggs, well-beaten

1 can Comstock blueberry pie filling

1 tablespoon lemon juice

1 tablespoon lemon rind

Whipped cream

Combine cream cheese, sugar, salt and eggs; mix well. Pour over crust, and bake 15 minutes at 375°. Cool thoroughly. To the blueberry filling add lemon juice and rind. Spread over the cream cheese mixture. Refrigerate overnight. Cut in squares and serve with cream. Serves 16.

Mrs. Wilbur Hawkins

PASKHA
Russian Easter Cheesecake

1½ pounds farmer cheese

1 cup butter, softened

6 egg yolks

2 cups plus 2 tablespoons confectioners' sugar, sifted

1 teaspoon vanilla

Grated rind of 2 lemons

½ cup glazed fruits, finely chopped (preferably pineapple and cherries)

⅓ cup slivered blanched almonds

1 new flowerpot

Force cheese through food mill or meat grinder. Stir in butter. Beat together egg yolks, confectioners' sugar, vanilla and lemon rind until mixture is light and fluffy. Combine with cheese mixture, glazed fruits and almonds. Neatly line a flowerpot (5 inches high by 5 inches in diameter, with 3 drainage holes in the bottom) with wet cheesecloth. Tightly pack in the cheese mixture. Cover mixture with overlapped ends of cloth. Place on rack on drainboard. Set a heavy weight on cheese mixture for about 1 hour. Excess moisture will drain from the holes in bottom of flowerpot. Place on a plate with heavy weight still on top. Refrigerate for at least 12 hours. Unmold. Garnish with cherries and almonds, if desired. Serves 8.

Gary Graffman

CHERRY BAKE

1 can (1 lb.) red pitted
   cherries, drained

½ cup sugar

1 teaspoon vanilla

1 teaspoon red food coloring

1 small package white or
   yellow cake mix

½ cup butter

¼ cup nuts, chopped

Mix cherries, sugar, vanilla and coloring well to dissolve sugar. Place in 9x9-inch cake pan. Sprinkle dry cake mix over top. Slice butter and spread over cake mix. Add nuts. Bake at 300° for 1 hour. Serves 8.

Mrs. Ellis M. Skinner, II

CHOCOLATE CAKE

½ cup margarine

4 tablespoons cocoa

½ cup shortening

1 cup water

2 cups sugar

2 cups flour

1 teaspoon soda

2 eggs, beaten

½ cup buttermilk

1 teaspoon vanilla

Put margarine, cocoa, shortening and water in saucepan. Bring to a boil; add sugar and flour, and mix well. Add soda, eggs, buttermilk and vanilla. Mix well. Pour into greased sheath cake pan, and bake at 350° for 20-25 minutes. Prepare icing while cake is baking. Pour hot icing over hot cake. Serves 10-12.

ICING

½ cup margarine

4 tablespoons cocoa

⅓ cup sweet milk

1 teaspoon vanilla

1 box confectioners' sugar,
   sifted

1 cup nuts, finely chopped

1 cup marshmallows (optional)

Put margarine, cocoa and milk in saucepan. Bring to a boil, stirring constantly. Remove from heat immediately. Add vanilla, confectioners' sugar and nuts. Stir all ingredients together, and spread over hot cake.

Mrs. David C. Conner

HERSHEY CAKE

4 (5¢) Hershey bars
1 cup butter
2 cups sugar
4 eggs
1 cup buttermilk

2½ cups flour
¼ teaspoon soda
1 can (5½ oz.) Hershey syrup
2 teaspoons vanilla
½ cup pecans

⅛ teaspoon salt

Melt Hershey bars over very low heat. Cream butter and sugar. Add eggs, 1 at a time, and beat after each addition. Add Hershey bars. Add buttermilk, mixed with soda, and dry ingredients alternately, then add syrup; stir in vanilla and beat well. Stir in pecans, and pour into greased and floured tube or bundt pan. Bake at 325° for 1¾ hours. Serves 15-20.

Jan Tyler

MARSHMALLOW CAKE

½ cup butter, melted
1 cup sugar
2 eggs, beaten
¾ cup flour

Pinch of salt
2 tablespoons cocoa
1 teaspoon vanilla
1 cup nuts

1 cup miniature marshmallows

Pour butter over sugar; stir, and add eggs. Mix flour, salt, cocoa, and combine with egg mixture. Stir in vanilla and nuts. Bake at 350° for 30 minutes in 6x8-inch pan. Remove from oven, and cover top of cake with marshmallows. Return to oven about 1 minute to allow marshmallows to melt. Remove from oven, and frost while still warm.

FROSTING

2 tablespoons butter
6 tablespoons Pet milk

2 cups confectioners' sugar
¼ cup cocoa

Heat butter and milk to boiling point. Remove from heat, and pour over the sugar and cocoa which have been sifted together. Mix well. Frost cake, and serve in squares with ice cream. Serves 8-12.

Mrs. John L. Smith

SOUR CREAM CHOCOLATE CAKE

4 ounces bitter chocolate
1 cup hot water
2 eggs
2 cups sugar

1 cup sour cream
2 cups sifted flour
1 teaspoon soda
1/8 teaspoon salt

2 teaspoons vanilla extract

Melt chocolate with hot water over low heat. Cream eggs and sugar thoroughly. Add sour cream, and mix. Add flour, soda and salt. Combine chocolate mixture with egg mixture. Add vanilla. Pour into two 8-inch, greased and floured cake pans. Place in cold oven. Set oven at 300°, and bake for 30-35 minutes; or cake may be baked 50-60 minutes in 9x13-inch pan. Cool and ice.

ICING

2 cups sugar
1/4 cup cocoa
1/2 cup margarine

1 tablespoon white Karo syrup
1/2 cup milk
1 cup pecans, chopped

1 teaspoon vanilla

Mix sugar and cocoa in saucepan. Add margarine, Karo and milk. Bring to boil. Boil two minutes. Cool five minutes. Beat until thick enough to spread. Add pecans and vanilla. Spread between layers and on top of cake. Serves 8-10.

Mrs. Richard Wray, Jr.

DATE CAKE

1 cup dates, finely cut
1 cup hot water
1 cup sugar
1 heaping tablespoon butter
1 egg, beaten

1 teaspoon vanilla
1 teaspoon soda
1/4 cup hot water
1 1/2 cups flour
1 cup nuts, chopped

Sweetened whipped cream

Cook dates and water together for 5 minutes. Let cool. Cream sugar and butter. Add egg and vanilla. Dissolve soda in hot water. Add to creamed mixture along with cooled dates. Blend flour into mixture. Add nuts. Pour into a 9x9-inch pan and bake at 375° for 35-40 minutes. Serve with cream. Serves 8-10.

Mrs. Eugene B. Mohr

FRUIT CAKE

½ pound candied cherries
½ pound candied pineapple
1 pound pitted dates
1 pound pecans
1 cup flour

1 teaspoon baking powder
½ teaspoon salt
4 eggs
1 cup sugar
1 teaspoon vanilla

Cut up all fruits and nuts. Sift flour, baking powder and salt over the fruit. Stir well until fruit is coated with flour mixture. Slightly beat together eggs, sugar and vanilla. Add to fruit mixture, and stir well. Put in angelfood cake pan lined with greased wax paper. Bake at 225° for about 2 hours. Put pan of water at bottom of oven while cake bakes. Serves 30-40.

Mrs. Peter N. Manos

JAPANESE FRUIT CAKE

4 eggs
1 cup butter or ¾ cup
   shortening
2 cups sugar
2 teaspoons vanilla
3 cups flour
3 teaspoons baking powder

1 teaspoon salt
1 cup sweet milk
1 cup pecans, chopped
1 teaspoon almond flavoring
1 cup raisins, chopped
1 teaspoon cinnamon
1 teaspoon allspice

1 teaspoon cloves

Beat eggs together one at a time. Add butter, sugar and 1 teaspoon vanilla; cream. Sift together flour, baking powder and salt. Add flour and milk alternately to the creamed mixture. Divide batter into 2 equal parts. Add pecans and almond flavoring to one part of cake batter. Pour into 2 9-inch square cake pans. Add raisins, cinnamon, allspice, cloves and remaining vanilla to the second part of the cake batter. Pour into 2 9-inch square cake pans. Bake at 350° for 30-40 minutes.

FILLING

2 cups sugar
1 cup hot water or part
   coconut juice

2 lemons, chopped
2 heaping tablespoons
   cornstarch

1 fresh coconut, grated

Put sugar, water and lemons in saucepan; when it begins to boil, add cornstarch. Cook until thick. Add coconut. Stir for a few minutes. Cool. Put filling between alternate layers of cake. Cover whole cake with a thin powdered sugar icing. Let stand for a few days before serving so that moisture of filling penetrates cake. This cake will keep in a cool place for 3 weeks. Serves 16-32.

Mrs. W. Harvey Sloan

KARETHOPETA

12 eggs, separated
12 tablespoons sugar
14 tablespoons Zwieback, finely ground
2 ounces whiskey

12 tablespoons pecans, coarsely chopped
3/8 teaspoon cinnamon
1/8 teaspoon cloves

Beat egg yolks with sugar until light and fluffy in electric mixer. Combine 12 tablespoons Zwieback, nuts, cinnamon and cloves; and add to creamed mixture. Mix well. Add whiskey; mix well. Beat egg whites until stiff. Fold egg whites into other ingredients in a large bowl. Butter an 11x16-inch pan and sprinkle 2 tablespoons Zwieback crumbs over bottom of pan, removing excess. Pour batter into pan, and place in a pre-heated 350° oven for 35-40 minutes or until lightly browned. Cool.

SYRUP

2 cups sugar
1½ cups water

1 orange slice (optional)
Maraschino cherry halves

Boil sugar, water and orange slice together for 10 minutes for a light syrup. Pour syrup across top of cake, and leave overnight. Cut into diamond-shaped pieces, and place cherry halves on top of each piece. Makes 30-40 pieces.

Mrs. Nick Zarafonetis

It is hard to believe that the English tea hour has not been an eternal custom, but its popularity is relatively recent. During the 18th century when the tea gardens were coming into vogue, some critics said this oriental brew caused nervous disorders and others said it was most "unwholesome and wickedly extravagant". In small towns tea was so unknown the leaves were cooked and the liquid thrown away.

LIGHTENING TEA CAKES

1/3 cup butter, melted
2 eggs
Sweet milk
1 cup flour

1 cup sugar
1 teaspoon baking powder
1/2 teaspoon vanilla
1/2 teaspoon lemon juice

Place cooled butter and eggs in a cup, and fill with sweet milk. Mix. Sift together flour, sugar and baking powder. Add milk mixture, vanilla and lemon juice. Mix, and bake at 350° in well-greased small muffin tins until done. If desired, nuts may be added when batter is mixed, but dredge nuts well with flour. Makes 48 small cakes.

Mrs. Peter N. Wiggins, Jr.

NORWEGIAN DELIGHT

1 cup sifted cake flour

¼ teaspoon salt

5 eggs, separated

Rind of 1 lemon, grated

1½ tablespoons lemon juice

1 cup sugar

Sift flour and salt together 4 times. Beat egg yolks, lemon rind and juice until thick. Beat egg whites until stiff, but not dry, and fold in sugar in small amounts. Fold in egg yolk mixture. Sift about ¼ cup of flour at a time over the surface, and fold in. Bake in ungreased tube pan at 350° for 1 hour.

FILLINGS AND FROSTING

2 teaspoons gelatin

2 tablespoons pineapple juice

1 cup crushed pineapple, crushed

Few drops of green coloring

4 cups confectioners' sugar

2⅓ cups heavy cream, whipped

1 can apricots, drained, reserving 1 tablespoon juice and 8 apricots

1 teaspoon sugar

Dissolve 1 teaspoon gelatin in pineapple juice over hot water. Add to pineapple and food coloring. Chill; then add 4 table-spoons cream. Set aside. Mash apricots to pulp after removing skin. Dissolve 1 teaspoon gelatin in apricot juice over hot water. Add to mashed apricots and sugar. Chill; then mix with 2 tablespoons cream. Set aside. Combine confectioners' sugar and remaining cream. Cut cooled cake into 4 layers, each about 1 inch thick. On first layer, spread half of pineapple mixture. On second layer, spread apricot mixture. On third layer, spread remaining pineapple mixture. Place fourth layer on top. Frost entire cake with whipped cream and sugar mixture. Garnish with apricot halves. Serves 12.

Mrs. Robert L. Johnson

SAUSAGE CAKE

1 pound unseasoned sausage

1 cup hot coffee

1 teaspoon baking soda

3 cups brown sugar, packed

3 cups sifted flour

1 cup raisins

1 teaspoon allspice

1 teaspoon cinnamon

1 teaspoon cloves

1 teaspoon nutmeg

1 cup nuts, coarsely chopped

Combine sausage, coffee and soda. Cream with brown sugar. Sift flour into spices, and add to sausage mixture. Mix thorough-ly. Add nuts and raisins. Bake in 350° oven for 45 minutes or until done in 2 8-inch square cake pans, greased and lightly floured. Serves 8-12.

Mrs. James E. Upfield

NUTTY CAKE

1½ cups butter
2 cups sugar
12 egg yolks
Grated rind and juice of
    2 oranges
1 pound chopped pecans
6 ounces Zwieback, crushed

½ teaspoon cinnamon
½ teaspoon nutmeg
½ teaspoon cloves
Pinch of salt
2 teaspoons baking powder
12 egg whites
Whipped cream

Cream butter with sugar. Add egg yolks, 2 at a time, creaming well. Add orange rind and juice and pecans. Blend Zwieback with spices and salt. Combine dry ingredients with creamed mixture, and add baking powder. Beat egg whites until they form peaks, and fold into mixture. Pour into buttered 18x12x2-inch pan, and bake approximately 40 minutes in 350° oven, or until toothpick inserted near middle comes out dry. Twenty minutes after cake is removed from oven, top with warm syrup and serve warm, or chill and serve topped with whipped cream.

SYRUP

2 cups sugar
1 cup water

1 tablespoon lemon juice
1 tablespoon apricot liqueur

Combine sugar, water and lemon juice, and bring to a boil until sugar dissolves and mixture thickens slightly. Remove from heat, and add liqueur. Pour over warm cake. Makes 35 squares.

Mrs. John D. Murchison

ORANGE SLICE CAKE

3½ cups flour
½ teaspoon salt
1 pound candied orange
    slices, diced
1 package (8 oz.) dates,
    chopped
2 cups pecans, chopped

1 teaspoon soda
½ cup buttermilk
1 cup butter
2 cups sugar
4 eggs, well-beaten
1 cup orange juice
2 cups powdered sugar

Thoroughly mix flour and salt together; reserve half. Sprinkle other half over orange slices, dates and nuts. Thoroughly combine soda and buttermilk. Cream butter and sugar; add eggs. Add reserved flour and buttermilk mixture alternately. Fold in orange slices, dates and pecans. Bake in a large tube pan at 300° for 1¾ hours. Mix orange juice and powdered sugar together, and pour over hot cake while still in pan. Let set until perfectly cold. Serves 12.

Mrs. Ben Barnes

PINEAPPLE CAKE

1½ cups sugar
2 cups sifted flour
½ teaspoon salt

2 teaspoons soda
½ cup oil
2 eggs

1 can (20 oz.) crushed pineapple

Mix all ingredients in bowl. Bake in greased 9x13-inch pan in 350° oven for 35 minutes.

ICING

½ cup evaporated milk
½ cup margarine
1 cup sugar

½ cup brown sugar
1 teaspoon vanilla
1 cup nuts

Combine ingredients, and cook about 4 minutes, or until sugar is dissolved. Add vanilla and nuts. Pour over warm cake. Cool and cut into squares. Serves 12-15.

Mrs. Roland Cazes

PRUNE CAKE

1 cup oil
2 heaping cups sugar
2 teaspoons cinnamon
2 teaspoons allspice
2 teaspoons nutmeg
2 teaspoons cloves
¾ teaspoon salt

3½ teaspoons vanilla
3 eggs
1 cup buttermilk
2 cups sifted flour
1 teaspoon soda
1 cup prunes, cooked, sweetened and drained

1¼ cups pecans, chopped

Combine oil, sugar, spices, salt and vanilla in large bowl of electric mixer. After mixing well, alternately add eggs, buttermilk and flour sifted with soda. Beat 2½ minutes at medium speed. Mash prunes with fork or potato masher. Add prunes and pecans to batter. Bake in a greased tube or bundt pan at 350° for 1 hour, or in 2 greased loaf pans at 350° for 50 minutes. This is a moist cake and will keep a long time if kept cool. Serves 20. *This cake is a family favorite and a delightful way to say "Happy Holidays" to dear friends.*

Mrs. William P. Crisler

PUMPKIN CAKE

½ cup shortening	½ teaspoon cinnamon
1¼ cups sugar	½ teaspoon ginger
2 eggs, beaten	½ teaspoon nutmeg
2¼ cups flour	1 cup cooked pumpkin
3 teaspoons baking powder	¾ cup milk
½ teaspoon salt	½ teaspoon soda

½ cup nuts, chopped (optional)

Cream shortening; add sugar; cream together. Blend in eggs. Sift together flour, baking powder, salt and spices. Mix pumpkin and milk. Stir in soda. Add the flour mixture and the pumpkin-milk mixture alternately to the creamed mixture. Blend in the nuts. Pour into tube or layer pans. Bake at 350° in layer pans for 35 minutes or in tube pan for 55 minutes.

Mrs. John R. Watson

RUM M M M CAKE

1 cup black walnuts	½ cup oil
1 box Duncan Hines yellow cake mix	½ cup rum (dark or light)
1 large box instant vanilla pudding	4 eggs

Grease and flour tube pan. Line bottom of pan with nuts. Mix cake mix and pudding. Add oil, rum and then eggs, one at a time. Beat well. Bake at 325° for 45-60 minutes.

SAUCE

½ cup butter	¼ cup water
1 cup sugar	¼ cup rum

Bring butter, sugar and water to a boil. Cool. Add rum. Poke holes in cake, and pour over. Serves 12.

Mrs. Paul G. Herrington

SOUR CREAM POUND CAKE

1 cup butter	1/4 teaspoon soda
3 cups sugar	3/4 cup sour cream
6 eggs	1/2 teaspoon vanilla
3 heaping cups flour	1/2 cup sweet milk

Have all ingredients at room temperature. Cream butter and sugar. Add eggs, 1 at a time, beating well after each addition. Sift flour with soda. Add 2 cups flour alternately with sour cream. Add vanilla with last cup of flour and milk. Pour into 3 loaf pans or 1 steeple cake pan. Bake at 325° for 1 hour for loaf cakes or 1 hour and 20 minutes for a steeple pan.

Mrs. Ben Barnes

WHITE CAKE

1 cup butter	1 cup milk
8 egg whites or 4 whole eggs	3 cups flour
2 cups sugar	3 teaspoons baking powder
Pinch of salt	1 teaspoon vanilla or lemon extract

Have ingredients at room temperature. Cream butter and sugar, adding sugar gradually. Put eggs in 1 at a time, if using whole eggs. If whites are used, beat separately, adding salt. Beat stiffly, and set aside. Sift flour 6 times, and measure after sifting. Mix flour and milk alternately into the creamed mixture, adding some flour last. If egg whites are used, fold in last. Oil and flour 2 8-inch cake pans. Bake at 350° for 45-60 minutes, or pour into loaf pans and bake at 325°.

ICING

3 egg whites	3/4 cup sugar
3/4 cup light corn syrup	1 1/2 tablespoons water

Coconut, freshly grated (optional)

Combine egg whites, syrup, sugar and water in top of double boiler. Cook over rapidly boiling water, while beating. When icing will stand in peaks, remove from fire. After icing cake, sprinkle with coconut.

Mrs. Trammell Crow

COCONUT WHITE CAKE

⅔ cup Crisco

1⅔ cups sugar

1¼ cups milk

3 eggs

2½ cups flour

3½ teaspoons baking powder

½ teaspoon salt

½ teaspoon vanilla

1½ teaspoons butter flavoring

Cream shortening and sugar. Add ¾ cup milk and one egg at a time, beating well. Add dry ingredients, flavoring and remainder of milk. Makes 2 9-inch layers. Bake at 350° for 25-35 minutes.

ICING

1¼ cups sugar

6½ tablespoons Karo syrup

⅔ cup water

3 egg whites, slightly beaten

1 can coconut

Put sugar, syrup and water in pan on high heat. Let boil until mixture forms drops. Do not let thread. Pour hot mixture over egg whites, continuing to beat until stiff peaks are formed. Put icing in center of bottom layer and spread to edge, add coconut. Add top layer; frost with icing, then coconut.

Mrs. Jim G. Bray

CARAMEL ICING

3 cups sugar

1 cup sweet milk

1 tablespoon butter

Combine 2 cups sugar with milk in large saucepan, and place over low heat, and bring to a boil. In the meantime, caramelize 1 cup sugar in skillet over medium heat until straw-colored. Add caramelized sugar to milk and sugar mixture, stirring constantly. Cook until a soft ball forms in cold water. Add butter. Remove from heat, and beat until thick.

Mrs. Robert L. Dillard, Jr.

CRÊPES SUZETTE

¼ cup butter	12 crêpes
¼ cup sugar	5 teaspoons Cointreau
Peel of 3 oranges	5 teaspoons Grand Marnier
Peel of 1 lemon	4 tablespoons brandy

Melt butter and sugar in shallow chafing dish, and mix well. Add orange and lemon peel, and simmer for approximately 15 minutes or until peel is very soft. This may be done in advance. At serving time, place chafing dish over flame, re-heat sauce and then remove peel. Place 3 crêpes in chafing dish. Allow them to absorb some of the sauce, then fold each crêpe in half twice. Repeat until all crêpes are used. Pour Cointreau, Grand Marnier and brandy evenly over crêpes. Tilt pan slightly, and move back and forth over flame until the liquor ignites. Continue moving pan until flame dies. Serve 3 crêpes per person, and pour remaining sauce over each serving. Serves 4.

Mrs. Joseph D. Zimmerman

According to history, a reknown French chef, Henri Charpentier, was busily concocting crêpes with liqueur for Edward VII. The elegant dish was accidently caught up in flames. Chef Henri proceeded to carry the flaming dish to the table to serve the king and his guests. The king simply raved over the taste, and when asked about the name of the dish, the chef replied, "They have just been invented, sir, and they shall be called Crêpes Princesse". The King replied, "Where is your gallantry, Henri?" Then he announced to his guests, "They shall be called Crêpes Suzette, in Mademoiselle's honor". Suzette was the young daughter of his host.

ALMOND TOFFEE

¾ pound blanched almonds   1 cup sugar
1 cup butter   4 packages German sweet
       chocolate

Toast almonds to light tan and thoroughly crisp. Coarsely grind ⅓ of the almonds. The other two-thirds should be split the long way, and set aside to go into the candy. Melt butter; add sugar, and cook to 250° on a candy thermometer. Cook over medium heat, stirring constantly. When the thermometer shows 250°, add the split almonds, and continue cooking to 290°. Pour on marble slab or greased flat platter. While still hot, cut into 1-inch squares. Make chocolate coating by melting chocolate in top of double boiler. Keep the water hot under the chocolate. When squares are cold, dip in chocolate coating. Immediately cover with ground almonds. Put on waxed paper, and allow to dry overnight.

Mrs. Samuel A. Shelburne

APRICOT-NUT ROLLS

1 pound dried apricots   Grated rind of 1 orange
2 cups sugar   1 cup nuts, chopped
Juice of 2 oranges   Powdered sugar

Run apricots through meat grinder. Combine with sugar, juice, rind; mix thoroughly. Cook 10 minutes, stirring constantly. Add nuts. Cool. Form into bite-sized balls, and roll in powdered sugar on wax paper. Store in tight tin.

Mrs. DeWitt Ray

CARAMELS

1¾ cups dark Karo syrup   2 cups whipping cream
2 cups sugar   1 cup butter
1 teaspoon vanilla

Put syrup, sugar, 1 cup cream and butter in large saucepan. Cook over medium heat, stirring constantly, until boiling well. Gradually stir in remaining cream. Cook to 245° on a candy thermometer or until it forms a ball in cold water. Add vanilla. Pour into buttered tins or 13x9-inch pan. Cut into squares when cold, and wrap in waxed paper.

Mrs. Samuel A. Shelburne

BLACK WALNUT CARAMELS

2½ cups sugar

½ teaspoon cream of tartar

¾ cup white corn syrup

1½ cups cream

4 tablespoons butter

1 cup walnuts

½ teaspoon vanilla

Mix 1 cup sugar with cream of tartar, and melt over slow fire, stirring constantly. When melted, add remainder of sugar, corn syrup and 1 cup cream. Lumps will cook out. Stir constantly over low fire; bring to a boil and boil 5 minutes. Add butter and remainder of cream, and cook slowly until hard ball stage. Remove from fire, and let cool a few minutes before adding nuts and vanilla. Turn into well-buttered pan, and let stand until firm. Cut into squares before candy becomes solid.

Mrs. R. J. Byrd

CHOCOLATE COVERED CANDY BALLS

½ cup butter, melted

2 boxes powdered sugar

1 can (15 oz.) Eagle Brand milk

2½ cups nuts, chopped in large pieces

1 teaspoon vanilla

⅛ pound paraffin

½-¾ pound semi-sweet chocolate

Mix butter, sugar, milk, nuts and vanilla together, and drop in balls on waxed paper. Set 3-4 hours or overnight. Melt paraffin in double boiler, and add semi-sweet chocolate. Mix well until completely dissolved and melted. Place toothpick in candy ball and dip into mixture, coating well. They may also be served without chocolate coating. Place on wax paper to set. Makes 5 dozen. *These are excellent to prepare in advance and freeze for holiday gifts.*

Mrs. Cloyd D. Young

DATE BALLS

2 cups sugar

1 cup milk

1 package dates, chopped

1 tablespoon butter

1 cup nuts

1 teaspoon vanilla

Confectioners' sugar

Combine sugar, milk and dates. Put in large saucepan, and bring mixture to soft ball stage (238°). Remove from heat, and add butter, nuts and vanilla. Form into small balls, and roll in confectioners' sugar. Makes 3 dozen.

Mrs. Alfred A. Holmberg

ANGELS DIVINITY À LA MAE

2½ cups sugar
½ cup light corn syrup
½ cup water
2 egg whites
¼ teaspoon salt

2 teaspoons vanilla
1 cup walnuts, coarsely chopped
12 candied cherries, halved (optional)

In saucepan combine sugar and corn syrup with water. Cook over low heat, stirring until sugar is dissolved. Cover and cook 1 minute or until crystals on side of pan melt. Uncover and cook to 238°, without stirring, or until a small amount forms a soft ball in cold water. Beat egg whites with salt until stiff. Beating constantly at top speed, pour ½ of hot syrup slowly over egg whites. Cook remainder of syrup to 256° or until it forms a hard ball when dropped in cold water. Pour hot syrup into meringue mixture, beating constantly with wooden spoon. Beat in walnuts and vanilla. Beat until mixture is stiff. Pour into a lightly greased 11x7x1¼-inch baking pan. Let stand until firm. Cut in pieces, and top with cherry halves. Makes 24 pieces.

Mrs. Lewis P. MacAdams

NEVER-FAIL FUDGE

2 cups sugar
3 heaping tablespoons cocoa
⅔ cup milk

1 package walnuts or pecans, chopped
2 tablespoons butter
1 teaspoon vanilla

In a large heavy saucepan blend sugar and cocoa. Add milk, and stir until smooth. Cook over medium heat, and do not stir after candy begins to boil. Cook candy until it forms a soft ball. Remove from stove, and add nuts, butter and vanilla. Cool until bottom of pan is cool to the touch. Beat until candy is not glossy. Pour into a greased 8x4-inch pan. Serves 4-5.

Mrs. Zelman Brounoff

SUPER SMOOTH HOLIDAY FUDGE

1 package (12 oz.) semi-sweet chocolate chips
⅔ can (10 oz.) sweetened condensed milk

¼ teaspoon vanilla
1 tablespoon cold water
½ cup nuts (optional)

Melt chocolate in a double boiler. After chocolate is smooth, remove from stove, and mix in milk, vanilla and water. Add nuts. Stir slowly, never beat. Pour into lightly greased 8-inch square pan. Place in refrigerator to cool. Do not freeze. Makes 2 pounds.

Howard M. Jarratt

SUGAR HONEY PECANS

1 cup sugar
1/4 teaspoon salt
1/4 cup honey

1/2 cup water
1/2 teaspoon vanilla
3 cups pecan halves

Combine sugar, salt, honey and water in medium saucepan. Cook over medium heat, stirring constantly, until sugar is dissolved. Continue cooking, without stirring, to 240° on candy thermometer or until mixture forms a ball. Remove from heat. Add vanilla and pecans. Stir gently until mixture becomes creamy. Put on wax paper. Separate with fork. Makes 24.

Mrs. Alfred A. Holmberg

PENUCHE

1 cup brown sugar
1 cup white sugar
1 cup milk
1 tablespoon white Karo syrup
Pecan halves

3 tablespoons butter
1/8 teaspoon salt
1/2 cup pecans, broken
Few drops of vanilla

Put brown sugar, white sugar, milk, syrup, butter and salt in deep heavy pan, and stir before cooking. Cook over medium heat, and stir occasionally. When it forms a soft ball (238°), remove pan from stove, and place in cold water for a few moments. Beat vigorously until it begins to thicken. Then add pecans and vanilla. Using 2 greased teaspoons, push candy off 1 spoon with the other spoon onto aluminum foil. Place a pecan half on top of each patty, if desired. Candy may be poured into a large pie plate. Cool slightly before cutting into squares. Do not make on a rainy day.

Mrs. Henry H. Patterson

PRALINES

2 cups sugar
1 tablespoon water
2 cups pecans
3/4 cup Pet milk
1 teaspoon vanilla

2 tablespoons white Karo corn syrup
Pinch of salt
1/2 teaspoon baking soda

Combine all ingredients except vanilla in heavy saucepan; stir until mixed. Heat over medium-high heat until mixture comes to a boil, then cook over medium heat, stirring continually, until candy forms a firm ball in cold water. Remove from heat, pour into glass or stainless steel bowls. Add vanilla, beat by hand until candy is creamy. Drop on wax paper from tablespoon. Store in a tin or cookie jar. *This recipe comes from New Orleans, yet it is different from most pralines.*

Mrs. Warner H. Lewis

BUTTERMILK PECAN PRALINES

1 teaspoon soda	Pinch of salt
1 cup buttermilk	2 tablespoons white corn syrup
3 cups sugar	1 teaspoon vanilla
1 cup butter	1½ cups pecan halves

Add soda to buttermilk. Mix sugar, buttermilk mixture, butter, salt and syrup. Cook until it forms a rather hard ball when dropped into water. Add vanilla and then the pecans, and stir a short time. Cool rapidly. Spoon pralines on waxed paper. Makes 22-48 pralines.

Mrs. William Plack Carr

BROWNIES

1 cup butter or part shortening and part butter	2 cups sugar
	1 cup sifted flour
2 ounces unsweetened baking chocolate	4 eggs
	2 teaspoons vanilla
2 ounces semi-sweet baking chocolate	1 cup pecans, chopped

Melt butter and chocolate in double boiler. Add sugar and then eggs, beaten in 1 at a time. Add flour; then add vanilla and pecans. Bake in a greased 8x12-inch pan at 350° for 40 minutes. While brownies are still warm, ice with a chocolate-powdered sugar icing. Brownies may also be iced with a can of Swel chocolate icing, substituting hot coffee for water and adding 1 tablespoon butter.

Mrs. Herman H. Stewart

BLONDE BROWNIES

1 box (16 oz.) brown sugar	1½ cups flour
4 eggs	1½ teaspoons baking powder
1 teaspoon vanilla	1½ cups nuts, chopped (pecans or walnuts)

Place sugar in top of double boiler. Add eggs, one at a time, stirring after each addition. Add vanilla. Cook until thick. Remove from heat. Stir in flour and baking powder which have been sifted together. Add nuts. Lightly grease 13x9x2-inch pan, and pour in the batter. Bake at 325° for 25 minutes. Do not overbake. Cut into squares while warm. Dust with powdered sugar. They are even more delicious if frozen, as they become chewy. Makes 48 squares.

Mrs. Joseph Somer

CHOCOLATE CHIP BROWNIES

1 cup sifted flour

½ teaspoon baking powder

⅛ teaspoon soda

½ teaspoon salt

½ cup nuts, chopped

⅓ cup butter, melted

1 cup brown sugar

1 egg, slightly beaten

1 teaspoon vanilla

½ package (8 oz.) chocolate chips

Sift flour once, measure; add baking powder, soda and salt; then sift again. Add nuts, and mix well. Combine butter and sugar, and mix well. Add egg and vanilla. Add flour mixture, a small amount at a time, mixing well after each addition. Turn into greased 9x9x2-inch pan. Sprinkle chocolate chips over top. Bake at 350° for 20-25 minutes. Cool and cut. Makes 1 dozen.

Mrs. John A. Henry, III

PEPPERMINT BROWNIES

2 squares unsweetened chocolate

½ cup margarine

2 eggs

1 cup sugar

¼ teaspoon peppermint extract

½ cup sifted flour

Dash of salt

½ cup nuts

Melt chocolate and margarine over hot water. Beat eggs until frothy. Beat in sugar, and add chocolate-margarine mixture and extract. Add flour, salt and nuts. Mix well. Pour into 10-inch greased and floured pan. Bake 20-25 minutes in 350° preheated oven. Cool well.

FROSTING

2 tablespoons margarine

2 cups sifted powdered sugar

3 tablespoons milk

½ teaspoon peppermint extract

Red food coloring

Combine all ingredients in mixer. Frost cooled brownies, and refrigerate.

GLAZE

1 tablespoon margarine

1 square unsweetened chocolate

Mix margarine and chocolate over hot water. Pour over frosted brownies. Do not use knife to spread. Roll and tilt pan until glaze covers frosting. Refrigerate, and serve cool. Makes 18 2-inch brownies.

Mr. Peppermint

BAKLAVA

1½ pounds filo (pastry sheets)

1½ pounds butter

1½ pounds pecans, chopped

1 teaspoon cinnamon

1 teaspoon cloves

Remove filo from refrigerator at least an hour before using. To remove salt from butter: melt butter over a slow heat, skim top, remove from heat, tilt pan and keep tilted until remaining salt has settled in bottom of pan. Pour clear butter into a bowl for spreading with pastry brush on filo sheets. Mix pecans and spices well. Butter the bottom and sides of a 15x10x2½-inch pan with melted butter. Place 10 sheets of filo, one at a time, brushing each second one evenly with butter. Sprinkle top sheet with thin layer of nut mixture. On top of this, place another pastry sheet with another layer of nuts, repeating this procedure until nut mixture is used and buttering each second sheet during this process. Then, one at a time, place 10 more sheets of pastry, buttering each one evenly and the last one very generously. Before baking, cut baklava into 1½-inch diamond-shaped pieces with a sharp knife. Bake in a 350° oven for 30 minutes. Lower to 300°, and continue baking another 30 minutes or until baklava is slightly browned. Cool.

SYRUP

5 cups sugar

4 cups water

2 cups honey

2 or 3 whole cloves

3 slices orange or lemon (including peel)

In a saucepan mix well all ingredients, and bring to a quick boil. Lower heat, skim, and simmer for 30 minutes. Pour slowly and evenly over baklava. Do not remove baklava from pan for 24 hours, or overnight, to enable the syrup to be absorbed. Before removing from pan, take sharp knife and cut through pieces again. Place wax paper on large cookie sheet, and let baklava pieces drain for several hours. Baklava can be frozen after baking. In case of emergency, it can be removed from freezer 2 hours before serving, but thawing overnight is preferable. Serves about 50. *Baklava is the finest and most famous of Grecian desserts.*

Mrs. Pepecha Booziotis

CHILDREN'S BUTTERSCOTCH BARS

2 cups graham cracker crumbs

1 can (15 oz.) sweetened condensed milk

1 package butterscotch bits

Combine ingredients, and spread in a 9-inch buttered pan. Bake at 350° for 20-25 minutes. Cut while still hot. Makes 25 bars. *These are quick and easy for the busy mother! Better yet, let the children do it.*

Mrs. Joseph B. Martin

DRIED FRUIT DREAM BARS

1 cup dried fruit, chopped (apricots, figs, prunes, raisins or peaches)

½ cup butter

¼ cup sugar

1⅓ cups flour

2 eggs

½ teaspoon vanilla

1 cup brown sugar, firmly packed

½ teaspoon baking powder

¼ teaspoon salt

½ cup nutmeats (optional)

Powdered sugar

Cut butter into sugar and 1 cup of the flour until mixture is crumbly. Press firmly into bottom of greased 8 or 9-inch square pan. Bake in a 350° oven for 20 minutes, until lightly browned. Beat eggs thoroughly with vanilla; gradually beat in brown sugar. Sift remaining ⅓ cup flour with baking powder and salt; add fruit and nuts, and mix. Stir flour mixture into egg mixture. Spread evenly over the baked layer. Bake at 350° for 30 minutes more. Cool on a rack. Cut into bars. Roll in powdered sugar. Makes 16-32 bars.

Mrs. David Grissom

HELLO DOLLY

½ cup butter

1 cup graham cracker crumbs

½ cup Angel Flake coconut

1 cup chocolate or butterscotch chips

1 cup pecans

1 can (15 oz.) Eagle Brand milk

Melt butter in 9x12-inch pan. Place crumbs, coconut, chips, pecans and milk, in order given, in the pan forming layers. Do not stir. Bake at 350° for 20-25 minutes. Cool before cutting. Makes 3 dozen.

Mrs. Bennett L. Smith

GREEK PAXIMADIA

1/2 cup butter	1 teaspoon soda
1/2 cup oil	3 teaspoons baking powder
3 eggs	2 teaspoons lemon extract
1 1/2 cups sugar	5 1/2 cups sifted flour

With electric mixer, beat butter and oil until well-blended. Add eggs one at a time. Beat until light and creamy. Add sugar. Stir in baking soda, baking powder and lemon extract. Remove from mixer. Gradually add flour, and knead until a soft dough is formed. Divide dough into 5 parts. Shape into long, narrow, flat loaves, about 2 1/2 inches wide and 1 inch thick. Place on a greased cookie sheet 2 inches apart to allow for baking, and cut diagonally about halfway in 1/2-inch slices. Bake loaves at 375° for about 20 minutes or until lightly browned. Remove from oven, and slice again through marks while warm. Cool slightly. Toast slices in oven on a cookie sheet, on both sides. Turn once, and leave in oven until light brown at 325°. Allow to cool before storing in covered container. Makes 80.

Mrs. Arthur L. Sarris

RITZY BARS

3 egg whites, stiffly beaten	1 teaspoon vanilla
1 cup sugar	20 Ritz crackers, finely rolled
1 cup pecans, chopped	

Add sugar and vanilla to egg whites. Fold in crackers and pecans. Pour into buttered, 8-inch square pan. Bake at 300° for 40 minutes. Remove from oven, and cut in squares immediately. Remove from pan, and put on waxed paper to cool. These keep well. Serves 10.

Mrs. A. W. Bourke

BROWN SUGAR COOKIES

1 cup shortening	2 1/2 cups flour
2 1/2 cups brown sugar	1/2 teaspoon soda
2 eggs, well-beaten	Pinch of salt
2 cups pecans, chopped	

Cream shortening and brown sugar well. Add eggs. Sift flour, soda and salt together. Add dry ingredients gradually to creamed mixture. Add pecans. Spoon onto greased cookie sheets. Bake at 375° for 12 minutes. Makes 5-6 dozen. *This is my grandmother's recipe and a favorite at Christmas time.*

Mrs. Manfred E. New

BUTTER STARS

2 cups butter
2 cups sugar

2 eggs, beaten
5 cups flour

2 tablespoons vanilla

Cream butter and sugar well. Add eggs, then flour and vanilla. Put in a star-shaped cookie press, and drop on an ungreased cookie sheet. Bake at 350° for 10-12 minutes or until golden brown. Makes 5 dozen.

Mrs. William M. Acker

FROSTED CASHEW COOKIES

1/2 cup butter
1 cup brown sugar, firmly
    packed
1 egg
1/2 teaspoon vanilla
2 cups sifted flour

3/4 teaspoon baking powder
3/4 teaspoon soda
1/4 teaspoon salt
1/3 cup dairy sour cream
1 3/4 cups salted whole
    cashew nuts

Cream butter and sugar until light and fluffy. Beat in egg and vanilla. Add sifted dry ingredients alternately with sour cream, mixing well. Carefully fold in cashew nuts. Drop by teaspoon onto greased cookie sheet. Bake at 350° for 12 minutes. Cool and frost.

FROSTING

1/2 cup butter
2 cups sifted confectioners'
    sugar

3 tablespoons coffee cream
1/4 teaspoon vanilla
Cashew nuts

Lightly brown butter, remove from heat; add sugar, cream and vanilla. Beat until smooth and thick enough to spread. Put cashew nut on top of each frosted cookie. Makes 3 dozen.

Lois Swan Jones

CHOCOLATE ALMOND BALLS

1/2 cup butter, softened
2 tablespoons brown sugar
2 tablespoons sugar
1 teaspoon vanilla
1 cup sifted flour

1/2 cup almonds, finely
    chopped and toasted
1/2 cup semi-sweet chocolate,
    finely chopped
Confectioners' sugar

Cream butter and sugars. Add vanilla and flour. Fold in almonds and chocolate. Chill in refrigerator for 20-30 minutes. Shape in 1-inch balls. Place on ungreased cookie sheet, and bake at 350° for 15 minutes. Roll in sifted confectioners' sugar, and cool on cake racks. Makes 3-4 dozen.

Arlene Hamley Tayloe

CORN FLAKE AND CHOCOLATE COOKIES

8 ounces Hershey chocolate
bar

1 square Baker's bitter
chocolate

1 tablespoon butter

3 cups corn flakes

Melt chocolate and butter in double boiler. Stir in corn flakes. Spoon out onto cookie sheet. Let cool or set slowly (not in refrigerator). Do not make in hot weather. Serves 6.

Mrs. Robert D. Stecker

CRY BABY COOKIES

¾ cup sugar

1 egg, beaten

½ cup butter or Crisco

2½ cups flour

1 teaspoon soda

¼ teaspoon salt

1 teaspoon cinnamon

1 teaspoon ginger

1 teaspoon nutmeg

½ teaspoon allspice

¼ cup molasses

½ cup milk or coffee

½ cup seedless raisins

½ cup nutmeats, chopped
(pecans or walnuts)

Cream together sugar, egg and butter. Sift flour, measure; then resift with soda, salt, cinnamon, ginger, nutmeg and allspice. Add to first mixture, alternately, with molasses and milk. Add raisins and nuts. Drop on greased cookie tin, and bake at 375° for 10-12 minutes. Makes 5 dozen.

Ralph B. Rogers

DATE COOKIES

1 pound dates, chopped

1 cup pecans, chopped

1 can Angel Flake coconut

¼ teaspoon salt

1 can (13 oz.) Eagle Brand sweetened condensed milk

Mix dates, pecans, coconut, salt and milk. Make into balls or shape with spoon, and place on slightly greased cookie sheet. Bake at 325° for 15-20 minutes. Remove from pan while hot.

Mrs. Harry L. Kaplan

FORGOTTEN COOKIES

2 egg whites

¾ cup sugar

1 teaspoon vanilla

Pinch of salt

1 package (6 oz.) chocolate bits

½ cup nuts

Beat egg whites until very stiff. Add sugar and continue beating. Spoon in vanilla, salt, nuts and chocolate bits. Drop by teaspoon on greased and floured cookie sheet. Put in 350° oven. Count slowly to 30 (30 seconds); then turn off oven. Leave in oven 6-8 hours or cool overnight. Makes 2 dozen.

Mrs. Charles E. Griffin

GRANDMOTHER'S SWEDISH GINGERSNAPS

1 cup butter

¾ cup sugar

¾ cup brown sugar

1 egg

1½ teaspoons soda

2 tablespoons boiling water

3¼ cups flour

1 teaspoon ginger

1 teaspoon cloves

1 teaspoon allspice

2 teaspoons cinnamon

1 tablespoon light Karo syrup

Cream butter and sugars until light and fluffy. Beat in egg. Add soda to water. Add all dry ingredients alternately with the soda-water and syrup. Roll out; cut into shapes. Bake on a cookie sheet at 375° for 12 minutes. Makes 4 dozen. *My great-grandmother actually brought this recipe from Sweden with her.*

Lois Swan Jones

KOURABIETHES

1 pound unsalted butter

1½ cups confectioners' sugar

2 egg yolks

2 pounds flour, approximately

½ teaspoon baking soda

3 tablespoons orange juice

Leave butter at room temperature until very soft. Place in electric mixer, and beat until light and creamy. Add ½ cup sugar, and beat for 5 minutes. Add egg yolks and orange juice, and beat until well-blended. Sift flour and baking soda gradually into butter mixture to make a soft dough that does not stick to fingers. Shape into small round balls, and press down in center. Place on buttered cookie sheet 1 inch apart, and bake at 375° for 20 minutes or until very lightly browned. Cool slightly; remove from baking sheet. Carefully place on flat surface which has been sprinkled with ½ cup sifted sugar. Sprinkle remaining sifted sugar over cookies. Allow cookies to cool completely, and place on serving dish. Makes 40-50.

Mrs. Steve Congas

MADELEINES

2 eggs

1 cup sugar

1 cup sifted all-purpose flour

¾ cup butter, melted and cooled

1 teaspoon lemon peel, grated

Confectioners' sugar

Preheat oven to 350°. Grease and lightly flour Madeleine pans. Place hot, not boiling, water in the bottom of double boiler. In top of double boiler, beat eggs and sugar with electric mixer or rotary beater just until lukewarm, about 2 minutes. Set double boiler top in cold water. Beat mixture at high speed 5 minutes or until very light and fluffy. With wire whisk, gently fold in flour until well-combined. Stir in butter and lemon peel. Pour into Madeleine pans, using about 1 teaspoon of batter for each form. Bake about 12 minutes at 325°-350°. Cool 1 minute; then remove from pans with small spatula. Cool completely. Lightly sprinkle with confectioners' sugar. Makes 3½ dozen.

Mrs. L. Rumsey Strickland

MAMA'S ORANGE COOKIES

2 cups sugar

1 cup butter

2 eggs

5 cups sifted flour

2 rounded teaspoons baking powder

1 teaspoon soda

1 cup sour milk

½ cup orange juice

Grated rind of 1 orange

Cream sugar and butter, and add eggs. Sift dry ingredients together. Add milk, orange juice and orange rind to creamed mixture alternately with dry ingredients. Drop batter by teaspoonfuls on a greased cookie sheet. Bake at 360° for 10-12 minutes. Cool and ice cookies. Makes 75.

ORANGE ICING

1 box powdered sugar

2 heaping tablespoons butter

Juice and grated rind of 1 orange

Combine sugar, butter, rind and juice with rotary beater. *Some years back I played the harp and was maid of honor at a girl friend's wedding in Portland, Oregon. Her grandmother had made plenty of these cookies to munch on, and during the 2 weeks I was there, I did. I loved them, and was impressed with how fresh they stayed.*

Julia Louise Herrmann

ORANGE SPARKLE COOKIES

2¼ cups sifted all-purpose flour

1 teaspoon soda

½ teaspoon salt

¾ cup butter

1 cup sugar

1 egg

1 teaspoon lemon extract

1 teaspoon orange extract

2 tablespoons orange rind, grated

¼ cup orange juice

½ cup black or English walnuts, chopped

Sugar

Sift together flour, soda and salt. Cream butter, and gradually add sugar, creaming well. Add egg, extracts, orange rind and juice, and mix well. Blend in dry ingredients, and mix thoroughly. Stir in walnuts, and chill 1-2 hours. Drop dough by teaspoonfuls into sugar; roll to coat. Place on lightly greased cookie sheets. Bake at 350° for 12-15 minutes until light golden brown. Cool 1 minute; remove from sheet. Makes 5 dozen. *Variation: For a more chewy cookie, omit egg.*

Mrs. Ronald Reagan

PAT'S SNICKER DOODLES

1 cup shortening

2 cups sugar

2 eggs

1 teaspoon vanilla

2¾ cups flour

2 teaspoons cream of tartar

1 teaspoon soda

½ teaspoon salt

½ cup sugar

½ teaspoon cinnamon

Mix shortening, 1½ cups sugar, eggs, vanilla and flour. Add cream of tartar, soda and salt. Form into small balls. Roll in mixture of ½ cup sugar and cinnamon. Bake on cookie sheet at 400° for 8-10 minutes. Makes 5 dozen.

Mrs. Leland L. Coggan

PECAN DREAMS

½ pound sweet butter, melted

4 tablespoons sugar

2 cups flour

2 teaspoons vanilla

2 cups pecans, finely chopped

Confectioners' sugar

Add butter to sugar, mix, and allow to cool. Gradually add flour, vanilla and pecans. Knead together slightly by squeezing and patting. Take small amount of dough, and shape crescents, about 2½ inches in length. Bake on cookie sheet for 20 minutes at 375°. Allow to cool a little. Carefully roll in confectioners' sugar. Makes about 30-35 crescents.

Mrs. Peter N. Manos

RUM BALLS

1 package (17½ oz.) vanilla
  wafers
1 can (14 oz.) walnuts, dried
  peanuts, filberts or almonds

2 tablespoons cocoa
½ cup light corn syrup
¼ cup dark rum or bourbon
Confectioners' sugar

Grind vanilla wafers and nuts very fine in a food grinder or electric blender. Mix with cocoa, syrup and rum until a thick paste is formed. Dust the palms of hands with the sugar. Pull off the dough in bits, and roll into balls the size of a big cherry. Set aside to dry for about an hour. Roll in sugar, and store in an air-tight container for several days to mellow. Makes 30 delicate balls.

Igor Gorin

SNOWBALLS

¾ cup sifted confectioners'
  sugar
⅔ cup nuts, coarsely chopped
  (almonds, walnuts, filberts)

1 egg white
Dash of vanilla

Place ½ cup sugar and nuts in an electric blender at high speed for 30 seconds. Work in the egg white and vanilla with a spatula. This will make a paste firm enough to roll into balls. Make little balls with about 1 teaspoon of the paste for each. Roll in remaining sugar, and place on ungreased baking sheet. Bake in preheated 325°-350° oven for 15-25 minutes, or until cookies are puffed. Makes 1 dozen. *This recipe was on a Christmas card I received from William North Jayme, who wrote the libretto for Douglas Moore's opera, "Carry Nation". These cookies are a wonderful addition to a Christmas cake-cookie platter.*

Beverly Wolff

WASP NESTS

1 package (8 oz.) chocolate
  chips
1 package (8 oz.) butter-
  scotch chips

1 teaspoon vanilla
1 large can Chow Mein
  noodles

½ cup nuts, chopped (optional)

Place chips in top of double boiler over very hot water. Stir occasionally to mix while chips are melting. Stir in vanilla, and remove from heat. Stir in Chow Mein noodles and nuts. Try to evenly coat the noodles. Drop by small teaspoonfuls onto wax paper. Will become firm at room temperature, but if in a hurry, place briefly in refrigerator. Makes 3 dozen. *These are marvelous at the bridge table.*

Mrs. George W. Taggart

DESSERTS

OLD COUNTRY WELSH COOKIES

6 cups flour

1 teaspoon baking soda

2 teaspoons baking powder

1 teaspoon salt

2½ cups sugar

1 teaspoon nutmeg

1 pound lard

1 pound currants

4 eggs, beaten

½ cup milk

Mix dry ingredients, and add lard. Wash, and drain currants; then add to dry mixture. Add eggs to milk. Then add eggs and milk to dry mixture. Combine thoroughly. When mixture is the consistency of dough, roll out, and cut in 3-inch circles. Bake on griddle, turning when slightly brown. Brown each side of cookie evenly. Makes 60 3-inch cookies. *I was told by my mother-in-law that a test of a true Welsh woman was how well she could make Welsh cookies. Needless to say, I learned to make them early in my marriage.*

Mrs. Irwin D. Parry

ANGEL PIE

4 egg whites

Pinch of salt

1 cup sugar

1 teaspoon vanilla

½ teaspoon almond extract

½ pint heavy cream, whipped

6 Hershey bars, grated

Beat egg whites with salt until whites stand in very stiff peaks. Slowly add sugar, beating continually. Add vanilla and almond extract. Pour into a greased and floured 9-inch glass pie plate. Bake at 375° until brown. Cool, and cover with cream. Top with Hershey bars. Chill. Serves 6.

Mrs. Sam P. Burford, Jr.

BLUEBERRY-BANANA CREAM PIE

2 baked 9-inch pie crusts

2 large bananas, thinly sliced

2 envelopes Dream Whip

4 packages (3 oz.) cream cheese

1½ cups sugar

Juice of ½-1 lemon

1 can blueberry pie filling mix

Line bottom of pie crusts with bananas. Prepare Dream Whip according to package directions. Combine cream cheese, sugar and lemon juice. Fold in Dream Whip. Spread over bananas. Then, over each pie, spread half of the pie filling mix in the center portion of the cream filling. Leave about 1 inch of the white cream showing around the edges. Serves 12. *This is a glamorous and easy pie.*

Mrs. Jerome E. Dawkins

APPLE PIE WITH CHEESE CRACKER CRUMBS

5 medium apples, sliced
3/4 cup sugar
1 teaspoon cinnamon

1/2 teaspoon nutmeg
8-inch pie shell
Butter

Mix apples, sugar and seasonings. Place in pie shell, and dot with butter.

TOPPING

1 cup cheese crackers, crumbled
1/3 cup butter

1/3 cup brown sugar
1 1/2 cups flour

Mix crumbs with butter, and add sugar and flour. Mix together. Pour over top of apples, and bake at 400° for 45 minutes or until brown and apples are cooked. Serves 6.

Mrs. John R. Watson

Charles Lamb said: "A man cannot have a pure mind who refuses apple dumplings." Most men today would say the same about the old-fashioned apple pie.

FRENCH APPLE PIE

3/4 cup sugar
2 tablespoons flour
1/4 teaspoon salt
1 teaspoon cinnamon

1/4 teaspoon nutmeg
1 can (1 lb. 4 oz.) pie sliced apples
1 unbaked pie crust

Flute edge of pie crust, and press into an upright rim to prevent juices from boiling over. Mix sugar, flour, salt, cinnamon and nutmeg. Add to apples. Stir gently until apples are coated with sugar mixture. Pour into pie crust.

TOPPING

1 cup flour
1/2 cup brown sugar, packed

1/2 cup margarine
1/4 cup pecans, chopped (optional)

Place flour, sugar and margarine in medium-sized bowl. Work with pastry blender or 2 knives until crumbly. Add pecans. Heap topping on pie, and bake at 425° for 40-45 minutes or until nicely browned. Make sure topping is firm around edges as it helps seal in juices. Serves 6-7.

Mrs. M. G. O'Dell

SOUTHERN APPLE PIE

9-inch pie crust
3/4 cup sugar
2 tablespoons flour
1 cup sour cream

1 egg, beaten
1/4 teaspoon salt
1/2 teaspoon vanilla
2 cups apples, finely chopped

Bake pie crust 7 minutes at 350°. Cool. Mix filling ingredients thoroughly, and add apples. Pour into partially baked shell, and continue baking at 450° for 30 minutes.

TOPPING

1/2 cup sugar
6 tablespoons flour

1 teaspoon cinnamon
1/4 cup butter

Blend sugar, flour, cinnamon and butter for topping. Spread on pie, and bake additional 10 minutes. Serves 6-8.

Mrs. Frank Pearcy

ALMOND CHERRY PIE

1 can (15 oz.) sweetened
    condensed milk
1/3 cup lemon juice
1 teaspoon vanilla

1/4 teaspoon almond extract
1/2 cup heavy cream, whipped
1 can (1 lb. 5 oz.) cherry pie
    glaze or filling

1 baked pastry shell or graham cracker crust

Mix condensed milk, lemon juice, vanilla and almond extract together, and stir until it thickens. Fold cream into the mixture. Pour this into cooled pie crust. Top pie with cherry glaze. Refrigerate until time to serve. Serves 6-8. *Donald received this recipe from a cook at the Kellogg Center, Michigan State University. He enjoyed one of her famous pies while serving as head of the Congress of Strings at Michigan State several summers ago.*

Mrs. Donald Johanos

FUDGE PIE

2 squares (1 oz.)
    unsweetened chocolate
1/2 cup butter
1 cup sugar
2 eggs, well-beaten
Pinch of salt

1/4 cup flour
1 teaspoon vanilla
3/4 cup pecans or walnuts,
    chopped
1 unbaked pie shell
Vanilla ice cream

Melt chocolate over hot water. Cream butter and sugar; add chocolate, eggs, salt, flour, vanilla and nuts. Pour into pie shell, and bake for 30 minutes at 325°. Serve with a scoop of ice cream on top. Serves 8.

Mrs. Slayden Diehl

GALATOPOURIKO
Greek Milk Custard Pastry

SYRUP

5 cups sugar

4 cups water

1 tablespoon lemon juice

Lemon peel

1 jigger brandy or rum (optional)

Prepare syrup in advance. Stir sugar and water together. Add lemon juice and peel. Bring to a boil, and cook over medium heat to 227° on a candy thermometer. Remove from heat; add brandy, and cool. Syrup must be cold when ready to pour over hot pastry.

FILLING

2 quarts milk

Orange peel

8 eggs

2 cups sugar

1 teaspoon vanilla

1 cup minus 2 tablespoons farina

2 cups plus 6 tablespoons butter, melted

1 pound filo

¼ pound almond slices, toasted

Place orange peel in pot with milk. Bring milk to scalding. Remove from heat. Cream eggs and sugar in electric mixer; add vanilla. Gradually add farina to egg mixture, blending well. Slowly add hot milk. Return this mixture to pot, and place over low heat, stirring constantly, until mixture thickens. Remove from heat, beating until cool. Add 6 tablespoons butter. Brush bottom and sides of 17x11x2½-inch pan with butter. Place about 15 sheets of filo in pan, 1 sheet at a time, brushing each with butter. Sprinkle almonds on alternate sheets. Be sure to extend some of filo over sides so that after custard is added, sides can be folded over, sealing in custard. Pour in all the custard. Sprinkle with 6 tablespoons butter. Fold filo edges over custard. Again place 15 sheets of filo on top, brushing each sheet with butter and sprinkling alternate sheets with almonds. Using a very sharp knife, cut through top layers of filo lengthwise, starting down the center making 6 strips. Then cut into squares. Be careful not to cut too deep and cause the filling to ooze out. Bake in a preheated 375° oven until lightly browned. Lower heat to 325°, and continue baking for a total of 45 minutes. Remove from oven, finish cutting pastry, and pour cold syrup over hot pastry. Serve slightly warm or cool. Serves 42 generously.

Evelyn Semos

BOB HOPE'S FAVORITE LEMON PIE

3 tablespoons cornstarch

1 cup plus 2 tablespoons sugar

1 cup boiling water

4 egg yolks, slightly beaten

2 tablespoons butter

Grated rind of 1 lemon

4 tablespoons lemon juice

Pinch of salt

3 egg whites, stiffly beaten

2½ tablespoons sugar

Baked pie shell

Combine cornstarch and sugar. Add water slowly, stirring constantly until thick and smooth. Add egg yolks, butter, lemon rind, juice and salt. Cook 2-3 minutes. Pour into shell. Cover with meringue made from egg whites and 2½ tablespoons sugar. Bake in slow oven 15 minutes, or until light brown. Serves 8.

Mrs. Bob Hope

EAGLE BRAND LEMON PIE

1 small box Nabisco vanilla wafers, crushed

¼-½ cup sugar

¼ cup butter, melted

1 can (15 oz.) Eagle Brand condensed milk

½ cup lemon juice

¼ teaspoon lemon extract

2 egg yolks

Heavy cream, whipped

Mix wafers, sugar and butter, and press into a 9-inch pie pan. Cook at 375° for 5 minutes. Cool. Mix milk, lemon juice, extract and egg yolks together, and pour into crust. Chill. Top with cream. Serves 10.

Mrs. R. Douglas Coffin

LEMON CHESS PIE

2 cups sugar

1 tablespoon corn meal

1 tablespoon flour

¼ cup butter, melted

4 eggs

1 tablespoon lemon rind, grated

⅓ cup lemon juice

⅓ cup milk

Unbaked 9-inch pie shell

Mix sugar, corn meal and flour. Stir in butter, add eggs 1 at a time, beating after each addition. Add lemon juice and rind. Beat well, and add milk. Pour into pie shell, and bake at 350° for 45 minutes. Serves 6.

Mrs. George D. Blaylock

FRENCH LEMON PIE

2 tablespoons butter
1½ cups sugar
3 eggs

Juice of 1½ lemons
Pinch of salt
Unbaked pie crust

Cream butter and sugar. Beat eggs until frothy, and add to creamed mixture. Then add lemon juice and salt. Pour into pie crust. Bake at 325° until firm. Serves 6.

Mrs. James M. Elder

Mint was a favorite herb of the Greeks. Mythological legend has it that Pluto, god of the underworld, turned a lovely girl into the herb, mint.

ICE CREAM SUNDAE PIE

CRUST

2 cups chocolate wafer crumbs   ⅓ cup soft butter

Combine crumbs and butter. Press into a 9-inch pie plate. Bake at 350° for 8 minutes. Cool.

FILLING

3 pints vanilla ice cream,
   slightly softened

3 tablespoons green Crème de Menthe

Turn ice cream into a large bowl. Pour Crème de Menthe over it. With a large spoon, swirl it into ice cream to give a marble effect. Do not overmix. Place bowl in freezer for 1-2 hours. Fill pie shell with ice cream, mounding high in center.

FUDGE SAUCE

3 squares unsweetened
   chocolate
¾ cup sugar
¼ teaspoon salt

4½ tablespoons butter
¾ teaspoon vanilla
½ cup water

Cook all ingredients 5 minutes. Cool. Pour ½ cup fudge sauce over top of pie, and place in freezer.

GARNISH

1 cup heavy cream, whipped   ¼ cup pecans, chopped

Before serving, garnish with cream sprinkled with nuts. Pass more sauce when serving. Serves 6.

Mrs. Gerald W. McCoy

PEACH CREAM CHEESE PIE

1 package Whip 'n Chill

1 package (8 oz.) cream cheese

½ cup sugar

1 graham cracker prepared crust

2 packages frozen sliced peaches, thawed and drained

¼ cup apricot preserves

Prepare Whip 'n Chill as directed on package. Soften cream cheese; beat with sugar until smooth. Blend Whip 'n Chill into cheese mixture. Pour into crumb crust. Chill 3 hours. Arrange layer of peaches in a circle on top of cream cheese mixture, all pointing towards the center. Melt apricot preserves, and brush over top of peaches. Cool and serve. Serves 8.

Mrs. Cecil H. Green

ROSY PEACH PIE*

6 cups fresh peaches and nectarines, sliced

Pastry for 2-crust pie

¾ cup brown sugar

4 tablespoons flour

¼ teaspoon salt

3 tablespoons red currant jelly

2 tablespoons rum

Whipped cream or vanilla ice cream

Be sure both fruits are of equal ripeness. Place fruit in pastry-lined 9-inch pie pan. Combine sugar, flour and salt, and pour over fruit. Dilute jelly with rum, and pour over other ingredients, distributing mixture evenly over all fruit. Cover with lattice crust, and bake at 425° for 35-40 minutes. Serve warm topped with cream. Serves 6-8.

Gianna d'Angelo

RUM PECAN PIE

3 eggs, well-beaten

½ cup half and half

½ cup dark corn syrup

1 teaspoon vanilla

3 tablespoons rum or brandy

1 cup sugar

⅛ teaspoon salt

2 tablespoons butter, melted

2 cups pecans, thinly sliced

Unbaked pie shell with fluted edge

Combine all ingredients, and pour into pie shell. Bake at 400° for 35 minutes or until crust is browned and filling is slightly puffed. Cool. Serves 8.

Mrs. David Varner

*From *The Bel Canto Cookbook*, by Peter Gravina, Published by Doubleday and Company

NEW ORLEANS PECAN PIE
FILLING

2 egg yolks

1 cup sugar

4 tablespoons sifted flour

1 cup sour cream

¼ teaspoon lemon extract

⅛ teaspoon salt

Baked 9-inch pie shell

Mix egg yolks, sugar, flour, sour cream, lemon extract and salt. Cook in double boiler for about 45 minutes until thickened. Spoon into pie shell, and cover with topping.

TOPPING

2 egg whites

1 cup brown sugar

1 cup pecan meats, broken

Beat egg whites until they form a soft peak. Add brown sugar, and stir in pecan meats. Spread over filling. Bake at 325° until brown, about 15 minutes. Serves 6-8. *This is a very different pecan pie.*

Mrs. John Stuart, III

PUMPKIN CHIFFON PIE

3 egg yolks, beaten

¾ cup brown sugar

1½ cups pumpkin

½ cup milk

½ teaspoon salt

½ teaspoon nutmeg

1 teaspoon cinnamon

1 envelope gelatin

¼ cup cold water

1 tablespoon bourbon (optional)

3 egg whites

¼ cup sugar

Baked 8-inch pie shell

Combine egg yolks, brown sugar, pumpkin, milk, salt, nutmeg and cinnamon. Cook in top of double boiler until thick, stirring constantly. Soak gelatin in cold water; stir into hot mixture. Chill until partially set; add bourbon. Beat egg whites; add sugar, and beat until stiff. Fold into gelatin mixture. Pour into pie shell. Makes 1 pie or 8 individual tarts. Serves 6-8. *This recipe was given to me by Bobbie Thomsen, who worked as a curator in the White House during the Eisenhower administration. This was Mrs. Eisenhower's recipe. Bobbie added the bourbon.*

Mrs. George S. Dutter

RITZ CRACKER PIE

2 cups water	24-30 Ritz crackers
1½ cups sugar	Butter
2 teaspoons cream of tartar	¾ teaspoon cinnamon

2 8-inch unbaked pie crusts

Bring water, sugar and cream of tartar to a boil. Add whole Ritz crackers, and let boil 2 minutes. Pour into pastry shell. Dot with butter, and sprinkle with cinnamon. Add top crust. Bake at 350° for 12-15 minutes or until pastry is golden brown. Serves 6. *This recipe has proven to be a real conversation piece as, after the Ritz crackers are cooked, they appear and taste exactly like apples. We've fooled many guests with this recipe.*

Norman Treigle

SHERRY CHIFFON PIE

1 envelope unflavored gelatin	⅔ cup sherry
⅓ cup cold water	¼ teaspoon salt
4 eggs, separated	Baked 9-inch pie shell
1 cup sugar	Whipped cream

Dash of nutmeg

Soften gelatin in cold water for 5 minutes. Beat egg yolks until light; gradually add ½ cup sugar, continuing to beat. Add sherry. Cook in top of double boiler over hot water, stirring constantly, until mixture is consistency of soft custard. Add gelatin; stir until dissolved; cool. Beat egg whites stiff; beat in remaining ½ cup sugar and salt. Combine with custard. Spoon into pastry shell. Chill until firm, about 3 hours. When ready to serve, garnish with whipped cream and dash of nutmeg. Serves 6-8.

Beverly Wolff

SHOO-FLY-PIE

1½ cups flour	½ teaspoon baking soda
½ cup sugar	¾ cup dark molasses
¼ cup butter	¾ cup boiling water

Unbaked 9-inch pie shell

Mix together flour, sugar and butter. In separate bowl mix soda, molasses and water. Put ⅓ molasses mixture into pie shell, add layer of crumbs, then alternate molasses and crumbs, ending with crumb mixture. Bake at 425° for 10 minutes, then at 350° for 40 minutes. Serves 6.

Mrs. Chapman Kelley

SUNDAE PIE

1½ cups evaporated milk
½ teaspoon nutmeg
3 eggs, separated
½ cup sugar
⅛ teaspoon salt
¾ tablespoon gelatin

½ cup water
½ teaspoon vanilla
1 cup heavy cream, whipped and sweetened
¼ cup semi-sweet chocolate, grated, or small amount of cocoa

Baked 9-inch pie shell

Heat milk and nutmeg in double boiler. Beat egg yolks with sugar and salt until light. Pour hot milk over egg mixture, return to double boiler, and cook until thick. Remove from heat, add gelatin which has soaked in water for 5 minutes. Add vanilla, and let cool. Beat with electric beater, and fold in stiffly beaten egg whites. Pour into pie shell, and refrigerate. When cold, cover with cream and sprinkle with chocolate or cocoa.

Mrs. Manfred E. New

ROUGH PUFF PASTRY

½ cup shortening
½ cup soft butter
2 cups flour
½ teaspoon salt

⅔ cup ice water or less
1 tablespoon lemon juice
1 egg
1 teaspoon milk

Cut shortening and butter into flour and salt. Add ice water and lemon juice. Stir to mix. Form into a ball, cover with wax paper, and chill. Roll out into a rectangle, fold in thirds, and roll into rectangle again. Refrigerate 30 minutes. Repeat 3 times folding and refrigerating. Roll to desired shape.

The Cookbook Committee

TARTLET SHELLS

½ cup soft butter
¼ cup sugar
¼ teaspoon salt

1 egg white
¼ teaspoon almond extract
¾ cup blanched almonds, ground

1 cup sifted flour

Blend butter, sugar, salt, egg white and almond extract in a bowl until smooth and well-combined. Add almonds and flour; mix until smooth. Wrap dough in waxed paper, and refrigerate for 1 hour. Preheat oven to 375°. Use 1 teaspoon dough for each tartlet. Using fingers, press dough evenly into 2x2-inch tart tins. Set tins on cookie sheet. Bake about 10 minutes or until golden brown. Let cool on rack about 10 minutes. Fill shortly before serving. Makes 30.

Mrs. Charles L. Caperton

CANNOLI

SHELLS

3 cups flour   3 heaping tablespoons Crisco

Scant ⅔ cup water

Mix flour and Crisco, blending well. Add water slowly. The dough should be quite stiff. Work and knead well, using additional flour, if necessary. This is dependent on humidity. Cover dough with wax paper and cloth, and let stand for at least 6 hours. Flour a board. Use small portion of dough, about the size of a large egg, and roll to paper thinness. This is very important. If the dough is not rolled thin enough it will not blister, and good cannoli should have a blistered surface. An unpainted, well-scrubbed broom handle, cut into 6-inch pieces and then seasoned by baking in a mixture of olive oil and Wesson oil, makes an excellent mold. The rolled out dough should then be trimmed into strips about 2 inches less in width than the mold. Mold around stick. Overlap ¾ inch, and trim excess. Press edges with back of a fork to seal. Have about ½ inch of melted Crisco in skillet, and keep at 390°. Fry shells, stick and all, beginning where dough is joined. Turn as each side browns. Place on paper towel to cool slightly, then gently push mold out. Shells will keep for weeks in an air-tight container. Makes 60 shells.

FILLING

Fresh ricotta cheese   Almond extract
Sugar   Cinnamon-sugar mixture

Use fresh ricotta, seasoned with sugar and almond extract to taste, mixing well with a fork. This can be prepared early in the day before serving. Just before serving, fill the shell with the flavored ricotta by pushing it in with a butter knife, first from 1 end, and then from the other. After the desired number of shells are filled, roll them in a cinnamon-sugar mixture. *These are best eaten with the fingers. We always find it advisable to suggest the best technique — which consists of eating around the edges, like an ice cream cone. If people are not familiar with these delicate pastries, the tendency is to bite completely across the shell which results in quite a disaster.*

Victor Alessandro

VIENNESE PASTRIES

½ cup butter

1 package (3 oz.) cream cheese

1 cup flour

2 tablespoons sugar

Grated lemon rind

Marmalade

Powdered sugar

Mix butter, cheese, flour, sugar and a small amount of lemon rind with hands. Wrap the dough in wax paper, and chill in refrigerator. (This will keep for several days.) Roll out dough onto a heavily-floured board. Cut the dough into squares 1½-2 inches. Put a little dab of marmalade mixed with more lemon rind in the center of each square. Fold the squares into triangles, and pinch the edges fast. Bake on an ungreased cookie sheet at 400°-425° for 5-8 minutes. Pastries should be light in color. Cool, then dip them in powdered sugar. Makes 24. *This is a favorite recipe of a dear friend who grew up in Vienna and escaped to London during World War II while still a young girl.*

Mrs. Donald Johanos

CHOCOLATE POPPY SEED TORTE

¼ cup butter

½ cup sugar

6 eggs, separated

½ cup bread crumbs

¼ pound semi-sweet chocolate, melted

⅓ cup ground poppy seeds

Apricot jam

Cream butter and sugar. Beat egg whites until stiff. Beat yolks until thick and lemon-colored. Add yolks to butter-sugar mixture. Add crumbs. Fold in chocolate. Fold in poppy seeds and then egg whites. Pour into 2 paper-lined, buttered 9x1½-inch round pans, and bake at 325° for about 20 minutes. Cool on racks. Put layers together with apricot jam. Top with following chocolate glaze.

CHOCOLATE GLAZE

8 ounces semi-sweet chocolate

6 ounces water

¾ cup sugar

1 tablespoon butter

Combine chocolate, water and sugar. Cook until soft ball stage. Remove from heat, and add butter. Beat for a few minutes. Serves 8. *Poppy seeds add an interesting dimension to this recipe.*

Mrs. Janos Starker

BLACK FOREST TORTE

1¾ cups unsifted all-purpose flour

1¾ cups sugar

1¼ teaspoons soda

1 teaspoon salt

¼ teaspoon baking powder

⅔ cup soft-type margarine containing liquid safflower oil

1¼ cups water

1 teaspoon vanilla

4 squares (1 oz.) unsweetened chocolate, melted and cooled

3 eggs

Measure flour, sugar, soda, salt, baking powder, margarine, water and vanilla into a large mixing bowl. Add chocolate. Beat at low speed to blend, then beat 2 minutes at medium speed, scraping sides and bottom of bowl frequently. Add eggs; beat 2 minutes longer. Brush sides and bottom of 4 9-inch layer cake pans with margarine. Pour ¼ of the batter (little over 1 cup) into each pan. Layers will be thin. Bake at 350° for 17-20 minutes, until wooden pick inserted in center comes out clean. Cool slightly, and remove from pans. Cool completely.

FILLING

2 packages (4 oz.) German sweet chocolate

½ cup soft-type margarine containing liquid safflower oil

½ cup sliced almonds, toasted

1 tablespoon sugar

1 teaspoon vanilla

2 cups heavy cream

Melt chocolate over hot water. Cool. Blend in margarine and almonds. Whip cream with sugar and vanilla until stiff; do not overbeat. Place bottom layer on serving plate. Spread with half of chocolate mixture. Add second layer and half of cream. Repeat layers, ending with cream on top. Do not frost sides.

TOPPING AND GARNISH

Flaked coconut

Candied cherries

Angelica

Sprinkle coconut over top. Garnish with cherries and angelica. Cover with Saran wrap, and refrigerate until ready to serve. Freeze torte uncovered. Wrap in Saran wrap, and store in freezer for as long as 2 weeks. Makes 16 servings. *Variation: Eliminate coconut, and use decorative glacé fruit right on whipping cream.*

Julie Benell

LINZERTORTE

1 cup butter

1 cup sifted flour

1½ cups almonds or pecans, chopped

⅛ teaspoon cloves

½ cup sugar

⅛ teaspoon cinnamon

2 tablespoons cocoa

2 egg yolks

⅓ cup black raspberry jam

2 egg whites, slightly beaten

Preheat oven to 325°. Blend butter into flour with pastry blender; add almonds, and knead into flour mixture. Mix sugar with cloves, cinnamon and cocoa, and mix into egg yolks. Add to flour mixture, kneading dough until smooth and well-blended. Spread about ⅔ dough onto bottom of ungreased 10-inch spring-form pan; spread with jam. Remaining dough should be rolled between palms to make long rolls about ½ inch in diameter. Chill rolls until firm. Arrange rolls lattice-style over jam. Brush with egg whites. Bake at 325° for 1¼ hours. When taken from oven, go around sides with a knife to prevent jam from sticking. Cool before removing from pan. Serves 12. *This recipe was given to me by Mrs. Hugo Adler, mother of Samuel Adler, who moved from Dallas to join the faculty of the Eastman School of Music in Rochester. It is a dessert that is different, very rich, and will bring many favorable comments.*

Mrs. Royal H. Brin, Jr.

FRESH PEACH TORTE

½ cup butter

¼ cup powdered sugar

1 cup flour

½ cup orange juice

1 tablespoon cornstarch

¼ cup sugar

3 drops of red food coloring

¼ cup red currant jelly

9 ripe peaches, peeled and halved

Pineapple or orange juice

Whipped cream

Blend butter, powdered sugar and flour into soft dough, and press into shallow pizza pan. Bake at 325° for 30 minutes or until golden. Cool. Mix orange juice, cornstarch and sugar. Cook slowly until thick. Add food coloring and jelly, and stir until dissolved. Cool. Dip peaches into pineapple or orange juice to preserve color. Then dip peaches into glaze, and arrange on top of pastry. Chill for about 1 hour. Top with cream. Serves 6.

Mrs. Jerry Bywaters

DELICATE INSTANT COCOA TORTE

MERINGUE

3 egg whites

1/2 teaspoon almond extract

1/4 teaspoon salt

3/4 cup brown sugar, firmly packed

1/2 cup English walnuts, finely chopped

Cut 4 8-inch circles from brown paper, and put them on cookie sheets. Beat egg whites, almond extract and salt until foamy. Gradually add the brown sugar, about 2 tablespoons at a time, and beat until stiff glossy peaks are formed. Reserve 1 tablespoon chopped walnuts, and fold the remaining nuts into the meringue. Spread meringue on paper circles. Sprinkle top of one circle with 1 tablespoon chopped walnuts, and bake in 300° oven for 30-35 minutes. Cool thoroughly; peel paper gently from meringue.

FILLING

1 package (3 oz.) cream cheese

1 1/2 tablespoons water

1 teaspoon vanilla

2/3 cup instant cocoa mix

1 1/2 cups heavy cream, whipped

Beat cream cheese, water and vanilla until smooth. Add cocoa mix, and beat well. Fold cream into cocoa mixture. Spread about 3/4 cup filling on each of the 3 plain meringue layers. Stack on top of each other. Top with nut-trimmed circle. Flute the top layer with remaining cream mixture. Chill several hours or overnight. Makes 12 servings.

Julie Benell

BANANAS FOSTER

1/2 cup brown sugar

4 tablespoons butter

1 teaspoon cinnamon

4 bananas, sliced lengthwise

2 jiggers banana liqueur

1 tablespoon dark rum

1 jigger brandy

1 quart vanilla ice cream

Melt sugar and butter in a skillet or chafing dish. Add cinnamon and bananas. Pour liqueur and rum over bananas. Cook until fruit is soft. Add brandy, and ignite. Pour over vanilla ice cream to serve. Serves 4-6.

Helen Corbitt

SHERRY BAKED BANANAS

4 ripe bananas, peeled
Apricot jam
½ cup sherry

2 tablespoons butter
2 tablespoons brown sugar
1 tablespoon lemon juice

Split bananas lengthwise, and spread with apricot jam. Pour the sherry, butter, brown sugar and lemon juice over them. Bake in a glass pie dish 20 minutes at 350°, basting occasionally. Serve hot over ice cream, or topped with whipped cream. Serves 4-6.

Mrs. Louis E. Harlan

BRANDY ICE

½ gallon French vanilla
   ice cream

1 cup brandy

½ cup Crême de Cocoa or Kahlua

Thaw ice cream in large mixing bowl until soft enough to use beaters. Add brandy and Crême de Cocoa, and blend thoroughly. Place in freezer until consistency of thick malt. Serve in champagne or sherbet glasses with small cocktail straws Serves 8.

Mrs. John J. Cadigan

BRIDE'S DELIGHT

1 can (15 oz.) Borden's Eagle
   Brand condensed milk

Whipped cream

Immerse unopened can in a pot of water, and boil for 4 hours. Cool the can, and refrigerate. Unmold, and serve in thin slices garnished with cream. Serves 6.

Loretta Young

CHEESE ROLL WITH STRAWBERRIES

Cream cheese
Brown sugar

Strawberries
Ritz crackers

Whip cheese, and form into a roll. Wrap in wax paper, and refrigerate. Immediately before serving, roll the cheese in brown sugar. Place on a serving tray with strawberries on one side and crackers on the other. *Delightful as a dessert or for brunch.*

Mrs. J. D. Williamson, Jr.

LUSCIOUS CHOCOLATE

10 graham crackers, crushed

3 eggs

½ cup butter

2 cups confectioners' sugar

3 squares bitter chocolate, melted and cooled

1½ cups pecans

Grease an 8-inch square pan with butter. Cover bottom with graham cracker crumbs. Combine remaining ingredients with electric mixer, and pour over crumbs. Crumble another couple of crackers, and sprinkle over the top. Refrigerate overnight. Serves 12.

Mrs. Wilbur E. Langkop

CHOCOLATE ANGEL STRATA

1 cup flour

½ teaspoon salt

⅓ cup shortening

3-4 tablespoons cold water

Sift flour and salt together. Cut in shortening until particles are the size of small peas. Sprinkle water over mixture, tossing lightly with fork. Add liquid to driest particles, until just moist enough to hold together. Roll into a ball, flatten to ½ inch thickness; roll out on floured surface until 1½ inches larger in diameter than an inverted 9-inch pie pan. Fit loosely into pan; fold edge to form a rim, and flute. Prick generously with a fork. Bake at 450° for 10-12 minutes until golden brown.

FILLING

2 egg whites

½ teaspoon white vinegar

¼ teaspoon salt

½ teaspoon cinnamon

¾ cup sugar

2 egg yolks, slightly beaten

¼ cup water

1 cup (6 oz.) semi-sweet chocolate chips, melted

1 cup whipping cream

Beat together egg whites, vinegar and salt. Add ¼ teaspoon cinnamon, if desired. Add ½ cup sugar gradually, beating until meringue stands in stiff glossy peaks. Spread on bottom and sides of baked pie shell. Bake at 325° for 15-18 minutes until lightly browned. Cool. Combine egg yolks, water and chocolate chips. Spread 3 tablespoons over meringue. Chill remainder. Combine remaining sugar, ¼ teaspoon cinnamon and cream. Beat until thick. Spread half over chocolate in pie shell. Combine remaining whipped cream with chocolate mixture, and spread over whipped cream in pie shell. Chill at least 4 hours, and serve cold. Serves 6-8.

James Oliver Buswell, IV

CHOCOLATE MOUSSE LADY FINGER CAKE

4 ounces Baker's chocolate

6 eggs, separated

¾ cup sugar

⅓ cup milk

⅛ teaspoon salt

1 cup confectioners' sugar, sifted

1½ cups butter

1 teaspoon vanilla

30 lady fingers, split

1 cup heavy cream, whipped

1 teaspoon instant coffee

1 teaspoon confectioners' sugar

Melt chocolate in double boiler. Beat egg yolks until lemon-colored. Gradually beat in sugar until smooth and thick. Beat in milk. Add egg mixture to chocolate. Cook, stirring until well-blended, 5-10 minutes. Let cool in large mixing bowl for 30 minutes. Add salt to egg whites, beat until stiff but not dry. Beat in ½ cup confectioners' sugar, 1 tablespoon at a time. Reserve. Cream butter. Gradually beat in rest of confectioners' sugar. Add to chocolate mixture, and stir until well-blended. Gently fold in egg whites and vanilla. Line bottom and sides of a 3-quart spring form with a single layer of lady fingers, placing them vertically around sides. Pour in ⅓ of chocolate mixture, then another layer of lady fingers, etc. There will be 3 layers. Refrigerate overnight. Next day wrap and freeze. Just before serving, add whipped cream, flavored with coffee and sugar, to the top. If frozen, allow 8 hours to thaw in refrigerator. Two hours before serving, remove spring form. Serves 12.

Mrs. James M. Degnan, III

OLD SOUTHERN EGG SPOONNOG

1 pint heavy cream

6 eggs, separated

6 tablespoons sugar

4 tablespoons whisky, brandy or wine

Nutmeg to taste

Whip the cream, and set aside. Whip whites until stiff. Set aside. Add sugar to egg yolks, and blend well. Add liquor. Blend all the mixtures together, adding nutmeg. Pour into sherbet glasses, and chill. Serves 6-8.

Mrs. Henry E. English

EGGS À LA NEIGE
MERINGUES

4 cups milk
6 egg whites

¾ cup sugar
¼ teaspoon salt

The day before or early in the day, prepare meringues. Scald milk in a large skillet. Beat egg whites until frothy. Gradually add sugar, then salt. Beat until stiff. Drop tablespoon-sized mounds of meringue into hot milk, 1 inch apart. Cook 5 minutes, turning once with slotted spoon. Drain on paper towels. Repeat until meringues are all cooked. Store on paper towels in an air-tight container. Refrigerate milk until needed.

CUSTARD SAUCE

1½ cups heavy cream
¾ teaspoon vanilla
6 egg yolks
½ cup sugar

1½ tablespoons flour
Pinch of salt
2 pints fresh strawberries
1 square unsweetened
   chocolate, shaved

In double boiler, scald cream with vanilla and 1½ cups milk used for cooking meringues. Beat egg yolks until light. Add sugar, flour and salt. Add a little of the cream-milk mixture. Stir this into the rest of the cream-milk mixture. Cook over hot water, stirring constantly, until sauce coats a metal spoon. Cool in refrigerator until 20 minutes before serving time. Wash, hull, and slice strawberries into individual serving bowls or 1 large serving bowl. Heap meringues over strawberries. Pour the custard sauce over meringues. Garnish with chocolate. Serves 8. *A nice dessert for a large dinner party or buffet, as it can be served individually.*

Mrs. Robert H. Mitchell

GRAPES WITH SOUR CREAM

1 pound white seedless grapes 1 pint sour cream
1 cup brown sugar

Rinse and drain grapes. Place in refrigerator to chill for 1 hour. Blend sour cream and grapes together. Sprinkle sugar over top of mixture. Do not mix in. The sugar will dissolve into the sour cream. Serve after about ½ hour. This may be prepared 24 hours in advance and refrigerated. Serves 4-6. *I heard about this dessert from Jean Martin, Manager-Chef of the Plimsoll Club in New Orleans.*

George London

JO JACOBSON'S DESSERT

3 fresh peaches, quartered

1 box fresh raspberries

1 box fresh blueberries

2 cups fresh bing cherries

1 cup almonds, chopped

1/2 cup Kirsch

2 1/2 dozen almond macaroons, crumbled

Vanilla ice cream

Place fruit and almonds into a bowl. Pour Kirsch over top. Mix in macaroons. Put in a frosted silver bowl; add spoonfuls of ice cream. Fold gently into fruit. Serves 8.

Mrs. Sheridan Thompson

LEMONADE-COCONUT DESSERT

1 1/2 cups flaked coconut

3 tablespoons margarine

1/3 cup sugar

1 envelope gelatin

3/4 cup water

1 can (6 oz.) frozen lemonade

1 package (2 oz.) Dream Whip

Few drops of yellow food coloring

Using an 8x8x2-inch pan, toast the coconut in the oven at 350° about 15 minutes, stirring often so that the coconut will brown evenly. Add the margarine, and stir when melted; then press evenly around the pan, and let cool. Blend sugar and gelatin, and add water; cook over boiling water until dissolved. Stir in lemonade, and chill until it begins to congeal. Prepare Dream Whip according to directions, and fold in. Add a few drops of yellow food coloring. Makes 9 large squares.

Mrs. Harry R. Vernon

LIPARI ISLAND DESSERT

1 medium or large round sponge or pound cake

1 bottle Oloroso sherry

2 cups butter

1 1/2 boxes confectioners' sugar

1/2 teaspoon almond extract

2 squares chocolate, melted

Grated rind of 1 orange

Cut cake horizontally into 3 layers. Sprinkle each layer liberally with sherry. Cream butter and sugar in mixing bowl. Add 2/3 cup sherry, almond extract, chocolate and the orange rind. Spread frosting over the entire cake; top, sides and in the center. Place in refrigerator for about 5 hours before serving so that the butter frosting sets. May be garnished with almonds or any other type of nuts. Makes a very rich dessert, and should be served in small portions. Serves 15-20.

Robert K. Sands

DESSERTS

ORANGE WINE JELLY

1 cup white wine	Grated peel of 1 lemon
Juice of 2 oranges	3 tablespoons sugar
Juice of 1 lemon	1 envelope gelatin
Grated peel of 1 orange	1/4 cup cold water

Whipped cream

Measure wine and juice together, and if necessary, add water to provide 2 cups of liquid. Stir in peels and sugar, and bring to a boil. Remove from heat. Dissolve gelatin in water, and stir into hot liquid. Turn into glass dish, and chill. Serve with cream. Serves 4. *This is a refreshing finale.*

Mrs. Peter E. Hirschfeld

PAVLOVA

3 egg whites	Bananas, chopped
Pinch of salt	Oranges, chopped
3/4 cup sugar	Pineapple, chopped
1 teaspoon vinegar	Peaches, chopped
1 teaspoon vanilla	Passion fruit, chopped

Whipping cream

Beat egg whites to a stiff froth with salt. Add sugar gradually, and beat well. Add vinegar and vanilla. Bake on a large greased pan or ring mold for 45 minutes in a slow oven. The inside should be like marshmallow. Serve with fruit and whipped cream. *If fresh fruit is not available, there is a brand of Australian fruit salad on the market under the brand name, "Enchanted Isle." As someone said, this dessert is as Australian as the kangaroo.*

Mrs. Edward Clark

History records that the ancient Chinese grew peaches over 3000 years ago. Traders brought the fruit to Persia where it was given its present name. Later the fruit became popular in Greece and Italy, before going to England by the 13th century. Spanish explorers brought the "pits" or seeds to the New World, where Captain John Smith noted in 1629 that peaches flourished in abundance in the Jamestown Colony.

PEACH FLAMBÉ

4 brandied peaches or large
black cherries, pitted

1½ tablespoons Grand
Marnier

1½ tablespoons Cointreau

3 tablespoons brandy

Ice cream

In a saucepan, place brandied peaches, and add Grand Marnier and Cointreau. Heat brandy; add to peaches, and flame. Pour peaches and sauce over ice cream, served in little bowls that are set in slightly larger bowls of chopped ice. *This is most effective when prepared in a chafing saucepan or deep skillet by the host or hostess while guests are watching. Dim the lights while brandy is flaming. Be sure all alcohol is burned out as the flavor is more delicate.*

Mrs. William W. Lynch

PEARS FILLED WITH CREAM CHEESE AND HOT FUDGE SAUCE

6 pears

1 package (3 oz.) cream
cheese, whipped

½ cup butter

2½ cups powdered sugar

⅔ cup evaporated milk

6 squares bitter chocolate

Fill pear halves with cream cheese, and place together. Refrigerate. Place butter, sugar, milk and chocolate in top of double boiler. Cook 30 minutes. Leave it alone. Remove, and beat. Add cream if you wish a thinner sauce, but never water. Pour over filled pears. Serves 6.

Helen Corbitt

RUM BUBBLE

1 tablespoon gelatin

2 tablespoons cold water

1 cup sugar

6 tablespoons boiling water

⅓ cup rum

2 tablespoons bourbon

2 egg whites, stiffly beaten

2 cups whipped cream

Strawberries or toasted slivered almonds and coconut

Soften gelatin in cold water for 5 minutes. Add boiling water; stir until dissolved. Add sugar, rum, bourbon, and stir until sugar has dissolved. Cool. When mixture begins to thicken, beat until foamy. Fold in egg whites and cream, two tablespoons at a time. Mix thoroughly. Pour in greased ring mold, and chill for several hours. Fill center, and decorate edge of serving dish with strawberries, or cover with almonds and coconut. Serves 6. *This recipe was given to me by Mrs. Chinn Ho, a Chinese friend living in Hawaii.*

Mrs. Dallas Gordon Rupe

SCOTCH FANTASY

2 cups fresh peaches,
    peeled and sliced
1 cup Drambuie

1 quart rich vanilla ice cream
Few sprigs of mint

If the peaches are a bit tart, add a little sugar. Place in quart mixing bowl, and saturate with Drambuie. Cover, and chill 1-2 hours. Serve over vanilla ice cream; garnish with fresh mint. Serves 4. *Variation: Pour Scotch Fantasy in a punch bowl over a block of ice with lots of champagne and gingerale, and you have a party! Use 1 cup strawberries, fresh pineapple, raspberries or papaya in place of half of the peaches.*

Jan Henney

STRAWBERRIES SUPREME

12 large strawberries
¼ jar guava jelly
2 dashes of grenadine
2 dashes of Cointreau

Toasted sliced almonds
Vanilla ice cream
Whipped cream
Grated orange rind

Powdered sugar

Wash strawberries. Run guava jelly through a sieve over strawberries, and add grenadine and Cointreau. Put into sherbet glasses. Add toasted almonds. Top with a small scoop of ice cream and cream. Sprinkle orange rind, and dust with powdered sugar. Serves 2.

Mrs. Robert McCulloch

SWEDISH CREAM WITH BERRIES

1 envelope gelatin
¼ cup cold water
2⅓ cups whipping cream

1 cup sugar
1 pint sour cream
1 teaspoon vanilla

1 carton frozen strawberries or 2 small boxes fresh berries

Dissolve gelatin in water, and let stand for 5 minutes to soften. Place cream in saucepan, and add sugar and gelatin. Heat gently until creamy consistency, stirring gently. Remove from heat, and cool until thick. Place in refrigerator 30-60 minutes to hasten thickening. When partially thickened, thoroughly fold in sour cream and vanilla. Pour into sherbets, leaving room for berries, and chill 8 hours. Remove from refrigerator, spoon berries over the top of the Swedish Cream. Juice from berries adds to flavor. Serves 8. *This is lovely for a luncheon.*

Mrs. Robert J. Crampton

TUACA HAMMER

1 scoop rich vanilla ice cream 1 jigger Tuaca

Mix in blender. Serve in champagne glasses. Serves 2.

Mrs. Alvin Zidell

It has been said that the best ices in the world can be found in the small village of St. Tropez. It seems that a Mme. Lamponi has developed with great gastronomical skill the truest and finest flavors to be found anywhere.

LEMON ICE CREAM

Juice of 8 lemons   1 pint heavy cream
4 cups sugar   Grated peel of 1 orange
2 quarts whole milk   Pinch of salt

Mix all ingredients together, and freeze in 6-quart ice cream freezer, churning for about 25 minutes until stiff. Makes 6 quarts.

Mrs. Clarence H. Dragert

MACAROON BOMBE

1 dozen almond macaroons,   ¼ cup coffee cream
    crumbled   ½ cup sugar
½ cup sherry
                1 cup heavy cream, whipped

Soak macaroons in sherry, coffee cream and sugar. When macaroons have been softened, stir into a smooth paste, and fold in cream. Freeze until firm, but not hard, in a 1-quart shallow casserole. Cut into squares, or spoon into dessert dishes. Serves 4-6.

Mrs. Thomas D. Broad

LOW CALORIE ORANGE-PINEAPPLE SHERBET

1 can (6 oz.) frozen unsweetened orange juice concentrate

1 can (6 oz.) frozen unsweetened pineapple juice concentrate

3½ cups cold water

2 teaspoons liquid Sucaryl solution, or 48 tablets crushed

1 cup non-fat dry milk solids

Set refrigerator control at coldest setting. Put all ingredients in a 2-quart mixing bowl in order given. Beat just enough to blend. Pour into ice trays; freeze 1-2 hours until half-frozen. Remove to large, chilled mixing bowl. Beat on low speed until mixture is softened, then beat on high speed 3-5 minutes until creamy but not liquid. Pour into freezer containers or ice cube trays. Freeze. Makes 20 ½ cup servings at 58 calories per serving.

Mrs. Robert A. Beyers

FROSTY STRAWBERRY SQUARES

1 cup sifted all-purpose flour

¼ cup brown sugar

½ cup pecans or walnuts, chopped

½ cup butter, melted

2 egg whites

1 cup sugar

2 cups fresh strawberries

2 tablespoons lemon juice

1 cup heavy cream, whipped

Stir together flour, sugar, nuts and butter. Spread evenly in shallow baking pan. Bake at 350° for 20 minutes, stirring occasionally. Sprinkle ⅔ of the crumbs in a 13x9x2-inch baking pan. Reserve 10-12 whole strawberries, and slice remainder. Combine egg whites, sugar, sliced berries and lemon juice in large bowl. Beat at high speed to stiff peak stage, about 10 minutes. Fold in cream. Spoon over crumbs, and top with remaining crumbs. Freeze 6 hours or overnight. Cut into squares. Trim with whole strawberries. Serves 10-12.

Mrs. Tom C. Cross

APRICOT TORTONI

⅓ cup almonds, chopped

3 tablespoons butter, melted

1 teaspoon almond extract

1⅓ cups vanilla wafer crumbs

3 pints vanilla ice cream, softened

1 jar (12 oz.) apricot preserves

Whipped cream

Toast almonds in butter, then mix with crumbs and extract. In 9-inch square pan press layer of crumb mixture, then layer of ice cream, drizzle apricot preserves over top; then repeat layers of crumb mixture, ice cream and preserves, ending with crumb mixture. This is usually 3 layers of crumbs, 2 of ice cream and 2 of preserves. Freeze several hours until firm. Cut in squares, and top with cream, if desired. Serves 10-12.

Mrs. Edwin H. Howell

Cortés found a very exciting drink in the New World. After much investigation, he discovered the secret ingredient was cacao, flavored with a small pod (vanilla), which the Aztecs called thelxochitl. The chocolate drink was an instant success in Spain but over a hundred years would pass before it was accepted in the rest of Europe. This could have been because the clergy denounced the drink as "immoral and provocative of immorality". In 1660, Maria Theresa became Louis XIV's queen and introduced the chocolate drink to the ladies of the French court. When they heard the drink had very definite aphrodisiac results, cacao and vanilla were in great demand.

MOCHA-NUT TORTONI

2 eggs, separated

½ cup sugar

2 cups whipping cream

2 tablespoons instant coffee

2 teaspoons vanilla

½ cup semi-sweet chocolate bits, melted and cooled

½ cup toasted almonds, minced

Beat whites until almost stiff; gradually add ¼ cup of sugar. Beat until stiff. Whip cream with remaining ¼ cup sugar and instant coffee. Add egg yolks, slightly beaten, and vanilla. Mix with egg whites. Fold in chocolate. Add almonds. Freeze in paper cups or parfait glasses. Take out of the freezer a few minutes before serving or earlier, according to your taste preference. Serves 12.

Mrs. H. Ross Perot

DESSERTS

INDIVIDUAL COFFEE WALNUT SOUFFLÉS

2 envelopes unflavored gelatin
1 cup sugar
4 tablespoons instant coffee
¼ teaspoon salt

4 eggs, separated
2½ cups milk
1 teaspoon vanilla
2 cups heavy cream

½ cup walnuts, finely chopped

Combine gelatin, ½ cup sugar, instant coffee and salt in 2½-quart saucepan. Beat egg yolks with milk. Add to gelatin mixture. Stir over low heat until gelatin dissolves, and mixture thickens slightly, about 10-12 minutes. Remove from heat; add vanilla. Chill, stirring occasionally, until mixture mounds slightly when dropped from spoon. Meanwhile, prepare collars on dessert glasses by binding a double strip of aluminum foil firmly around top of each glass, extending 1 inch above top rim of each glass. Beat egg whites until stiff, but not dry. Add remaining ½ cup sugar, gradually. Beat until very stiff. Fold in gelatin mixture. Whip cream; fold in with walnuts. Spoon into prepared dessert glasses. Chill until firm. Remove collars. Garnish with additional chopped walnuts, if desired. Half the recipe may be molded in 5-cup mold or turned into 9-inch baked pie shell. For 8-12 servings with "top hat", use 4-6-ounce goblets or demi-tasse cups. If 8-ounce glass or dish is used, "top hat" will be eliminated or number of servings will be reduced to 4-6.

Julie Benell

SOUFFLÉ FLAMBÉ AU RHUM

4 eggs, separated
2 tablespoons sugar

6 dessert spoons rum, warmed
Butter

Add sugar to egg yolks, and beat to ribbon consistency. Whisk the egg whites vigorously until stiff. Gradually fold in whites, and mix well. Butter a skillet. Pour in the egg mixture, and bake at 350° for 10 minutes. Heat a serving dish, and tip the soufflé into it carefully. Quickly sear the outside of the soufflé criss-cross fashion with a hot poker. Sprinkle with sugar. Pour the warmed rum over the top, and blaze at the table. Serves 4. *This is certainly the simplest recipe possible for a soufflé. However, the use of the skillet for cooking it is most important.*

Robert Casadesus

THE DESSERT SOUFFLÉ

⅓ cup plus 2 tablespoons
sugar

3 tablespoons all-purpose
flour

¾ cup milk

5 eggs, separated

2 tablespoons butter, melted

2 tablespoons vanilla extract
or Cointreau or other
liqueur

¼ teaspoon cream of tartar

½ cup powdered sugar

Preheat oven to 400°. Butter a 6-cup soufflé dish lavishly. Put
the 2 tablespoons sugar in it, and evenly coat inside of dish.
Tap out excess. Put flour in a saucepan, and pour in just enough
milk to blend, using a wire whip. Gradually add remaining
milk and sugar, and stir over heat until it thickens. Add 4 egg
yolks, butter and flavoring. Beat egg whites to as stiff a
point as possible. Blend ¼ of the egg whites into the sauce
to lighten it. Then very carefully fold in remainder of egg
whites. Pour into soufflé dish, and put dish in deep center of
oven. Immediately reduce heat to 375°. After 15 minutes the
soufflé should be rising and browning. Sprinkle powdered sugar
over top, and continue baking for 5-10 minutes longer. *Person-
ally I love a soufflé just "underdone" with a thin cone of liquid
left in the center. Thus, the soufflé makes its own sauce. This
soufflé with the exception of egg whites may be prepared in
advance, covered, and refrigerated. There is nothing like a
soufflé to make an evening special.*

John Ardoin

GRAND MARNIER SOUFFLÉ

3 tablespoons butter

4 tablespoons flour

1 cup milk

Pinch of salt

6 tablespoons sugar

2 tablespoons honey (orange
blossom or other wild-
flower honey)

2 tablespoons lemon juice

Rind of 1 lemon, grated

Rind of 1 orange, grated

4 egg yolks

⅓ cup Grand Marnier

6 egg whites

Melt butter in enameled saucepan. Sprinkle in flour; mix, and
cook without stirring 2-3 minutes. Do not brown. Add milk; stir
with whisk until thick. Add salt, sugar, honey, juice and rinds.
Remove from heat; add egg yolks, 1 at a time, whisking in
thoroughly. Let cool a bit; add Grand Marnier. Whip egg whites
until in soft peaks and still moist. Fold mixture into whites with
spatula. Pour into buttered and sugared 6-cup soufflé dish.
Place in upper third of preheated 400° oven. Turn heat to 375°
immediately; cook 20-25 minutes. Serve immediately. Serves 4.

Mrs. Jack W. Lively

SOUFFLÉ EDWARD CLARK

4 ounces mixed glacé fruits

2 ounces Kirsch

½ cup milk

Scant ⅔ cup castor sugar

Scant ⅓ cup finest cocoa

Scant 1 teaspoon nutmeg

1 tablespoon French ground ginger

3 tablespoons instant coffee

5 tablespoons unsalted butter

5 tablespoons flour

5 egg yolks

6 egg whites

2 ounces Benedictine

Marinate chopped glacé fruits in Kirsch. Dissolve and mix in milk, ½ cup sugar, cocoa, nutmeg, ginger and instant coffee. In a saucepan melt butter, add flour, and cook until it does not stick to the bottom of pan. Add milk mixture, and cook until the resulting paste is again free from the saucepan. Remove from heat, and add egg yolks one by one. Beat the egg whites until stiff, and add the remaining sugar. Fold the whites into the chocolate mixture. Pour into a soufflé dish. Allow the fruits, drained of the liqueur, to sink into the mixture, and bake at 400° for 25 minutes. Have a little Benedictine and Kirsch mixture ready, warmed, and when the soufflé comes out of the oven, light it, and pour on top. Serve promptly together with a sauce boat of Chantilly cream flavored with Benedictine. *This recipe was created by the chef of Mrs. Fairfax in honor of their Excellencies, U. S. Ambassador to Australia, Edward Clark, and Mrs. Clark.*

Mrs. W. O. Fairfax

LEMON SOUFFLÉ

1 envelope gelatin

¼ cup cold water

4 eggs, separated

½ cup lemon juice

1 cup sugar

½ teaspoon salt

1 teaspoon lemon rind, grated

1 cup heavy cream, whipped

Slivered almonds, toasted (optional)

Sprinkle gelatin over cold water to soften. Mix yolks, lemon juice, ½ cup sugar and salt in double boiler, stirring constantly until thick. Remove from heat, and stir in gelatin and lemon rind. Cool. Beat egg whites until soft peaks form. Add ½ cup sugar, and beat until stiff and shiny. Add cream to whites, and fold cream into egg whites gently. Fold in gelatin mixture. Pour into 2-quart soufflé dish, and chill. Sprinkle with almonds before serving. Serves 4-6.

Mrs. Jonathan Kutner

CUSTARD

1 quart milk

4-5 eggs

Nutmeg

Cinnamon (optional)

2 tablespoons sugar

Beat eggs into milk. A blender is good for a smooth mixture. Add sprinkling of nutmeg and cinnamon. Place mixture in top of a double boiler with water already boiling. Cover, and let cook for 13-15 minutes. Remove from heat, and cool. Serves 10. *For people like me who know the great food value of eggs, but are not entranced by them in their plainer forms, it was valuable to learn, from my Italian mother-in-law, a very simple and speedy way to prepare custard.*

Eugene Cook

PLAIN BAKED CUSTARD

5 tablespoons sugar

3 eggs

⅛ teaspoon salt

½ teaspoon vanilla

2 cups milk, scalded

Mix sugar, eggs, salt and vanilla; combine with milk. Pour into custard cups or baking dish. Set in pan of hot water, and bake at 300° until firm, about 30-40 minutes. A knife blade run into the center of custard will come out clean.

Mrs. Dan Hughes, Jr.

ORANGE CUSTARD PUDDING

2 oranges

Sugar

1 quart milk

3 tablespoons flour

3 eggs, separated

1 cup sugar

1 teaspoon vanilla

Peel and skin the sections of oranges, and marinate in a little sugar. Let set while mixing other ingredients. Simmer milk, but do not boil. Mix flour, egg yolks and sugar. Add slowly to milk, stirring constantly. Cook to desired thickness. Pour into a 1½-quart Pyrex casserole, and add vanilla. Stir in orange sections. Beat whites until stiff, and use as a topping. A fourth egg white may be added, if desired. Brown quickly in a very hot oven. Chill, and serve ice cold.

Mrs. John Connally

CHOCOLATE MOUSSE

½ cup sugar

½ pound semi-sweet chocolate

¼ cup water

5 eggs, separated

1 teaspoon vanilla

Pecan halves or shaved chocolate

Melt sugar, chocolate and water together in top of double boiler. Put top of boiler in pan of cold water to cool. Meanwhile, beat yolks, and add vanilla, continually beating. Pour yolks into cooled chocolate, and mix well. If mixture seems too firm, add 1-2 tablespoons milk. Beat whites until stiff, and fold chocolate mixture into whites. Pour into individual molds, and chill. Garnish with nuts or chocolate. Chill at least 8 hours. Serves 6.

Ann Donaldson

RASPBERRY MOUSSE

1 package (3 oz.) red raspberry Jello

1 cup boiling water

1 package frozen red raspberries

1 pint vanilla ice cream

Whipped cream

Dissolve Jello in water. Chill until partially set. Whip with electric beater until frothy. Whip partially thawed red raspberries and vanilla ice cream into the Jello. Spoon into parfait glasses, and freeze. When serving, top with cream. Serves 6-8. *Variation: Add 1 tablespoon raspberry or other fruit liqueur of your choice to the mixture before freezing. Dribble a little liqueur over the whipped cream when serving.*

Mrs. Reginald P. Tull

FRUIT COBBLER

½ cup butter

1 cup flour

2 teaspoons baking powder

Pinch of salt

1 cup sugar

¾ cup milk

3-4 cups fruit

Melt butter in 2-quart casserole. Mix rest of ingredients except fruit, and beat well. Pour into melted butter. Pour in fruit. Bake at 350° for 45 minutes. Serves 6.

Mrs. Cullis R. Reese

MANHATTAN PUDDING

1½ cups fresh orange juice
1 cup sugar
¼ cup lemon juice

1 pint heavy cream
½ cup powdered sugar
½ tablespoon vanilla

⅔ cup walnut meats, finely chopped

Mix fruit juices and sugar. When sugar is dissolved, turn into mold. Then whip cream; add powdered sugar, vanilla and nuts. Spoon on top of juices. Freeze. When frozen, unmold, slice, and serve. Serves 8.

Mrs. Philip K. Bates, Jr.

PLUM PUDDING

¼ cup flour
½ cup bread crumbs
½ cup brown sugar
½ teaspoon allspice
¼ teaspoon salt
½ cup beef suet, finely chopped
1 ounce blanched almonds, chopped
2 ounces Sultana raisins
4 ounces raisins

4 ounces currants
2 ounces candied orange peel, chopped
2 ounces candied pineapple, chopped
1 sour apple, peeled and grated
3 eggs, beaten
Rind and juice of ½ lemon or orange
Irish whisky or bourbon to taste or ½ bottle Guiness beer

Mix dry ingredients well. Combine dry ingredients with suet, almonds and fruit in a large mixing bowl. Mix well. Add eggs to lemon juice and whiskey, and stir all ingredients together. Leave overnight. Fill a large well-greased bowl ¾ full, and cover with foil. Steam for 4 hours. When cold, it may be stored or frozen indefinitely. Steam for 2 hours before serving. Turn onto a hot dish. Decorate top with sprig of holly. Just before serving, shake castor sugar on top and around sides, then pour a little whiskey or brandy over the pudding and light. Serves 12. *This is the traditional British Christmas dinner dessert.*

Mrs. Stanley W. Blanchard

DESERTS

QUICK FRUIT PUDDING

1 can (1 lb. 5 oz.) Comstock
    apple, peach or cherry
    pie filling
1 Jiffy package yellow
    cake mix

½ cup butter
Pecans (optional)
Whipped cream or ice cream

Place pie filling in 8-inch pan. Prepare cake mix, and pour over filling. Dot with butter. Sprinkle with pecans. Bake according to cake directions. Serve warm with cream. Serves 6.

Mrs. Finis D. Wilkins

ENGLISH TRIFLE

4 sponge cakes,
    thickly sliced
Raspberry or strawberry
    preserves
6 macaroons
½ cup sherry or milk
Grated rind of ½ lemon

2 ounces almonds, blanched
    and slivered
½ pint custard sauce
½ pint cream
2 egg whites
Fine sugar
Angelica

Glacé cherries

Spread half of sponge cake slices with preserves, cover with remainder of slices, and arrange alternately with macaroons in a glass dish. Soak cake thoroughly with wine. Sprinkle with lemon rind; add almonds, and cover with custard sauce. Combine cream and egg whites; whip stiffly, and sweeten to taste with sugar. Pile cream mixture lightly on top of custard. Garnish with angelica, almonds and cherries. Serves 4.

Greer Garson

TEXAS

NOCHE SPECIALS
A Mexican Appetizer

Tortillas or tostados

Crisco oil or shortening

Cheese, grated

Jalapeño peppers, sliced

Cut tortillas into quarters and fry in deep hot fat until brown and crisp on both sides, or buy ready-made tostados. Drain, and put about 1 teaspoon of cheese and a slice of jalapeño pepper on each quarter. Place in hot oven until well-heated and cheese begins to melt. Serve at once.

Mrs. Lyndon B. Johnson

CHILI CON QUESO

1 cup onions, chopped

1 tablespoon shortening

1½ cups tomatoes, chopped and well-drained

1 can (4 oz.) long green chilies, reserving liquid

1 teaspoon salt

½ teaspoon pepper

1 pound Velveeta cheese, grated

Toasted tortilla chips

Sauté onions in shortening until tender. Add tomatoes, chilies, salt, pepper and cheese. Cook in double boiler slowly for 30-40 minutes. Add liquid from chilies if mixture becomes too stiff. Serve hot as a dip with tortilla chips. Serves 12.

Mrs. Ralph G. Greenlee

GUACAMOLE DIP

4 large avocados, finely chopped

1 tablespoon onion, finely chopped

2 tablespoons salad oil

1 tablespoon wine vinegar

1 tablespoon lemon juice

¼ teaspoon ground oregano

¼ teaspoon pepper or hot peppers

1 large tomato, finely chopped

Dash of garlic powder or 1 small clove garlic, finely minced

Salt to taste

Fritos or potato chips

Mix all ingredients except Fritos about 1 hour before serving and season to taste. Will keep overnight if covered tightly. Serve with Fritos.

Mrs. Robert McCulloch

TEXAS CRAB GRASS

1/2 cup butter

1/2 medium onion, finely chopped

1 package frozen chopped spinach, cooked and drained

1 can (7 oz.) crabmeat

3/4 cup Parmesan cheese, grated

Melba rounds or crackers

Slowly melt butter in heavy saucepan. Add onion and sauté until soft. Add spinach to onion mixture. Add crabmeat and cheese. Transfer to chafing dish and serve with Melba rounds.

Mrs. Warren H. Hall

AVOCADO COCKTAIL

2 tablespoons lemon juice

4 tablespoons orange juice

1/2 cup mayonnaise

1/2 cup well-seasoned chili sauce

1/8 teaspoon onion, grated

1/2 teaspoon salt

Dash of Tabasco

1 hard-boiled egg

2 small avocados, peeled and cubed

1 cup crabmeat

2 cans grapefruit sections

Combine lemon juice, orange juice, mayonnaise, chili sauce, onion, salt and Tabasco. Force egg through a ricer or sieve and stir into mixture. Arrange avocado in cocktail glasses with crabmeat and grapefruit sections. Use grapefruit sparingly. Pour sauce over the top and chill thoroughly before serving. Serves 8.

Mrs. Robert J. Crampton

XATÓ

3 cloves garlic

7-8 almonds, peeled and toasted

1 or more sharp chili peppers or powdered cayenne pepper to taste

1/2 cup olive oil

1/4 cup wine vinegar

3/4 teaspoon salt

2 heads curly endive

Put all ingredients, except endive, into blender and mix until well-blended. Separate endive into leaves and marinate in sauce for at least 1 hour before serving. Xató is a traditional Catalan dish and is generally served as a first course. Serves 6. *This was served to us in Spain accompanied by platters of thinly sliced ham, a variety of cold sausages, filets of anchovy and a white bean omelet.*

Mrs. Dallas Gordon Rupe

CEVICHI
A Mexican Fish Appetizer

1 teaspoon oregano

1 teaspoon gumbo filé

1 teaspoon celery seed

8 ounces lime juice

8 ounces lemon juice

½ pound frozen or fresh haddock or halibut, skinned and boned

1 jar (4 oz.) yellow chili peppers, seeded and halved

1 jalapeño pepper, seeded and minced

Salt to taste

1 small onion, diced

2 large fresh tomatoes, cut in small pieces

1 bottle (3 oz.) Spanish olives

¼ cup olive oil

Tie oregano, gumbo filé and celery seed in a small piece of cheese cloth. Chill lime and lemon juices. Cut haddock in ½-inch strips. Mix peppers with fish, salt lightly, and place in a glass dish. Add onion and sack of spices to fish, cover completely with lime and lemon juice. Cover dish and refrigerate 12 hours, stirring occasionally with silver spoon. After 12 hours, pour off liquid and add tomatoes and juice. Stir in olives and olive oil. Squeeze spice sack over fish, bury it deep in mixture, adjust salt to taste, and refrigerate an additional 2-3 hours. Serve in a glass dish with Doritos or crackers. Makes 3 cups. *I first ate this dish in Acapulco, at Caleta Playa in 1940. Orders were taken by little barefoot boys who raced over the sand. Often, we saw a fisherman selling a freshly caught fish to the women who prepared the Cevichi by throwing the ingredients into an earthen bowl and setting it in a block of ice.*

Mrs. William H. Beasley

GRILLED GARLIC SHRIMP

½ cup oil

¼ cup lemon juice

½ cup parsley, chopped

3 cloves garlic, chopped

Salt and pepper to taste

Cayenne to taste

2 pounds large shrimp, shelled and deveined

Combine oil, lemon juice, parsley, garlic, salt, pepper and cayenne. Marinate shrimp for 30 minutes at room temperature. Place on skewers and broil close to coals for 5 minutes or until shrimp turn pink, basting frequently with marinade. Serves 8. *These are really delicately flavored, simple to prepare and always a success.*

Mrs. Morris A. Galter

GRINGO SOUP

1 package (2 lb.) red pinto beans

3 quarts hot water

1½ cups cooked ham, cut in 1-inch cubes

Freshly ground black pepper to taste

White pepper to taste

Salt to taste

2-3 tablespoons chili powder

Dash of cooking sherry

Green onions and stems, finely chopped

Bacon bits

Thoroughly wash beans. Place beans in water. Boil at medium, then low-medium heat for about 3 hours. Add hot water as required until beans boil down to a fairly thick juice. Add ham when beans are about half-done. Continue to boil and stir frequently. When beans are almost done, season with black pepper, white pepper, salt and chili powder. Stir well and continue to boil until done. Add sherry. Cool. Put in blender and homogenize to a coarse texture. When ready to serve, reheat and serve piping hot. Sprinkle onions and bacon on top of soup. Serves 6-8. *Serve in colorful pottery or crockery bowls. We like to serve either hush puppies or jalapeño cornbread sticks with this soup and a green salad with avocado dressing.*

Charles Cullum

AVOCADO-GRAPEFRUIT MOLDED SALAD

1 package lime gelatin

1 scant cup hot grapefruit juice

1 ripe avocado, sliced

1 package (3 oz.) cream cheese

¼ teaspoon MSG

½ teaspoon celery juice

1 scant cup mayonnaise

Dash of salt

1 cup grapefruit sections, well-drained

Dissolve gelatin in grapefruit juice. Let cool until almost ready to jell. Blend avocado with cream cheese, and add MSG, celery juice, mayonnaise and salt. Add gelatin mixture, then fold in grapefruit sections and mold. Serves 8. *This is a beautiful and delicious salad from the old Stagecoach Inn at Salado, Texas.*

Mrs. R. F. Schermerhorn

MOLDED GRAPEFRUIT SALAD

⅓ cup sugar

⅓ cup water

1½ teaspoons gelatin

2 tablespoons cold water

¾ cup grapefruit juice

1 tablespoon lemon juice

½ teaspoon salt

Lettuce

Philadelphia cream cheese

Walnuts, chopped

French dressing

Boil sugar and water for 3 minutes. Dissolve gelatin in cold water. Combine both with juices and salt. Pour into mold and refrigerate until set. Serve on lettuce with a dab of cheese to which walnuts have been added. Top with a light French dressing. Serves 6-8.

Mrs. DeWitt Ray

The cooking of the hill country around the Pedernales River came entirely from Germany, the Old South, and the Mexican regions of Texas. The traditions of these regions flowed together easily, and the characteristic cooking was simple and sturdy. It followed the Southwestern tradition of serving few soups and salads.

WESTERN SALAD

2 garlic cloves, peeled and halved

½ cup salad oil

2 small heads iceberg or Romaine lettuce or ½ and ½

½ cup grated Parmesan cheese

¼ cup blue cheese, crumbled

½ teaspoon salt

¼ teaspoon pepper

1 egg

3½ teaspoons lemon juice

1 teaspoon Worcestershire sauce

2 cups croûtons

Soak garlic in salad oil for 1 hour. Break up lettuce and put in salad bowl, and sprinkle with Parmesan, blue cheese, salt and pepper. Drizzle oil, then break egg over lettuce. Add lemon juice and Worcestershire sauce. Toss. Add croûtons, and toss lightly. Serve immediately. Serves 8.

Mrs. Richard A. Erb

CHARCOALED FISH

2 pounds fish steaks
½ cup oil
½ cup sesame seeds
⅓ cup lemon juice

⅓ cup Cognac
3 tablespoons soy sauce
1 teaspoon salt
1 clove garlic, crushed

Place steaks in a single layer in a shallow baking dish. Combine remaining ingredients. Pour sauce over fish and let stand for 30 minutes, turning once. Remove fish, reserving sauce for basting. Place fish in well-greased hinged wire grills. Cook on a barbecue grill about 4 inches from moderately hot coals for 8 minutes. Baste with remaining sauce. Turn and cook for 7-10 minutes longer or until fish flakes easily when tested with a fork and sesame seeds have browned. Serve any remaining sauce with fish. Serves 6. *The sesame seed gives a nutty, toasted flavor.*

The Cookbook Committee

ANGELS ON HORSEBACK

24 plump raw oysters, drained
¼ cup lemon juice
3 dashes of Tabasco

1 teaspoon Worcestershire sauce
½ teaspoon salt
12 slices bacon

Preheat oven to 450°. Place oysters in a mixing bowl and add lemon juice, Tabasco, Worcestershire sauce and salt. Stir briefly to coat oysters with sauce. Cut each bacon slice in half, and use each half to wrap 1 oyster. Secure with toothpicks and place on a rack in a baking dish. Bake until bacon is crisp. *This is a favorite of ours for Sunday evenings.*

Mrs. Jerrold M. Trim

FRESH BOILED SHRIMP, PADRE ISLAND STYLE

Chili sauce
Onion salt
Lime or lemon juice
Dehydrated onion flakes

Horseradish
¾ pound fresh shrimp per person
1 package Rex crab boil

Mix chili sauce, onion salt, lime juice and onion flakes to prepare red sauce. Chill. Bring water to a boil in a very large pot. Add crab boil. Boil water 5-10 minutes longer. Add shrimp and cover. Remove from heat and let stand until shrimp turn soft pink and rise to the top. Do not overcook. Drain. Serve shrimp on a large platter on the floor with newspapers in front of everyone so they can shell the shrimp on the paper. Serve with red sauce. *A green salad and hot bread complete the meal.*

Mrs. Duncan E. Boeckman

SHRIMP AND AVOCADO MOUSSE

2 envelopes gelatin

½ cup cold water

1 cup boiling water

1½ teaspoons salt

⅛ teaspoon curry powder

2 teaspoons Worcestershire sauce

1 tablespoon lemon juice

1½ tablespoons chives, chopped

2 cups avocado, mashed

1½ cups cooked shrimp, chopped

¾ cup heavy cream, whipped

¾ cup mayonnaise

Soak gelatin in cold water to soften and stir in boiling water to dissolve. Cool slightly and add salt, curry powder, Worcestershire sauce, lemon juice, chives, avocado and shrimp. Chill until it begins to set, then fold in cream and mayonnaise. Adjust seasoning to taste and pour into oiled 8-9 cup ring mold. Chill. Serves 8-10. *Fill with parsley, shrimp and avocado slices, and serve with broiled tomato halves and cheese straws.*

Mrs. Jerry W. Peterman

CHICKEN ENCHILADAS

3-4 cups cooked chicken breasts, cut in chunks

2 cans cream of chicken soup

1 can (6 oz.) evaporated milk

½ cup onion

1 can green chili peppers

1 dozen tortillas, broken in small pieces

8 ounces Swiss cheese, grated

Mix chicken, soup, milk, onion and chili peppers. In casserole place a layer of tortillas, layer of chicken mixture and a layer of Swiss cheese. Repeat layers and end with cheese on top. Bake at 350° until hot and cheese is melted. Serves 6-8.

Mrs. Oakley W. Cheney, Jr.

CHICKEN ESPAÑOLE

2 large fryers or 1 large hen

1 green pepper, chopped

1 onion, chopped

¼ cup olive oil

2 cans tomato soup

1 jar (8 oz.) green olives, sliced

1 jar (8 oz.) ripe olives, sliced

2 cans (4 oz.) sliced mushrooms, or 1 pound fresh mushrooms, sautéed

Cook chicken until tender, bone, cut in pieces. Sauté green pepper and onion in olive oil. Add soup, olives and mushrooms. Combine thoroughly. Add chicken, and warm. Serve over rice. Serves 12. *This is a piquant chicken dish enhanced by olives.*

Mrs. Gene W. Rogers

CREAM CHICKEN TACOS

1 large onion, chopped

3 cups tomato juice

1 cup enchilada sauce

¾ cup Ro-Tel tomatoes

3 cups American cheese, grated

2¼ cups heavy cream

3 cups mushrooms

1 package tortillas

Hot oil

2 chickens, cooked, boned, and cut in chunks

Sauté onions until yellow. Add tomato juice, enchilada sauce, tomatoes, cheese and cream, and simmer for 1 hour. Add mushrooms. Fry tortillas in oil until crisp. Layer tortillas, chicken and mushroom sauce in large oven-proof casserole. Refrigerate overnight. Bake at 350° for 1 hour, and serve immediately. Serves 10.

Mrs. Robert A. White

POLLITO RELLENO

4 large chicken breasts, boned

2 cans (4 oz.) small sliced mushrooms

¼ cup butter

¾ cup coarse dry bread crumbs

1 tablespoon instant minced onion

¾ teaspoon chili powder

2 teaspoons Mei Yen powder

⅛ teaspoon garlic powder

Flatten chicken breasts with mallet. Sauté mushrooms in butter until golden. Remove mushrooms, reserving butter in pan. Combine mushrooms, bread crumbs, onion, chili powder, Mei Yen and garlic powder. Spoon ¼ cup crumb mixture onto each chicken breast. Roll up breasts, fastening with metal poultry pins, and place in covered glass baking dish. Spoon melted butter over chicken rolls, cover, and bake at 375° for 1 hour. Remove cover and baste with drippings. Place under broiler for 5 minutes, or until golden brown. Serves 4.

Mrs. Thomas C. Walker

WILD DOVE COOKOUT

16 doves

Wesson oil

Port or sherry

16 bacon slices

Marinate doves overnight in mixture of ½ oil and ½ wine (enough to cover). When ready to cook, remove from marinade, wrap each bird with a slice of bacon and secure with a toothpick. When fire under grill is moderately hot, place pan with birds over fire and baste with marinade until tender, approximately 1 hour. Serves 4-5.

Mrs. Walter F. Smith, Jr.

ROTISSERIE WILD DUCK

2 wild ducks, preferably
  Mallards
1 cup Burgundy, Rosé or
  pale dry sherry

Salt to taste
½ pound Gaylord salty
  bacon

Marinate ducks about 30 minutes in wine. Wash ducks inside and out. Drain well and pat dry. Season lightly with salt inside only. Wrap each duck completely in bacon (3-4 slices) and secure with toothpicks. Insert rotisserie rod in ducks and cook at 300° for 2 hours, basting occasionally with wine. These ducks can be cooked in a pan at 300°. If done this way, allow another hour for cooking and baste more frequently. *If cooked on an oven rotisserie, you will never have a more tender duck.*

Mrs. Oscar W. Ponder

QUAIL FOSTER

8 quail
¼ cup butter, melted
½ cup olive oil
1½ tablespoons flour

Salt and pepper to taste
1 cup cooking sherry
1 can chicken broth
1 cup shortening

8 slices French bread

Brown birds on all sides in butter and olive oil in an 8-quart Dutch oven. Remove birds from pan. Add flour to pan and brown well, stirring constantly. Return birds to pan. Add salt, pepper and sherry, and simmer, covered, for 15 minutes. Add chicken broth and simmer, covered, over low heat for 45 minutes. (Do not overcook.) While the birds are cooking, melt the shortening in a frying pan, and fry the bread until golden brown. Place bread on a paper towel to allow grease to drain. To serve, place toast on platter, and cover with enough gravy to soften toast. Place each bird on a slice of toast, and add more gravy on birds. Serves 4. *Variation: Substitute doves or partridges for quail.*

Mrs. Memnon K. Foster

BARBECUED BRISKET

7-10 pound brisket

Meat tenderizer

2 onions, chopped

2 garlic cloves, minced

2 teaspoons salt

1/4 teaspoon pepper

2 teaspoons chili powder

1 teaspoon celery salt

1 teaspoon dry mustard

2 tablespoons Worcestershire sauce

1/2 cup brown sugar

1/2 cup vinegar

4 cans tomato sauce

Juice of 2 lemons

1/4 teaspoon Tabasco

Tenderize brisket several hours prior to cooking. Build barbecue fire to 1 side of pit, using large quantity of hickory. Place brisket over low heat (200°), and cover pit with lid. Combine remaining ingredients and cook for 30 minutes to prepare sauce. Baste brisket with sauce every hour for 8-9 hours. Serves 10.

John W. Turner

MEXICAN STUFFED ROAST

4-5 pound rolled roast of beef

1 onion

1 green pepper

2 whole pimentos

1/2 pound ham

1 clove garlic

2 tablespoons wine vinegar

2 teaspoons salt

Pepper to taste

1/2 teaspoon oregano

Stuffed olives

1 can (8 oz.) tomato sauce

1/2 cup beef bouillon

Tie roast and make large deep holes in top. Grind together onion, green pepper, pimentos, ham and garlic. Add vinegar, salt, pepper and oregano. Stuff holes in meat with this mixture and plug each hole with a stuffed olive. Refrigerate at least 12 hours. Put in roasting pan with tomato sauce, bouillon, and leftover stuffing mixture. Roast at 350° until done. Serves 6.

Mrs. John D. Heard

TEXAS BARBECUE

3 pounds lean chuck, cut
   into ¾-inch cubes

Salt

Water

3 tablespoons liquid smoke

3 tablespoons Worcestershire
   sauce

1 bottle (14 oz.) catsup

2 tablespoons vinegar

2 tablespoons prepared
   mustard

Dash of Tabasco (optional)

1 regular size Coca Cola

Cook meat with salt and 1 cup water slowly for about 2 hours until very tender. Add more water, if necessary. Shred meat with forks while warm, being sure to remove all fat and skin. Add remaining ingredients except Coca Cola. Stir and let simmer for 30 minutes. Add Coca Cola. This may be prepared in advance.

Mrs. Mark Schooler

CHALUPAS

1 pound ground beef

2 medium onions, chopped

2 tablespoons bacon grease

2 tablespoons flour

2-3 tablespoons chili powder

1 can tomato soup

1 can (3 oz.) evaporated milk

1½ cups Cheddar cheese,
   grated

Salt to taste

12 tortillas, cut in pieces

Sauté beef and 1 onion in bacon grease until brown, sprinkling with flour and chili powder during cooking. Add water to cover and simmer for 30 minutes. Combine tomato soup, milk, cheese, remaining onion, and season with salt. Cover the bottom of a greased, 2-quart casserole with a layer of tortillas, then a layer of meat, and top with cheese mixture. Repeat until all ingredients are used, ending with cheese mixture. Bake at 325° for about 40 minutes or until cheese has melted and browned. The meat mixture may be made the day before serving. Serves 6. *This recipe was given in* Dining with the Murchisons, *an English-Spanish Cookbook for the excellent kitchens of Ranchos Marquita y Toro, copyright, 1950, published by J. C. Thompson, Dallas. It was given to me when we were guests at El Toro, the Murchison Island.*

Mrs. Joseph T. Nance

CHALUPAS LAREDO

1½ pounds ground round
Garlic salt to taste
Pinch of pepper
1 large can ranch-style
   beans, drained
Round crisp tortillas
1 teaspoon wine vinegar
2 teaspoons olive oil
1 cucumber, thinly sliced

1 head iceberg lettuce,
   shredded
2 medium tomatoes, diced
4 green onions, chopped
1 avocado, sliced
American cheese, grated
   (optional)
Jalapeño peppers, chopped
   (optional)

Ripe olives, chopped (optional)

Brown meat in large skillet for approximately 20 minutes. Add garlic salt, pepper and beans, and simmer 10 minutes. Spoon onto tortillas. Mix vinegar, olive oil, cucumber, lettuce, tomatoes, onions and avocado together and spoon over meat mixture. Top with cheese, jalapeños and olives. Serves 6-8.

Mrs. Don Malouf

As the gusty northers blew, chili was cooked in every kitchen, and a pepper went into every pot.

CHILI DEL TORRE

2 pounds ground chuck or
   ground round
2 onions, diced
2 cloves garlic, finely chopped
1 tablespoon chili powder

2 cans (1 lb. 4 oz.) Ro-Tel
   tomatoes
2 cans (1 lb. 4 oz.) pinto beans
1 teaspoon salt
1 teaspoon black pepper

Sauté meat, onion and garlic until golden brown. Add chili powder, tomatoes, beans, salt and pepper. Simmer for 1 hour. Serves 6-8. *Serve with tostados or crackers.*

John Tower

PEDERNALES RIVER CHILI

4 pounds chili meat

1 large onion, chopped

2 cloves garlic

1 teaspoon ground oregano

1 teaspoon comino seed

6 teaspoons chili powder
(more if desired)

1½ cups canned whole
tomatoes

2-6 generous dashes liquid
hot pepper sauce

Salt to taste

2 cups hot water

Place meat, onions and garlic in large, heavy skillet or Dutch oven. Cook until light-colored. Add oregano, comino seed, chili powder, tomatoes, hot pepper sauce, salt and water. Bring to boil, lower heat and simmer about 1 hour. Skim off fat during cooking. Serves 8. *Chili meat is coarsely ground round steak or well-trimmed chuck meat. If specially ground, ask meat man to use ¾-inch plate for coarse grind.*

Mrs. Lyndon B. Johnson

RANCH-HAND CHILI

3 pounds ground beef

1 large onion, chopped

1 tablespoon comino seeds

1 teaspoon garlic salt or
garlic powder

4 tablespoons Gebhardt's
chili powder

4 tablespoons Worcestershire
sauce

1 large red pepper pod,
seeded and cut into small
strips

2 cans (8 oz.) Hunt's tomato
sauce

1 quart hot water

Salt to taste

Cook meat, stirring until brown, in a large, heavy Dutch oven or iron skillet with a lid. Add onion. Keeping heat as low as possible, add comino seeds, garlic salt, chili powder, Worcestershire sauce, pepper pod, tomato sauce, hot water and salt. Simmer, covered, over very low heat for at least 3 hours, stirring occasionally. *This is a mild and flavorful chili, recommended for the faint-hearted.*

Bob Lilly

COWBOY CASSEROLE

1 package (8 oz.) spaghetti
1 onion, diced
Butter
1½ pounds ground round
Salt and pepper to taste

Garlic powder or chili powder
or Lawry's salt (or all 3)
1 can mushroom soup
1 can tomato soup
Dash of Worcestershire sauce

Cheese, grated

Cook spaghetti until just tender. Brown onion in butter. Add ground round and cook until browned. Add salt, pepper and seasonings to taste. Add mushroom soup, tomato soup and Worcestershire sauce. Mix spaghetti and meat sauce together; cover, and simmer 15 minutes. Put into a casserole, top with cheese, and heat in oven until cheese melts. Serves 6. *For Sunday afternoon football fans, you can prepare this in the morning, put it in the oven to warm at the start of the game on TV, run and take it out at half-time, put it on the table, hand everyone a plate, fork and piece of garlic bread, and eat it during the second half. You will never miss a single play.*

Mrs. Don Meredith

MEXICAN MEAT BALLS

2 cans (17 oz.) tomatoes,
reserving 2 tablespoons
juice
1 cup water
2½ teaspoons chili powder

1½ pounds ground beef
1 pound ground lean pork
1 teaspoon salt
1 egg

1 cup raw rice

Put tomatoes, water and 2 teaspoons chili powder into a 3-quart saucepan. Bring to a boil over medium heat. Mix meat, salt, egg, rice, remaining ½ teaspoon chili powder and tomato juice. Form meat mixture into balls, and add to sauce. Bring to a boil, reduce heat, and cook 2 hours or until liquid is a rich gravy consistency. Serves 6. *It is delicious with a tossed green salad and buttered broccoli.*

Mrs. William M. Elliott, Jr.

TACOS

1 pound ground round beef	1 cup Cheddar cheese, grated
1 large onion, chopped	32 taco shells
1 large tomato, chopped	Lettuce
1/2-1 jar (8 oz.) picante sauce	Tomatoes

Italian dressing

Brown meat in skillet. Add onion, tomato and picante sauce. Simmer until mixture has cooked down, approximately 30 minutes. Add cheese and toss mixture. Warm taco shells and spoon half full with meat mixture. Fill the rest of shell with lettuce-tomato salad, mixed with Italian dressing. Serve immediately. Makes 32.

Mrs. John D. Worley

BARBECUED PORK CHOPS

1/4 cup vinegar	1 medium onion, sliced
1/2 cup water	1/2 cup catsup
1 tablespoon mustard	2 tablespoons Worcestershire sauce
2 tablespoons sugar	
1 lemon, sliced	1-2 tablespoons liquid smoke

8 pork chops

Simmer vinegar, water, mustard, sugar, lemon and onion for 20 minutes. Add catsup, Worcestershire sauce and liquid smoke, and bring to a rapid boil. Pour over the chops and bake for 1 hour and 25 minutes at 350°, turning once. Serves 4.

Mrs. W. H. Goldsmith

VENISON CHILI

1 pound suet	4 pounds ground venison
2 large onions, chopped	1 quart boiling water
6 bay leaves	1 teaspoon red pepper
1 can (6 oz.) tomato paste	2 tablespoons chili powder
4 teaspoons salt	2 tablespoons ground comino

2 garlic cloves

Render suet; add onion and brown. Add bay leaves, tomato paste and salt. Cook 1 minute. Crumble meat into this. Add water, red pepper, chili powder, comino and garlic. Bring to a boil, reduce heat, and simmer 2 hours. Add more boiling water if too dry. Serves 8-10.

Mrs. Milton H. Thomas, Jr.

NOREEN'S BARBECUED RIBS

4 pounds lean backbone
or ribs

1-2 large onions, sliced

Several stalks of celery

2 cups Noreen's Barbecue
Sauce

Salt to taste

Place backbone in glass casserole and salt both sides. Place onions on top. Lay celery over onions. Cover with Barbecue Sauce. Bake 3 hours in a 250° oven. Turn; cook 3 more hours. Serves 4.

NOREEN'S BARBECUE SAUCE

2 bottles (1 pt. 10 oz.)
Heinz catsup

1 bottle (10 oz.)
Worcestershire sauce

¾ cup (packed) McCormick's
dry mustard

¼ cup vinegar

3 cups water

⅓ cup (packed) dark
brown sugar

⅓ cup sorghum molasses

2 cups water

2 medium onions, quartered

6 medium garlic cloves,
quartered

¼ cup Mazola oil

1 teaspoon salt

Pour all ingredients into a 6-quart kettle with cover. Use water and vinegar to rinse out catsup bottles and molasses measuring cup. Cook slowly, covered, at about 225°-250° for 2 hours, then take off cover. Stir occasionally. Adjust seasonings to taste. After sauce has thickened as desired, remove onion and garlic and strain into jars. Sauce will keep several weeks or longer if refrigerated. Heat sauce before serving with meat.

Mrs. William F. Nicol

CHEESE 'N CHILI RICE CASSEROLE

2 cups long-grain instant rice

2 cups water

½ teaspoon salt

1 tablespoon butter

8 ounces Monterrey Jack
cheese, cubed

½ pint sour cream

1 can (4 oz.) green chilies,
diced

Paprika

Cook rice with water, salt and butter. Let stand 5 minutes. Mix in cheese, sour cream and chilies. Pour into a buttered 2-quart casserole. Sprinkle paprika over top. Cook at 350° for approximately 30 minutes. Serves 6. *This is best served with grilled steak, chicken or brisket.*

Mrs. Robert H. Hodge

CHEESE GRITS CASSEROLE

3 eggs

3 teaspoons salt

1½ teaspoons Tabasco

1 teaspoon paprika

6 cups boiling water

1½ cups quick-cooking grits

1 pound mild Wisconsin cheese, grated

¾ cup butter

Beat eggs, salt, Tabasco and paprika together. Set aside. Add grits to water and cook as directed on the box. When cooked, add cheese, butter and egg mixture to grits and mix well. Pour into a 2-quart casserole and bake at 350° for 1 hour or until firm. Serves 16.

Mrs. Alex F. Weisberg, Jr.

EGGS À LA SAND BOX RESTAURANT

4 slices bacon

1 tomato, coarsely chopped

2 medium onions, coarsely chopped

1 jalapeño pepper, finely chopped

½ teaspoon salt

6 eggs

Cut bacon into ¼-inch pieces and fry in a skillet until soft but not brown. Add remaining ingredients, except eggs. Place eggs on top, letting them run through the vegetables. Turn occasionally with a spatula until eggs are cooked and somewhat scrambled. Serves 2-3.

Mrs. Duncan E. Boeckman

QUESO BEANS

6 cans (1 lb.) whole salad-style green beans, drained

2 cans mushroom soup

2 cans (6 oz.) peeled green chilies

½ cup cream

2 cups sharp Cheddar cheese, grated

½ teaspoon garlic salt

2 cans French fried onions

Place beans in buttered casserole. Mix other ingredients except onions and pour over beans. Sprinkle onions on top and bake at 350° for 30 minutes. Serves 24.

Mrs. John N. Savage

FRIJOLES

1 pound pinto beans

1/4 pound salt pork, cut into 1/2-inch squares

1 can (20 oz.) tomatoes, cores removed

Freshly ground pepper

1 clove garlic

Hot chili peppers to taste

Soak beans overnight. Cook beans over low heat until tender. Render salt pork. Add juice to the beans as it cooks out. When the juice stops flowing, add browned salt pork cubes to the beans. Add tomatoes. Season with ground pepper, garlic and hot peppers to taste. *At their best these beans should be hot-hot!*

Mrs. Bernard Fulton

CORN PUDDING

1 cup cooked rice

1 cup cream-style corn

1 green pepper, finely chopped

2 eggs, beaten

3/4 cup milk

1 cup cheese, diced or grated

1/2 teaspoon salt

1/2 teaspoon pepper

3 tablespoons butter

Mix rice, corn, pepper, eggs, milk, cheese, salt and pepper, and pour into buttered 2-quart casserole. Dot with butter. Bake at 350° for 1 hour or until firm. Serves 4.

Mrs. Fred W. Erhard

HOMINY CASSEROLE

1 small onion, diced

1 small bell pepper, diced

1 tablespoon margarine, melted

1 can Ashley green enchilada sauce

Large quantity mild Cheddar cheese, grated

4 cans yellow hominy, drained

Sauté onion and pepper in margarine until soft. Add enchilada sauce and simmer for 15 minutes. Combine majority of cheese, hominy and sauce in casserole, and top with remaining cheese. Bake at 350° until cheese is bubbly and light brown. Serves 12.

Mrs. Morton H. Meyerson

TEXAS CAVIAR
Pickled Black-Eyed Peas

4 cups cooked, dried
  black-eyed peas

1 cup salad oil

1/4 cup wine vinegar

1 clove garlic

1/2 cup onion, diced

1/2 teaspoon salt

Freshly ground black pepper to taste

Drain liquid from peas. Mix together thoroughly all other ingredients and add peas. Store in covered container in refrigerator, removing garlic clove after 1 day. Wait 3 days before serving peas, chilled and arranged in attractive bowl for buffet supper.

Mrs. Joe L. Bergin

LONESOME ACRES COMBINATION

7 medium yellow squash,
  sliced

1 medium onion, chopped

1 green pepper, chopped

1/2 cup margarine

1 can (1 lb. 1 oz.) cream-style
  corn

Salt and pepper to taste

1 egg, beaten

Ritz cracker crumbs, buttered

Cook squash in slightly salted water until soft. Drain. Sauté onion and green pepper in margarine until transparent. Combine squash, corn and sautéed vegetables. Add salt, pepper and egg. Pour into a buttered 2-quart casserole and sprinkle with cracker crumbs. Bake at 350° for 1 hour until firm. Serves 8. *This is my great grandmother's recipe which I enjoy serving with baked ham, pork or chicken.*

Mrs. Richard Wray, Jr.

TARTAR SAUCE

1 cup Hellman's mayonnaise

1 medium-sized dill pickle,
  finely chopped

1 teaspoon instant minced
  onion, softened in few
  drops water

1 teaspoon parsley flakes

Juice of 1 lemon

Dash of Tabasco

Mix all ingredients and refrigerate 1 hour or longer before serving. Makes 1½ cups. *Serve with fried shrimp or broiled snapper.*

Mrs. Lester D. Leatherberry

A TEXAS RATATOUILLE

1 can (28 oz.) tomatoes

1 medium onion, cut in small pieces

1 large green pepper, cut in strips

4 large stalks celery, cut in small pieces

1 pint fresh mushrooms, sautéed (optional)

1 large eggplant, peeled and cut in 1-inch chunks

2 teaspoons salt

Dash of garlic powder

1 teaspoon oregano

¼ cup margarine

Put tomatoes, onion, green pepper and celery in 4-quart saucepan. Over medium-low heat cook for 30 minutes, covered, stirring occasionally, until vegetables are tender. Add mushrooms, eggplant, seasonings and margarine, and cook for another 30 minutes over low heat, stirring gently occasionally. Put in a 3-quart casserole dish. Serve warm. Serves 6. *The definition of the French word "ratatouille" is given as a "coarse stew." This can mean a vegetable as well as a meat stew. Often times, other vegetables are added such as zucchini, squash and beans.*

Dorothea Kelley

INSTANT BARBECUE SAUCE

½ cup butter, melted

½ cup catsup

½ cup water

1 tablespoon Worcestershire sauce

3 tablespoons vinegar or lemon juice

Combine ingredients. Serves 6-8.

Mrs. William M. Osborne

BARBECUE SAUCE

1 cup margarine

½ bottle chili sauce

½ bottle Worcestershire sauce

½ cup catsup

2 whole garlic buds

Hot pepper sauce (optional)

Juice of 6-7 lemons

Combine all ingredients in a saucepan and simmer 10 minutes. Let cool and refrigerate in jar. Makes 2½ cups.

Mrs. Edwin L. Rippy

HUSH PUPPIES

1 cup corn meal	1/2 teaspoon sugar
1 teaspoon salt	1 tablespoon bacon drippings

1 cup boiling water

Sift together corn meal, salt and sugar. Add bacon drippings and water. Drop in hot fat and fry until done. Serves 4-6.

Mrs. James L. Terry

MEXICAN CORN BREAD

2 eggs, beaten	1 1/2 teaspoons salt
1 cup cream-style corn	2/3 cup shortening, melted
3 teaspoons baking powder	1 cup cottage cheese
1 cup corn meal	1 cup cheese, grated

1 can (4 oz.) Mountain Pass green chilies

Combine eggs, corn, baking powder, corn meal, salt, shortening and cottage cheese. Pour half of mixture into 9x12-inch pan. Lay chilies and 1/2 cup cheese over batter; pour on remaining batter, and top with remaining cheese. Bake at 350° for 1 hour. Serves 8.

Mrs. Agnes Muller

SOUTHERN SPOON BREAD

1 cup corn meal	1 cup milk
2 cups boiling water	3 eggs, beaten
2 tablespoons butter	3 teaspoons baking powder
1 teaspoon salt	1 can small green chilies

1/2 cup sharp cheese, diced

Sprinkle corn meal slowly into boiling water, stirring constantly. Cook until thick. Add butter, salt and milk. Cool. Add eggs, baking powder, chilies and cheese. Turn into well-greased casserole and bake at 350° for 45 minutes. Top with big lump of butter and serve at once. Serves 4.

Mrs. James C. Reid

CARROT CAKE

1⅓ cups Wesson oil
2 cups sugar
4 eggs, well-beaten
3 cups carrots, grated

2 cups sifted cake flour
½ teaspoon salt
2 teaspoons soda
2 teaspoons cinnamon

2 teaspoons allspice

Cream oil and sugar. Add eggs and carrots, and mix well. Sift dry ingredients. Add flour mixture to carrot mixture, a small amount at a time, beating well. Pour into 10x14-inch greased and floured loaf pan and bake at 325° for 1 hour. Cool.

ICING

½ cup margarine, melted
1 package (8 oz.) cream
  cheese, softened
1 box powdered sugar

½ cup pecans, chopped
½ cup raisins, chopped
½ cup coconut
1 teaspoon vanilla

Combine margarine and cheese with sugar, and beat well. Add other ingredients, mix well, and spread on cooled cake. Serves 20.

Mrs. Harold L. Crites, Jr.

FRUITED PECANS

2 cups sugar
1 tablespoon flour
½ cup plus 2 tablespoons milk
1 tablespoon butter

Juice of ½ lemon
Juice of 1 orange
Grated rind of 1 orange
4 cups pecan halves

Mix sugar and flour thoroughly. Put in saucepan, and add milk and butter. Bring to boil; add juices and rind. Reduce heat, and cook to soft ball stage. Add pecans and beat until creamy and the nuts fall apart. Pour onto brown paper and separate with 2 forks. Two pecan halves may be joined to make a full-sized nut. *These are delicious for holiday nibbling.*

Dorothy Sinz

PERFECT PRALINES

2 cups sugar	1/8 teaspoon salt
1 teaspoon soda	2 tablespoons butter
1 cup buttermilk	2 1/2 cups pecan halves or pieces

In large, heavy saucepan combine the sugar, soda, buttermilk and salt. Cook over high heat for 5 minutes or to 210° on candy thermometer. Stir constantly, scraping bottom of pan. Add butter and pecans. Continue cooking, stirring constantly and scraping pan, until candy reaches soft ball stage at 234°. Remove from heat and cool slightly. Beat until thick and creamy. Drop from tablespoon onto waxed paper and cool. Makes about 18 2-inch pralines. *Choose a clear, dry day to make candy. These pralines will not harden on a damp day.*

Mrs. Glen Gatlin

CHESS PIE

4 eggs, beaten slightly	1 tablespoon vinegar
1 1/2 cups sugar	1/2 cup margarine, melted
1 teaspoon vanilla	Unbaked 9-inch pie shell
Nutmeg	

Combine ingredients and pour into pie shell. Sprinkle with nutmeg. Bake at 375° for 45 minutes.

Mrs. Preston Smith

SOUTHERN PEACH SKILLET PIE

7 tablespoons shortening	2 tablespoons sugar
2 cups flour	1/8 teaspoon salt
3 tablespoons milk	1/4 teaspoon cinnamon
5 cups fresh or frozen peaches, peeled and sliced	2 tablespoons butter

Cut shortening into flour until finely blended. Add enough milk to make a soft dough. Roll out to 1/8-inch thickness and pat into a heavy iron skillet. Fill with peaches, drained if frozen, and sprinkle with sugar, salt and cinnamon. Dot with butter. Fold dough to the center. Bake at 450° for 10 minutes; reduce heat to 375°, and bake 15-20 minutes longer until well-browned Serves 6-8.

Mrs. John C. Smith, Jr.

PECAN PIE

2 tablespoons butter	½ cup sugar
3 eggs, well-beaten	1 teaspoon vanilla
Dash of salt	1-2 cups pecans
1 cup Karo syrup	Unbaked pie shell

Melt butter and cool. Combine eggs, butter, salt, Karo, sugar, vanilla and pecans. Put into pie shell and bake 40-50 minutes at 350°. Serves 6-8.

Mrs. George L. MacGregor, Jr.

PEACH ICE CREAM

4 eggs	½ gallon milk
2 cups sugar	1 tablespoon vanilla
1 can (15 oz.) Eagle Brand sweetened condensed milk	1 pint very ripe peaches, cut into pieces

Beat eggs until fluffy. Place eggs and sugar in a 2-quart saucepan. Place over medium heat. As sugar begins to dissolve, add condensed milk. Add about 1 quart milk to mixture, then add vanilla. Heat for about 10 minutes to dissolve sugar. Put mixture into a 4-quart ice cream freezer container, add the rest of milk and stir. When milk is mixed with other ingredients, put in freezer paddle and cover with lid. Put ice and ice cream salt in freezer. When ice cream begins to firm, remove lid and add peaches. As it continues to freeze, peaches will mix throughout the ice cream. Serves 8-12.

Mrs. William B. Dunaway

Napoleon offered a prize to the person who could find a method of preserving food for his soldiers. A French chef, Nicholas Appert, experimented with wide-mouthed bottles, filling them to the top, corking them tightly, and boiling them on the spot before allowing them to cool completely. He received the reward for his successful venture, only after writing a book explaining his method in accordance with the prize rulings. Today, after 150 years, he is known as the "Father of Canning".

PEPPER JELLY

1 cup jalapeño peppers	1½ cups cider vinegar
½ cup bell or sweet banana peppers	6 cups sugar
	1 bottle Certo

Grind peppers. Proportions of jalapeño and bell pepper may be varied to control hotness. Put in blender using ½ cup vinegar to blend. Refrigerate overnight to marinate. Place peppers, sugar and 1 cup vinegar in kettle over medium heat, and stir until fully boiling and until impossible to stir down. Remove from heat and let stand exactly 5 minutes. Skim off foam and stir in Certo quickly and thoroughly. Pour in jars and let stand to jell before sealing.

Josephine Travis

WINES

WINES BY VICTOR WDOWIAK

WINE TASTING PARTY

A Wine Tasting Party may have many forms according to the number of people and their personal knowledge of wine. I find this particular format useful for a large group of 50 or over as it helps to keep the crowd moving in a well-defined traffic pattern.

As the guests come in the first room, have a table set up with Scandinavian-type cold hors d'oeuvres and chilled dry white wines, one type of wine or more depending on your plans and budget. The second room should have an assortment of mild cheeses and one or more red wines served at room temperature. (Remember to bring the cheeses also to room temperature ahead of time.) To keep the crowd moving, the dessert table in the third room should offer a sweet dessert wine.

The big problem, of course, is wine glasses. You should have one glass per person per wine, and you can see how quickly that multiplies. Rent the necessary glasses as this business of rinsing them in the room, even in a silver bowl, is not very elegant, but naturally becomes a necessity if your crowd numbers 200 to 300 and up.

Figure on each guest consuming 3 to 4 ounces of each wine or between 9 to 12 ounces per evening. It comes out to between ⅓ and ½ bottle of wine per person for the evening.

CHECK LIST

A few good corkscrews

Sufficient number of wine glasses

Paper napkins

Bowls for chilled wines

Crushed ice

Help to pour wines and pick up glasses

RECOMMENDED WINES

White Wines:

> Germany: Graacher Himmelreich, 1966
>
> France: Mersault, 1966; Sancerre, 1967; or the ultimate Montrachet, 1966
>
> California: Pinot Chardonnay, Wente Bros.; Joe Heitz; or the very rare Hanzell

Red Wines:

> California: Cabernet Sauvignon, Beaulieu Vineyards, Concannon; or the legendary Martin Ray (The best California wines do have a vintage year on the label.)
>
> France: A must is a better Beaujolais, 1967, such as Moulin-A-Vent or Fleurie; full-bodied Pommard, 1962; and if you feel rich, Clos de Vougeot, 1961.

Dessert Wines:

> Hungary: Tokaji Aszu, any vintage
>
> France: Château Latour Blanche, Château d'Yquem, 1961 or 1962
>
> Germany: The rarest of all wine jewels: a Trockenbeeren Auslese, any vintage

CHEESES

Cheeses to accompany wines should be mild: Port Salut, Bel Paese, Gourmandise with walnuts; Délice de Savoie; Monterrey Jack.

WINE FACTS

Alcohol in wine evaporates during cooking, leaving only the delicate flavor in the dish. Extra dividend: Calories evaporate with the alcohol!

Open bottles of table wine (14% of alcohol or less) do not keep. Consume them within two days.

Red wines age and improve in the bottle, but the majority of white wines do not. So, pick your reds at least four years old, but drink the youngest good vintage of whites.

Serve red wines at about 65° (roughly a few degrees below room temperature) and the white wines chilled to 50°-55°. Why? Because they taste best that way.

Open red wines and let stand without cork one hour before serving. Whites do not need this breathing period.

Store your extra stock of wines laying the bottles flat so the corks stay wet and airtight.

In case the wine pleases you more than usual, please soak off the label and keep it. It is the easiest way to find the same bottle of wine again.

Keep a few month's supply of wine at home so you will not have to buy this bottle for tonight and shake the daylights out of it carrying it home from the wine shop.

For that very, very special dinner you are going to serve, a few suggestions for the wine service. Serve:

  White wine before red

  Light before full-bodied wine

  Young before older vintages

  Dry wine before sweet

  Champagne before dinner

Champagne is wonderful as the only wine to go through the whole dinner, but really does not go too well with desserts.

WINE SUGGESTIONS

With Appetizers: Manzanilla-type sherry; dry Vermouth on the rocks; dry white wine stirred with ½ teaspoon of Crême de Cassis cordial

With Soups: No wine except at very elaborate dinners, when dry sherry or Sercial Madeira may be served. On the other hand, a few ounces of dry sherry will add zest to most soups, if added during the last five minutes of cooking time

With Fish: Dry white wines, chilled to 50°-55°, for instance: white Burgundy, Rhine or Moselle, Portuguese white Vinho Verde, California Johannisberger Riesling

With Poultry: California Semillon or Pinot Chardonnay, French Graves, Italian Soave

With Game: With venison: red wines from the Rhone Valley

With Game Birds: red Bordeaux

With Meats: Dry red wines from France, California or Italy

With Barbecue or Mexican Food: The only wine that can stand up to these dishes is Italian Chianti

With Salads: No wine should be served with any dishes flavored with vinegar

With Desserts: Sweet wines like French Sauternes, Hungarian Tokaji, or a California Château Sauterne

Wines for Cooking: Dry Sherries, Madeira, Marsala; or the same wine you are going to serve with the dish

VENISON BOURGUIGNON

3 pounds trimmed venison, cut in 1½-inch cubes

2 cups dry red wine

1 cup dry sherry

½ cup olive oil

2 teaspoons soy sauce

2 cloves garlic

½ teaspoon thyme

2 bay leaves

Dash of Tabasco

3 medium onions, thinly sliced

1 cup flour

Salt and pepper to taste

Accent to taste

Butter

1 cup beef stock

2 large carrots, sliced

½ pound fresh mushrooms, sliced

Place venison in a glass or stainless steel bowl. Combine red wine, sherry, oil, soy sauce, garlic, thyme, bay leaves, Tabasco and 1 onion. Pour over meat and marinate for 4 hours, shaking and turning meat a few times. If desired, tenderize the venison and keep in marinade for 2 more hours. Drain and dry meat, reserving marinade. Season flour with salt, pepper and Accent, and put in a plastic sack. Dredge a few cubes of venison at a time. Brown meat in a heavy skillet without crowding. Remove and keep warm while browning rest of meat. Add 1 cup of strained marinade to heavy skillet and scrape all brown bits, which will form base of stew. Return all meat to skillet, and add rest of marinade and beef stock. If there is not enough liquid to cover meat, add wine or sherry. After simmering for 1 hour, add carrots, 2 onions, and mushrooms, sautéed in butter. Simmer for 2½ hours or until meat is tender. Serves 6. *Serve with rice and a good bottle of Chateauneuf-du-Pape.*

Victor Wdowiak

GRAPES IN SOUR CREAM

2 pounds very ripe seedless grapes

2 cups French Sauternes or Hungarian Tokaji

Sour cream

Fresh mint leaves (optional)

Toasted slivered almonds (optional)

Place grapes in a shallow pan or bowl, and puncture each grape with a fork. Pour Sauternes over grapes and place in refrigerator for 4-5 hours, shaking the bowl occasionally. Just before serving, drain grapes and roll, not fold, in sour cream. Serve in chilled individual bowls, garnished with mint leaves and sprinkled with almonds.

Victor Wdowiak

MISCELLANEOUS

BAKED FRUIT WITH CHUTNEY

2 cans (1 lb. 4 oz.) pineapple chunks, drained

1 can (1 lb. 13 oz.) sliced yellow cling peaches, drained

1 can (1 lb. 13 oz.) pears, drained

1 can (1 lb. 13 oz.) unpeeled apricot halves, drained

½ cup butter

1 cup brown sugar

½ cup chutney

Place all ingredients except apricots in a casserole. Melt butter with brown sugar and chutney. Pour over fruit in casserole. Bake, uncovered, at 300° for 20 minutes. Add apricot halves the last 5 minutes of baking. Drain most of syrup. Serves 10.

Mrs. Victor E. Barlow

BAKED ORANGES

3 whole thin-skinned oranges

1 cup sugar

1 cup water

6 tablespoons corn syrup

1 stick cinnamon

Boil oranges in enough water to cover for 30 minutes. Drain and cool. Cut in slices or quarters. Simmer sugar, water and corn syrup until sugar is dissolved. Cover orange segments with syrup in a casserole, cover tightly, and bake 1½ hours at 350°, basting at least 3 times. For a darker color and a spicier taste, place stick of cinnamon in bottom of casserole before baking. Serves 6. *Baked oranges may be served warm or cold, and are excellent with turkey, ham or duck.*

Mrs. Robert D. Boren

PEACH SURPRISE

1 can cling peach halves

1 jar Smucker's orange marmalade

Place peach halves hollow side up in a shallow pie pan. Fill the crevice of each peach with 1 tablespoon marmalade. Place in middle of broiler. Allow marmalade to melt and bubble. Serves 4-6.

Mrs. Walter M. Kilgo

Cranberries may have been so named because it was a favorite food of the cranes which lived in the New England bogs. Ships always carried a large supply of cranberries, "the bogland medicine", for they were known to prevent scurvy.

RUBY BANANAS

1 cup fresh cranberries

1/2 cup cold water

1/2 cup sugar

3 large bananas, halved lengthwise

2 tablespoons lemon juice

Wash berries and cover with cold water. Cook quickly 10 minutes. Press through sieve. Add sugar to hot cranberry juice and stir well. Place bananas in shallow, open, oven-proof casserole, and sprinkle with lemon juice. Pour cranberry juice over bananas. Bake at 375° for 10 minutes or until bananas are tender. Serves 6. *This versatile dish may be served hot with meat or cold as a dessert.*

Mrs. Ralph B. Rogers

APPLE BUTTER

4 pounds Jonathan or
    Winesap apples

2 cups cider

½ cup sugar

2 teaspoons cinnamon

1 teaspoon cloves

½ teaspoon allspice

Juice and grated rind of 1 lemon

Remove stems from apples; quarter and cook in cider until soft. Put through a strainer, and add other ingredients. Cook the apple butter very slowly, stirring often, until butter falls in sheets from a spoon. This does not have to be sealed and will keep in the refrigerator. Makes 2 quarts.

John W. Turner

PEACH CHUTNEY

1⅔ cups sugar

1¾ cups vinegar

8 large peaches, peeled
    and sliced

7 sweet red peppers, seeded
    and chopped

3 medium onions, peeled
    and chopped

1 clove garlic, peeled
    and chopped

4 ounces candied ginger,
    chopped

1 teaspoon salt

1 cup seedless raisins

Peel and pulp of 1 orange,
    chopped

Peel and pulp of 1 lemon,
    chopped

⅔ cup almonds, blanched
    and split

1 teaspoon powdered ginger

Moisten sugar with 1¼ cups vinegar. Bring to a boil and cook for 5 minutes. Skim well. Add peaches and cook for 10 minutes, skimming again. Add peppers, onions, garlic, ginger, salt, raisins, orange and lemon peel and pulp. Cook for 30 minutes, stirring frequently and skimming as necessary. Add almonds, powdered ginger and remaining vinegar. Continue cooking for 30 minutes, watching carefully and stirring frequently to prevent sticking. Immediately pour into well-drained, sterilized, 1-pint jars. Adjust rubbers and seal tightly. Makes 3 pints.

Sandra Rose

STRAWBERRY PRESERVES

1 quart strawberries   2 tablespoons vinegar

4 cups sugar

Boil the berries and vinegar hard for 3 minutes. Add sugar and boil hard for 10 minutes. Pour into crock and stir frequently. Let stand 24 hours. Pour into sterilized Ball jars and seal. Makes 1 quart.

Mrs. Alvin M. Owsley

PICKLES

1 gallon sour or dill pickles   1 pint white vinegar

5 pounds white sugar   ½ box pickling spices

1 clove garlic

Cut pickles and let stand in ice cubes for 2-3 hours. Drain. Place in a 2-gallon crock with sugar, vinegar, spices and garlic. Stir, cover, and keep in a cool place, stirring daily, for 6 days. Then put into clean jars.

Mrs. Miles McInnis

PICKLED OKRA

Whole okra   Fresh red or green peppers

Salt   Sugar

Garlic   Dill seed (optional)

White or red vinegar

Wash okra and pack in 1-pint jars. Add 1 teaspoon salt, 1 garlic clove, 1 pepper, ½-1 teaspoon sugar and dill seed to each jar. Pour boiling vinegar over contents. Seal jar and let stand 6 weeks before using.

Mrs. Leo F. Corrigan

HOT BEER

3 eggs	1 teaspoon cloves
1½ cups sugar	Juice and rind of 2 lemons
1 teaspoon cinnamon	Juice and rind of 1 orange
1½ teaspoons cardamon	1 cup water
	3 cans beer

Beat eggs and sugar until light and foamy. Add spices. Boil lemon and orange rind in water for 5 minutes. Strain. Bring beer to boiling point; add strained lemon and orange water, and beat in egg mixture. Do not boil. Fill heavy mugs and serve hot.

Margaret Gulbis

CAFÉ BRÛLOT

1 stick cinnamon	3 lumps sugar
8 whole cloves	3 jiggers brandy
Peel of 1 lemon, thinly cut	3 cups strong coffee

Place cinnamon, cloves, lemon peel and sugar in silver brûlot bowl or chafing dish. Pour brandy in large ladle; ignite brandy and pour over ingredients in bowl. Keep ladling ingredients until sugar is dissolved. Gradually add coffee, ladling the mixture until the flames fade. Serve immediately. Serves 4.

Mrs. Eugene L. Fry

Johann Sebastian Bach created a "Coffee Cantata," which musically expressed the emotions felt by women protesting the coffee consumption of their men. These social revolters did not want to be ignored by their coffee-house frequenters.

COFFEE

Medaglia D'Oro coffee	Mountain Valley water

Combine 1 teaspoon coffee with 1 cup cold water for each cup desired. Add 1 extra teaspoon coffee to the pot, preferably an Italian turnover coffee pot. After water comes to a boil, turn off heat, and flip coffee pot over. Serve when water has dripped through grounds. *In my opinion, coffee is the most difficult of all food or beverages for the average American to make. This is a recipe for coffee snobs, for those who like a clear, flavorful Italian type of coffee. It can be served with milk or cream, but it is better black.*

Stanley Marcus

GRAPEFRUIT DRINK APPETIZER

1½ cups sugar

1 cup water

Mint or mint flavoring

1 large can (16 oz.) pink grapefruit juice

Combine sugar and water, and boil until sugar is dissolved. Crush a large handful of fresh mint in above mixture. Pour in grapefruit juice. Put in freezer. Remove from freezer 2 hours before serving. Drink should be slushy when served. Serve in Manhattan glasses with sprig of mint. Serves 8. *This is very refreshing and extremely cool for the summer.*

Mrs. Richard C. Bower

HOT CIDER

2 quarts cider

1 cup pineapple juice

1 cup orange juice

1 small bottle maraschino cherries and juice (optional)

⅛ teaspoon salt

½ cup sugar

3 sticks cinnamon

6 whole cloves

Juice of 1 lemon

Combine all ingredients in a 4-quart saucepan. Heat; stir until sugar dissolves. Serves 15.

Mrs. Milton H. Thomas, Jr.

LIME SHERBET PUNCH

2 cans (6 oz.) frozen orange juice

2 cans (6 oz.) frozen lemonade

2 cans (6 oz.) frozen limeade

18 cans water

1 can (41 oz.) unsweetened pineapple juice

1 can (20 oz.) crushed pineapple

2 quarts lime sherbet

2 large bottles ginger ale

Mix all ingredients except ginger ale. Pour over large ring of ice in punch bowl. Add ginger ale just before serving. Serves 40.

Mrs. Frank E. Sommerfield

MILK PUNCH

1 ounce bourbon   ½ teaspoon vanilla
1 teaspoon sugar   ¾ cup milk
                    Nutmeg

Place bourbon, sugar, vanilla and very cold milk in blender, and mix until light and frothy. Pour into a tall, chilled glass and top with nutmeg. Serve with a straw. Serves 1.

The Cookbook Committee

LOW CALORIE ORANGE JULIUS

2 ounces frozen orange juice   2 packages Sweet 'n Low
5 ounces skim milk   5 crushed ice cubes

Place orange juice, skim milk, sugar substitute and ice in blender, and beat on high for 1 minute. Makes 1½ cups.

Mrs. Kenneth Weil

The origin of "giving a toast" was originated in the days of Catherine de' Medici. It was customary to drink to one's health, to issue a challenge while holding a wine glass, and to salute the king's glory by raising a glass. It became a popular custom to place a crust of bread in the bottom of a wine goblet from which everyone drank in turn until all of the wine was gone and only the moist toast was left. Then all would bow to the fortunate next person who would take the honored bite with much delight.

POOR MAN'S CHAMPAGNE

1 gallon Sauterne   4 ounces vodka

3 ounces lemon juice   3 quarts ginger ale

Add chilled ingredients to a large punch bowl. Keep chilled during serving by adding an ice ring made by freezing water in 1-quart ring mold. Serves 50.

Mrs. Lloyd M. Gilmore

SANGRITA

1 cup orange juice

2 cups tomato juice

Dash of Tabasco

Dash of Worcestershire sauce

Salt to taste

Juice of 1 lemon

Tequila añejo

Mix orange juice, tomato juice, seasonings and lemon juice together. To drink, use 2 small glasses. Pour sangrita in one and tequila in the other. Take a sip of sangrita and without swallowing, immediately take a sip of tequila. *This is the true Mexican way to have sangrita.*

Eugene Locke

INSTANT SPICED TEA

1½ cups Tang

½ cup lemon-flavored instant tea

½ cup sugar

½ teaspoon cinnamon

½ teaspoon ground cloves

Mix well; store in an airtight jar. Use 1 tablespoon tea mixture to 1 cup of water, or to taste.

Mrs. A. Ray Edsel

RUSSIAN TEA

1 teaspoon cinnamon

1 teaspoon nutmeg

1 teaspoon allspice

1 clove

Juice of 3 lemons

Rind of 1 lemon

Juice of 3 oranges

Rind of 1 orange

2 cups sugar

1 cup pickled peach juice

½ cup tea leaves

5 quarts water

Tie cinnamon, nutmeg, allspice and clove in a small bag. Combine bag of spices, juices, rinds, sugar and 1 quart water; and boil for 5 minutes. Before serving, mix this with strong tea made by using tea leaves and 1 gallon water. Serve either hot or cold. Serves 24.

Mrs. L. H. Maloy

MISCELLANEOUS

TEA PUNCH

2 teaspoons Lapson Schong
  tea

3 Orange Pekoe tea bags

Sugar

Juice of 1 lemon

Juice of 2 oranges

Juice of ½ grapefruit

Water

½ cup white rum

Peel of 1 orange

Peel of 1 lemon

Peel of ¼ grapefruit

Make a strong tea extract from Lapson Schong and Orange Pekoe, and sweeten to taste. Add lemon, orange and grapefruit juices. Pour in a pitcher, and add enough water to fill ⅔ full. Add ice cubes, rum and orange, lemon and grapefruit peels. Let steep for 1 hour while chilling, and serve ice cold.

Serge Fournier

HOT BUTTERED RUM

1 pound brown sugar

½ cup butter

Pinch of salt

¼-½ teaspoon nutmeg

¼-½ teaspoon cinnamon

¼-½ teaspoon cloves

Rum

Boiling water

Mix sugar, butter, salt, nutmeg, cinnamon and cloves. Preheat mugs. Put a generous teaspoon of batter in each mug, add 1½ ounces rum, and fill with boiling water. Stir well to mix. This mixture keeps indefinitely.

Mrs. Warren H. Hall

BIRCHERMUESLI

2 tablespoons precooked oats	1 glass jar yogurt
2 tablespoons brown sugar	Juice of 2 oranges
Juice of ½ lemon	½ apple, grated
½ banana, mashed	1 pound berries in season, hulled
2 tablespoons thin cream or 1 tablespoon thick cream	Almonds, finely chopped

Mix oats, brown sugar, lemon juice, banana and cream, and blend well. Add yogurt, orange juice and apple immediately to prevent browning. Mash ¾ of the berries, and add to mixture. Decorate with remaining whole fruit, sprinkle with almonds, chill slightly, and serve either in a glass bowl or in individual glass ice cream dishes. *This recipe was invented by the famous vegetarian doctor, Bircher, and literally means "Bircher-porridge", and is as healthy as it is delicious.*

Yehudi Menuhin

GRAPEFRUIT IN HOT CLARET

4 seedless grapefruit	¼ cup water
1 cup sugar	1 cup Claret
	½ teaspoon lemon juice

Peel and section grapefruit. Place in a china or ceramic bowl. Chill. Boil sugar and water. Cool. Add Claret and lemon juice. Pour over grapefruit. Serves 4. *This is for a breakfast party or brunch.*

Helen Corbitt

ORANGES WITH SOUR CREAM

6 large California seedless
oranges

1 tablespoon brown sugar

1 cup sour cream

1/2 teaspoon cinnamon

2 tablespoons orange peel, grated

Peel and section oranges. Place in shallow serving dish and sprinkle with brown sugar. Cover with sour cream and sprinkle with cinnamon and orange peel. Garnish with mint if available. Serves 4-6.

Helen Corbitt

ONION SANDWICH

1 large onion

Rye bread or pumpernickel,
sliced medium thick

Butter

Mustard spread (optional)

Salt

Freshly ground black pepper

Peel onion and thinly slice, being careful not to break slices. Spread butter on bread at least 1/4 inch thick. Place onion slice on top of butter and sprinkle with salt and pepper. *Then stay out of crowded elevators.*

Herc Ficklen

PANCAKE SYRUP

1 cup white corn syrup

1/2 cup water

1/2 cup brown sugar

Few drops of maple flavoring

Butter

Combine corn syrup, water and brown sugar. Heat until sugar dissolves and mixture comes to boiling point. Add maple flavoring and as much butter as desired.

Dale Zimmerman

RECIPE INDEX

RECIPE INDEX

RECIPE INDEX

RECIPE INDEX

RECIPE INDEX

RECITE INDEX

CONTRIBUTOR INDEX

CONTRIBUTOR INDEX

NOTED COOKERY

Dallas Symphony Association, Inc.
P. O. Box 8472
Dallas, Texas 75205

Office: McFarlin Memorial Auditorium

Please send me_____copies of **NOTED COOKERY**
@ $5.00 plus .35 handling for each copy. Enclosed please
find a check or money order for $_____, payable
to **NOTED COOKERY.**

Name_____

Street_____

City_____State_____ _____Zip_____

All proceeds benefit the Dallas Symphony Orchestra.

NOTED COOKERY

Dallas Symphony Association, Inc.
P. O. Box 8472
Dallas, Texas 75205

Office: McFarlin Memorial Auditorium

Please send me_____copies of **NOTED COOKERY**
@ $5.00 plus .35 handling for each copy. Enclosed please
find a check or money order for $_____, payable
to **NOTED COOKERY.**

Name_____

Street_____

City_____State_____Zip_____

All proceeds benefit the Dallas Symphony Orchestra.